BIRDS OF LOUDOUN

A Guide Based on the 2009-2014
Loudoun County Bird Atlas

Published by Loudoun Wildlife Conservancy
Written and Designed by Spring Ligi
Edited by Mary Ann Good
Cover Design and Consulting by Bob Schamerhorn of Infinity Graphics, Richmond, VA
Printed by PIP Printing, Lynchburg, VA

Atlas Committee:
Bill Brown
Joe Coleman
Mary Ann Good
Bruce Hill
Spring Ligi
Linda Millington
Christine Perdue
Allison Sussman
Mark Wimer

ISBN 978-0-9839458-3-3-53495

The Loudoun Wildlife Conservancy is a nonprofit 501(c)(3) group of volunteers who share a common goal of protecting and perpetuating natural habitats for the benefit of both people and wildlife. Contributions are tax-deductible to the extent allowed by the law.

A project of the Loudoun Wildlife Conservancy in partnership with the USGS Patuxent Wildlife Research Center, with a contribution from the Virginia Society of Ornithology.

Photo credits on cover:
Great Horned Owl with nestlings by Liam McGranaghan
Bald Eagle by Laura McGranaghan
Blue-winged Warbler by Laura McGranaghan

Barred Owl feather logo (shown above) by Karen Coleman

TABLE OF CONTENTS

INTRODUCTION

Birds provide an easy yet powerful way to connect to our natural world and serve as important indicators of the overall health of our environment. Loudoun County, Virginia has a wide variety of bird species, and is characterized by a diversity of habitats that provide breeding, migration, and overwintering sites for its bird population. However, Loudoun has experienced tremendous growth over the past two decades, leading to its ranking by the U.S. Census Bureau as one of the fastest growing counties in the U.S. This growth in human population has resulted in habitat loss due to development, forest fragmentation, increased vehicular traffic, noise, communication towers, pesticides, and an increase in the numbers of house cats. Other environmental changes include habitat degradation from white-tailed deer and invasive exotic plant species.

In order to learn more about the impacts of population growth and associated environmental changes on Loudoun's birds, the Loudoun Wildlife Conservancy (Loudoun Wildlife) embarked on a 5-year bird atlas, from 2009 to 2014. The atlas was designed to establish a comprehensive list of species and determine their distribution throughout the county. Atlases provide a powerful opportunity to study all species of birds – from common to rare, secretive to approachable, localized to widespread – in a way that reveals changes in the distribution of species on a fine scale (Kamm et al. 2013a). Bird atlases are usually conducted at the state level and collect data only during the breeding season. However, the Loudoun County Bird Atlas is unique in that the project focused on a single county and collected year-round data for all bird species. By comparing this atlas (Atlas 2) to data from the 1985-1989 Virginia Breeding Bird Atlas (BBA) (Atlas 1), the impact of environmental change on Loudoun's bird population may be better understood. Loudoun Wildlife can then devise strategies to identify and protect species-rich areas and guide future conservation activities.

LOUDOUN'S GEOGRAPHY AND HABITATS

All 521 square miles of Loudoun County lie within the Piedmont physiographic region and are characterized by rolling hills bisected by rapidly flowing streams in the west and slower moving ones in the east as the county gradually sinks down to coastal plains. The county's elevation varies from 1,900 feet in the Blue Ridge Mountains to 180 feet in the east (along the Potomac River). On the north, Loudoun is separated from the counties of Frederick and Montgomery, Maryland by the Potomac River. The Blue Ridge Mountains serve as Loudoun's border on the west, with Clarke County, Virginia and Jefferson County, West Virginia on the western side of the mountains' crest. The Virginia counties of Prince William and Fauquier border Loudoun on the south and Fairfax on the east. The Bull Run Mountains and Catoctin Mountain bisect the county, with Loudoun Valley and Short Hill Mountain to their west. Approximately 1% of the county is water.

The western half of Loudoun includes a variety of habitats because of the rich diversity of soil types there. Pastures, farmland, and abandoned fields attract species such as Northern Harrier, American Woodcock, American Kestrel, Eastern Meadowlark, and Grasshopper Sparrow. The abandoned fields often include native brambles and non-native Autumn Olive. Farm buildings and silos are used as nesting and roosting sites by Barn Owls and Barn Swallows. Hedgerows provide a welcome habitat for Brown Thrasher and Blue Grosbeak. Upland second-growth hardwood forest provides habitat for species such as Wood Thrush, Cerulean Warbler, Ovenbird, and Scarlet Tanager. The upland forest is most extensive along the Blue Ridge and Short Hill Mountains and includes mainly oak, hickory, tulip, ash, and maple trees. Lowland second-growth hardwood forest is also present, consisting of sycamore trees along streams and willow and maple trees in wetlands. Ducks, geese, and shorebirds use the ponds scattered throughout the farms, golf courses, and suburban areas of western Loudoun. Neighborhoods, with their scattered trees and bird feeders, are attractive to species such as Mourning Dove, Carolina Chickadee, Carolina Wren, Northern Cardinal, and House Finch.

Eastern Loudoun has many of the same habitats as the western half of the county, but the patches of forest, farmland, and pasture are smaller and there are notably more suburban areas and parks with Eastern Red Cedar and a variety of shrubs. Eastern Loudoun is close to a second physiographic region in Virginia, the Coastal Plain, and includes the Potomac River, wetlands, and large ponds found throughout the suburban developments. Dulles International Airport, located on the county's southeastern border, provides large open space for species such as Snowy Owl during irruptive years. The highly productive, privately-owned Dulles Greenway Wetlands Mitigation Project, located in the central part of the county, attracts species rare to Loudoun such as Tricolored Heron, Virginia Rail, Stilt Sandpiper, Short-billed Dowitcher, and Marsh Wren.

PROCEDURES

From April 2009 through April 2014, volunteer field observers (atlasers) systematically surveyed different habitats throughout Loudoun, documenting birds and their full range of behaviors. A detailed description of the methodology is available in the Loudoun County Bird Atlas Handbook (Ligi 2011), located on the Loudoun Wildlife Conservancy website (https://loudounwildlife.org). The methods are comparable to the 1980s Virginia BBA and modeled after contemporary statewide atlases such as Maryland/District of Columbia, Delaware, and Massachusetts.

Loudoun was divided into a grid of 73 blocks, approximately 10 square miles each, based on U.S. Geological Survey 7.5-minute quadrangle maps. Atlasers were assigned to different blocks throughout the county to obtain county-wide coverage. Participants were encouraged to conduct a survey in all accessible habitat types within their block at least once every 10-15 days during the peak breeding months (May through August) and once a month during the remaining months (September through April). Incidental observations were also accepted from atlasers as they surveyed opportunistically outside of their assigned blocks within the county.

Atlasers used a pre-printed field card to consistently record the occurrence and behavior of all birds. Each sighting was assigned an evidence code based on the behavior, habitat, and time of year the bird was observed. The evidence codes were classified into four distinct categories as shown in Table 1: Observed (O) for all non-breeding observations, Possible (PO) breeder, Probable (PR) breeder, and Confirmed (CO) breeder.

Table 1. Evidence codes and definitions. Safe dates indicate the dates during the breeding season that a species is no longer in migration and can be presumed to be on breeding territory. These dates are not nesting or egg dates. Refer to the atlas handbook for a complete list of species and their corresponding safe dates.

Category	Code	Observed Behavior
OBserved	E	Observed outside of safe dates, not exhibiting breeding behavior (winter birds and migrants)
OBserved	O	Observed within safe dates, not in breeding habitat
POssible	X	Heard or seen in breeding habitat within safe dates
PRobable	A	Agitated behavior or anxiety calls
PRobable	P	Pair seen within safe dates
PRobable	T	Bird holding territory (counter-singing, chasing, etc.)
PRobable	C	Courtship or copulation
PRobable	N	Bird visiting a probable nest site
PRobable	B	Adult wren or woodpecker carrying nesting material or nest building
COnfirmed	NB	Adult carrying nesting material or nest building (except wrens and woodpeckers)
COnfirmed	DD	Distraction display
COnfirmed	UN	Used nest or eggshells found
COnfirmed	FL	Recently fledged young
COnfirmed	CF	Parent carrying food, feeding young, or removing fecal sac
COnfirmed	RC	Raptor performing a courting display or repeatedly carrying food to a specific area
COnfirmed	ON	Parent entering/exiting nest site or on nest
COnfirmed	NE	Nest with eggs
COnfirmed	NY	Nest with young

Five factors provided a set of guidelines to determine when a block was considered completely surveyed: 1) 25 hours of coverage, 2) 50 PO, PR, or CO breeding species, 3) two-thirds of all breeding species considered PR or CO breeders, 4) 25% of all species considered non-breeding birds, and 5) when applicable, missing no more than 15% of breeding species observed in that block during Atlas 1. The coordinators reviewed and processed the data through BBA

Explorer, an online data repository and web-based data entry and management portal hosted by the USGS Patuxent Wildlife Research Center. Verification forms were required for species considered rare or sensitive.

While the field methods for Atlas 2 followed those of Atlas 1 for comparability of results, additional information was collected during Atlas 2 to add value. Notably, Atlas 2 included all species while Atlas 1 focused solely on breeding birds. Furthermore, Atlas 2 covered every block within the county, with each block receiving significantly more thorough coverage and a higher level of effort. Atlas 1 participants submitted one field card per block at the end of each breeding season, while Atlas 2 participants completed and electronically submitted a new field card for each survey, allowing the results to be viewed online in real time. Knowing the current state of each block allowed better targeting of effort and provided feedback for all participants. One final enhancement to Atlas 2 was the designation of seven special areas throughout the county. These areas included Algonkian, Bles, and Claude Moore Parks, the Blue Ridge Center for Environmental Stewardship, Banshee Reeks Nature Preserve, and the privately owned Dulles Greenway Wetlands and Horsepen Preserve. Observations within each special area were recorded on a separate field card in order to measure habitat value.

RESULTS
A Snapshot

Atlas Statistics	
Total species	262
Total breeding species	120
Confirmed breeders	104
Probable breeders	13
Possible breeders	3
Migrant only species	76
Winter only species	66
Year-round species	68
Average species per block	110
Average field hours recorded per block	83
Total field hours reported	5,931
Total sightings	64,813
Participants	85

Species (out of total species) reported in all 73 blocks

Turkey Vulture
Red-bellied Woodpecker
Downy Woodpecker
Great Crested Flycatcher
Blue Jay
Carolina Chickadee
Tufted Titmouse
Carolina Wren
Gray Catbird
Cedar Waxwing
American Goldfinch
Eastern Towhee
Chipping Sparrow
Northern Cardinal

Species reported exclusively within 7 special areas*

Red-necked Grebe
Stilt Sandpiper
Short-billed Dowitcher
Tricolored Heron
Yellow-crowned Night-Heron
Glossy Ibis
Western Kingbird
Northern Shrike
Marsh Wren
Mourning Warbler

*85% of all atlas species were found non-exclusively in these special areas (areas named in paragraph above)

Confirmed breeder highlights	Probable breeder highlights	Winter and migratory highlights
Hooded Merganser (county first)	Black-billed Cuckoo	Brant
Barn Owl	Eastern Whip-poor-will	Black Rail
Loggerhead Shrike	Horned Lark	Sandhill Crane
Vesper Sparrow	Marsh Wren	American Avocet
Bobolink	Cerulean Warbler	Red Phalarope
Blue-winged Warbler	Yellow-throated Warbler	Cattle Egret
Dickcissel	Summer Tanager	Mississippi Kite
		Snowy Owl
		Northern Saw-whet Owl
		Alder Flycatcher
		Red Crossbill
		White-winged Crossbill
		Connecticut Warbler

Comparing Datasets: Then and Now

Comparing the Atlas 1 and Atlas 2 datasets revealed a variation in species between atlases. According to Table 2, seven species reported as breeding in Atlas 1 were not reported as breeding during Atlas 2, whereas 15 species reported as breeding during Atlas 2 were not reported as breeding during Atlas 1. Table 3 draws attention to species that increased or decreased in total percentage of presence over all blocks from Atlas 1 to Atlas 2. Comparing the number of species per block (Figure 1) reveals an average of 110 total species and 71 breeding species per block for Atlas 2 and 50 breeding species per block for Atlas 1. The number of effort hours per block differed substantially from one atlas to the other, with Atlas 2 averaging 80 effort hours per block and Atlas 1 averaging 10 hours per block.

Drawing comparisons between the Loudoun datasets in Atlas 1 and Atlas 2 can provide valuable insight. However, these comparisons should be interpreted with caution. It is not likely that the higher number of breeding species in Atlas 2 was entirely driven by new species colonizing a block. Rather, a variety of factors are likely at play, with a significant factor being the more thorough coverage and higher level of effort per block in Atlas 2.

Upon examining the 25 most widespread breeding species from both atlases (reported in the most blocks with respect to all breeding species), we discovered a change in 7 of these top 25 species (Table 4). Grassland species, such as Northern Bobwhite and Eastern Meadowlark, slipped from the top 25 list in Atlas 2, and were replaced with suburban and open woodland species such as Downy Woodpecker, White-breasted Nuthatch, and Blue Jay.

Further examination of breeding species by habitat revealed relatively no change between atlases in the number and percentage of species in woodland and urban/suburban habitats. However, Table 5 shows a noteworthy decline in grassland species and increase in species affiliated with water from Atlas 1 to Atlas 2.

Table 2. Possible (PO), probable (PR), and confirmed (CO) species found exclusively during either Atlas 1 or 2.	
Present in Atlas 1, not Atlas 2	Present in Atlas 2, not Atlas 1
Ring-necked Pheasant (PR)	Hooded Merganser (CO)
Ruffed Grouse (PR)	Pied-billed Grebe (PO)
Upland Sandpiper (CO)*	Black-billed Cuckoo (PR)
Spotted Sandpiper (PO)	Virginia Rail (PR)
Veery (PO)*	Great Blue Heron (CO)
Henslow's Sparrow (PR)	Green Heron (CO)
Chestnut-sided Warbler (PO)*	Osprey (CO)
	Sharp-shinned Hawk (PO)
	Bald Eagle (CO)
	Broad-winged Hawk (PR)
	Brown Creeper (PO)
*This species was observed	Marsh Wren (PR)
in Atlas 2 with no evidence	Swamp Sparrow (CO)
of breeding.	Prothonotary Warbler (CO)
	Yellow-throated Warbler (PR)

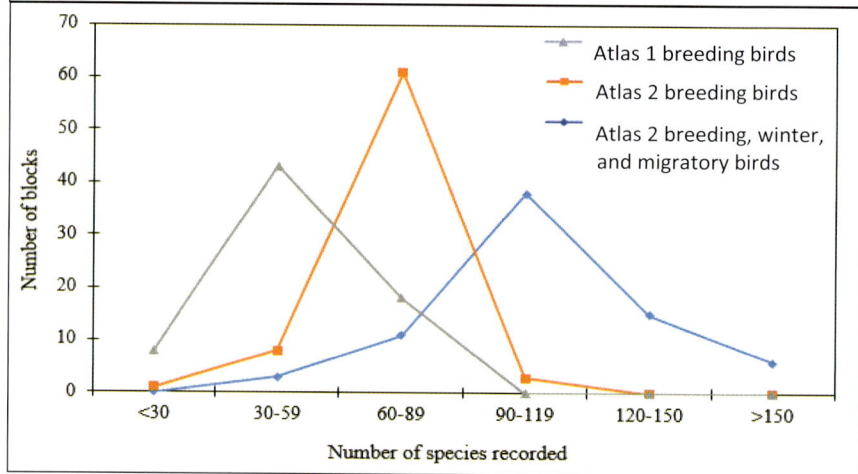

Figure 1. Species per block comparison between Atlas 1 and Atlas 2.

Table 3. Sampling of species that increased or decreased in total percentage of presence over all blocks since Atlas 1. Numbers in parentheses indicate the percentage of blocks documented as breeding out of the total number of blocks for each atlas (i.e. Atlas 1 to Atlas 2).

Increase	Decrease
Wild Turkey (16 to 81%)	Northern Bobwhite (87 to 26%)
Green Heron (0 to 82%)	Ring-necked Pheasant (14 to 0%)
Black Vulture (1 to 84%)	Ruffed Grouse (7 to 0%)
Turkey Vulture (3 to 96%)	Loggerhead Shrike (11 to 1%)
Cooper's Hawk (3 to 63%)	Eastern Meadowlark (86 to 78%)
Bald Eagle (0 to 10%)	Kentucky Warbler (29 to 18%)
Red-shouldered Hawk (1 to 95%)	
Red-tailed Hawk (3 to 89%)	
Tree Swallow (17 to 84%)	
Eastern Bluebird (80 to 96%)	

The decline in grassland species may be largely attributable to habitat loss and degradation. Loudoun's agricultural land use decreased from 70% in Atlas 1 to 40% in Atlas 2, while developed land use increased from 5% in Atlas 1 to 20% in Atlas 2 (Price et al. 2006; Jin et al. 2013). The increase in water species is likely due to increased access to wetlands, ponds, riparian, and similar habitat by both observers and birds compared to the 1980s. Loudoun now contains easily accessible ponds throughout more developed suburbs, designated areas to view the Potomac River and other waterways, as well as the large, privately-owned Dulles Greenway Wetlands Mitigation Project, which attracts many types of birds.

Table 4. Top 25 breeding species (reported in the most blocks with respect to all breeding species). Numbers in parentheses indicate the percentage of blocks in which the species exhibited breeding behavior. Species that occur in the top 25 list in one atlas but not the other are in bold font.

Atlas 1	Atlas 2
Northern Cardinal (97%)	**Downy Woodpecker (100%)**
American Crow (96%)	**Great Crested Flycatcher (100%)**
Red-bellied Woodpecker (93%)	Carolina Wren (100%)
American Robin (93%)	Northern Cardinal (100%)
Gray Catbird (93%)	Red-bellied Woodpecker (99%)
Chipping Sparrow (93%)	American Crow (99%)
Field Sparrow (93%)	Carolina Chickadee (99%)
Indigo Bunting (93%)	Tufted Titmouse (99%)
House Wren (91%)	**White-breasted Nuthatch (99%)**
Common Grackle (91%)	American Robin (99%)
Mourning Dove (90%)	Gray Catbird (99%)
Northern Mockingbird (90%)	Eastern Towhee (99%)
European Starling (90%)	Chipping Sparrow (99%)
Eastern Wood-Pewee (89%)	Indigo Bunting (99%)
Barn Swallow (89%)	American Goldfinch (99%)
Carolina Chickadee (89%)	Mourning Dove (97%)
Eastern Towhee (89%)	Eastern Wood-Pewee (97%)
Red-winged Blackbird (89%)	Northern Mockingbird (97%)
Northern Bobwhite (87%)	**Turkey Vulture (96%)**
Tufted Titmouse (87%)	**Eastern Phoebe (96%)**
American Goldfinch (87%)	**Blue Jay (96%)**
Carolina Wren (86%)	**Eastern Bluebird (96%)**
Song Sparrow (86%)	European Starling (96%)
Eastern Meadowlark (86%)	Field Sparrow (96%)
House Sparrow (86%)	Common Grackle (96%)

Species Richness

The four most species-rich blocks (158-192 total species) were all located in more-developed eastern Loudoun (Figure 2, pg. 6). An astounding 190 species were documented in the Brambleton area and also in southern Leesburg (areas in and around Banshee Reeks Nature Preserve and the Dulles Greenway Wetlands). The Sterling area, including Algonkian and Bles Parks, proved to be another bird-rich area, hosting over 165 species. These results are surprising and do not hold true for breeding-only birds, whose most species-rich blocks were located in more rural western and northern Loudoun.

Several possible factors may explain why eastern Loudoun hosts the four most species-rich blocks. Its position within the Piedmont region and close proximity to the Coastal Plain provides ample habitat for a diversity of species within a relatively limited area. Eastern Loudoun includes the Potomac River, several rich wetlands and large ponds, and rich green open space in a suburban setting. Suburban areas often have more bird diversity than large rural areas, especially if those rural areas are heavily forested or in intensive agricultural use (Marzluff and DeLap 2015). Whereas some species disappear as land is transformed by human development, other species thrive in altered habitats.

Unlike the more rural western half of the county, eastern Loudoun is undergoing rapid development. As habitat becomes developed, birds are often forced into smaller pockets of suitable habitat, perhaps making them easier to observe and document. The majority of species in the top four species-rich blocks were reported in protected areas and preserves, suggesting that these protected areas provide

Table 5. Number of breeding species by habitat. Numbers in parentheses indicate the percentage of total species that use the habitat.

Habitat	Atlas 1	Atlas 2
Grassland	18 (14%)	15 (11%)
Woodland	34 (27%)	37 (27%)
Open Woodland	41 (32%)	41 (30%)
Water	7 (5%)	15 (11%)
Urban, Suburban, Rural Development	24 (19%)	24 (18%)
Other	4 (3%)	4 (3%)

important stop-overs for migratory species and resource-rich areas for wintering species.

Though these smaller pockets of suitable habitat may result in higher species diversity, they offer fewer opportunities for establishment of territories and breeding success. When migrants and winter birds are excluded in Atlas 2, the most species-rich blocks are located in relatively rural western and northern Loudoun (Figure 3). Interestingly, Figure 4 reveals that the most species-rich blocks in Atlas 1 (before the building boom) are fairly evenly distributed throughout the county.

It is important to note that many of the grassland and uncommon species reported in high richness areas of eastern Loudoun were observed during the early years of Atlas 2 in abandoned fields awaiting development. Most of these fields have since been developed.

Figure 2. Total number of species documented in Atlas 2 during all seasons.

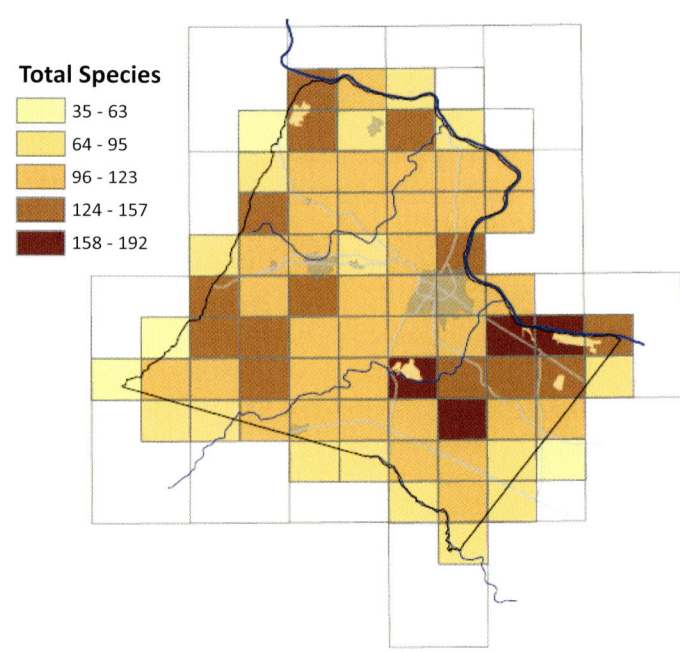

Figure 3. Number of breeding species documented in Atlas 2 during the breeding season.

Figure 4. Number of breeding species documented in Atlas 1 during the breeding season.

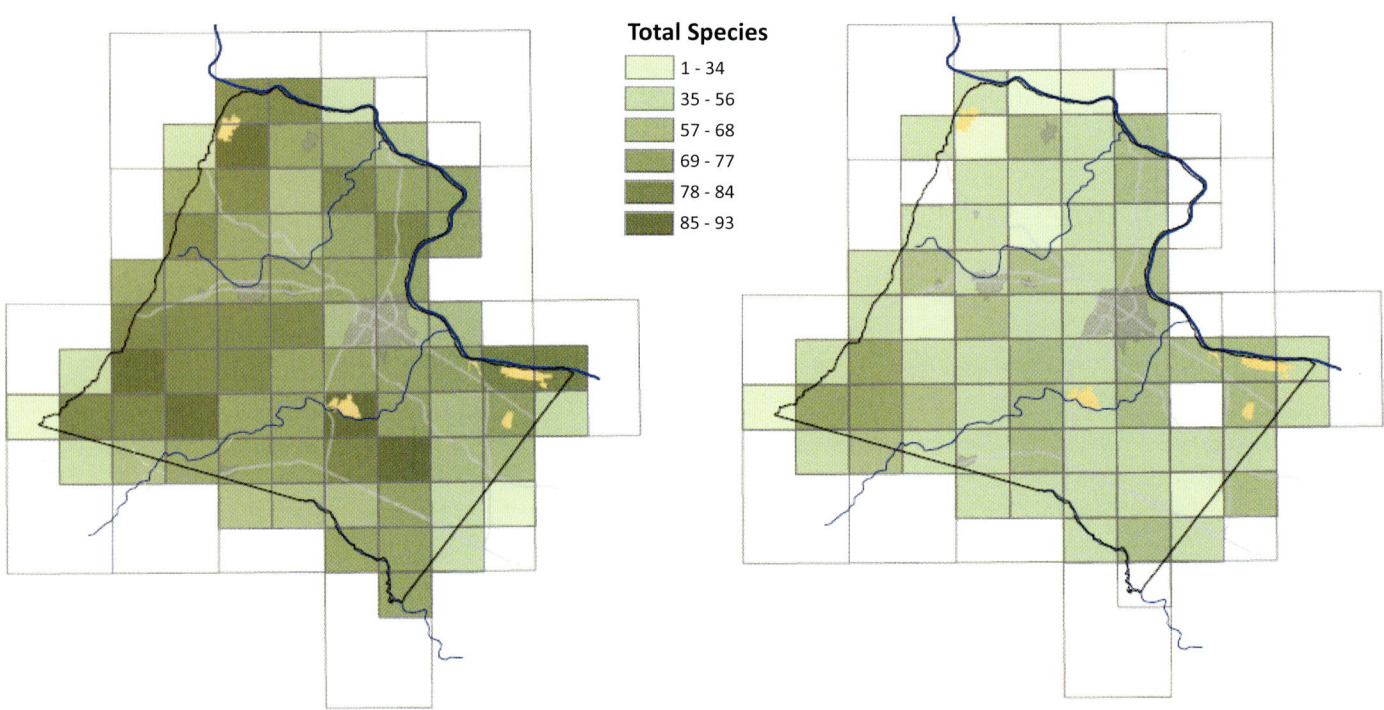

USING THE SPECIES ACCOUNTS

The species accounts provide information regarding the appearance, habitat, breeding behavior (when applicable), and conservation status for the 262 Atlas 2 species*. Written by local birders, each account emphasizes the species' connections to Loudoun and includes a distribution map. Photographs taken by mainly local photographers bring the accounts to life. Accounts for non-breeding and rare species are more abbreviated than those for breeding species. All species are arranged taxonomically according to the 2018 59th supplement to the American Ornithological Society's Checklist of North American Birds.

Each account covers the general occurrence of the species in Loudoun, indicating how likely the bird is to be detected in appropriate habitat in the correct season. Species occurrence (common, rare, etc.) may not correlate directly with the number of atlas blocks in which the species was documented, since appropriate habitat is not always evenly distributed across the county. Breeding accounts highlight the earliest and latest dates that breeding was confirmed during Atlas 2. Non-breeding (winter and migrant) accounts highlight the earliest and latest seasonal sightings or northerly/southerly migration periods as documented during the atlas. Occasionally, a species was documented outside its typical time period; such sightings are noted within the text of the account. All documented species have an International Union for Conservation of Nature (IUCN) status of "Least Concern" unless otherwise noted. Definitions for commonly used terms and abbreviations are provided in Tables 6 and 7.

Table 6. Definitions for commonly used terms.	
Abundant	Hard to miss; a common species which is very numerous
Common	Likely to be observed in suitable habitat
Uncommon	Present in suitable habitat, but not always observed
Occasional	Observed only a few times during the season
Rare	May be present, but not every year; occurs irregularly
Vagrant	Range (breeding, winter, and migratory) is outside Loudoun and surrounding area
Spring	March through May
Summer	June through August
Fall	September through November
Winter	December through February
Breeding evidence	Includes possible, probable, and confirmed breeding species unless otherwise stated
Earliest breeding confirmation[†]	Earliest date (month and day) breeding was confirmed during Atlas 2. Applies to birds that breed in Loudoun. See Table 1 for confirmation codes.
Latest breeding confirmation[†]	Latest date (month and day) breeding was confirmed during Atlas 2. Applies to birds that breed in Loudoun. See Table 1 for confirmation codes.
Earliest seasonal sighting[†]	Earliest date (month and day) recorded during a particular season (spring, summer, winter, or fall) in Atlas 2. Applies to Loudoun's winter birds, vagrants, and a few migrants.
Latest seasonal sighting[†]	Latest date (month and day) recorded during a particular season (spring, summer, winter or fall) in Atlas 2. Applies to Loudoun's winter birds, vagrants, and a few migrants.
Southerly migration period[†]	Earliest and latest dates (month and day) recorded during fall migration in Atlas 2. Applies to most migrants that pass through Loudoun.
Northerly migration period[†]	Earliest and latest dates (month and day) recorded during spring migration in Atlas 2. Applies to most migrants that pass through Loudoun.

[†] Earliest and latest dates were determined solely from Atlas 2 data and were included only for species with 5 or more sightings. As such, these dates may not provide a complete picture of the earliest and latest dates for a species.

* The Rufous/Allen's Hummingbird account was combined with Ruby-throated Hummingbird for 261 total accounts.

Distribution Maps

Every species account includes a distribution map, which illustrates the blocks in which a species was observed or documented as a possible, probable, or confirmed breeder. Refer to the color-coded key accompanying each map. The highest category of evidence reported during the 5-year atlas is the one displayed for that block. A "change by block" comparison is included for breeding species, comparing results from the Atlas 1 and Atlas 2 datasets. Filled circles (●) indicate a gain from Atlas 1 to Atlas 2 while open circles (○) reveal a loss from the first to the second atlas. *Note that 26 of the 73 blocks were excluded from comparison due to insufficient effort in Atlas 1.* Insufficient effort was defined as 3 or fewer effort-hours per block, as shown by the lightest blue blocks in Figure 6 (see Figure 5 for comparison with Atlas 2 effort). A base map of Loudoun is provided to orient readers with Loudoun's major highways, waterways, and towns (Figure 7). Names in green are the names of groupings of 6 blocks (quadrangles). All maps were created by the USGS Patuxent Wildlife Research Center using ArcGIS software by ESRI.

Figure 5. Atlas 2 effort.

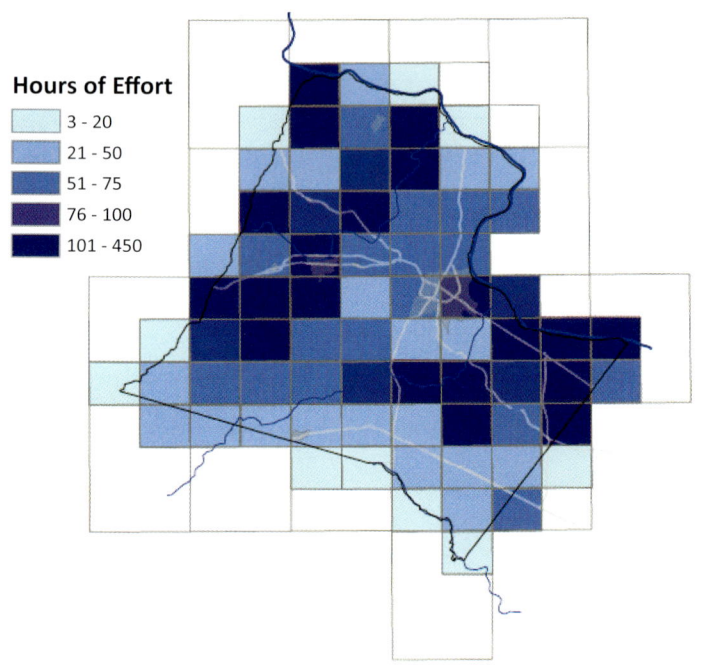

Hours of Effort
- 3 - 20
- 21 - 50
- 51 - 75
- 76 - 100
- 101 - 450

Figure 6. Atlas 1 effort. Note the different color scale from Figure 5.

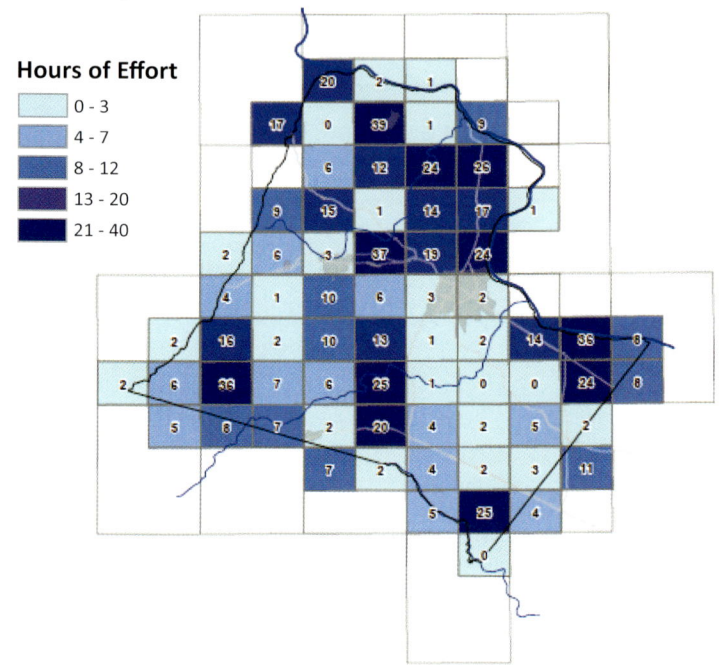

Hours of Effort
- 0 - 3
- 4 - 7
- 8 - 12
- 13 - 20
- 21 - 40

Figure 7. Base map for Loudoun County.

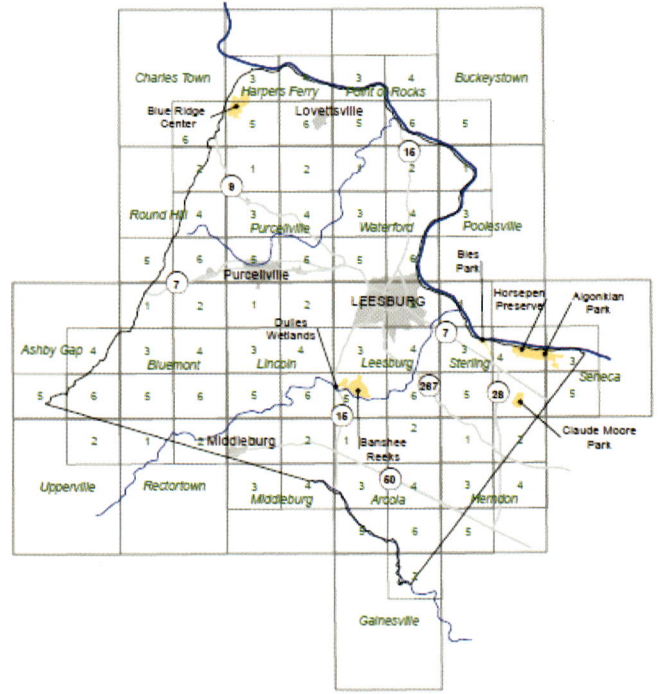

Table 7. Commonly used abbreviations.	
Atlas 1	1985-1989 Virginia Breeding Bird Atlas
Atlas 2	2009-2014 Loudoun County Bird Atlas
BBA	Breeding Bird Atlas
BBS	Breeding Bird Survey
CBC	Christmas Bird Count
Dulles Greenway Wetlands	Dulles Greenway Wetlands Mitigation Project
IUCN	International Union for Conservation of Nature
Loudoun Wildlife	Loudoun Wildlife Conservancy
NWR	National Wildlife Refuge
PIF	Partners In Flight
USGS	United States Geological Survey
USFWS	Unites States Fish and Wildlife Service

SPECIES ACCOUNTS

Photo by Gerco Hoogeweg

SNOW GOOSE
Chen caerulescens

Occurrence: rare migrant and winter visitor

Earliest fall sighting: October 31

Latest spring sighting: March 17

It's an unforgettable spectacle — a sound like the distant baying of hounds that calls attention to wave after wave of Snow Geese flying onto their wintering grounds. Rare in Loudoun, where 15 sightings were documented in 13 blocks scattered throughout the county, Snow Geese are often reported in flocks of a thousand or more on East Coast refuges such as Chincoteague NWR. Larger populations of this bird, which breeds in colonies in the Arctic tundra, winter in central U.S. and in the Pacific Coast states, all supported by a variety of wetland habitats and agricultural fields.

Snow Geese consist of two color morphs. The light morph has completely white plumage except for black wingtips. It sports a pinkish bill with a distinctive black "grin patch." The dark morph, or Blue Goose, has a dark brown body with a white head and neck. It appears more frequently in western populations than in Atlantic coastal regions.

Written by Bill Brown

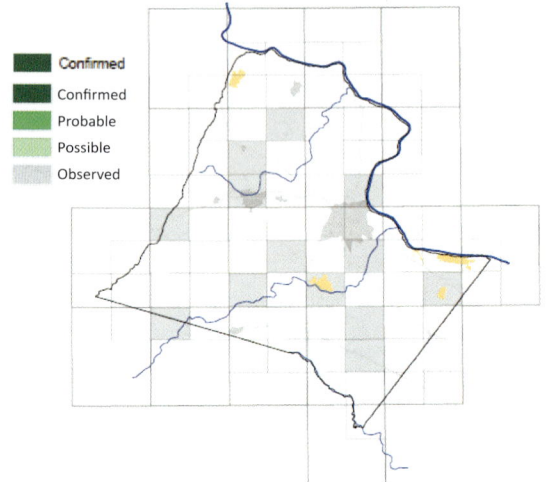

Confirmed
Confirmed
Probable
Possible
Observed

GREATER WHITE-FRONTED GOOSE
Anser albifrons

Occurrence: rare migrant and winter visitor

Earliest/latest seasonal sightings: fewer than 5 atlas sightings, see account for details

Named for the white band around its pinkish bill, the Greater White-fronted Goose is a gray-brown bird with bright orange legs. Its undertail feathers are white, and a narrow white lateral stripe across its flank is visible when the bird is at rest. Only 2 atlas sightings were reported, one in Waterford 6 during the Central Loudoun CBC and another in mid-September in Point of Rocks 5.

In North America, the Greater White-fronted Goose breeds from Alaska across northernmost Canada to the western coast of Hudson Bay. In winter, the Pacific population of the species moves south to Washington, Oregon, and California, while a separate mid-continent population migrates over a broad swath of the Great Plains to winter in Texas, Louisiana, and Mexico. A subspecies that breeds in Greenland and usually winters in Ireland and Scotland is the source of many of the occurrences in the Atlantic Coast states.

Written by Bill Brown

Photo by Michael Bowen

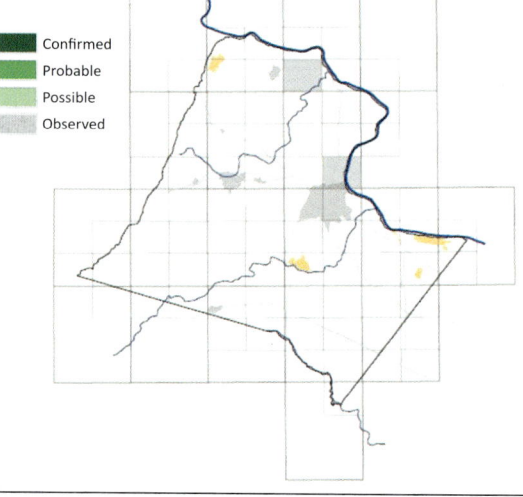

Confirmed
Probable
Possible
Observed

Photo by Deb Calhoun

BRANT
Branta bernicla

Occurrence: rare migrant and winter visitor

Earliest/latest seasonal sightings: fewer than 5 atlas sightings, see account for details

The Brant is a small goose with a black head, neck, and breast. Adults have a characteristic white "necklace" patch, missing from juvenile birds. The belly of the eastern subspecies is pale, while the western "Black Brant" subspecies is dark. Like other geese, male and female adults are identical and maintain the same coloration year-long.

The Brant is seldom seen in Loudoun and was reported only once – a group of 35 were observed flying over Snickers Gap Hawkwatch in Bluemont 1 on November 28, 2010. Unlike other North American geese, the Brant winters almost exclusively in coastal habitats. Furthermore, its normal migration route runs south along the coast of Virginia rather than inland. It feeds primarily on marine eelgrass and green algae, and only recently has it begun to venture onto cultivated fields to graze on grass and clover. This species breeds in the Arctic tundra. Loudoun residents wishing to see Brant might want to visit coastal hotspots such as Ocean City, Maryland, where the birds begin arriving in October and departing in early February.

Written by Bill Brown

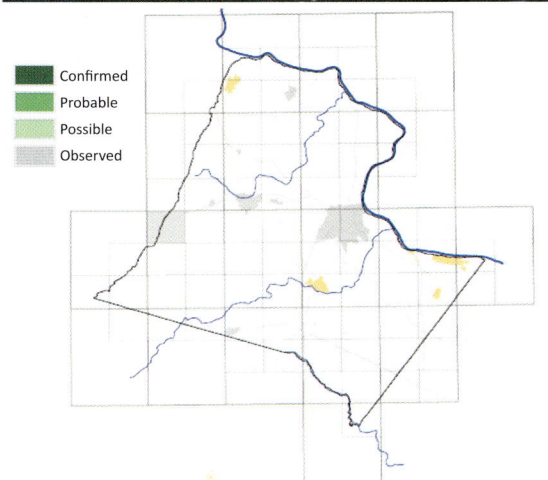

Confirmed
Probable
Possible
Observed

CACKLING GOOSE
Branta hutchinsii

Occurrence: rare winter visitor

Earliest/latest seasonal sightings: fewer than 5 atlas sightings, see account for details

In 2004, the Canada Goose's four smallest subspecies were split off and lumped together as a new species, the Cackling Goose. In addition to their size, these four subspecies were distinguished by being the northernmost breeders – all nesting in the tundra along the Arctic Coast of North America.

The Canada and Cackling Goose have similar coloration and share their distinctive field marks – a black head and neck and white chinstrap. They can often be distinguished by their size, but there is some overlap, so that the largest Cackling Goose can be larger than the smallest Canada. The Cackling has a rounder head with a steeper forehead and shorter bill; the Canada has a more wedge-shaped head.

Only 4 sightings of the Cackling Goose were reported during the 5-year atlas, reflecting the fact that its principal wintering areas are localized in Washington, Oregon, and California, and in the south-central states around Texas.

Written by Bill Brown

Cackling Goose in front of Canada Geese
Photo by Dave Boltz

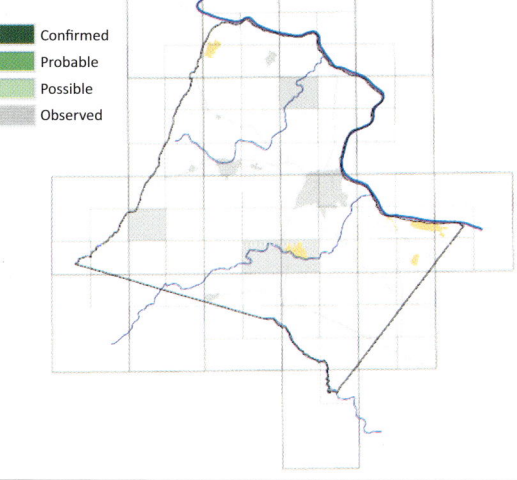

Confirmed
Probable
Possible
Observed

CANADA GOOSE
Branta canadensis

Occurrence: abundant breeder, migrant, and year-round resident

Earliest breeding confirmation: April 1, parent entering/exiting nest site or on nest (ON)

Latest breeding confirmation: August 18, recently fledged young (FL)

The Canada Goose, large and widespread, may well be the most readily identifiable bird in the county. Even most non-birders recognize its distinctive black head and neck and white chinstrap, which distinguish it from all other North American geese, except for the noticeably smaller, rare Cackling Goose. Males and females are nearly identical, though the female is often slightly smaller than her mate. Adults maintain the same plumage coloration throughout the year.

Photo ©Dick Rowe

Canada Geese were observed in virtually all 73 atlas blocks. Evidence of confirmed or probable breeding was reported in 58 blocks, an increase of 22 blocks from Atlas 1. This species is found in a wide variety of natural and man-made habitats including rivers, floodplains, marshes, wetlands, ponds, parks, and almost anywhere with a significant expanse of open lawn.

Canada Geese mate for life, with males and females sharing responsibilities of raising the young. Most begin to breed in their fourth year. The female selects the nest site and builds the nest, starting with a simple scrape in the ground. The female also incubates the eggs. The pair jointly defends the nest against predators, with the male taking primary responsibility during incubation. Goslings hatch fully covered with down, and they are able to leave the nest, walk, and swim within 24 hours of hatching. Both parents lead the young to food but do not feed them directly. The young can fly within 6 to 9 weeks, but remain with their parents for up to a year.

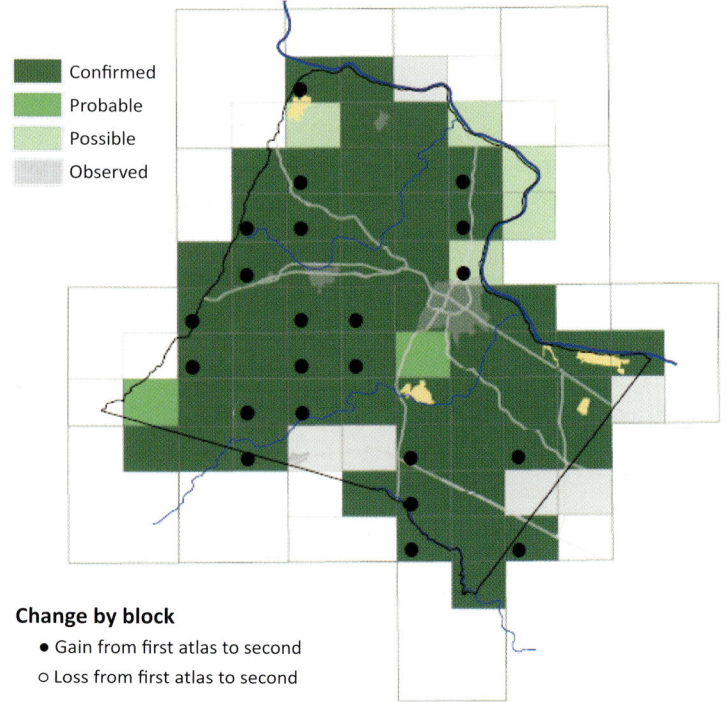

Confirmed
Probable
Possible
Observed

Change by block
- Gain from first atlas to second
○ Loss from first atlas to second

In Virginia, and elsewhere along the Atlantic Flyway, there are distinct migratory and resident populations of Canada Geese. The migratory population breeds in northern Canada and migrates southward in the winter. The resident population breeds and winters from southern Canada southward. The resident population has grown dramatically over the past half century, due to a lack of natural predators and ready source of food in farm fields and in suburban lawns, parks, and golf courses. The geese have increasingly come into conflict with humans, concerned about perceived health hazards, crop destruction, and threats to aviation. Management policies, which successfully protected Canadas in the mid-twentieth century because of low population numbers, have given way to efforts to control the population through a variety of lethal and non-lethal measures.

Written by Bill Brown

MUTE SWAN
Cygnus olor

Occurrence: occasional year-round resident

Earliest/latest seasonal sightings: atlas sightings in every season, see account for details

Mute Swans are non-native to North America, imported from Europe to decorate ponds and lakes in towns and cities. Though elegant, swimming with its long neck held in a graceful S and wings slightly raised, this swan's aggressive behavior displaces native species and disturbs local ecosystems. Its voracious appetite for aquatic vegetation damages feeding habitat. This swan has an orange bill with a black knob which helps distinguish it from native Trumpeter and Tundra Swans. Contrary to its name, the Mute Swan makes a variety of vocalizations, though its call is muffled compared to other swans. Pairs mate for life and remain on the breeding grounds year-round.

With few natural predators, North American populations have increased over the past 50 years, creating a problem for wildlife and habitat. Efforts have been made in Virginia and other states to reduce the scattered populations that have become established in the wild. Individual Mute Swans were observed in 5 blocks along Loudoun's border, including the Potomac River, with no evidence of breeding, though given the right circumstances breeding is a possibility.

Written by Spring Ligi

Photo by Gerco Hoogeweg

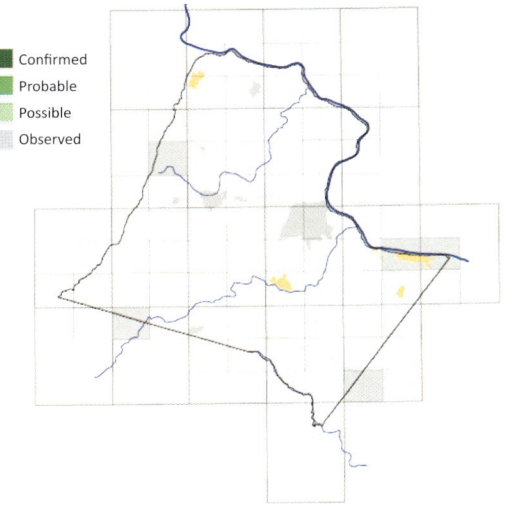

- Confirmed
- Probable
- Possible
- Observed

TRUMPETER SWAN
Cygnus buccinator

Occurrence: rare migrant and year-round resident

Earliest summer sighting: July 22

Latest fall sighting: November 10

Trumpeter Swans, once present throughout North America, included a population that wintered on the Eastern Shore of the Chesapeake Bay. After European colonization, overhunting for feathers for hats and writing quills and agricultural conversion of wetlands led to their dramatic decline. In the 1990s, a partnership between Environmental Studies at Airlie and Defenders of Wildlife attempted to restore a migratory population in the eastern U.S. by training swans reared at Airlie to follow ultra-light planes to the Eastern Shore where it was hoped they would winter. Today, non-migratory Trumpeter Swans, some with visible neck bands, are seen in Virginia's Piedmont and were observed in 3 atlas blocks in southwestern Loudoun. Although they breed in neighboring counties, breeding has not been documented in Loudoun. Trumpeter Swans, North America's heaviest flying bird, weigh an average of 26 pounds. They hold their long necks straighter than Mute Swans. Black facial skin forms a V on the forehead, unlike the Tundra Swan's black facial skin which is straight across.

Written by Linda Millington

Photo ©Dick Rowe

- Confirmed
- Probable
- Possible
- Observed

TUNDRA SWAN
Cygnus columbianus

Occurrence: occasional migrant and winter visitor

Earliest fall sighting: November 13

Latest spring sighting: April 20

The Tundra Swan is the smallest and most numerous swan in Loudoun. It is typically observed in large flocks on lakes, ponds, wetlands, and rivers, often in close proximity to agricultural fields where it feeds. The Tundra Swan's distinctively straight-necked posture, along with its flocking behavior, helps distinguish it from the native Trumpeter and non-native Mute Swans. Most Tundra Swans have a yellow spot at the base of their black bill. The whistling sound produced when air flows through the wings in flight has earned this species the name "whistling swan." They are often first noticed during migration when their bugling calls are heard from their straggling 'U'-shaped line far overhead.

Pairs breed on the Arctic tundra, mating for life and remaining together year-round. Tundra Swans were observed in 21 of the 73 atlas blocks. Overall, populations in North America appear to be stable. However, oil and gas drilling in Arctic breeding habitats and loss of wetlands in Loudoun and other migratory stop-over sites pose potential threats to this species.

Written by Spring Ligi

Photo ©Dick Rowe

Confirmed
Probable
Possible
Observed

Photo by Dave Boltz

WOOD DUCK
Aix sponsa

Occurrence: common breeder and migrant, occasional winter resident

Earliest breeding confirmation: April 19, recently fledged young (FL)

Latest breeding confirmation: August 8, recently fledged young (FL)

While fairly common in the right habitat—wooded ponds and marshes as well as rivers and creeks of all sizes with plenty of cover, sightings of these beautiful ducks are nevertheless uncommon and memorable. The male Wood Duck is arguably North America's most stunning and distinctive bird. He sports a bright green, drooping crest, red eye and red markings on the short bill, and a sharply outlined white "bridle" on an otherwise black head. Coloration on his body includes a chestnut chest, green on back and wings, and yellow sides, with white belly seen in flight. The much duller female may be easily distinguished by a white "comet" shape around her eye, drooping crest, and short bill.

Wood Ducks nest in cavities or in nest boxes often quite high (up to 60 feet) in trees usually near but sometimes some distance from water. After the 6 to 16 eggs hatch, the precocial young jump out of the nest to the ground or water a day later. Egg-dumping, where the female lays eggs in other Wood Duck nests and leaves them to be raised by the

WOOD DUCK (continued)

other female, is common; some very full nests have been found containing as many as 29 eggs, especially where other nest boxes are easily found nearby. The Wood Duck is the only North American duck that will commonly raise two broods.

While Wood Ducks can reside year-round as far north as New England and Minnesota, they only occasionally are found in winter in Loudoun. Small numbers are found in about half of the Central Loudoun CBCs. During the atlas period, there were only a dozen reports during the months of November through February. Presumably eastern birds simply move further south in winter, not venturing further than Florida, the Caribbean, or northern Mexico.

After a dramatic decline in their numbers in the late 19th century, the North American BBS found Wood Duck numbers to have increased between 1966 and 2015, good news for this beloved species. This increase is supported by a net gain in over 20 blocks from Atlas 1 to Atlas 2, when they were observed in 50 of the 73 blocks.

Written by Mary Ann Good

Change by block
- ● Gain from first atlas to second
- ○ Loss from first atlas to second

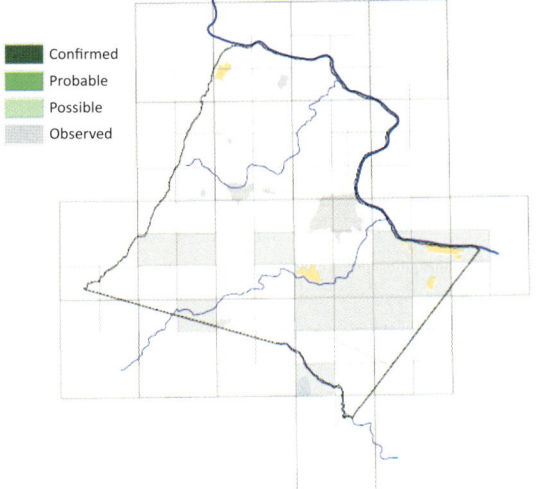

Photo by Dave Boltz

BLUE-WINGED TEAL
Anas discors

Occurrence: uncommon migrant, rare summer and winter visitor

Southerly migration period: October 10 – November 13

Northerly migration period: March 21 – May 2

One of the smallest dabbling ducks, the Blue-winged Teal is usually found swimming through emergent vegetation in marshes and shallow ponds. The male in breeding plumage is easily recognized by its dark bluish-gray head with a large white crescent behind its bill and white hip patch. The large blue wing patch normally shows only in flight. Females and males in non-breeding plumage show a tight, uniform pattern of brown feathers with black centers.

Blue-winged Teal were recorded in about one-fifth of the atlas blocks, mostly in southeastern Loudoun where there are many water bodies. The majority of sightings occurred in April. Reports of Blue-winged Teal on two Central Loudoun CBCs indicate that, though rare, they may linger in Loudoun during mild winters, unlike many ducks that readily withstand our colder winters. Breeding is concentrated heavily in the prairie pothole region of the northern Great Plains and central Canada, but extends through most of the U.S., absent only in the southeast and far southwest of the country. This species is the second most abundant duck in North America.

Written by Bill Brown

Photo by Bill Brown

NORTHERN SHOVELER
Anas clypeata

Occurrence: uncommon migrant and winter resident

Earliest fall sighting: November 29

Latest spring sighting: May 7

The Northern Shoveler is a dabbling duck distinguished from others of its genus by a noticeably longer bill that widens at the end. The bill is lined with fine projections that filter small invertebrates from the water. A breeding male has a metallic-green head, white breast, and chestnut belly and flanks. Female shovelers and non-breeding males have rather dull mottled brownish plumage. In flight, both sexes show a pale blue patch on the upper forewing, but that is not always visible when the bird is at rest.

In Loudoun, the shoveler is most often seen in shallow ponds and wetlands, less frequently in the Potomac River. Almost half of the atlas sightings were reported at the Dulles Greenway Wetlands, including 1 aberrant summer sighting in mid-August. The Northern Shoveler breeds widely through the western U.S. and Canada, with populations remaining relatively stable over the past five decades. On its breeding ground, it is more territorial than the other dabbling ducks and forms stronger pair bonds, often lasting well into the egg incubation period.

Written by Bill Brown

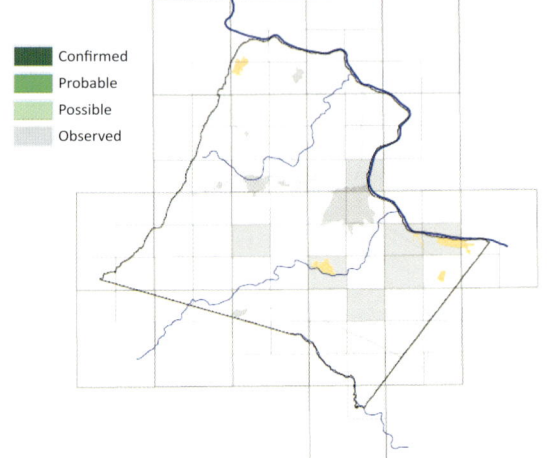

Confirmed
Probable
Possible
Observed

GADWALL
Anas strepera

Occurrence: uncommon migrant and winter resident

Earliest fall sighting: October 29

Latest spring sighting: May 9

This medium-sized dabbling duck is not known for its flashy colors and can be easily overlooked. If you find a quiet pond or marsh with Mallards, check carefully to make sure some of the "females" aren't Gadwall! Male Gadwall are brown and gray with a black patch at the tail; females are brown and buff, resembling female Mallards, but with a thinner, darker bill. In flight, both sexes have a white wing-patch. They feed on submerged vegetation and often steal food from diving ducks.

Gadwall breed mainly in the Great Plains and Canadian prairies. Loudoun residents may observe courtship behavior, which occurs in fall and early winter. This species was observed in 16 blocks, with 14 of the 34 total sightings (40%) located in the calm, open water areas of the Dulles Greenway Wetlands. Despite being the third most hunted duck species in the U.S., its numbers remain strong due to careful management of duck harvests and conservation of wetlands and nesting habitat.

Written by Spring Ligi

Photo by Dave Boltz

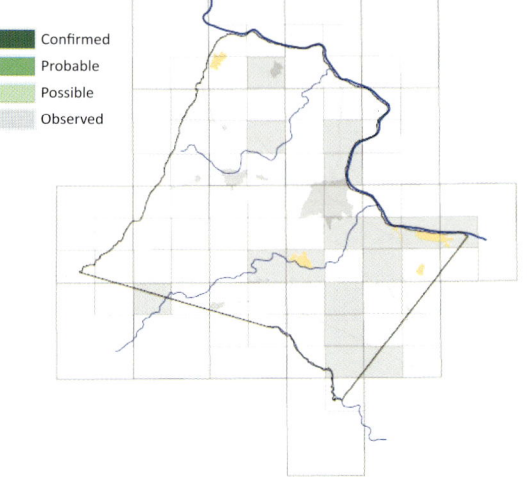

Confirmed
Probable
Possible
Observed

Photo by Bill Brown

AMERICAN WIGEON
Anas americana

Occurrence: uncommon migrant and winter resident

Earliest fall sighting: November 25

Latest spring sighting: April 5

The American Wigeon can be distinguished from all other North American dabbling ducks by its shorter bill, which is pale bluish-gray with a black tip. In breeding plumage the male is unmistakable, with its white forehead and crown and broad green band curving up and back from its eye to the nape of its neck.

The American Wigeon was observed about 25 times throughout 14 blocks, mostly in February and March, and largely in the shallow ponds and wetlands of southeastern Loudoun. It winters coast to coast across the southern half of North America in freshwater, brackish, and saline habitats. It breeds further north than any other dabbling duck, from Alaska across the Canadian tundra and boreal forest to Nova Scotia. In the Great Plains region its breeding extends south to New Mexico, while in the East it breeds almost entirely north of the Great Lakes. Though widely hunted, federal waterfowl surveys indicate that the overall population has remained stable, with a recent increase in 2013 and 2014.

Written by Bill Brown

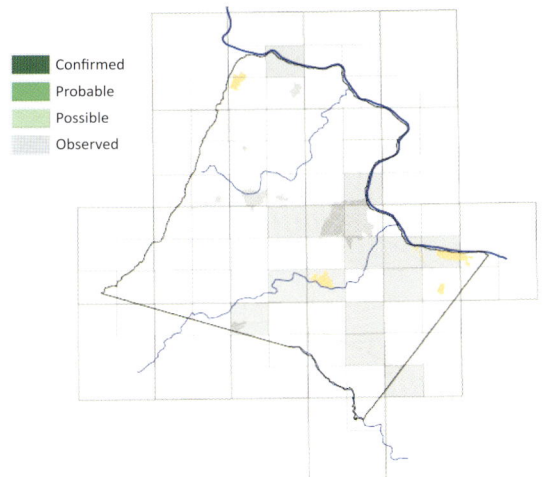

- ■ Confirmed
- ■ Probable
- ■ Possible
- ■ Observed

MALLARD
Anas platyrhynchos

Occurrence: common breeder and year-round resident

Earliest breeding confirmation: April 21, recently fledged young (FL)

Latest breeding confirmation: September 11, recently fledged young (FL)

The Mallard is the most familiar wild duck in North America as well as the ancestor to most domestic breeds. They are extremely adaptable birds and can be found almost anywhere there is a body of fresh water nearby, from city parks and golf courses to grain fields, bays, lakes, and secluded ponds.

Photo by Dave Boltz

Mallards are large ducks, with males easily identified most of the year by an iridescent green head, yellow bill, and distinctive curly black tail coverts. Females are dull gray-brown with a yellow-orange bill. Both males and females have a blue wing speculum bordered in black and white. Females *quack* while males give a quieter and more raspy call. As with other ducks, Mallards shed all their flight feathers after breeding and remain flightless for 3-4 weeks. During this "eclipse" period they are dull in color and can be difficult to distinguish from other species.

Mallards are dabbling ducks; they do not dive but tip forward in the water to find food. Their diet includes plants, nuts, seeds, and pretty much any small insect, mollusk, and fish that can be eaten. They'll readily forage below bird feeders and in grain fields. Chances are if you've seen someone feeding the ducks, it is Mallards taking the handouts. Please

MALLARD (continued)

note: Feeding ducks is harmful and pollutes water.

Pairs form in fall and winter. Courtship involves many ritualized behaviors including the male dipping his bill in the water and then flinging it while grunting and whistling. Many males may court one female. Mallards are notorious hybridizers and will mate with other dabbling ducks. Females choose nesting sites that can be some distance from water. The nest is a shallow bowl of plant material lined with down; up to 15 creamy grayish or greenish eggs may be laid. Incubation is by the female only for about 26 days. When the young hatch they move to a body of water within a day.

In Atlas 2 the Mallard was observed in 59 blocks, with breeding evidence documented in 47, a net gain of 25 blocks from Atlas 1. The more thorough coverage and higher level of effort per block in Atlas 2 are likely

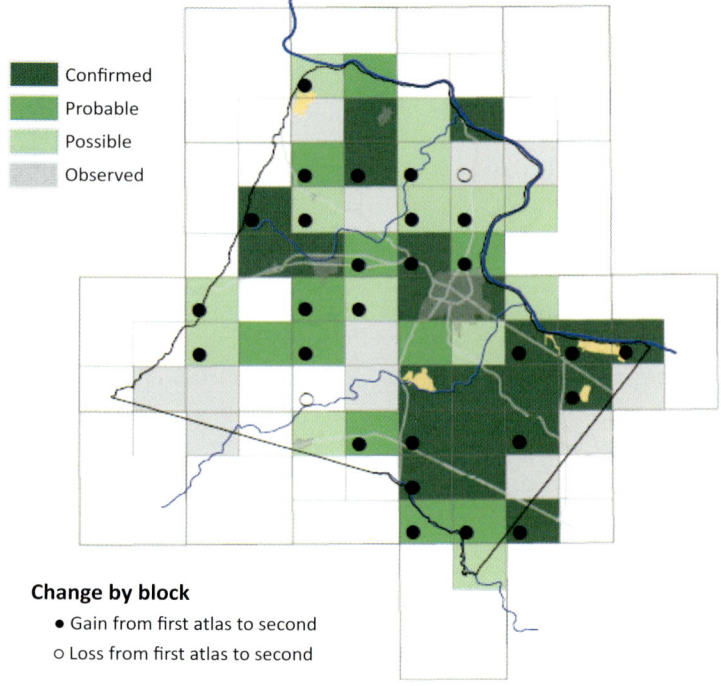

Confirmed
Probable
Possible
Observed

Change by block
- Gain from first atlas to second
○ Loss from first atlas to second

significant factors in this species' apparent expansion. Mallards have been reported in large numbers on every Central Loudoun CBC. This species earns the distinction of most abundant and widespread duck in North America, as well as the most hunted.

Written by Donna Quinn

Photo by Dave Boltz

Confirmed
Probable
Possible
Observed

AMERICAN BLACK DUCK
Anas rubripes

Occurrence: uncommon migrant and winter resident, rare summer visitor

Earliest fall sighting: October 30

Latest spring sighting: May 12

Found in ponds, rivers, and wetlands, the American Black Duck is nearly identical in size and structure to the Mallard. Its drab, nondescript plumage resembles a female Mallard but is noticeably darker. Its olive-colored bill is paler than the female Mallard's bill, but similar to the male Mallard's bill in non-breeding plumage. The speculum, when visible, is distinctive. This vivid wing-patch is violet with black borders on the Black Duck, but blue with white borders on the Mallard. The two species often flock together and hybridize, producing individuals with mixed or blended coloration. American Black Ducks were observed in 29 blocks throughout Loudoun, with no evidence of breeding. However, there were 2 July sightings of this shy dabbling duck in Leesburg 5 (2011) and Waterford 2 (2012). Black Ducks breed in the coastal plain of Virginia, spreading northward through eastern North America nearly to the Arctic Circle. Hunted intensively in the '60s and '70s, stricter regulations have helped stabilize their numbers, although habitat loss remains an issue.

Written by Bill Brown

NORTHERN PINTAIL

Anas acuta

Occurrence: occasional migrant and winter visitor

Earliest fall sighting: November 13

Latest spring sighting: April 13

Loudouners are fortunate when they get the infrequent sighting of this handsome duck. The male has a stately appearance with his long slender neck and very long, pointed tail. These, together with his dark brown head, pale gray body, and white "bib," appearing to be tied behind his head, make him unmistakable. The female, although very plain, also has a long neck, slender shape, and pointed, shorter tail. Among the first ducks to migrate north in the spring and south in the fall, this species breeds in the northern Midwestern states, Canada, and Alaska, and winters from the southern U.S. south to northern Colombia.

In addition to dabbling and filter-feeding in shallow lakes or ponds, sometimes tipping bottom-up, pintails may forage for the seeds, aquatic insects, snails, and crustaceans they prefer at the water's edge. This species was found in only 5 blocks during Atlas 2 and reported in 8 of the past 20 Central Loudoun CBCs. The North American BBS showed a population decline of 72% from 1966 to 2012.

Written by Mary Ann Good

Photo by Dave Boltz

Confirmed
Probable
Possible
Observed

Photo by Dave Boltz

Confirmed
Probable
Possible
Observed

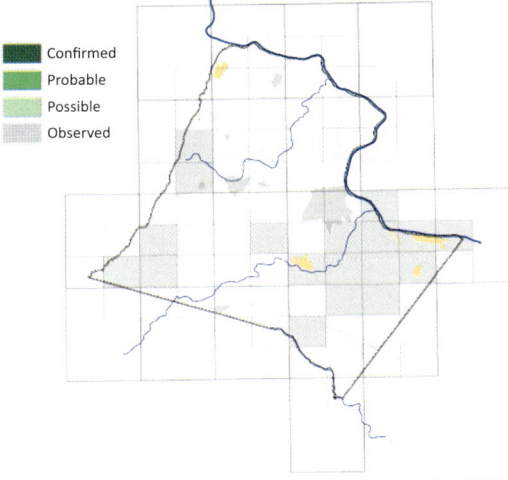

GREEN-WINGED TEAL

Anas crecca

Occurrence: uncommon migrant and winter resident

Earliest fall sighting: September 22

Latest spring sighting: May 3

The Green-winged Teal, about 14 inches in length, is the smallest North American dabbling duck. The male in breeding plumage is easily recognized by its rich chestnut-colored head, broad green crescent arcing from each eye to the nape of its neck, and vertical white bar at each shoulder. As with most dabblers the female is less distinctive, with a pale gray head and mottled tan and brown back and flanks.

The Green-winged Teal may be found throughout Loudoun in shallow water and mud flats with thick emergent vegetation. It filter-feeds along the surface of the water, seldom upending itself like other dabbling ducks. It also probes the mud for small invertebrates. This duck winters from coast to coast across the southern U.S. Its breeding range stretches from Alaska through much of the Great Plains and Great Lakes region and on to the Maritime provinces of Canada. Populations have increased in recent decades, despite being the second most hunted duck in the U.S.

Written by Bill Brown

CANVASBACK

Aythya valisineria

Occurrence: occasional winter visitor, rare migrant

Earliest winter sighting: December 29

Latest spring sighting: March 19

Photo by Deb Calhoun

The Canvasback, the largest of the diving ducks, was mostly found on water bodies of eastern Loudoun, near the Potomac River. They are more common along the coast, though degradation of their wintering habitat, especially in the Chesapeake Bay, has impacted them. They feed on the leaves and roots of bay grasses, with a fondness for wild celery. This fast flyer forms pair bonds in early spring and migrates to its breeding grounds in the Midwest's prairie pothole region. The Canvasback was found in 5 atlas blocks and on less than half of the Central Loudoun CBCs over the past 20 years. Its sloped head and long, tapered bill are very distinctive.

While the current population appears to be stable, their population fluctuates substantially, which has made them a species of concern in the past. As a result, the USFWS closely monitors how many Canvasbacks may be hunted every year (Baldassarre 2014).

Written by Joe Coleman

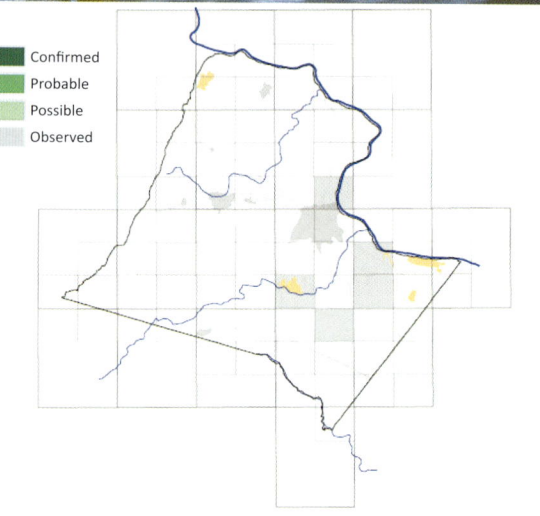

Confirmed
Probable
Possible
Observed

Photo ©Dick Rowe

Confirmed
Probable
Possible
Observed

REDHEAD

Aythya americana

Occurrence: uncommon winter resident, rare migrant

Earliest winter sighting: December 25

Latest spring sighting: March 17

Redheads, a medium-sized diving duck with a chestnut-colored head and neck offset by a black and gray body, are stunning. This sociable duck had 17 sightings in 12 atlas blocks and was found on only 4 of the 20 Central Loudoun CBCs. More common along the coast as they prefer shallow waters with lots of seagrass, they can occasionally be found on lakes and rivers in our area. Pairs form on the wintering grounds and breed mainly in the Midwest's prairie pothole region. Female Redheads take brood parasitism to the extreme, laying eggs in the nests of other Redheads as well as 10 other duck species.

Their population experienced a dramatic decline in the early 1900s and was precarious enough in the middle of the century for Redheads to warrant special protection (Baldassarre 2014). However, their numbers have increased appreciably since 1966, likely due to carefully managed hunting seasons and restoration of duck habitat.

Written by Joe Coleman

RING-NECKED DUCK

Aythya collaris

Occurrence: common migrant and winter resident

Earliest fall sighting: October 30

Latest spring sighting: May 15

Photo by Bill Brown

Ring-necked Ducks, smallish diving ducks, are common winter residents in our area, becoming more common as the winter progresses and peaking in March. They were found in 44 atlas blocks and on all 20 of the Central Loudoun CBCs, with over 300 individuals twice. There was 1 aberrant summer atlas sighting (June 20, 2009) in the Bluemont area. Of all the diving ducks, they are the most likely to utilize small ponds but are also found on lakes and rivers in our area. The ring on their neck, for which they are named, is actually rather difficult to see in the field; their peaked head, the ring on the bill, and the white spur on males between their sides and chest are the easiest features to use for identifying them.

Ring-necked Ducks breed on freshwater marshes and bogs across North America's boreal forest. Their population has "prospered more than any other species of North American diving duck" (Baldassarre 2014).

Written by Joe Coleman

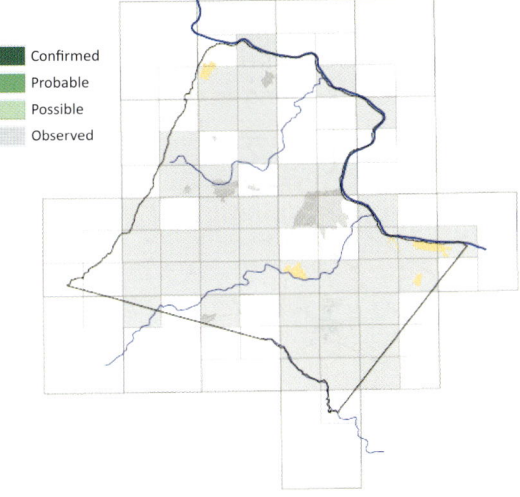

- Confirmed
- Probable
- Possible
- Observed

Photo by Dave Boltz

- Confirmed
- Probable
- Possible
- Observed

GREATER SCAUP

Aythya marila

Occurrence: rare migrant and winter visitor

Earliest/latest seasonal sightings: fewer than 5 atlas sightings, see account for details

The Greater Scaup is typically found on open bays and estuaries along the Atlantic Coast in winter, but sometimes comes inland to lakes and rivers. This medium-sized diving duck was documented only 3 times during the 5-year atlas (closer to the Potomac River in eastern Loudoun) and once over the past two decades of Central Loudoun CBCs. Greater Scaup are often found with the more common Lesser Scaup, and indeed, both species were reported together for every atlas sighting. The slightly larger size of the Greater Scaup and the male's more rounded, green-black head helps distinguish the two species. Unlike the Lesser Scaup, this species is found across Eurasia in addition to North America.

According to the USFWS, Greater Scaup numbers have declined significantly over the past few decades. Factors contributing to their decline may include pollution in coastal areas as well as changes in breeding habitat or food resources.

Written by Spring Ligi

LESSER SCAUP
Aythya affinis

Occurrence: uncommon migrant and winter resident

Earliest fall sighting: November 4

Latest spring sighting: May 11

This fast-flying, medium-sized diving duck may be seen on freshwater lakes and ponds in more coastal eastern Loudoun. The Lesser Scaup was reported in 14 blocks, 11 more than Loudoun's other scaup species, the Greater Scaup, which is more common along the coast and on large bodies of water. The Lesser Scaup's slightly smaller size and peaked head (versus Greater Scaup's more rounded head) help distinguish these two very similar species.

Lesser Scaup were documented in 11 of the past 20 Central Loudoun CBCs, with numbers ranging from 1 to 29 individuals each of those years. Though this species is widespread throughout North America, numbers have declined by approximately 60% over the past few decades according to the North American BBS. Factors contributing to their decline are little understood, but may include contaminants and changes in breeding habitat or food resources.

Written by Spring Ligi

Photo by Deb Calhoun

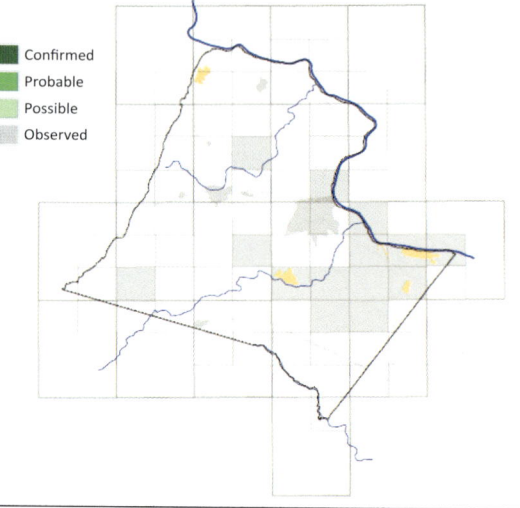
Confirmed
Probable
Possible
Observed

Photo by Dave Boltz

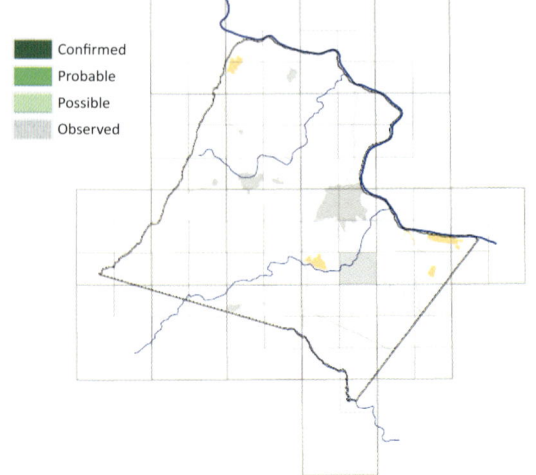
Confirmed
Probable
Possible
Observed

SURF SCOTER
Melanitta perspicillata

Occurrence: rare migrant

Southerly/northerly migration periods: fewer than 5 atlas sightings, see account for details

Documented only once during the atlas (April 2012), this diving duck overwinters along the Atlantic and Pacific coasts and breeds on freshwater lakes in the boreal forest and tundra of Canada and Alaska. During migration, the Surf Scoter occasionally stops on inland lakes to rest. This amazing sea bird teaches surfers a thing or two about diving through ocean wave crests. When a wave is about to crash down, the scoter dives (typically no deeper than 30 feet) and swims under the crest, popping up on the other side. The churning action of the crashing waves can expose mollusks, crustaceans, and other food.

Nicknamed "skunk-headed coot" for its boldly patterned head, the male is all black except for its orange and white bill and white patches on the forehead and nape. Little is known about population trends, though winter populations are vulnerable to oil spills and other pollution. Two other species of scoters have been documented in Loudoun, both also rare – the White-winged Scoter (2014) and Black Scoter (prior to atlas).

Written by Spring Ligi

WHITE-WINGED SCOTER

Melanitta fusca

Occurrence: rare migrant and winter visitor

Earliest/latest seasonal sightings: fewer than 5 atlas sightings, see account for details

The White-winged Scoter is the largest of the three scoter species found in the U.S. and the most likely to be found on inland lakes and rivers when migrating from its breeding grounds in northwestern Canada and Alaska to the Atlantic and Pacific coasts. This species was reported 3 times between January and March 2014, an unusual year with multiple sightings on or near the Potomac River throughout the region. In comparison, Surf Scoter was reported once during Atlas 2 and Black Scoter, generally observed less than the other scoters, was documented once prior to the atlas.

Male White-winged Scoters have a white, comma-shaped patch around the eyes and orange bill tip, while females have whitish patches on the face and a dark bill. The white speculum on the wing helps distinguish this species from other scoters, especially in flight. This diving duck forages for mollusks, crustaceans, insects, and fish. Little is known about population trends for any of the scoter species, though winter populations are vulnerable to oil spills and pollution.

Written by Spring Ligi

Photo by Nicole Sudduth

Confirmed
Probable
Possible
Observed

LONG-TAILED DUCK

Clangula hyemalis

Occurrence: rare migrant and winter visitor

Earliest/latest seasonal sightings: fewer than 5 atlas sightings, see account for details

Unlike most ducks, which have two plumages annually, the Long-tailed Duck has three plumages and is in a nearly constant state of molt from April through December. In winter plumage, the one most likely to be seen in Loudoun, males have a white head and neck with a gray cheek patch and darker neck patch. Their most distinctive feature is a long spiked tail. Females, which lack the long tail feathers, have a white face and brown neck patch.

The Long-tailed Duck breeds in the Arctic tundra and prefers to winter in coastal marine waters or large freshwater lakes. It was reported only 4 times and in only 2 years during Atlas 2, with 3 of those sightings on the Potomac River. This duck dives up to 200 feet while foraging, deeper than any other diving duck. Unlike most diving ducks, it uses its wings as well as its feet to swim underwater. Listed as "Vulnerable" by the IUCN, the Long-tailed Duck is considered a species of high conservation concern, though little information is available on population trends.

Written by Bill Brown

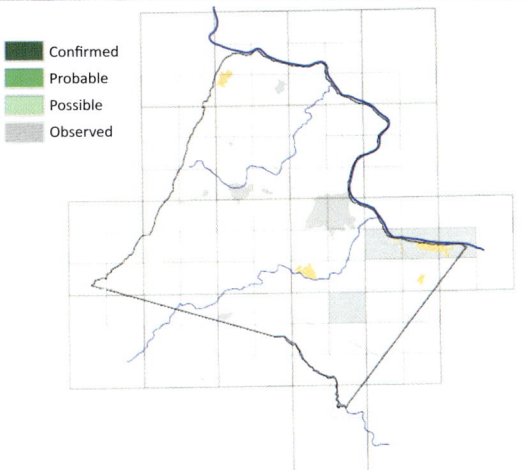

Photo by Gerco Hoogeweg

Confirmed
Probable
Possible
Observed

BUFFLEHEAD

Bucephala albeola

Occurrence: uncommon migrant and winter resident

Earliest fall sighting: November 6

Latest spring sighting: April 22

Photo by Michael Bowen

The smallest North American diving duck, the Bufflehead is a common winter visitor to Loudoun's ponds, lakes, and rivers. The breeding male has a relatively large blackish head, which in good light glistens with iridescent purple and green, with a striking white patch. Its flanks and underparts are white, and its back is black. The female is dull brownish overall, with a small white ear patch. Bufflehead feed primarily on aquatic invertebrates: insects, in fresh water; crustaceans and mollusks, in saltwater. They capture their food in frequent short dives of 10 feet or less, averaging about half their foraging time underwater.

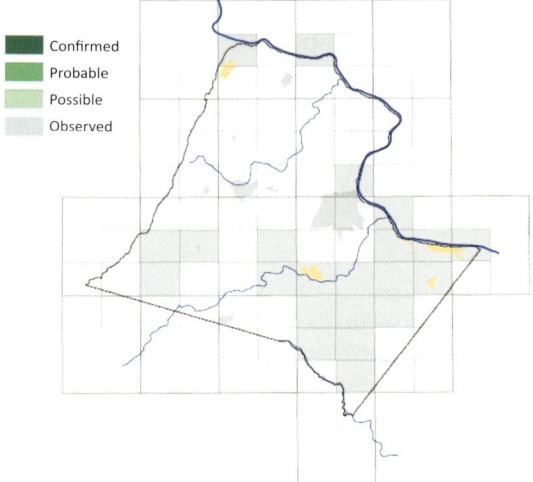

Confirmed
Probable
Possible
Observed

Bufflehead breed mostly in the boreal forest and parklands of Canada, and to a lesser extent in the northwestern U.S. They nest in cavities, usually Northern Flicker holes, but occasionally in Pileated Woodpecker holes. Numbers have increased in Loudoun, according to the Central Loudoun CBC. Only 80 individuals were documented during the 1997-2006 counts whereas 544 individuals were documented during the 2007-2016 counts, with a high of 131 individuals in 2012.

Written by Bill Brown

Photo by Michael Bowen

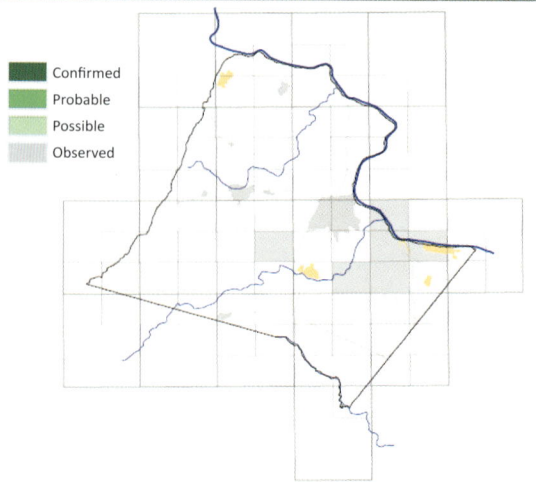

Confirmed
Probable
Possible
Observed

COMMON GOLDENEYE

Bucephala clangula

Occurrence: rare migrant and winter visitor

Earliest fall sighting: November 29

Latest spring sighting: March 30

The Common Goldeneye is a fast-flying, medium-sized diving duck. The breeding male's iridescent blackish-green head has a tall peaked crown and a diagnostic circular white patch at the base of its bill. The female has a brown head and grayish body. Both sexes have the amber irises for which the bird is named.

Though infrequently seen in the ponds and reservoirs of eastern Loudoun, the Common Goldeneye is more often found in the deeper waters of the Potomac River and the Chesapeake Bay. It was reported on 6 of the past 20 Central Loudoun CBCs. The Goldeneye is a cavity nester that breeds in the boreal forest across Canada and Alaska. A brood parasite, the female often lays her eggs in the nests of other Common Goldeneyes, as well as Hooded and Common Mergansers and Bufflehead. Conversely, the Common Goldeneye is often parasitized by those species. Overall, populations appear stable and are increasing in some breeding areas where nest boxes are provided.

Written by Bill Brown

HOODED MERGANSER
Lophodytes cucullatus

Occurrence: rare breeder, uncommon migrant and winter resident

Earliest/latest breeding confirmations: fewer than 5 atlas confirmations, see account for details

Hooded Merganser is a new breeding species for Loudoun, with the first confirmation of breeding documented during Atlas 2. Hooded Mergansers are diving ducks, best recognized by their small size, thin bill, and a fan-shaped crest that they can raise and lower. The adult male Hooded Merganser is boldly patterned, with a prominent white patch on its head, a white breast, chestnut flanks, and black back. Females and immatures are more subdued in

Photo by Gerco Hoogeweg

coloration, gray and brown, with warmer-toned cinnamon crests. Hooded Mergansers dive to catch aquatic insects, crayfish, and small fish. Unlike dabbling ducks, Hooded Mergansers swim low in the water. They run across the water on takeoff, and fly with fast, shallow wingbeats. When landing, they tend to drop quickly onto the water and skid to a stop. Hooded Mergansers are usually seen in pairs or small groups of up to 40 birds.

Hooded Mergansers nest in holes in trees near freshwater ponds or rivers (like Wood Ducks) and may also use man-made nest boxes instead of trees where they are available. If you are in the right place at the right time, you might see the young leap from their nest cavities to the ground, typically within a day or so of hatching. Such rapid fledging may help them avoid nest predators, such as snakes, raccoons, and other birds. Once out of the nest, females and their ducklings may be seen foraging in shallow, secluded bodies of water with adequate cover. In the late fall, winter, and early spring, migrant and wintering Hooded Mergansers can frequently be found on open waters of the Potomac River, as well as smaller lakes, ponds, marshes, and creeks throughout Loudoun.

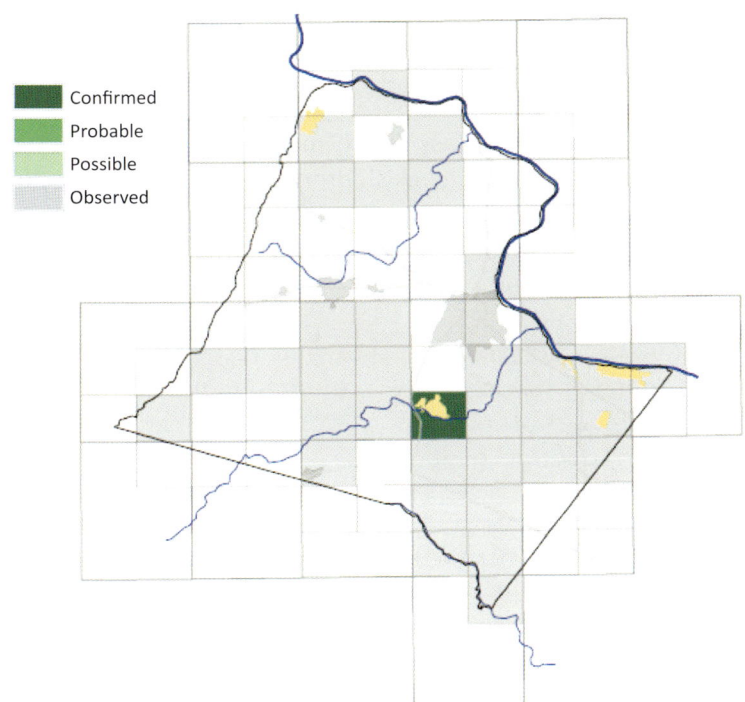

Confirmed
Probable
Possible
Observed

Hooded Merganser was confirmed as breeding in only 1 block, Leesburg 5. All 3 breeding confirmations (June 2011 and 2012) were reported in the healthy, rich Dulles Greenway Wetlands. This species was observed much more regularly throughout Loudoun as an uncommon migrant or winter visitor, found in 34 blocks. It was not documented during Atlas 1. As both a breeding and a wintering species, the Hooded Merganser may be benefiting from an increase in man-made ponds and wetlands in Loudoun. At least two separate females with young have been documented in eastern Loudoun since Atlas 2, both times in man-made drainage ponds in the Ashburn area in 2016. On a continental scale, numbers of this widespread species are thought to be increasing.

Written by Bruce Hill

Photo by Dave Boltz

COMMON MERGANSER
Mergus merganser

Occurrence: uncommon migrant and winter resident, rare summer visitor

Earliest fall sighting: October 3

Latest spring/summer sighting: June 9

Common Mergansers are the largest merganser and among the largest ducks in North America. Males are stunning birds, with dark green heads, white bodies, and long, slender, red bills. In addition to being uncommon winter residents and migrants, they also likely nest in Loudoun in small numbers in tree cavities. There was a single June sighting in Harpers Ferry 4, but no breeding evidence has been documented, during Atlas 2 or otherwise. They are secretive nesters, and females with ducklings have been found on the Potomac and Shenandoah Rivers in neighboring counties. They prefer freshwater rivers and lakes and turned up in 18 atlas blocks and on the last 17 Central Loudoun CBCs, with more than 100 individuals on 5 counts.

Because they feed high (mainly fish) on the food chain, they are important indicators of environmental health. Though their population has declined over the past 50 years, they are expanding "to the south in the eastern U.S." due to "improved water quality of large rivers and availability of nesting cavities as forests age" (Baldassarre 2014).

Written by Joe Coleman

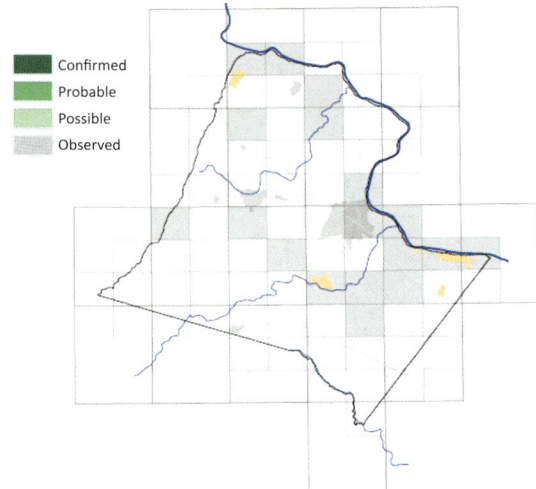

- Confirmed
- Probable
- Possible
- Observed

RED-BREASTED MERGANSER
Mergus serrator

Occurrence: uncommon spring and rare fall migrant, rare winter visitor

Earliest fall sighting: November 19

Latest spring sighting: May 12

Red-breasted Mergansers, slender and long-bodied, are a little smaller than Common Mergansers; though both have slender red bills, the males are otherwise quite easy to distinguish. The females of the two species can be difficult to separate in the wild; Red-breasted Merganser females are a little smaller, have a more pronounced crest, and the white throat blends into the brown head while there is a sharp contrast where the throat and head meet on Common Merganser females. The Red-breasted Merganser is found diving for fish in a wide variety of wet habitats, but prefers salt and brackish water more than the Common and Hooded Mergansers. This ground nester breeds farther north than the Common Merganser, around lakes and rivers in the tundra and boreal forest.

Because their population status is difficult to assess, some researchers believe their numbers are stable while others believe they are decreasing. They were reported in 12 atlas blocks throughout Loudoun, but were seen on only 3 of the 20 Central Loudoun CBCs.

Written by Joe Coleman

Photo by Dave Boltz

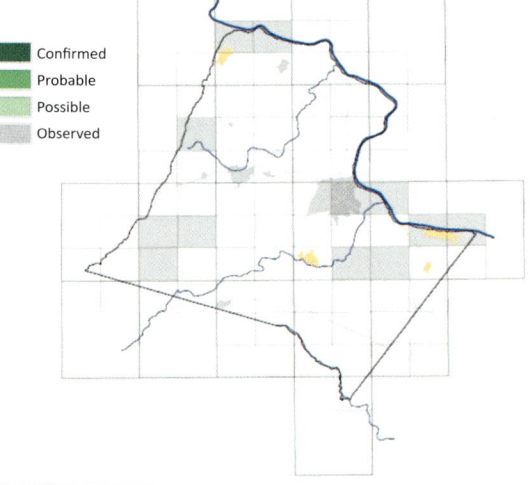

- Confirmed
- Probable
- Possible
- Observed

Photo by Bob Schamerhorn

RUDDY DUCK
Oxyura jamaicensis

Occurrence: uncommon migrant and winter resident

Earliest fall sighting: September 22

Latest spring sighting: May 11

The "bluebill" (an apt colloquial name) is a small, stiff-tailed diving duck often spotted in winter and spring on ponds and lakes across Loudoun. Ruddy Ducks prefer larger ponds to avoid close approach by threats and typically swim away from danger rather than fly, since they need a running start along the water to get airborne. The male in breeding plumage is rust colored, with a black cap and nape, white cheeks, and blue bill. The female has a similar but more subdued pattern and dark bill. In non-breeding plumage, the birds are drab, appearing brownish overall. The large head and bill, small overall size, and stiff cocked tail remain distinguishing features.

Ruddy Ducks dive to the bottom of shallow to medium-depth ponds to feed on insects, crustaceans, and plants. This endearing bird is gregarious, with flocks generally staying together, especially when resting at night. North American populations appear stable, though threats include poor water quality and loss of wetlands on their breeding grounds, the prairie pothole region of Canada and the U.S.

Written by Bruce Hill

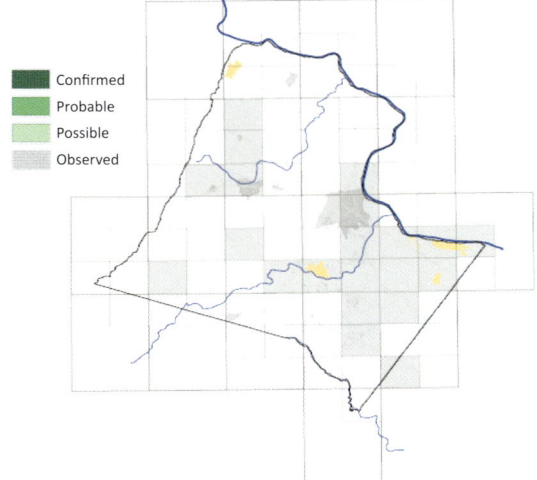

Confirmed
Probable
Possible
Observed

NORTHERN BOBWHITE
Colinus virginianus

Occurrence: occasional breeder and year-round resident

Earliest/latest breeding confirmations: fewer than 5 atlas confirmations, see account for details

Populations of this once-common breeder in Loudoun have plummeted in recent decades. The Northern Bobwhite is now about as rarely encountered as a dairy farm in Loudoun, where its loud, upward-inflected whistling of its name, *Bob-White!,* was once a familiar sound. This bird provides one of the most dramatic changes from Atlas 1, as shown by a loss of 29 blocks from Atlas 1 to Atlas 2. Of the 19 blocks with breeding evidence in Atlas 2, only 1 block had confirmed breeding (Middleburg 3,

Photo by Bill Walsh

in late June 2013). While it is a year-round resident, only 3 of the 35 reports occurred outside of the May 15 – August 15 window, perhaps due in part to their lack of vocalization then. The Northern Bobwhite was reported in 5 of the past 20 Central Loudoun CBCs, with all reports prior to 2005. Reasons for the bobwhite's decline include habitat loss, changes in agriculture, and fire suppression. Its IUCN status is "Near Threatened." Efforts are underway in many eastern states to bring back the Northern Bobwhite through reintroduction of native ground cover, controlled burning, and management of upland pine forests.

NORTHERN BOBWHITE (continued)

The bobwhite, or "quail," has always been more easily heard than seen, as its handsome dappled plumage provides excellent camouflage. Intricately patterned in rufous, brown, black, and white, the male has a bold head pattern with a slight crest and white throat; the female's throat and eye stripe are buffy. This small gamebird is plump with rounded wings, short tail, and very small bill. It forages in small coveys in brushy habitat and overgrown fields, flushing suddenly if alarmed; it also likes open pine or pine/hardwood forests.

Where conditions are good, bobwhites make up for their short lifespan (less than 6 years) by producing two to three broods totaling 25 or more offspring. They nest on the ground, which may be partially responsible for their decline. Young are highly precocial, walking and foraging within hours of hatching. Bobwhites feed on seeds and leaves, as well as insects during the breeding season.

Written by Mary Ann Good

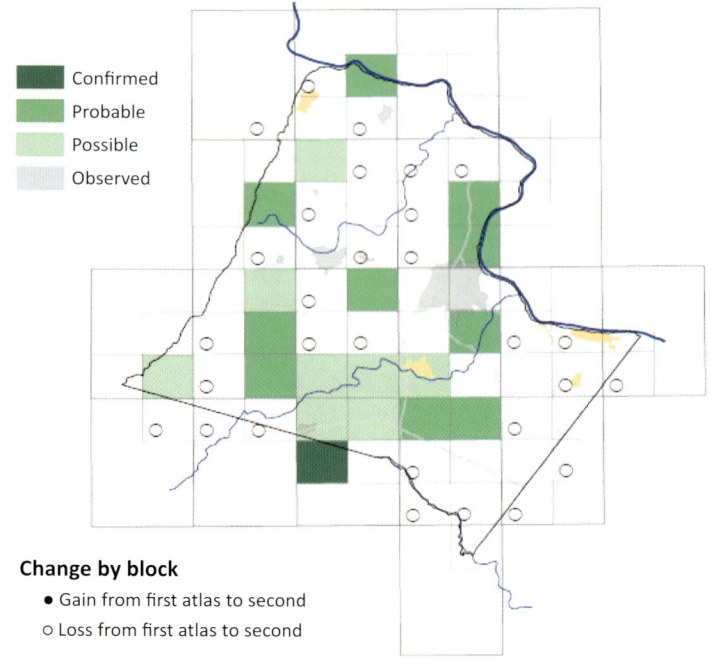

Confirmed
Probable
Possible
Observed

Change by block
● Gain from first atlas to second
○ Loss from first atlas to second

Photo by Bob Schamerhorn

WILD TURKEY
Meleagris gallopavo

Occurrence: uncommon breeder and year-round resident

Earliest breeding confirmation: April 20, nest with eggs (NE)

Latest breeding confirmation: September 21, recently fledged young (FL)

After over-hunting caused drastic declines in numbers a century ago, the Wild Turkey has rebounded to healthy numbers, and they may be seen foraging in small groups or flocks as large as three to four dozen in fields and wild clearings throughout Loudoun. Atlas data emphasizes this success story, with a net gain of almost 30 blocks from Atlas 1 to 2. Breeding was confirmed in 29 blocks in Atlas 2, with probable or possible breeding evidence in 30 more; there were only 2 full blocks where this bird was not observed. The Wild Turkey has been reported on every Central Loudoun CBC. They are most often seen walking or foraging on the ground, and they rely on their strong legs rather than wings to escape predators. They will freeze to conceal themselves or run to brushy cover; however, they do take flight as a last resort and to roost in trees at night.

Wild Turkeys are very large, with a heavy body and long legs and an incongruously small, unfeathered head. Despite their ungainly appearance, their dark feathers have a bronze-green iridescence, and the male (tom) when displaying for his harem of females (hens) raises and spreads his handsome tail in the manner of a peacock. He also struts and

WILD TURKEY (continued)

gives the characteristic *gobble-gobble-gobble* call, especially early in the morning. The hen turkey is similar but is less dark and iridescent and doesn't have the elaborate tail; she also lacks the wattle and "beard" of the male.

Wild Turkeys live in or near mature deciduous forests, especially those with nut or oak trees, and use their strong feet to scratch through leaf litter and in weedy fields. They raise a large brood (6-20), typical of ground and game birds subject to heavy predation and hunting pressure. Newly hatched chicks (poults) are precocial and follow the female, who feeds them for a few days until they can find food on their own. Several hens and their broods will often band together into a roving "turkey nursery."

Bet you didn't know: Wild Turkeys can swim if necessary, by holding their wings close, spreading their tails, and kicking their legs.

Written by Mary Ann Good

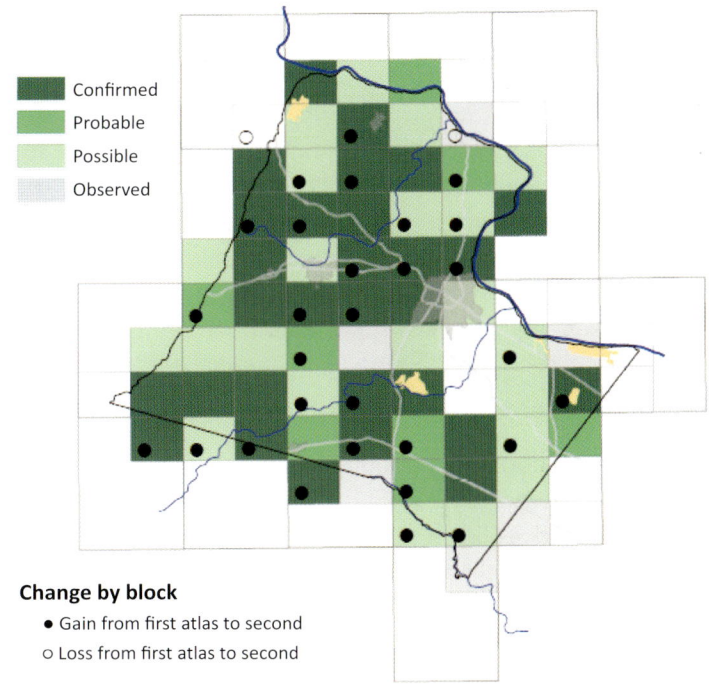

Confirmed
Probable
Possible
Observed

Change by block
● Gain from first atlas to second
○ Loss from first atlas to second

Photo ©Dick Rowe

PIED-BILLED GREBE
Podilymbus podiceps

Occurrence: rare breeder, uncommon year-round resident

Earliest/latest breeding confirmations: highest breeding evidence in Possible category, see account for details

Unique, small, chunky, thick, plain – these are some of the adjectives that best describe the Pied-billed Grebe. The only extant species in its genus, its bill is much shorter and thicker than Loudoun's other grebes and it is also the smallest. It has the amazing ability (like other grebes) to adjust its buoyancy to sink deeply or ride just below the water's surface with its unique water-trapping feathers. During the breeding season, it lives up to its name, pied-bill, with a dark vertical band on a light bill. The mostly brown body is slightly lighter underneath with white under the tail. In spring and summer, the throat is black.

The Pied-billed Grebe spends a lot of time diving and often hides among vegetation. Its distinctive whooping/barking call may be heard during courtship. Both prospective parents help build the nest to hold their 2 to 10 eggs – a floating bowl about 5 inches in diameter made of aquatic plant material hidden among emergent vegetation. They typically place it with enough water underneath the nest to allow them to approach from below. Once born, the chicks can swim, but will often ride on mom's back for safety.

PIED-BILLED GREBE (continued)

They are residents year-round in much of the southern U.S. and South America though some migrate to the northern U.S. and large parts of Canada to breed. In Atlas 2, Pied-billed Grebes were documented throughout the year in 22 blocks, mainly in southeastern Loudoun, with only a single possible breeding sighting at Horsepen Preserve in Sterling 4. Their hidden nest sites and time spent under the water may make breeding difficult to document. Post-atlas (late May 2015), a sighting of recently fledged young confirmed breeding at the Dulles Greenway Wetlands in Leesburg 5. This species was not documented in Atlas 1.

Pied-billed Grebes inhabit slow-moving water bodies, including ponds, marshes, estuaries, bays, and rivers. Their thick bill allows them to eat crustaceans in addition to fish, frogs, and other invertebrates. They are widespread throughout their range, likely because of their generalist nature.

Written by Bryan Henson

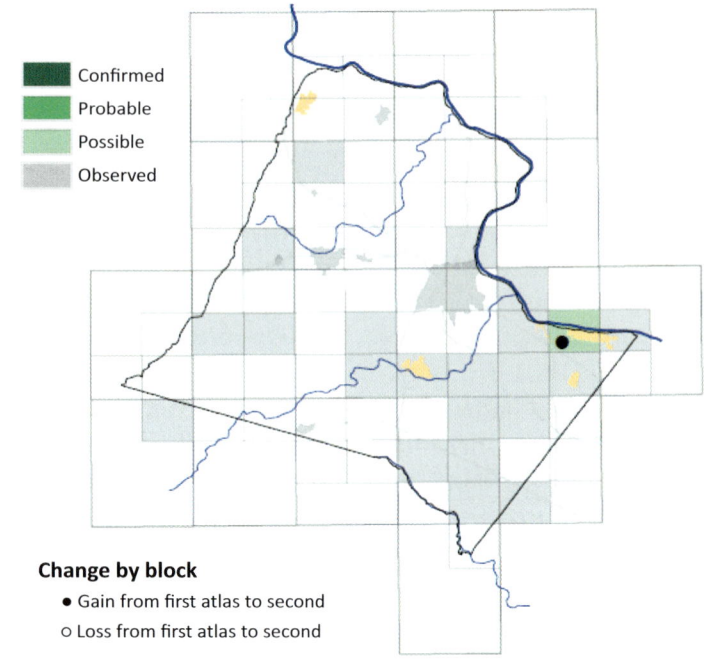

Confirmed
Probable
Possible
Observed

Change by block
- Gain from first atlas to second
- Loss from first atlas to second

Photo by Dave Boltz

Confirmed
Probable
Possible
Observed

HORNED GREBE
Podiceps auritus

Occurrence: occasional migrant, rare winter visitor

Earliest fall sighting: October 22

Latest spring sighting: May 7

The Horned Grebe is an unlikely find in Loudoun, but is seen a few times each year and was reported in 8 atlas blocks (including 2 rare mid-June 2012 sightings in western Loudoun). Found on only 3 of the 20 Central Loudoun CBCs, it more commonly winters in rivers, bays, and open ocean waters of the Chesapeake Bay region. This small to medium-sized grebe is often solitary, but may be found in small, loose groups, diving to feed on fish and other prey. The Horned Grebe's winter plumage is drab, gray above and white below, with red eyes, a small gray bill, and white cheeks and neck below a black cap. In spring, its plumage is transformed, with creamy-white tufts (or "horns") behind the eyes, offset by a black crown and cheek patches and a rich reddish-brown neck and flanks. Like other grebes, its legs are located well back on its body, ideal for swimming and diving but ill-suited for walking on land. This bird is listed as "Vulnerable" by the IUCN and, though populations are not well understood, is thought to be a species of high conservation concern.

Written by Bruce Hill

RED-NECKED GREBE
Podiceps grisegena

Photo ©Dick Rowe

Occurrence: rare winter visitor and early spring migrant

Earliest/latest seasonal sightings: fewer than 5 atlas sightings, see account for details

A rare winter treat in Loudoun, with occasional irruption years, the Red-necked Grebe was reported only twice during the atlas (February and March 2014). This species more commonly winters on the Atlantic and Pacific oceans and occasionally large lakes. Beginning as early as February, its drab gray non-breeding plumage transforms into a rufous neck, black cap, and white cheeks. In all seasons, it has a long, pointed yellow bill, a long-necked appearance, and is larger than Loudoun's other grebes (Horned and Pied-billed). The Red-necked Grebe defends its breeding territory with loud, complex displays and builds a floating nest on marshy lakes in Canada and Alaska.

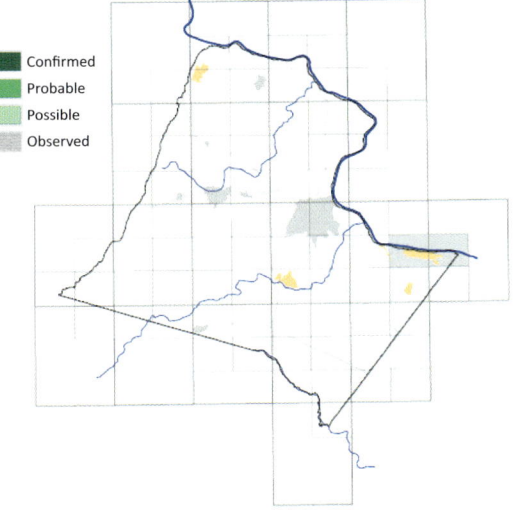

Confirmed
Probable
Possible
Observed

This grebe rarely leaves the water and infrequently flies, except during migration. It sometimes swims with its head submerged, looking for fish to dive for. It also gleans insects off vegetation. Like other grebes, this grebe may eat its own feathers, possibly to protect the digestive tract from bones and other indigestible material. Little is known about Red-necked Grebe population trends, but pollution in coastal wintering areas may pose a threat to this species.

Written by Spring Ligi

Photo by Larry Meade

ROCK PIGEON
Columba livia

Occurrence: abundant breeder and year-round resident

Earliest breeding confirmation: April 20, parent entering/exiting nest site or on nest (ON)

Latest breeding confirmation: July 12, adult carrying nesting material or nest building (NB)

The adage "familiarity breeds contempt" goes a long way to describing the relationship between much of the birding community and the feral Rock Pigeon. Most birders immediately recognize this plump bird with a small head, short bill, and variable gray plumage, but seldom give it a second look. The Rock Pigeon is larger and pudgier than its cousin, the Mourning Dove.

Widely seen in Loudoun, often in flocks, the Rock Pigeon was reported in nearly every block and all regions of the county during Atlas 2. Found in urban settings, small towns, and farms, it roosts and nests on the ledges and crevices of farm buildings, skyscrapers, and highway overpasses. Its ability to thrive in a wide range of human habitat is due in large part to over 5,000 years of domestication and selective breeding — which has given the pigeon a lot of time to adapt. In fact, the entire North American population of Rock Pigeons is considered feral — that is, descended from domesticated birds that escaped captivity.

ROCK PIGEON (continued)

The span of time within which breeding was confirmed during Atlas 2 – April to mid-July – is surprisingly short, given that the Virginia Society of Ornithology's "Gold Book" records May 3 and December 22 as the earliest and latest egg dates for the Virginia Piedmont (Rottenborn and Brinkley 2007) and other sources report the bird breeding year-round. A reliable supply of food supports breeding throughout the year. In the first days of a young pigeon's life, parents feed their young with "crop milk," a semi-solid substance, rich in fat and protein, that both parents produce in the lining of their crop and regurgitate into the mouth of the young. After a few days of crop milk, the adults introduce solid foods readily available near human habitation – corn and other grains around farms, and food scraps and handouts in cities.

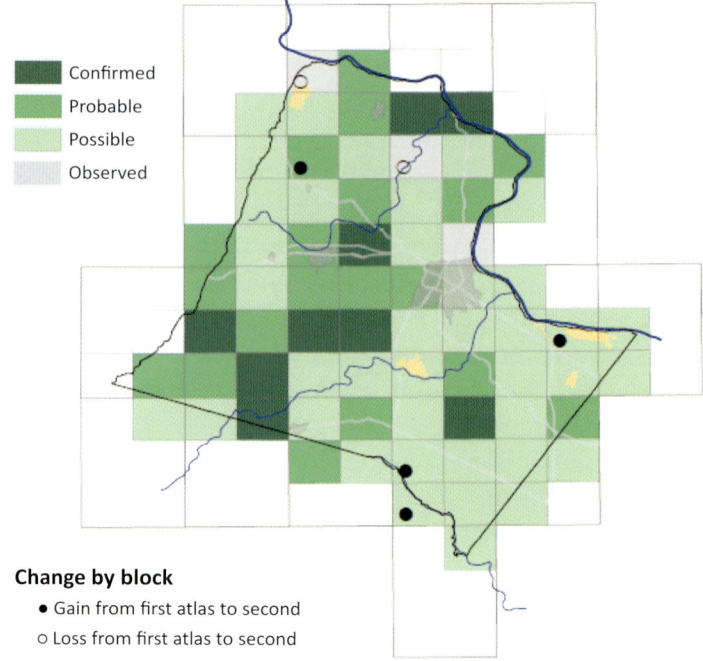

Confirmed
Probable
Possible
Observed

Change by block
● Gain from first atlas to second
○ Loss from first atlas to second

Though Rock Pigeons are abundant and widespread, data from the North American BBS shows a 46% population decline from 1966 to 2015. In the sector that includes Loudoun, the population trend map shows an average annual decline of over 1.5%.

Written by Bill Brown

Photo by Dave Boltz

MOURNING DOVE
Zenaida macroura

Occurrence: abundant breeder and year-round resident

Earliest breeding confirmation: March 22, adult carrying nesting material or nest building (NB)

Latest breeding confirmation: September 30, nest with young (NY)

Named for its mournful cooing, the Mourning Dove is commonly seen and heard year-round in Loudoun. Mourning Doves have small heads, plump bodies, and long, pointed wings and tails. They are stunning birds to those who take the time to appreciate their beauty. Their upper body is a soft shade of brown with black spots on the wings; their belly is buffy with gray under the wings. Both sexes have an iridescent blue eyering, and males sport a striking purple-pink neck patch.

Mourning Doves are regular visitors to bird feeders and can be found almost anywhere except dense forest. They subsist almost entirely on seeds, though they may occasionally eat snails. Sometimes maligned for their small heads and slow reaction to threat, their habit of suddenly springing into flight with loud wing beats likely serves to startle prey, buying precious seconds for this fast flyer to escape.

Males court females with a flight upward on noisy wing beats followed by a slow, circular glide down. On the ground,

MOURNING DOVE (continued)

males approach with their chest puffed out and head bowed down, giving emphatic cooing sounds. Nesting sites are typically in trees or shrubs but sometimes found on building ledges or other structures. The nests are flimsy; males provide material (pine needles, twigs, and grass) and the female builds. Two white eggs are incubated by both parents for approximately 14 days. Mourning Doves mate for life and can breed year-round, though breeding confirmations in Loudoun were limited to March through September.

Mourning Doves are part of a select group of birds that produce milk to feed their young. The curd-like secretion is produced by both sexes in the crop. Young are fed this protein- and fat-rich milk which fuels their rapid development. Young are weaned and fledge around 12 days of age.

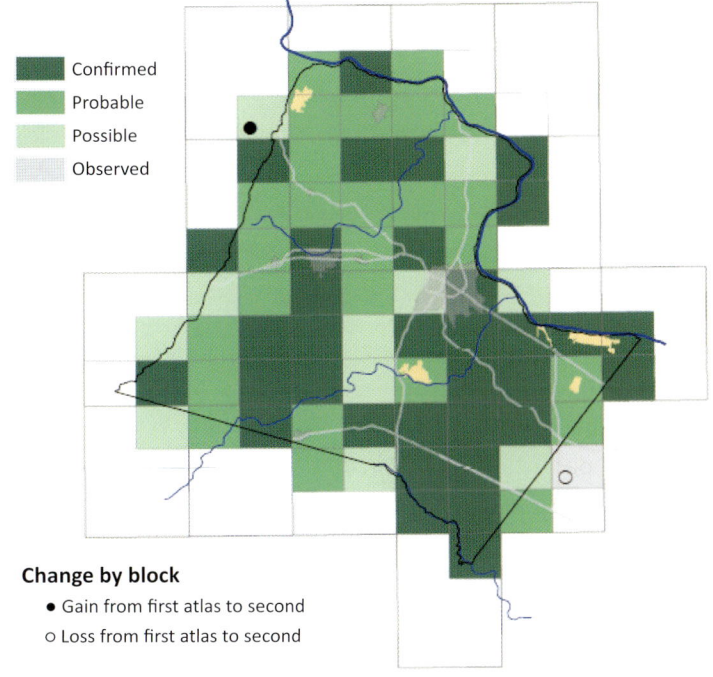

Confirmed
Probable
Possible
Observed

Change by block
● Gain from first atlas to second
○ Loss from first atlas to second

Despite holding the title of most frequently hunted species in North America, Mourning Doves are common across the continent. They were documented in virtually every atlas block and are reported by the hundreds on every Central Loudoun CBC. Many of the blocks with breeding confirmations are in more urban/suburban areas of Loudoun, indicating this species' ability to thrive in human-dominated landscapes.

Written by Donna Quinn

Photo by Joe Wolf

YELLOW-BILLED CUCKOO
Coccyzus americanus

Occurrence: uncommon breeder and migrant

Earliest breeding confirmation: June 12, parent entering/exiting nest site or on nest (ON)

Latest breeding confirmation: August 17, recently fledged young (FL)

The Yellow-billed Cuckoo is a long, slender bird with a heavy, down-curved bill. Its plumage is plain grayish-brown on the head, back, and wings, with a creamy white breast and rufous on its outer wing feathers. Its most distinctive feature is its long tail, lined in dramatic black and white checkered spots. Although its plain coloration may render it inconspicuous in the tree canopy, the Yellow-billed Cuckoo is often recognized by its vocalizations, typically a series of *knock-knock* calls on one pitch, and later in the breeding season, a dove-like cooing.

The Yellow-billed Cuckoo inhabits dense thickets, orchards, and wooded stream banks, where it may sit motionless as it looks for prey. The cuckoo's diet consists chiefly of large insects, notably caterpillars, cicadas, and grasshoppers. It is an especially beneficial species due to its consumption of destructive insects such as tent caterpillars, web worms, and gypsy moths.

YELLOW-BILLED CUCKOO (continued)

Cuckoos move widely in search of insect infestations, so their population densities vary greatly from year to year. Their nesting cycles may also correlate with insect outbreaks, ensuring that there is sufficient food to raise their young. Yellow-billed Cuckoos build a shallow, rather flimsy nest in a tree, vine, or shrub, usually 10-20 feet above ground. They especially favor wild grape vines. When food is abundant, they may deposit eggs in the nests of other bird species.

Yellow-billed Cuckoos are nocturnal migrants, wintering in northern and eastern South America, largely east of the Andes. They tend to arrive late in spring. First and last observations of the species in Loudoun were on April 26 and October 11, respectively.

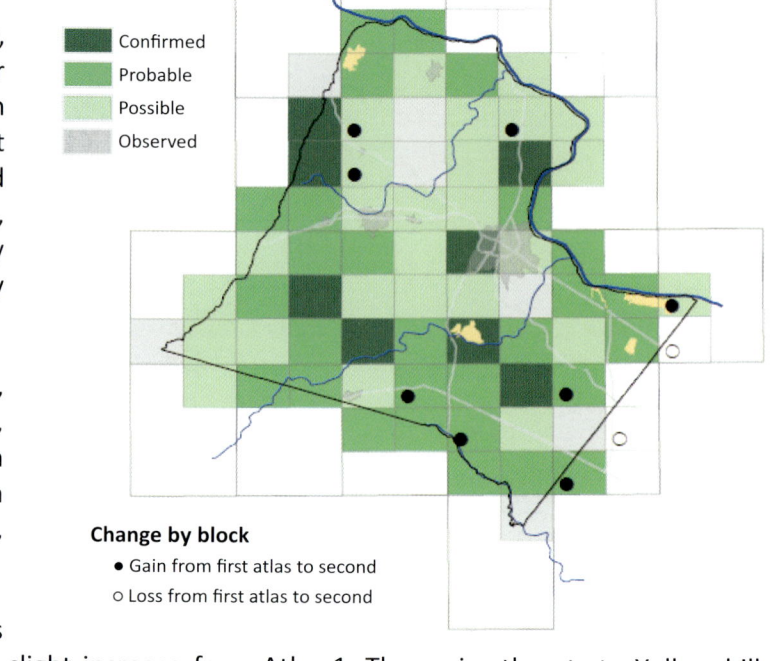

Confirmed
Probable
Possible
Observed

Change by block
- Gain from first atlas to second
○ Loss from first atlas to second

Breeding evidence for Yellow-billed Cuckoos was documented in 62 blocks, with confirmation in 8, a slight increase from Atlas 1. The major threats to Yellow-billed Cuckoos are from habitat loss, pesticide use, and hazards of migration. Although the Yellow-billed Cuckoo population in Loudoun appears stable, populations are on the decline in the far-western U.S., where this species is now listed as "Threatened" (USFWS 2017).

Written by Christine Perdue

Photo by ©Dick Rowe

BLACK-BILLED CUCKOO
Coccyzus erythropthalmus

Occurrence: rare breeder, occasional migrant

Earliest/latest breeding confirmations: highest breeding evidence in Probable category, see account for details

The Black-billed Cuckoo shares the same plain, gray-brown and white coloration as its close relative, the Yellow-billed Cuckoo, but the Black-billed is slighter overall, has a curved black bill and a red eyering, and displays smaller and less conspicuous checkered bands on its tail. Although the ranges of the two species overlap, the Black-billed Cuckoo is a forest dweller that occupies a more northerly range than the Yellow-billed.

The vocalizations of the two species are quite distinct. In contrast to the unmusical knocking call of the Yellow-billed, the Black-billed Cuckoo gives a rhythmic, stuttering version of its name: *cu-cu-coo, cu-cu-coo*. Sometimes it will call throughout the night.

The Black-billed Cuckoo nests in trees several feet off the ground. It may also lay eggs in the nests of Yellow-billed Cuckoos or other bird species. Like the Yellow-billed, its favored diet consists of large insects, particularly caterpillars, and it prefers deciduous forests where caterpillars are most abundant. Both cuckoo species are specially adapted to digest hairy caterpillars which other birds find unpalatable.

BLACK-BILLED CUCKOO (continued)

The Black-billed Cuckoo overwinters in western South America, in an area ranging from Colombia to Peru. Slow flyers and nocturnal migrants, they are especially vulnerable to collisions of all kinds during migration. The first and last observations of Black-billed Cuckoos occurred in Loudoun on April 24 and September 16, respectively.

More often reported as a migrant, Black-billed Cuckoos were not confirmed as breeding in Loudoun, though there was documentation of probable breeding in Harpers Ferry 4 and possible breeding in 3 blocks. This species is heard more often than seen, making breeding difficult to confirm. There was no breeding evidence reported during Atlas 1.

Confirmed
Probable
Possible
Observed

Change by block
- Gain from first atlas to second
- ○ Loss from first atlas to second

According to the North American BBS, the population of Black-billed Cuckoos is estimated to have declined by nearly two-thirds between 1966 and 2015. Although habitat loss and migration casualties are probable factors, it is likely that the widespread use of pesticides has played a major role in species mortality. Black-billed Cuckoos may be adversely affected both by ingestion of poisoned insects and by the depletion of caterpillar populations by pesticide use.

Written by Christine Perdue

Photo by Gerco Hoogeweg

COMMON NIGHTHAWK
Chordeiles minor

Occurrence: rare breeder, uncommon migrant

Earliest/latest breeding confirmations: highest breeding evidence in Probable category, see account for details

The Common Nighthawk is a slender bird, with long, pointed wings, large eyes, and the small beak and cavernous mouth characteristic of the nightjar family. Its mottled gray-brown plumage provides ideal camouflage when perched or nesting. This nighthawk's most recognizable feature is a white wing patch visible during flight. The male also has a white throat patch and tail stripe, while the female has a buffy throat patch and lacks the tail stripe.

Common Nighthawks are aerial insectivores, hunting chiefly at twilight and in the early morning. They forage on the wing, performing aerobatic swoops and dives as they chase insects. Their call, given often in flight, is a nasal *peent*, resembling that of the woodcock; however, their most dramatic sound effect comes at the end of a display dive, used in courtship and territorial defense. The bird may plunge from several hundred feet, creating a booming sound as it checks its dive and air moves through its primary wing feathers. Common Nighthawks inhabit a variety of open habitats in both rural and urban areas. They nest on the ground, depositing two eggs on surfaces that may include gravel, rock outcrops, sand dunes, and open fields. In cities, they often nest on gravel rooftops and hunt insects attracted to street lamps and other light sources.

COMMON NIGHTHAWK (continued)

Common Nighthawks winter throughout eastern and northern South America and have one of the longest migration routes of any neotropical migrant. They are one of the last migrants to arrive in spring and leave fairly early. They were observed in Loudoun as early as May 1 and as late as September 22. Almost three-quarters of the atlas sightings were reported in August and September when nighthawks form large flocks and commence southerly migration.

There were no breeding confirmations for Common Nighthawks in Loudoun. They were observed in 16 blocks and documented as a probable breeder in Round Hill 4 and possible breeder in Arcola 2. Only one report of possible breeding occurred during Atlas 1. Their cryptic colors and nocturnal habits make them difficult to detect during atlas surveys and may result in undercounting.

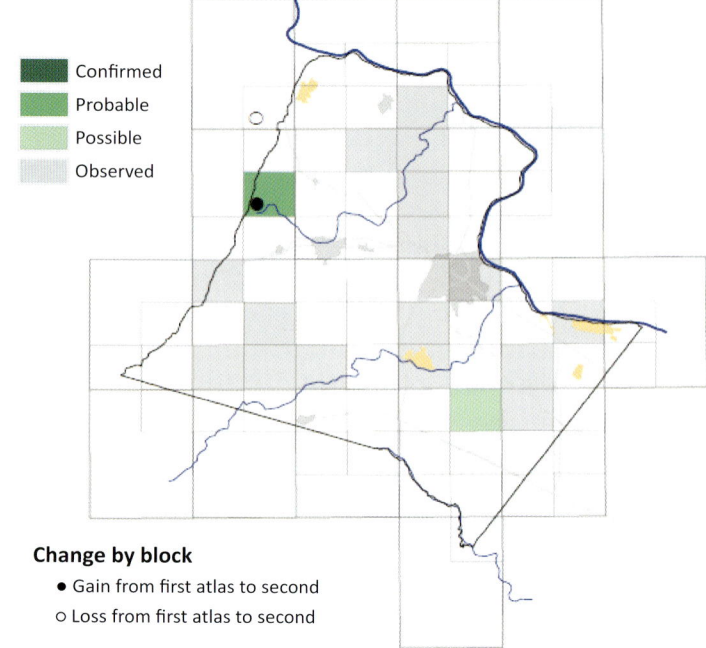

Confirmed
Probable
Possible
Observed

Change by block
- Gain from first atlas to second
- Loss from first atlas to second

Common Nighthawks have suffered significant declines in portions of their historic range, most notably in the eastern U.S. Habitat loss and pesticides, particularly use of neonicotinoids, are believed to be primary factors (American Bird Conservancy 2017). Urban numbers have also been reduced by the replacement of gravel roofs with other materials and by predation.

Written by Christine Perdue

Photo ©Dick Rowe

EASTERN WHIP-POOR-WILL
Antrostomus vociferus

Occurrence: rare breeder and spring migrant

Earliest/latest breeding confirmations: highest breeding evidence in Probable category, see account for details

The Eastern Whip-poor-will is a nocturnal, medium-sized nightjar of open forests. The whip-poor-will's common name derives from its insistent song, often repeated throughout the night. Its species name, *vociferus,* meaning "strong voice," also reflects the whip-poor-will's prowess as a singer.

Found in open woodland with little or no underbrush, whip-poor-wills are aerial insectivores that forage only at night. Aided by large eyes and keen night vision, they hunt insects by sight, scooping them into their cavernous mouths. Whip-poor-wills rest during the day, camouflaged by stippled brown and gray plumage which blends perfectly with the leaf litter of the forest. They are motionless and can even enter a state of torpor if weather conditions do not favor foraging. The sexes can be distinguished by white edges on the outer corners of the male's tail. Corresponding markings in the female are buffy.

Whip-poor-wills lay two eggs directly on the forest floor. Their breeding is synchronized with the lunar cycle, so that nestlings typically hatch a few days before a full moon. This permits the parents to hunt all night, maximizing foraging

EASTERN WHIP-POOR-WILL (continued)

when the nestlings' food demands are greatest. Whip-poor-wills winter in Florida, along the Gulf Coast of the U.S. and Mexico, and into Central America. In general, they are late migrants, arriving only when conditions support a plentiful insect supply. The earliest observation in Loudoun occurred on April 23. As insect populations and temperatures diminish, they are among the first birds to migrate, beginning in late summer.

Whip-poor-wills were documented 5 times in 4 blocks during Atlas 2. There were no breeding confirmations, but 2 reports of probable breeding, detected in Harpers Ferry 5 and Round Hill 4 during supplemental Owl and Nightjar surveys. This represented no appreciable change from Atlas 1, in which 3 reports of probable breeding were documented with no confirmations.

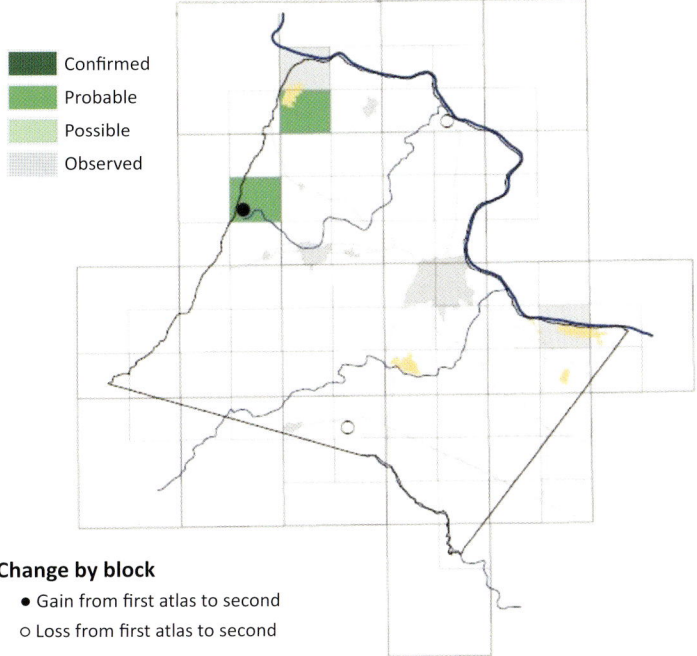

Confirmed
Probable
Possible
Observed

Change by block
● Gain from first atlas to second
○ Loss from first atlas to second

Once common throughout the eastern U.S., whip-poor-wills have now disappeared from large parts of their range. According to the North American BBS, the cumulative decline is estimated at 75% from 1966 to 2015, and the species is on the 2016 State of North America's Birds' Watch List. Loss of open understory forest habitat is considered the primary cause, but declines in the populations of nocturnal insects and night vehicle collisions are also posited as factors in the species' decline.

Written by Christine Perdue

Photo by Nicole Sudduth

CHIMNEY SWIFT
Chaetura pelagica

Occurrence: common breeder and migrant

Earliest breeding confirmation: May 25, parent entering/exiting nest site or on nest (ON)

Latest breeding confirmation: August 1, nest with young (NY)

Welcome envoys announcing warm, buggy weather is soon upon us, Chimney Swifts return to Loudoun in mid-April from their winter home in eastern Peru. Their soaring aerial ballet and exuberant twittering calls seem to celebrate spring and the summer ahead. These small dark gray-brown birds spend most of their lives airborne, landing only to rest at night and to nest. Even when not flying, Chimney Swifts do not perch like other birds, rather, they cling to vertical surfaces. Their "flying cigar" silhouette and distinctive chittering make them easy to identify.

Chimney Swifts are found in open sky over cities, towns, lakes, rivers, and meadows. They hunt insects on the wing; prey includes flying insects and those that can be gleaned from leaf tips or the surface of water. A pair of Chimney Swifts feeding young will consume 12,000 insects per day.

Before the arrival of Europeans in North America, Chimney Swifts nested in caves and hollow trees. However, as human dwellings became available, chimneys and other man-made structures such as sheds became their preferred

CHIMNEY SWIFT (continued)

nesting sites. Chimney Swifts were detected in virtually all 73 atlas blocks; however, confirming breeding for this species proved difficult. Breeding confirmations were limited to less than 10% of the blocks (6 blocks), largely due to inaccessibility of nest sites and non-breeding swifts also in residence. Unfortunately, now that chimneys are often capped and the use of pesticides is widespread, Chimney Swift numbers have declined 72% since 1966 (Sauer 2017) and these beneficial bug eaters are considered a "Near Threatened" species by the IUCN.

Shortly after returning to breeding grounds in spring, a pair performs an aerial dance with both snapping wings into a V-shape and gliding downward together. The mated pair break off twigs as they fly and build a half-saucer-shaped nest attached to the interior of a chimney glued together with their saliva. While only

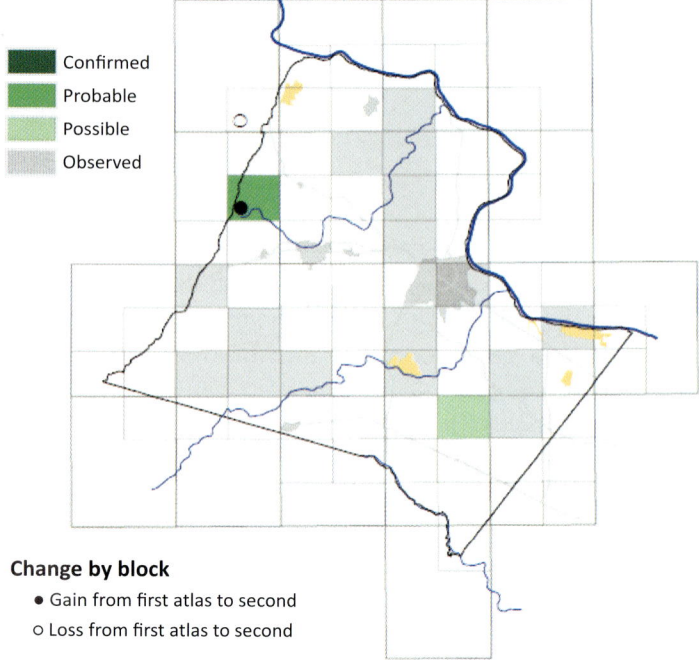

Confirmed
Probable
Possible
Observed

Change by block
- Gain from first atlas to second
○ Loss from first atlas to second

one breeding pair will inhabit a chimney, other non-nesting swifts may also be in residence. Both parents feed the young sometimes assisted by a non-mated helper. After the young fledge (28-30 days), groups of swifts form staging flocks. By late summer large groups gather to begin their migration to South America. In a magnificent spectacle, as many as 10,000 swifts will create a tornado-like swirl funneling into a roosting chimney to spend the night before or during their migration. They leave Loudoun by mid-October.

Written by Donna Quinn

Photo by Linda Millington

RUBY-THROATED HUMMINGBIRD
Archilochus colubris

Occurrence: common breeder and migrant

Earliest breeding confirmation: May 13, adult carrying nesting material or nest building (NB)

Latest breeding confirmation: August 27, recently fledged young (FL)

Ruby-throated Hummingbirds were found in every atlas block, from mid-April through mid-October. They live in woodlands, grasslands, meadows, parks, and backyards, and feed on nectar, especially from tubular-shaped flowers such as honeysuckle, as well as small insects. Many Loudoun residents attract hummingbirds by hanging feeders with sugar water.

The male Ruby-throated Hummingbird has a metallic green back, an iridescent ruby-red throat, and a black chin that extends below the eyes. The female has a green back, whitish throat, grayish-white underparts, and a black mask with white just behind its eye. Females and immatures have black tails with white spots at the tips. Hummingbirds are the only birds capable of flying backwards.

Adult male Ruby-throated Hummingbirds, like all other hummingbird species, migrate earlier than the females and juveniles. They also migrate individually, not in flocks. Despite their small size, Ruby-throated Hummingbirds migrate impressive distances from as far north as Canada down to their wintering grounds in Central America, with many flying nonstop across the Gulf of Mexico. After the males return to their Loudoun breeding grounds in early May and the

RUBY-THROATED HUMMINGBIRD (continued)

females in mid- to late May, courtship begins. Females build a thimble-size nest on a tree branch, typically 10-40 feet above the ground. The nest, made of thistle or dandelion down, spider silk, and moss, holds 1-3 tiny white eggs. Ruby-throated Hummingbird males can be extremely territorial, going so far as to adopt feeders as their own and attack other hummingbirds trying to drink. Home owners can accommodate more hummingbirds by using feeders with multiple ports or hanging several feeders, as well as by planting their favorite flowers. When preparing the sugar water, Cornell's Project FeederWatch website (2016) recommends using ¼ cup pure cane sugar to 1 cup hot non-distilled drinking water. The sugar water does not need to be red; in fact, food coloring may be harmful. The feeder, however, should have some red parts.

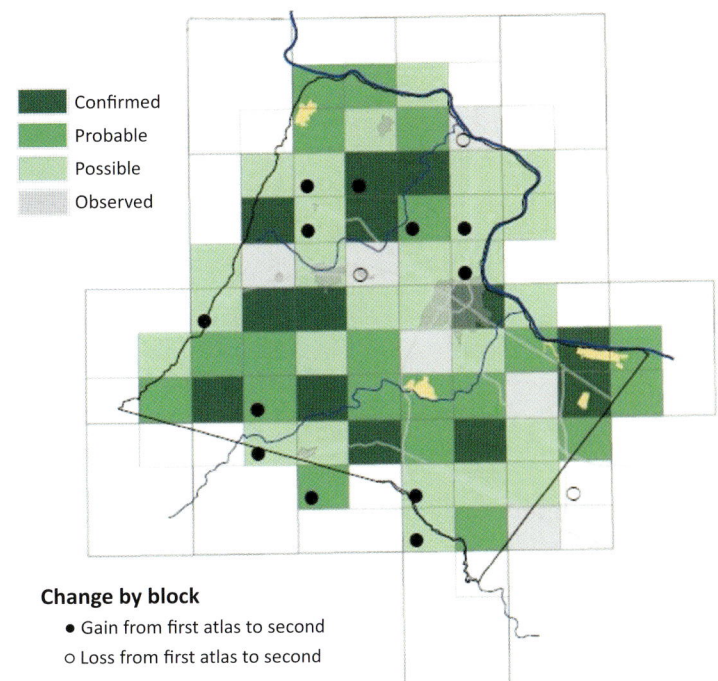

Change by block
- Gain from first atlas to second
- ○ Loss from first atlas to second

Though the Ruby-throated Hummingbird is eastern North America's only breeding hummingbird, western hummingbird species have been reported on rare occasion in Loudoun. A Rufous/Allen's Hummingbird was observed at a feeder in Bluemont 4 on November 15, 2012 (banding is usually required to pin down the species, especially for females and immatures). Unlike Rufous and Allen's Hummingbirds, whose populations are in decline, Ruby-throated Hummingbird populations have steadily increased over recent decades, according to the North American BBS.

Written by Linda Millington and Spring Ligi

Dullas Greenway Wetlands
Photo by Nicole Sudduth

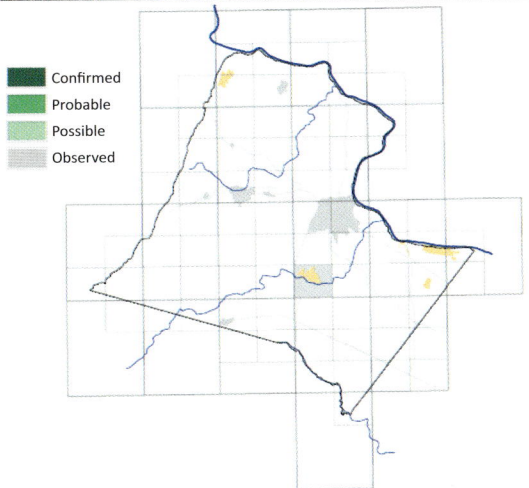

BLACK RAIL
Laterallus jamaicensis

Occurrence: rare migrant

Southerly/northerly migration periods: fewer than 5 atlas sightings, see account for details

Arguably the most unexpected bird found during Atlas 2 was the Black Rail, identified by several birders on May 9, 2009 based on its diagnostic *kick-ee-poo* vocalizations. This small, secretive, and seldom seen resident of freshwater and brackish marshes was discovered in Leesburg 5 in the cattail wetlands of the Dulles Greenway Wetlands, perhaps the only location in Loudoun with habitat that might attract this species.

Sparrow-sized and almost never emerging from cover, the Black Rail much prefers to run or walk instead of fly. It is thought to feed mostly on small insects, snails, and seeds found in its preferred habitat. In our region, it is known to occur and breed in coastal wetlands, but its inland distribution is poorly understood. The Black Rail is listed as "Near Threatened" by the IUCN and considered an at-risk species, primarily due to loss of habitat.

Written by Bruce Hill

Photo ©Jim Clark

VIRGINIA RAIL
Rallus limicola

Occurrence: uncommon breeder and migrant, occasional early winter visitor

Earliest/latest breeding confirmations: highest breeding evidence in Probable category, see account for details

Hearing its descending grunt call or repeated *kid-dik* in a freshwater marsh is about the only way to find the secretive and hard-to-see Virginia Rail. If actually seen, this bird's gray cheeks and reddish bill and legs help distinguish it from other rails. The Virginia Rail's small size, long toes, and thin body minimize its disturbance of the marsh vegetation, making detecting it by sight that much harder. The males and females are similar in appearance with size being the most noticeable difference. As with other rails, it seems to prefer to walk around the marsh rather than fly, yet often migrates hundreds of miles.

In Loudoun, the best place to find this species is the Dulles Greenway Wetlands in Leesburg 5; 85% of all Atlas 2 reports occurred there. The first spring record was April 17. Though breeding is difficult to confirm for this elusive species, documentation of probable breeding on June 9 and 10 (of two different years) suggests likely breeding in Loudoun. This species was not documented in Atlas 1. Surprisingly, the Central Loudoun CBC found a Virginia Rail in 4 of the 5 atlas years (but just 1 additional year, out of 20). These observations and the rail's secretive nature suggest that it is possible some rails overwinter in Loudoun.

The Virginia Rail normally breeds in the more northern U.S. and some parts of Canada. It winters in the southern U.S. and Mexico. In the winter, it is more likely to choose saltwater marshes than freshwater marshes. Some West Coast Virginia Rail populations have become year-long residents instead of migrants.

This rail's diet consists of aquatic invertebrates, fish, frogs, and snakes extracted from the wetland mud with its long bill. Its nest is made from marsh grasses and reeds forming a basket-style nest. It may create many nest sites, but lays anywhere from 4 to 13 eggs in only one nest. Precocial young develop rapidly and forage on their own shortly after hatching. More than 30 states, including Virginia, allow game hunting of Virginia Rails. Although their population is generally considered stable, as with other wetland species, they are threatened by habitat loss.

Written by Bryan Henson

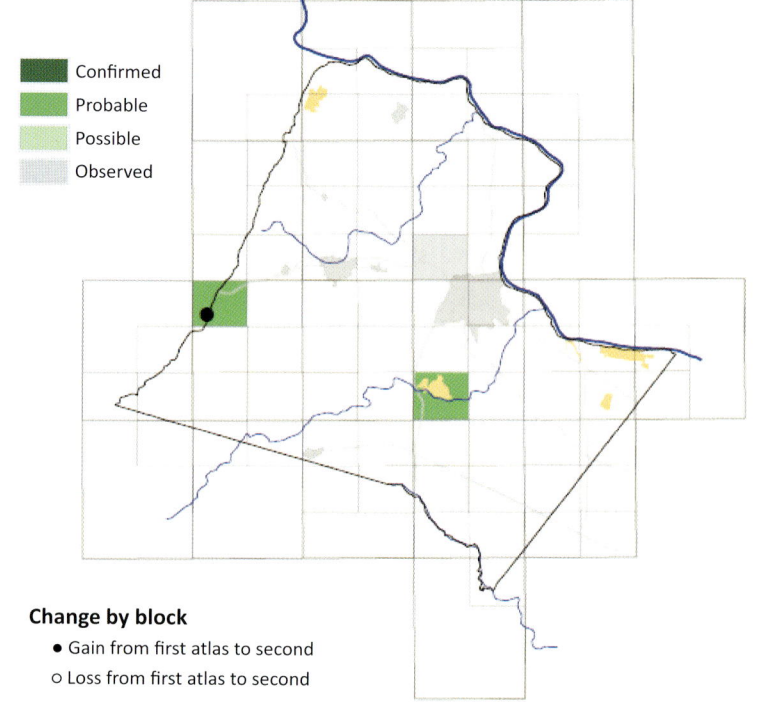

Confirmed
Probable
Possible
Observed

Change by block
● Gain from first atlas to second
○ Loss from first atlas to second

SORA
Porzana carolina

Occurrence: occasional migrant

Southerly/northerly migration periods: fewer than 5 atlas sightings, see account for details

The descending whinny of the Sora is more often heard than the small, sneaky marsh denizen is actually seen. However, when seen, the distinctive black face and yellow bill make it hard to confuse with other birds of the freshwater marshes. Soras feed on seeds and invertebrates of the marsh with a fondness for wild rice. Loudoun is just to the south of their breeding territory, which extends into the boreal forest of northern North America. Wintering grounds include the southern U.S. in addition to Central and South America. Atlasing efforts resulted in 3 early May reports at the Dulles Greenway Wetlands in Leesburg 5 and a single September report in Waterford 3.

Soras are game hunted in 31 states including Virginia. They are considered widespread throughout North America and not generally threatened, but as a wetland inhabitant their major threat is the loss of wetland habitat to development.

Written by Bryan Henson

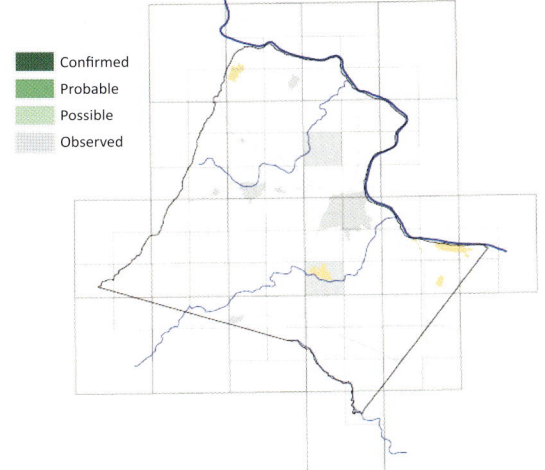

Confirmed
Probable
Possible
Observed

COMMON GALLINULE
Gallinula galeata

Occurrence: rare migrant

Southerly/northerly migration periods: fewer than 5 atlas sightings, see account for details

The Common Gallinule, formerly known as the Common Moorhen, is a medium-sized member of the rail family found in freshwater and brackish marshes, ponds, and canals. It is a dark brown to blackish bird with a prominent white stripe along its flank. It has a bright red forehead shield and a yellow-tipped red bill. Males and females have similar plumage. In winter, the shield and bill darken somewhat, but otherwise the coloration is similar year-round. This gallinule has long legs and long toes that enable it to walk through and on top of emergent marsh vegetation.

Though the Common Gallinule breeds throughout much of the eastern U.S., *Birds of North America* (2002) notes that it is "largely absent" from the Piedmont of Virginia and the Carolinas. It was reported only once during Atlas 2, in May 2009 at the Dulles Greenway Wetlands. Common Gallinule populations have decreased over the past 50 years due to loss of wetland habitat throughout their range.

Written by Bill Brown

Photo by Gerco Hoogeweg

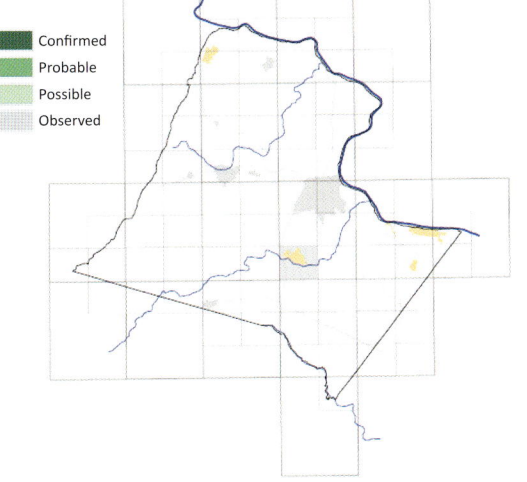

Confirmed
Probable
Possible
Observed

AMERICAN COOT

Fulica americana

Photo by Dave Boltz

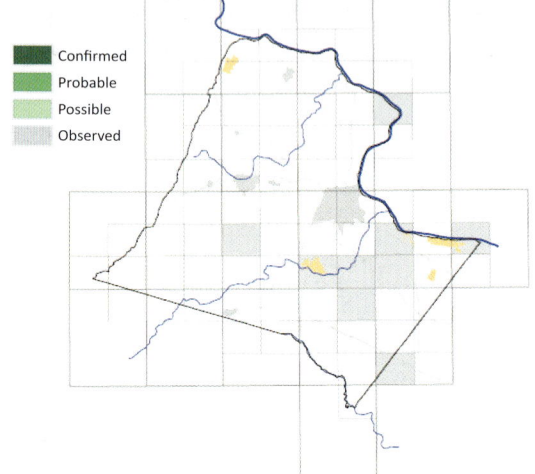

Confirmed
Probable
Possible
Observed

Occurrence: uncommon migrant and winter resident

Earliest fall sighting: October 22

Latest spring sighting: May 9

The American Coot is Loudoun's most commonly seen member of the rail family. It is easily identifiable, thanks to its plump shape and white bill set off against a dark head and body. Males and females look alike and retain a single plumage coloration year-round. The coot is usually seen swimming like a duck, sometimes dabbling for food on the surface and sometimes diving for submerged vegetation. It occasionally grazes on land for grasses and grains. Its diet also includes aquatic invertebrates and insects.

During Atlas 2, the American Coot was seen mostly in the southeastern quadrant of the county. It was sometimes found on the Potomac River, but more often in shallow, man-made ponds. Good places to look for coots, sometimes in flocks of 30-50 birds, include the Dulles Greenway Wetlands and Alder Lake in Ashburn. The coot breeds throughout much of the western U.S. and southern Canada. Populations appear to be stable according to the North American BBS.

Written by Bill Brown

SANDHILL CRANE

Antigone canadensis

Occurrence: rare migrant and winter visitor

Earliest winter sighting: December 15

Latest spring sighting: April 25

As Cornell's All About Birds website (2015) states, Sandhill Cranes have an "elegance that draws attention" whether in the sky or on the ground. Preferring Loudoun's pastures and grasslands, these tall, crimson-capped gray birds have long, distinctive, rolling trumpet calls. While found 5 times in only 4 atlas blocks (mainly in March and April, but once in mid-December) and on none of the Central Loudoun CBCs, post-atlas, they have begun turning up more often during our colder months in both the Lucketts area and on or near Algonkian Regional Park. Even though they are always in small numbers in our area, they are quickly noticed because of their striking appearance.

Photo by Gerco Hoogeweg

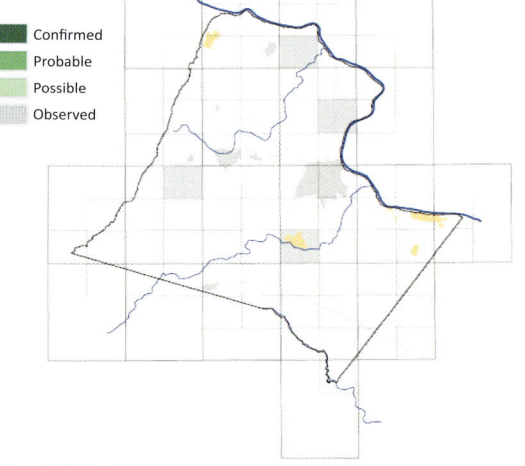

Confirmed
Probable
Possible
Observed

Most Sandhill Cranes migrate from their prime wintering grounds in the southern U.S. to where they nest in the north-central U.S. and throughout much of Canada. The migration of hundreds of thousands of them through Nebraska in late March is a natural phenomenon and wonderful to see and hear. While some isolated populations are at risk, sandhill populations are generally thriving, with a gain of about 4.5% from 1966 to 2014 according to the North American BBS.

Written by Joe Coleman

Photo by Gerco Hoogewig

AMERICAN AVOCET
Recurvirostra americana

Occurrence: rare migrant

Southerly/northerly migration periods: fewer than 5 atlas sightings, see account for details

A striking large, black and white shorebird with a long, upturned bill and rusty or gray (non-breeding) head and neck, the American Avocet can hardly be confused with any other bird. In fact, it is so unique that "shorebird with upturned bill" is often used as a crossword clue. They feed on aquatic invertebrates in shallow water. The American Avocet was documented only once during Atlas 2 (October 2010 in Seneca 3), when three individuals were observed flying around and landing on a pond at a golf course in easternmost Loudoun.

American Avocets breed in the midwestern U.S. and winter in the southern U.S. and Mexico. Interestingly, they sometimes lay eggs in other avocet nests and even the nests of other species; similarly, other species sometimes lay eggs in avocet nests. Avocet populations are considered stable, but their wetland habitat is generally at risk to both development and climate change.

Written by Bryan Henson

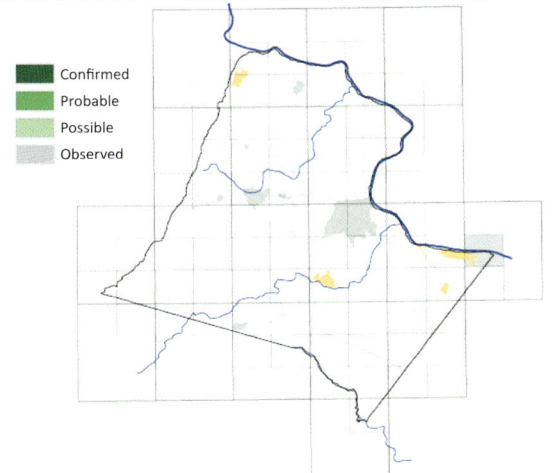

- Confirmed
- Probable
- Possible
- Observed

BLACK-BELLIED PLOVER
Pluvialis squatarola

Occurrence: rare migrant

Southerly/northerly migration periods: fewer than 5 atlas sightings, see account for details

Breeding along the Bering Sea and Arctic Ocean, and wintering on the coasts of the Atlantic Ocean and the Gulf of Mexico, the Black-bellied Plover is seen in Loudoun strictly during migration. The only atlas sighting was in September 2012, in southern Ashburn on a sod field – a habitat type that regularly attracts various plovers that migrate through this region.

In breeding plumage, the male Black-bellied Plover has solid black underparts extending from its belly up through its chin and over its cheeks, with a wide white border from head to midriff. The female is often a paler version of the male. In basic plumage, the bird has dull gray upperparts and a paler breast and belly. In flight it shows black axillaries (under-wing or "armpit" feathers), which distinguish it from similar-looking American Golden-Plovers. Black-bellied Plovers are the largest plover in North America, with populations considered stable throughout their range.

Written by Bill Brown

Photo by Bob Schamerhorn

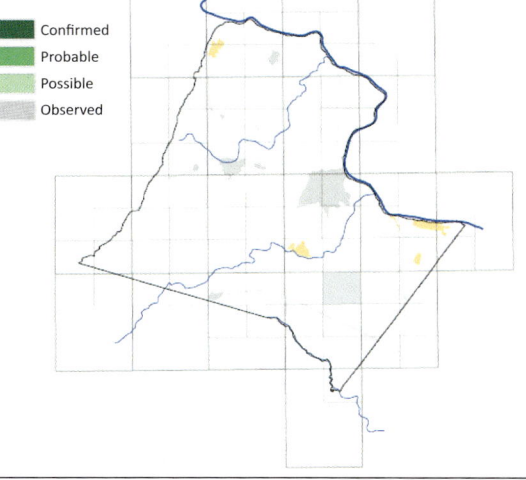

- Confirmed
- Probable
- Possible
- Observed

Photo ©Dick Rowe (non-breeding)

AMERICAN GOLDEN-PLOVER
Pluvialis dominica

Occurrence: rare migrant

Southerly/northerly migration periods: fewer than 5 atlas sightings, see account for details

Rarely seen in Loudoun, the American Golden-Plover breeds in the Arctic tundra and migrates primarily offshore over the Atlantic on its journey to wintering grounds in southern Brazil and Argentina. On the northbound leg, most individuals travel up the middle of North America, feeding on insects in open areas such as pastures, sod farms, farmland, and airports. Only 1 atlas sighting was recorded, in September 2010, on a Sterling golf course. Though populations have rebounded after being hunted excessively in the late 19th century, this species appears on the 2014 State of the Birds Watch List as a species in danger of extinction without significant conservation action.

The breeding American Golden-Plover has striking black and gold speckled upperparts, and its black cheek and underparts resemble the Black-bellied Plover's. On this bird, however, the black plumage extends through the under-tail coverts, whereas the Black-bellied Plover has white under-tail coverts and rump. The American Golden-Plover is smaller than the Black-bellied and has white, rather than black, axillaries (armpits).

Written by Bill Brown

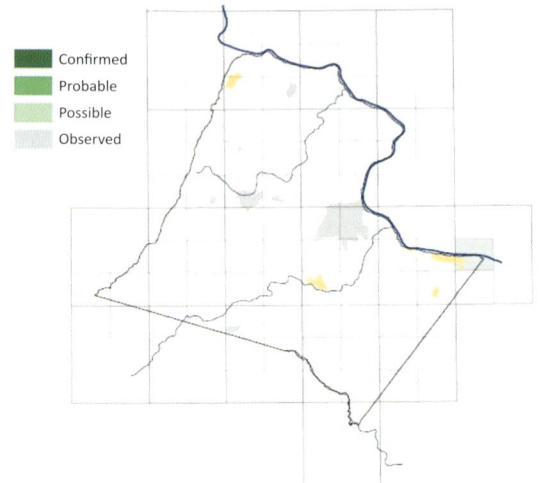

Confirmed
Probable
Possible
Observed

SEMIPALMATED PLOVER
Charadrius semipalmatus

Occurrence: rare migrant

Southerly/northerly migration periods: fewer than 5 atlas sightings, see account for details

The Semipalmated Plover is a small plover, named for the partial webbing between its toes, visible only at close range. It has a short, black bill, which is orange at the base in breeding birds, and a single complete black breast band that contrasts with its otherwise white throat and underparts.

The Semipalmated Plover was recorded 4 times, in 4 separate years, during the atlas. Three of those sightings were in May, presumably during northbound migration to its Arctic breeding grounds, and one was in August, when the bird would have been moving to its coastal wintering area. Typical migration stop-over habitat in and around Loudoun includes wetlands, such as the Dulles Greenway Wetlands, as well as sod farms. Though rare in Loudoun, the Semipalmated Plover is one of the most common and widespread plovers on migration throughout North America.

Written by Bill Brown

Photo by Nicole Sudduth

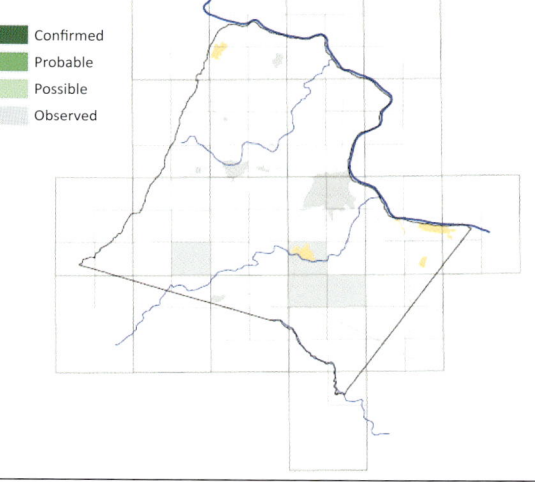

Confirmed
Probable
Possible
Observed

Photo by Laura McGranaghan

KILLDEER
Charadrius vociferus

Occurrence: uncommon breeder and migrant, occasional winter resident

Earliest breeding confirmation: April 14, distraction display (DD)

Latest breeding confirmation: July 18, recently fledged young (FL)

Killdeer are large plovers, approximately 10 inches long with an 18-inch wingspan. These tall, elegant shorebirds may be seen and heard throughout Loudoun. They are easily identified by their unique double breast band and plaintive *kill-dee* call. Killdeer are tawny brown in the upper body, white below, have an orange rump, and distinctively long tail. They are slim and angular in flight, and their strident cries, often given in flight, are far-reaching. Despite their status as a shorebird, Killdeer can be found quite far from water.

Throughout the year, Killdeer can be seen on the ground in open habitat such as pastures, plowed fields, airports, industrial parks, ballparks, and large lawns. Their diet consists primarily of insects, although they also eat seeds and hunt for minnows and frogs. They run in spurts, pausing to see what was flushed, and have been observed following farmers plowing fields to feed on insects, grubs, and earthworms turned up by the plow.

In breeding season, males fly over nesting territory in a wavering flight pattern with slow wing beats, calling repeatedly. Courtship involves a ritualized scrape ceremony in which the male scrapes a shallow depression in open ground. The female proclaims her acceptance by lowering herself in the scrape while the male stands over her and calls repeatedly. Killdeer lay three to five, typically four, eggs in the scrape in open ground; incubation is by both parents, 24-28 days. Scrapes have been observed in unexpected locations such as gravel driveways and clay tennis courts, often in places where they can be easily trodden upon. Females protect the nesting site with a convincing broken-wing display to draw predators away. Young leave the vulnerable nesting site shortly after hatching. Downy young Killdeer have a single breast band.

This species was reported as breeding in 59 of the 73 blocks and observed in 4 additional blocks. Central Loudoun CBC numbers ranged from zero to 29 individuals over the 20 years of counts, averaging 9. Comparisons to Atlas 1 reveal an overall gain in blocks due, in part, to the higher level of coverage per block in Atlas 2, but perhaps also due to the Killdeer's willingness to nest close to people in human-modified habitats. This affiliation with people has obvious benefits, but leaves them vulnerable to pesticide poisoning, collisions with vehicles and buildings, and roaming pets. In general, Killdeer populations have declined over the past 50 years, especially in Canada and the West.

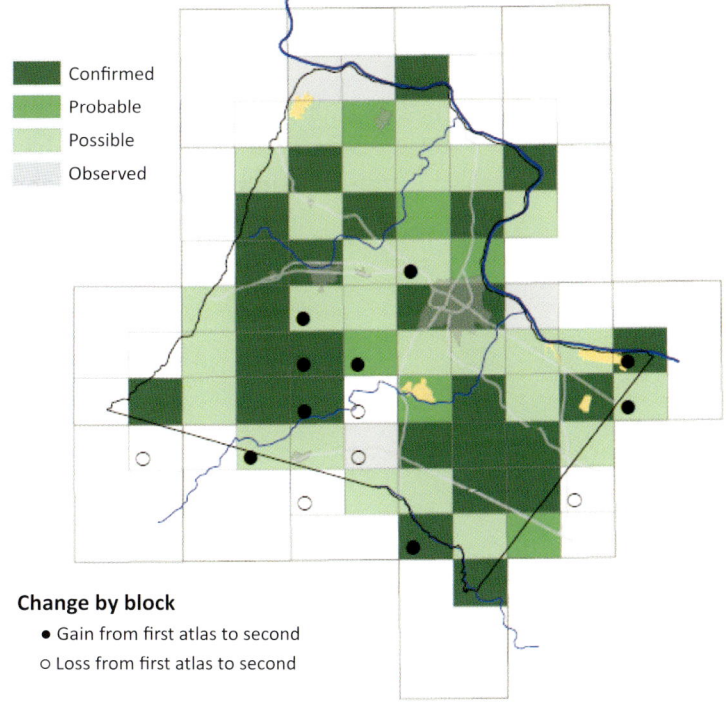

Confirmed
Probable
Possible
Observed

Change by block
● Gain from first atlas to second
○ Loss from first atlas to second

Written by Donna Quinn

STILT SANDPIPER

Calidris himantopus

Occurrence: rare fall migrant

Southerly/northerly migration periods: fewer than 5 atlas sightings, see account for details

In its non-breeding plumage, the Stilt Sandpiper looks very similar to other more common long-legged shorebirds found in Loudoun. One look-alike, the Lesser Yellowlegs, fortunately has eponymous yellow legs to help differentiate it. Gray on top and white below, its long bill, long greenish legs, and long neck are key features of the Stilt Sandpiper. It breeds in sedge tundra of the Arctic and winters throughout South America. Migrating mainly through the Great Plains, the Stilt Sandpiper is uncommonly found along the East Coast and is a rare treat for Loudoun birders. Found in freshwater marshes and ponds probing the mud, it uses an oil drill-type motion to grab insects and mollusks.

This shorebird was found only once during Atlas 2, in September 2009, likely attracted by the rich, thriving habitat of the Dulles Greenway Wetlands in Leesburg 5. Population trends are not well understood, but its limited breeding range may leave this species naturally vulnerable to environmental change.

Written by Bryan Henson

Photo ©Dick Rowe (juvenile)

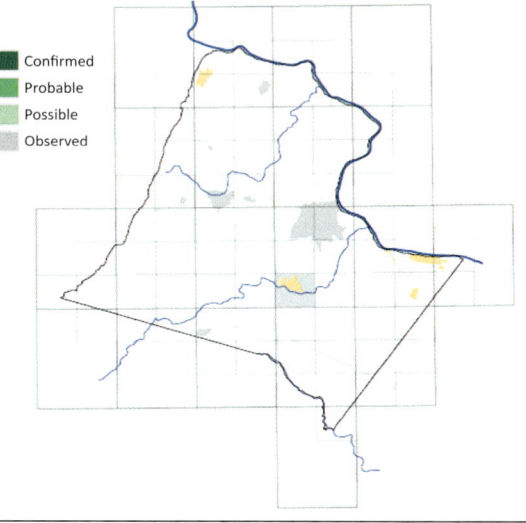

Confirmed
Probable
Possible
Observed

LEAST SANDPIPER

Calidris minutilla

Occurrence: uncommon migrant

Southerly migration period: July 9 – September 7

Northerly migration period: May 4 – May 19

The smallest of all shorebirds, the diminutive Least Sandpiper transits our region on its way to and from its breeding grounds in the tundra and forest of northern North America. It winters in the southern U.S. and South America. Although observed in 9 blocks, more than a third of the 16 atlas sightings were from a single site, the Dulles Greenway Wetlands in Leesburg 5. This habitat exemplifies the environment this sandpiper seems to prefer: edge habitat around shallow water bodies.

The most obvious identification trait may be its size, although only about half an inch separates it from the very similar Semipalmated and Western Sandpipers. In addition, their legs are black as opposed to the Least Sandpiper's yellow-green legs. Least Sandpipers often are found in smaller groups and forage lower to the ground than other sandpipers, seeking invertebrates in the mud and seeds from marsh grasses and cautiously watching their surrounding environment. Though widespread, populations across eastern North America are declining, likely due to wetland loss and degradation.

Written by Bryan Henson

Photo by Gerco Hoogeweg

Confirmed
Probable
Possible
Observed

WHITE-RUMPED SANDPIPER

Calidris fuscicollis

Occurrence: rare migrant

Southerly/northerly migration periods: fewer than 5 atlas sightings, see account for details

Photo by Bob Schamerhorn

White upper-tail coverts, commonly only seen during flight, provide the namesake feature of the White-rumped Sandpiper. Slightly larger and with a longer wing projection than our common sandpipers, these features help pick this sandpiper out in a crowd.

A single sighting during Atlas 2 (late July 2011) is not surprising considering the White-rumped Sandpiper's very long migration route – one of the longest of any American bird. They breed in the mossy/grassy tundra of the Arctic and winter in the southern tip of South America. During migration, they prefer the shores of ponds and lakes and grassy marshes. The single atlas observation was on the muddy edges of a large pond in the Brambleton area of Arcola 2 – an area that is now under development. Post-atlas (September 2018), this rarity was observed in a muddy field north of Leesburg. White-rumped Sandpipers are especially vulnerable to the disappearance of key migratory stop-over points where they build fat reserves for their long flights.

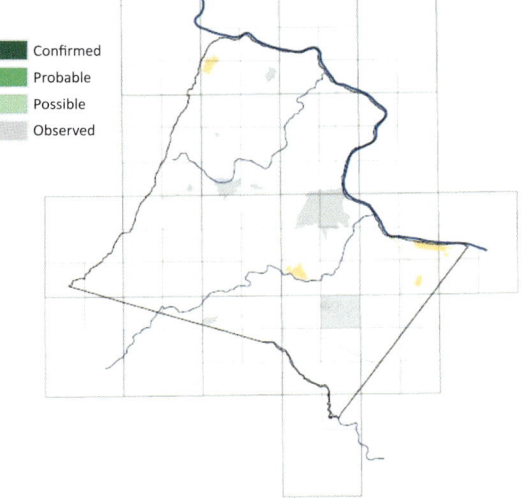

Confirmed
Probable
Possible
Observed

Written by Bryan Henson

PECTORAL SANDPIPER

Calidris melanotos

Occurrence: occasional migrant

Southerly/northerly migration periods: fewer than 5 atlas sightings each way, see account for details

Photo ©Dick Rowe

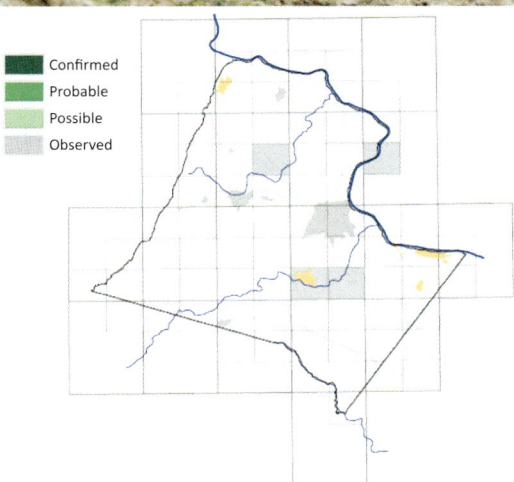

Confirmed
Probable
Possible
Observed

This medium-sized shorebird has yellowish-green legs, a fairly long neck, a stout, medium-length bill that may droop slightly, and a generally upright posture. On its underside, the chest shows fine dark markings that end abruptly along a clean line at its white belly, a distinctive field mark for the species. This high-Arctic tundra breeder is seen only occasionally in Loudoun as it stops over during its migrations between North and South America. It was reported 5 times in 4 blocks during Atlas 2, in early May and late July/early August.

The usually solitary Pectoral Sandpiper prefers grassy mudflats and weedy pond edges, where it hunts for insects above and below the waterline. This bird's tendency to avoid open areas may allow it to go unseen and be under-reported. It was historically a much more common bird in the early 1900s, but intense market hunting significantly reduced its population. It has since rebounded somewhat, but is watch-listed (NABCI 2016) as being at risk of becoming threatened or endangered without adequate conservation measures.

Written by Bruce Hill

SEMIPALMATED SANDPIPER

Calidris pusilla

Occurrence: uncommon migrant

Southerly migration period: July 14 – September 17

Northerly migration period: May 2 – May 11

In Loudoun, the Semipalmated Sandpiper is one of two sparrow-sized sandpipers with *black* legs (the Least Sandpiper has yellow legs). This small "peep" is an uncommon but seasonally regular visitor to our county, spending time during migration feeding actively on mudflats and pond edges. It was reported in 7 blocks during Atlas 2. This tiny bird has a short neck, medium black bill, and fairly long legs for its size. It sports a gray to brown back and crown and a clean white underside, with only limited and indistinct markings on its neck and chest.

An accomplished long-distance migrant, this small shorebird breeds in the high Arctic tundra and winters along the coasts of South America and the Caribbean islands. This can entail non-stop flights of up to 2,500 miles between the two continents, quite a feat for a bird just over 5 inches long that weighs in at about one ounce. This species is considered "Near Threatened" by the IUCN, with the eastern population in particular in apparent decline.

Written by Bruce Hill

Photo by Dave Boltz

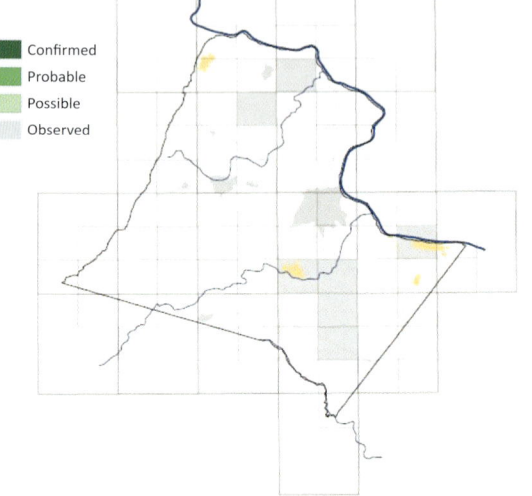

Confirmed
Probable
Possible
Observed

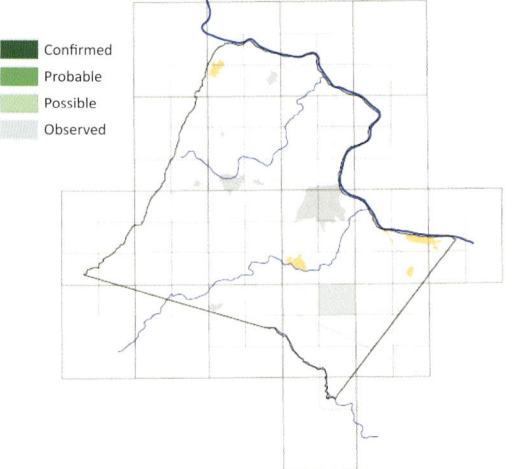
Photo by Gerco Hoogeweg

Confirmed
Probable
Possible
Observed

WESTERN SANDPIPER

Calidris mauri

Occurrence: rare summer/fall migrant

Southerly/northerly migration periods: fewer than 5 atlas sightings, see account for details

Though Loudoun does not offer much habitat for this species, one post-breeding migrant was observed on July 18, 2010 foraging with other "peeps" on the mudflats of a large pond in the Brambleton area of Arcola 2. This ground nester breeds in the tundra of western Alaska and winters along both coasts of North and South America. The majority migrate in large flocks along the Pacific Coast, though many reach the Atlantic Coast and can be found on mudflats, shores, lakes, ponds, and wetlands probing for crustaceans, mollusks, and insects.

In non-breeding plumage, this small sandpiper looks similar to the Semipalmated and Least Sandpipers, found more commonly in Loudoun, but it has a longer, more drooping bill. Western and Semipalmated have black legs whereas the Least's legs are yellow. In breeding plumage, the Western has distinctive chestnut patches on its back, crown, and face. The Western Sandpiper population is stable across its range, but is vulnerable to disturbances to key migratory stop-over sites that are vital to a large percentage of the population.

Written by Spring Ligi

SHORT-BILLED DOWITCHER

Limnodromus griseus

Occurrence: rare migrant

Southerly/northerly migration periods: fewer than 5 atlas sightings, see account for details

The Short-billed Dowitcher is a plump, medium-sized shorebird, frustratingly similar to the Long-billed Dowitcher (not documented during the atlas). Both dowitchers are noted for their distinctive foraging action – a deep, rapid probing motion that may remind one of a sewing machine. Despite the names, bill length is an unreliable method of identification. Females of both species tend to be larger with longer bills, so larger female Short-billed Dowitchers can have longer bills than smaller male Long-Billeds. In breeding plumage, the Short-billed tends to have a paler belly and vent, varying from white to orange, whereas the Long-billed has brighter, brick-red underparts.

Photo by Dave Boltz

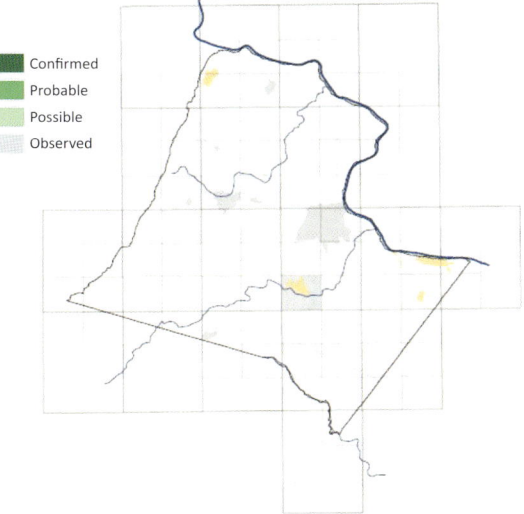

Confirmed
Probable
Possible
Observed

Recorded only once during Atlas 2, at the Dulles Greenway Wetlands in July 2010, the Short-billed Dowitcher is more reliably found on mud flats along the Atlantic Coast as it migrates between its breeding grounds in the boreal forest and its South American wintering grounds. This species is on the 2014 State of the Birds Watch List as a species at risk of becoming threatened or endangered without conservation action.

Written by Bill Brown

Photo by Dave Boltz

AMERICAN WOODCOCK

Scolopax minor

Occurrence: uncommon breeder and year-round resident, occasional migrant

Earliest/latest breeding confirmations: fewer than 5 atlas confirmations, see account for details

This cryptic shorebird can be difficult to find as it spends its days in damp forests or thickets in overgrown fields, using its long, flexible bill to probe for earthworms and other prey items underground. It is one of few shorebird species occurring in upland habitats and away from coastlines. Its habitat can be helpful in distinguishing it from the somewhat similar-looking Wilson's Snipe, a species much more strongly tied to wetlands.

American Woodcocks are round-bodied and short-legged, with mottled brown, buff, and gray plumage. Their large black eyes (useful during nocturnal flights) stand out on a generally plain gray face, save for a darker cap and brown line running from the eye to the base of the bill. They have broad, rounded wings, allowing them to take off nearly vertically (seemingly helicopter-like). When you come upon one, it will frequently freeze until you are nearly on top of it, exploding into flight. This habit may be intended to briefly startle any predator long enough to make its escape.

The Woodcock is still hunted as a gamebird throughout the eastern and central U.S. They are most commonly encountered at dusk or dawn in late winter or early spring, during their unique courtship ritual. Around twilight, the

AMERICAN WOODCOCK (continued)

males make incredible display flights, flying high into the air then spiraling back to earth while making a variety of chirps, as well as non-vocal twittering sounds made by air rushing through their primary feathers. Once back on the ground, they make nasal *peent* calls for several minutes, rotating 90 degrees with each utterance, before launching into their display flights again, all in hopes of attracting a nearby female. Open field habitats adjacent to woodlands are prime locations to look for this behavior. Outside of breeding season, this ground-nesting bird is generally solitary.

Though breeding is difficult to confirm for this master of camouflage, one nest with young was found during Atlas 2 in late March 2011 at the National Beagle Club Institute Farm in Lincoln 6. Two instances of birds performing a distraction display

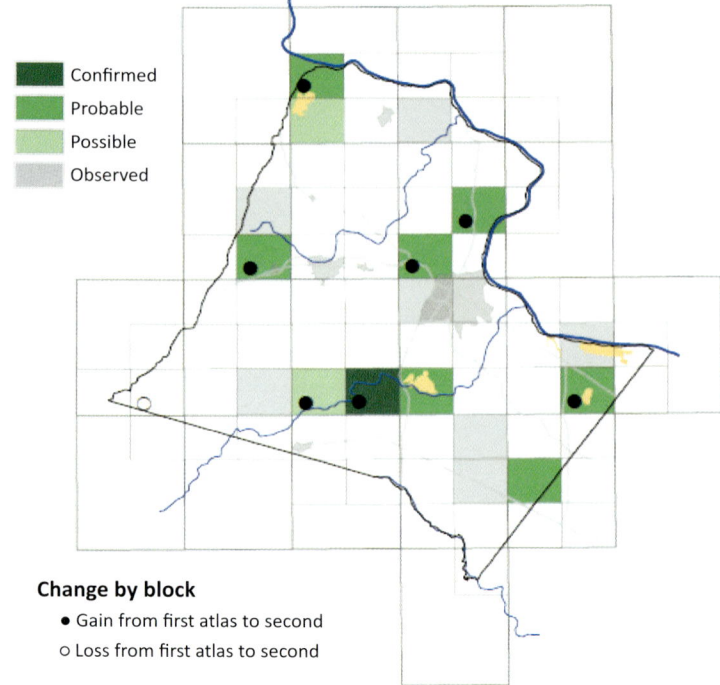

Change by block
- Gain from first atlas to second
○ Loss from first atlas to second

(likely to protect young) were reported almost simultaneously at other places on the property. Courtship displays (probable breeding) were reported in 7 other blocks throughout Loudoun. One report of possible breeding was documented in Atlas 1. Woodcocks were found in 7 of the past 20 Central Loudoun CBCs. They remain fairly common throughout their range, but are considered a declining species.

Written by Bruce Hill

Photo by Gerco Hoogeweg

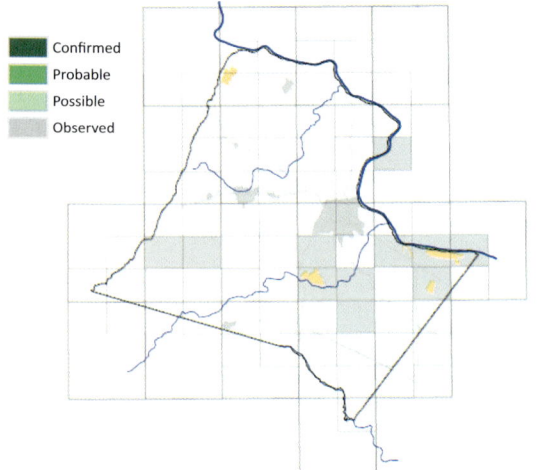

WILSON'S SNIPE
Gallinago delicata

Occurrence: uncommon migrant, occasional winter visitor

Earliest fall sighting: September 6

Latest spring sighting: May 12

Wilson's Snipe are medium-sized shorebirds with short, stocky legs and a very long, straight, flexible-tipped bill with which they probe the mud for earthworms and other invertebrates. They have long buffy streaks on their mottled brown back and brown and buff stripes on their head. Paulson, in his Shorebirds of North America (2005), writes there is "no other shorebird as vividly striped above…" Because of this cryptic coloration, they are very easy to miss in the muddy areas along pond edges and damp fields that they frequent in our area during the colder months. When they are seen, they explode into a zigzag flight uttering their flight call which vaguely sounds like snipe.

Wilson's Snipe were documented 29 times in 11 atlas blocks and on 13 of the 20 Central Loudoun CBCs. They are common and widespread throughout their range, breeding in most of Canada and the northern U.S. and wintering throughout much of the rest of the U.S. down to northern South America. They are found as frequently inland as along the coast.

Written by Joe Coleman

SPOTTED SANDPIPER

Actitis macularius

Occurrence: common spring, uncommon summer/fall migrant

Southerly migration period: July 1 – September 7

Northerly migration period: March 25 – May 30

Spotted Sandpipers are observed along the shorelines of lakes, rivers, and ponds in Loudoun, walking deliberately on land or in very shallow water while searching for insects and other invertebrates. This medium-sized sandpiper has bright yellow to orange legs and matching bill with a dark tip, and in breeding plumage, shows black spotting on its white breast and flanks. Spotted Sandpipers frequently bob the back half of their body up and down, which can help distinguish this species from the other common Loudoun migrant, the Solitary Sandpiper. When flushed, they fly away low over the water, alternating shallow wingbeats with short glides.

While not recorded as a breeder in Atlas 2, it breeds nearby in adjacent counties and states, and was recorded as a possible breeder in Atlas 1 (Purcellville 6). It was confirmed as breeding once in eastern Loudoun in the post-Atlas 2 timeframe (July 2016). Spotted Sandpipers are the most widespread breeding sandpiper in North America, but populations are declining, likely from habitat loss and other environmental factors.

Written by Bruce Hill

Photo by Gerco Hoogeweg

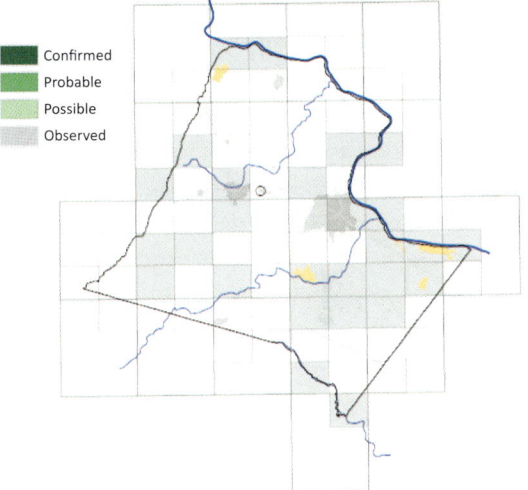

Confirmed
Probable
Possible
Observed

Photo by Gerco Hoogeweg

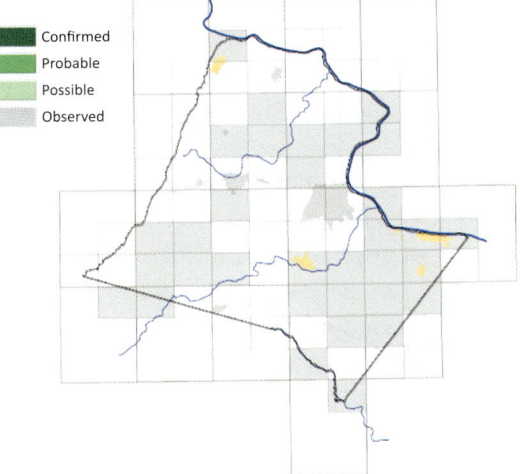

Confirmed
Probable
Possible
Observed

SOLITARY SANDPIPER

Tringa solitaria

Occurrence: common spring, uncommon summer/fall migrant

Southerly migration period: July 9 – October 6

Northerly migration period: April 21 – May 19

The Solitary Sandpiper seems to invade the margins of almost every small pond, stream, and ditch in Loudoun for a few weeks in late April and early May. It then heads northward to breed throughout Canada and Alaska. It has the unusual habit for a shorebird of nesting in trees, reusing the nests of similarly sized species. It reappears in smaller numbers in late summer and early fall en route to its winter haunts in the Caribbean and Central and South America. Though several may congregate at a given location, seemingly belying its name, it is a solitary traveler that doesn't group into flocks like many shorebirds.

This medium-sized shorebird has a relatively long neck and legs, thin bill, and dark olive back with white speckling. It has white undersides with an indistinct band across its chest. The barred tail can be a good field mark. It walks along freshwater shorelines and in shallow water, feeding on small invertebrates and frequently bobbing its head, especially when alarmed. Though common, populations appear to be declining according to the North American BBS.

Written by Bruce Hill

LESSER YELLOWLEGS
Tringa flavipes

Occurrence: uncommon spring, occasional summer/fall migrant

Southerly migration period: July 10 – October 23

Northerly migration period: April 18 – May 19

The Lesser Yellowlegs may be seen singly or in small numbers in or around shallow ponds or marshes where it probes both underwater and along the shoreline for aquatic and terrestrial insects and the occasional small fish. If seen alongside Loudoun's other yellowlegs species, Greater Yellowlegs, the Lesser is notably smaller and more slender; but this is difficult to judge without a direct comparison. Its straight, markedly shorter black bill, along with long yellow legs, should also be noted. Perhaps the best way to separate it from its larger cousin is its typically two-note call, a sharp *keew-keew*.

Found in 9 atlas blocks, the Lesser's distribution looks very similar to that of the Greater Yellowlegs, with the majority of the 24 sightings in southeastern Loudoun. The Lesser Yellowlegs breeds in northern Canada and Alaska, placing its nest on the ground within boreal forests and wetland habitats. This species has declined over the past 50 years, but still has a significant population of over 660,000 birds (Andres et al. 2012).

Written by Bruce Hill

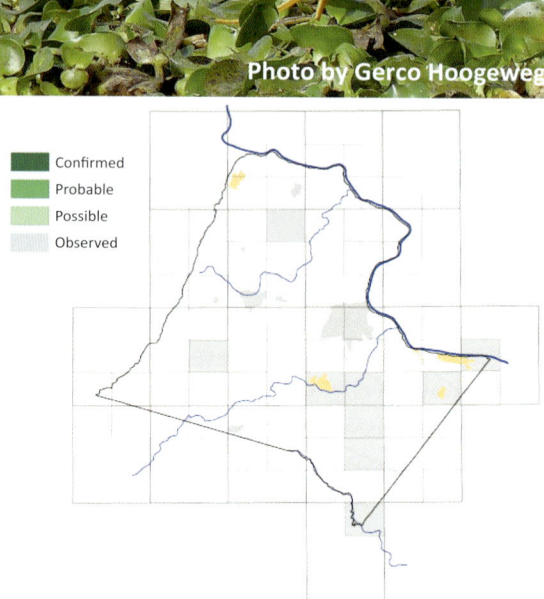
Photo by Gerco Hoogeweg

Confirmed
Probable
Possible
Observed

GREATER YELLOWLEGS
Tringa melanoleuca

Occurrence: uncommon spring, occasional summer/fall migrant

Southerly migration period: August 19 – November 20

Northerly migration period: April 8 – May 19

The Greater Yellowlegs, using its long yellow legs to its advantage, may be spotted wading in various water depths of both fresh and saltwater habitats, hunting for insects or small vertebrates. During Atlas 2, this regular visitor was reported 27 times across 10 blocks. Noticeably larger and heavier than the similar Lesser Yellowlegs, the Greater's bill is visibly longer than its head and is slightly upcurved, while the Lesser's is straight and about the same length as its head. An even better clue is its rapid, sharp call, which is almost always given in threes (or more) – *kew-kew-kew*. Remember "Greater" for its higher number of call notes.

This species is thought to have increased slightly in number over the past 50 years. Greater Yellowlegs breed in remote bogs and muskeg forest areas in the far North, which has been a factor in it being one of the least studied shorebirds. It is much easier to observe away from the breeding grounds – it winters throughout the southern U.S., Caribbean, and Central and South America.

Written by Bruce Hill

Photo by Dave Boltz

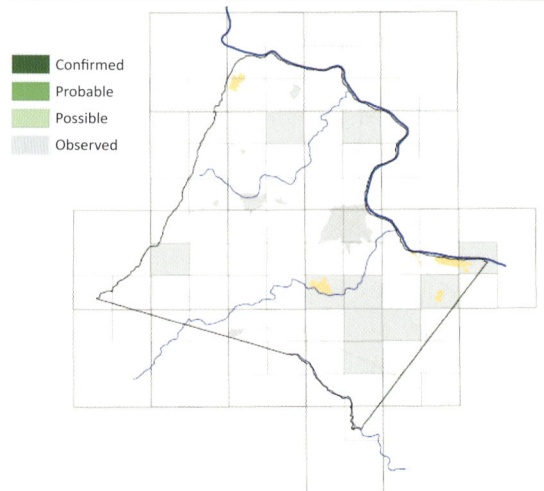
Confirmed
Probable
Possible
Observed

RED PHALAROPE
Phalaropus fulicarius

Photo by Gerco Hoogeweg

Occurrence: vagrant

Earliest/latest seasonal sightings: fewer than 5 atlas sightings, see account for details

Phalaropes have a very distinctive behavior that makes them easy to pick out of a crowd; while feeding, they spin in circles in shallow water. The spinning brings food, mostly aquatic insects, to the surface for them to feed on. The Red Phalarope can be distinguished from the Wilson's Phalarope by its thicker and shorter bill. It can be separated from the Red-necked Phalarope in breeding season by its white cheek and in non-breeding plumage by its paler and non-streaked neck. The Red Phalarope is sexually dimorphic, but it is the females who are more colorful and court several mates per season while the males raise the young.

There was a single surprising atlas sighting of this species on October 30, 2010 on the Potomac River in Seneca 3. The Red Phalarope breeds in the Arctic of North America and winters on the southern oceans surrounding North America, so it is rarely seen inland. Climate change could impact its population, which is thought to be declining.

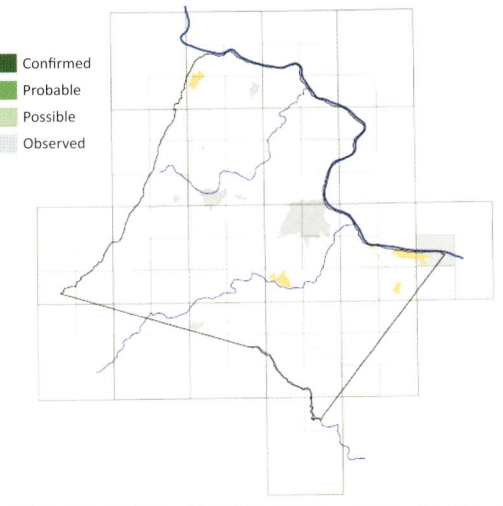

Confirmed
Probable
Possible
Observed

Written by Bryan Henson

Photo ©Dick Rowe

Confirmed
Probable
Possible
Observed

BONAPARTE'S GULL
Chroicocephalus philadelphia

Occurrence: occasional migrant, rare winter visitor

Southerly migration period: no atlas sightings, see account for details

Northerly migration period: March 10 – April 26

Among the smallest of North America's common gulls, the Bonaparte's Gull was found in the Potomac River and Goose Creek atlas blocks of eastern Loudoun mainly during its north-bound migration and twice in the winter. There were no south-bound atlas sightings, though it was reported within the broader coastal region. A black-headed gull during its breeding season, it has a thin black bill, pinkish to reddish legs and feet, and white outer primaries. It prefers the proximity of strongly flowing water where it can surface-fish for its prey and seldom scavenges at landfills like other gull species. It does not mix much with other gulls, but can flock at a good food source, often in the thousands.

A remote and solitary nester, the Bonaparte's Gull is unique among gulls for nesting in the coniferous trees of the boreal forest. It moves south with the coming of the freeze to winter in the Southeast, Cuba, and along the Atlantic seaboard. Populations are vulnerable to habitat destruction. No national, state, or provincial studies of this species' life cycle and breeding habits have been undertaken.

Written by Chris White

RING-BILLED GULL
Larus delawarensis

Photo by Gerco Hoogeweg

Occurrence: common migrant and winter resident, rare summer visitor

Earliest summer/fall sighting: August 20

Latest spring sighting: May 23

This medium-sized larid is the most commonly seen gull in Loudoun. It was reported in 37 blocks, especially from developed areas or near the Potomac River. Ring-bills nest colonially across the northern U.S. and Canada, then migrate further south for the rest of the year. Shopping centers, plowed fields, and the County Landfill are good bets to see this undiscriminating feeder, especially airborne.

Adults have a light gray mantle, white head, body, and tail, yellow legs, and a yellow bill with a dark ring near the tip. Their long wings have dark tips with small white spots; when sitting, their wingtips project well beyond the tail. They are strong and agile flyers. In our area, they often travel in large flocks, and may be seen early and late streaming to or from their overnight resting locations. Severely reduced by the feather trade a century ago, this species has recovered well and is expanding its breeding range. Numbers in Loudoun are expanding: 1997-2006 Central Loudoun CBCs averaged 290 Ring-bills per count, compared to 2,290 in the 2007-2016 counts.

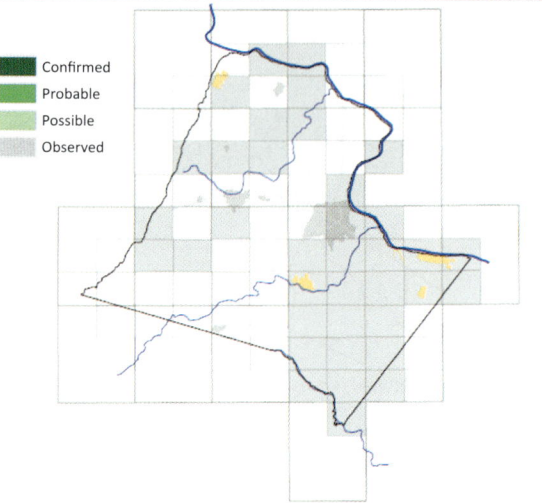

Confirmed
Probable
Possible
Observed

Written by Bruce Hill

Photo ©Dick Rowe

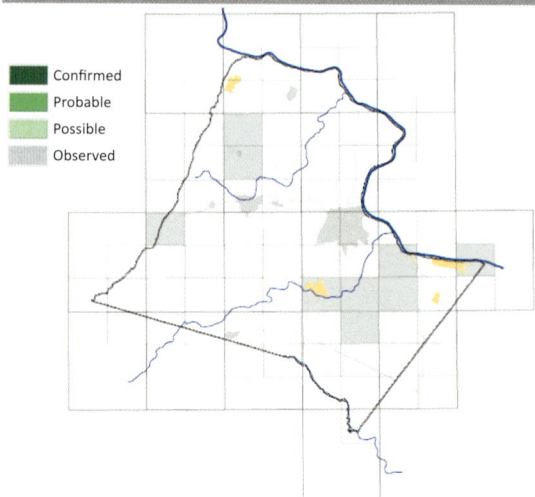

Confirmed
Probable
Possible
Observed

HERRING GULL
Larus argentatus

Occurrence: occasional migrant and winter resident

Earliest fall sighting: November 4

Latest spring sighting: March 23

The large and opportunistic Herring Gull occurs regularly in Loudoun in migration and during the winter months, but in much lower numbers than the smaller Ring-billed Gulls it associates with. The 2009-2013 Central Loudoun CBCs show an annual average of only 24 Herring Gulls compared to 1,169 Ring-billed Gulls, most having been counted at the County Landfill. They were reported in only a fourth as many atlas blocks as Ring-bills. The bulk of their population breeds well to the north throughout boreal regions of inland Canada; some also breed along the Atlantic Coast south to Virginia. They winter in the U.S. and Mexico, primarily in coastal regions.

When identifying Herring Gulls on the ground, note their size, large yellow bills, and light gray wings. In flight they are noticeably larger, and young birds darker, than the Ring-bills. Their many vocalizations include a loud, drawn-out *keeyer* call. This species was severely reduced by feather and egg hunting in the 1880s. They rebounded, only to decline again, dropping by 83% between 1966 and 2015 (North American BBS).

Written by Bruce Hill

LESSER BLACK-BACKED GULL

Larus fuscus

Occurrence: rare winter visitor

Earliest/latest seasonal sightings: fewer than 5 atlas sightings, see account for details

Photo by Dave Boltz

The Lesser Black-backed Gull breeds along the Atlantic coasts of Europe and Iceland, but appears annually in the U.S. along the eastern and Gulf coasts and the Great Lakes region in fast-growing numbers. Thousands are seen each year in the U.S, with at least some in all months of the year. Their rapid expansion in recent decades hints at their becoming a U.S. breeding species, though no firm evidence of this is yet established. Species populations in Europe appear relatively stable.

This medium-sized gull is much darker-backed and about two-thirds the weight of the Herring Gull, and is much smaller and not quite as dark-backed as the Great Black-backed Gull. Its bright yellow legs differentiate it from both species. The bill is yellow. Its diet is quite varied, ranging from fish and insects to other birds, carrion, and garbage, which it readily steals from others. Its call is a deep *kyow*. Single birds seen at the County Landfill during the Central Loudoun CBC in 2010 and 2012 account for the only 2 atlas records.

Written by Bruce Hill

Confirmed
Probable
Possible
Observed

Photo by Dave Boltz

Confirmed
Probable
Possible
Observed

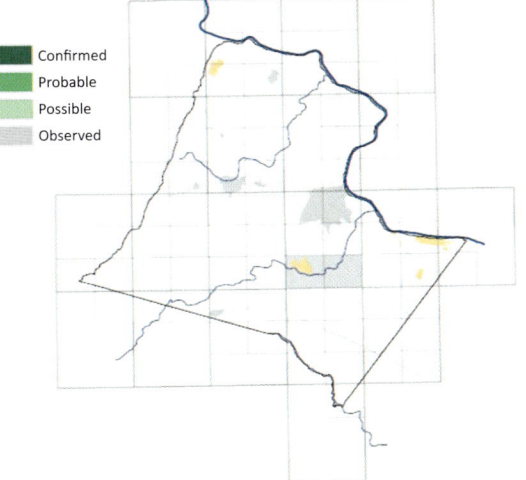

GREAT BLACK-BACKED GULL

Larus marinus

Occurrence: rare winter visitor

Earliest/latest seasonal sightings: fewer than 5 atlas sightings, see account for details

The Great Black-backed Gull is the largest gull in the world. An opportunistic hunter and scavenger, this aggressive bird eats almost anything. Besides man-made food sources (garbage, fishing discards), they regularly steal food from or even make a meal of other birds. Adults have a black back and upper wings, white head, big yellow bill, and flesh-colored legs.

Ranging from the Atlantic seaboard and Great Lakes to Greenland, Iceland, and western Europe, this bird breeds alone or in loose colonies in isolated areas near water, often with other species. In winter, they frequent tidal rivers, bays, and beaches. This maritime visitor was reported only twice in Atlas 2, both times in the vicinity of Beaverdam Reservoir and the County Landfill. Like other gulls, Great Black-backs were hunted for feathers for decoration and quills in the 19th and early 20th centuries. Numbers have since rebounded, and they are now found regularly as far south as North Carolina. Of the 9 Central Loudoun CBCs that recorded this gull, 7 were from 2007 on.

Written by Bruce Hill

CASPIAN TERN
Hydroprogne caspia

Occurrence: rare migrant

Southerly/northerly migration periods: fewer than 5 atlas sightings, see account for details

Caspian Terns are the largest tern in the world, the size of a large gull, and can seem more gull-like in appearance and behavior than their smaller relatives. Besides size, their heavy red bill is a striking and recognizable feature. They sport a black cap, light gray back and wings, white undersides, and black legs. To feed, they plunge into fresh or salt water to catch small fish.

Caspian Terns breed in a limited number of colonies in Canada and the western U.S., nesting close together and aggressively defending their young. They winter in Florida, the Gulf Coast, Mexico, and the Caribbean. In Loudoun, they are most likely to be seen during migration, as they move up or down the Potomac River and sometimes stray to smaller water bodies. Of the 4 April atlas sightings (all different years), 3 were near Algonkian Park along the Potomac; the other over a pond in the Sterling area. Little is known about Caspian Tern population trends, but according to the North American BBS this species appears to be stable.

Written by Bruce Hill

Photo by Gerco Hoogeweg

- Confirmed
- Probable
- Possible
- Observed

COMMON TERN
Sterna hirundo

Occurrence: rare migrant

Southerly/northerly migration periods: fewer than 5 atlas sightings, see account for details

A single Common Tern was observed at a large pond in the Ashburn area in September 2012. This is the only atlas record, though this species is reported with some regularity in our region, especially in the spring and fall near the Potomac River and Chesapeake Bay. The Common Tern is the most widespread tern in North America, nesting on the ground in fresh and saltwater habitats in Canada, then migrating throughout the eastern U.S. as it works its way to the coastal Caribbean and South America for the winter. Populations have declined over the past 5 decades, with the Common Tern listed as endangered or threatened in many states.

This tern appears white overall in flight, with a deeply forked tail and long, pointed wings showing black on the outer primaries. It has a light gray mantle and wings, black crown, orange/red bill with a black tip, and red legs. This medium-sized tern has an agile, buoyant flight, and can often be seen hovering before plunging into the water after small fish.

Written by Bruce Hill

Photo by Gerco Hoogeweg

- Confirmed
- Probable
- Possible
- Observed

RED-THROATED LOON
Gavia stellata

Occurrence: rare migrant

Southerly/northerly migration periods: fewer than 5 atlas sightings; see account for details

Photo ©Dick Rowe

The Red-throated Loon is unique in that it can take flight directly from the water or even land, unlike other loons which need to "run" along the water's surface on a long takeoff. This allows it to use smaller bodies of water. It is also the smallest of the loons, with a fairly short and sharp bill. While more monochromatic than the handsome breeding plumage, its winter plumage sports striking white speckles on a black background, thus its species name *stellata* (stars).

The Red-throated Loon breeds on the tundra wetlands in the far north, including the Arctic Circle in North America, and also across Eurasia. In the winter, they are commonly found up and down both U.S. coasts, and in rare instances may wander widely during migration. There was a single atlas sighting in November 2011 at Beaverdam Reservoir (Arcola 2), a protected, relatively shallow body of water characteristic of their winter habitat. Red-throated Loons are on the 2014 State of the Birds Watch List as a species in danger of extinction without significant conservation action.

Written by Bryan Henson

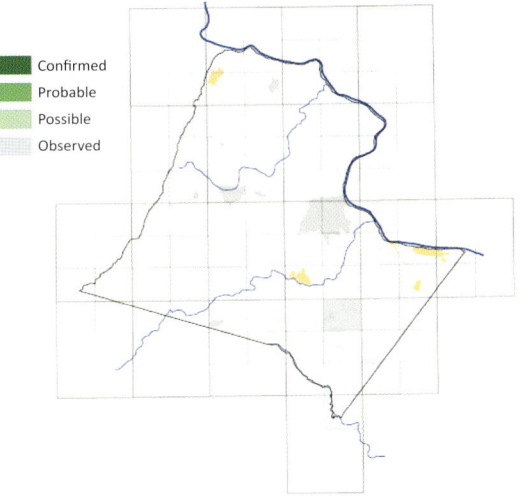

- Confirmed
- Probable
- Possible
- Observed

COMMON LOON
Gavia immer

Occurrence: occasional migrant, rare winter visitor

Earliest fall sighting: November 2

Latest spring sighting: May 22

Photo by Bob Schamerhorn

The haunting wail of a Common Loon is so iconic of the large, remote lakes of its Canadian and far northern U.S. breeding grounds that it is often used to set the scene in movies. Its breeding plumage, as seen locally in spring migration, is strikingly handsome, often likened to a tuxedo, sporting black and white checkers on the back and pinstripes on its neck. Adults in non-breeding plumage are mainly gray with a white throat. Their hefty bill is a characteristic feature.

Common Loons generally overwinter along the coastline, but are sometimes found inland on rivers and lakes. There were 23 atlas sightings along the Potomac River and larger water bodies; they were reported on just 1 of the past 20 Central Loudoun CBCs. Loons hunt for fish by diving quickly through the water, propelling themselves with their feet. Their success is dependent upon clear water, which makes them good indicators of water quality. They have declined in more populated breeding areas of the northern U.S., but in general their population is considered stable.

Written by Bryan Henson

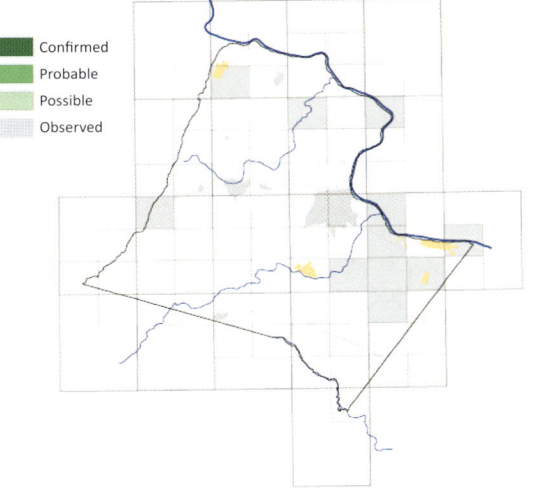

- Confirmed
- Probable
- Possible
- Observed

DOUBLE-CRESTED CORMORANT
Phalacrocorax auritus

Occurrence: uncommon migrant, occasional summer and rare winter visitor

Earliest spring sighting: March 11

Latest fall sighting: November 19

Photo by Deb Calhoun

The Double-crested Cormorant is the only cormorant likely to be seen in our area and the most common one in North America. They eat a wide variety of fish that they catch while swimming underwater. They are best known for their posture when they stand upright out of the water with their wings spread out to dry. This large, brownish-black water bird has a long neck and hooked bill; juveniles have paler undersides. Adults in breeding plumage have small tufts on the sides of their head and bright yellow-orange skin around the base of their bill and chin. They were almost extirpated from the northeastern U.S. in the 19th century due to hunting and pesticides, but populations have since rebounded and continue to increase. Double-crested Cormorants were found in 31 atlas blocks throughout the county on ponds, streams, and rivers. While rare in the winter, they have been found on two Central Loudoun CBCs.

Written by Joe Coleman

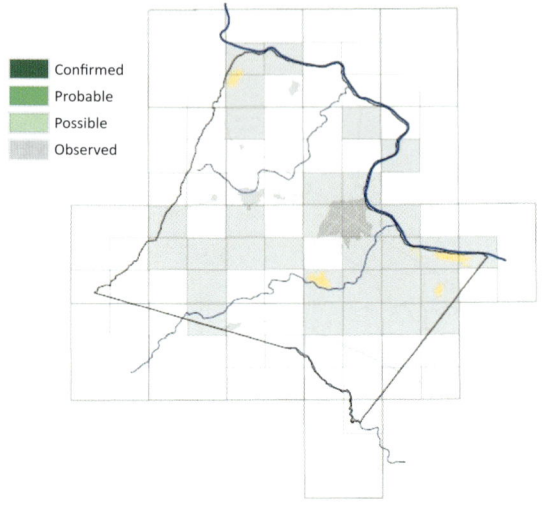
- Confirmed
- Probable
- Possible
- Observed

Photo ©Dick Rowe

- Confirmed
- Probable
- Possible
- Observed

AMERICAN BITTERN
Botaurus lentiginosus

Occurrence: occasional migrant

Southerly migration period: no atlas sightings, see account for details

Northerly migration period: April 5 – May 3

The American Bittern is a bird of stealth, often going undetected to humans and to the prey in its wetland habitat. Its coloration is mottled warm-brown on its back, with wide rufous striping on its neck and front. It is short-legged, with its longish neck usually hunched, including in flight. When alarmed, it stands with its long, sharp bill pointed to the sky, blending in with the marsh grasses. Encountering this bird is more often by flushing it or by hearing the strange springtime call of the male, a gulping, pumping *oong-ka-chunk*. It is a stealthy predator, moving imperceptibly until swiftly stabbing at its prey of insects, frogs, fish, or even voles.

This species is a year-round resident along the coast to the east of Loudoun, but most breed in Canada and the northern half of the U.S., wintering on the southern U.S. Atlantic, Gulf, and Pacific Coasts and in Mexico. There were 7 scattered atlas sightings in April and early May, with 1 in mid-June (Lincoln 2). Its numbers are steady or declining slightly in some areas.

Written by Mary Ann Good

GREAT BLUE HERON
Ardea herodias

Occurrence: common breeder, year-round resident

Earliest breeding confirmation: March 6, parent entering/exiting nest site or on nest (ON)

Latest breeding confirmation: June 19, adult carrying nesting material or nest building (NB)

Great Blue Herons are icons of the bird world due to their size and stately presence and their tendency to show up at almost any river, pond, lake, creek, or marsh. They are patient hunters who often stand vigil at a river's edge or walk along a shoreline in search of prey. While their diet consists primarily of fish and frogs, they take crayfish, snakes, small mammals, and even an occasional bird. Their size

Photo by Gerco Hoogeweg

and overall pale blue coloration make them unmistakable for any other bird in Loudoun, whether perched near water or flying overhead nearly anywhere, with slow, elegant wingbeats, legs outstretched and neck pulled in.

In Loudoun, Great Blue Herons nest in single-species colonies that are usually far from human dwellings and are generally hard to find. Loosely constructed stick nests are built in trees which, if reused, become more substantial over time. Because nest-building Great Blue Herons may carry sticks for long distances and even the young disperse long distances to feed, the breeding codes for this species are limited to confirmations and were only used when one was actually able to see nests. No ground-nesting Great Blue Herons were found in Loudoun.

The largest known colony in Loudoun, almost 70 nests, is along Broad Run in Sterling 3 in an area experiencing tremendous growth. Numerous studies have shown that human disturbance, from land development to recreation, can affect the success of Great Blue Heron rookeries (Quinn and Milner 1999, Vermont Fish and Wildlife Department 2002). While there is a lot of continuing development near the colony, this rookery was probably begun when there were few people visiting the area. Loudoun County has put a number of protections in place to keep people away from the colony during nesting season which will, hopefully, result in the birds continuing to nest there.

According to the North American BBS, Great Blue Herons increased in the U.S. between 1966 and 2014. While there was no evidence of breeding in Loudoun in Atlas 1, Great Blue Herons were found in Atlas 2 in 67 blocks and confirmed in 6 of those. It is likely that there were more nests that were not found because of the bird's secretive nature. As long as buffer zones are established around rookeries and water quality is kept clean and is rich with prey, Great Blue Herons should remain common in the county.

Written by Joe Coleman

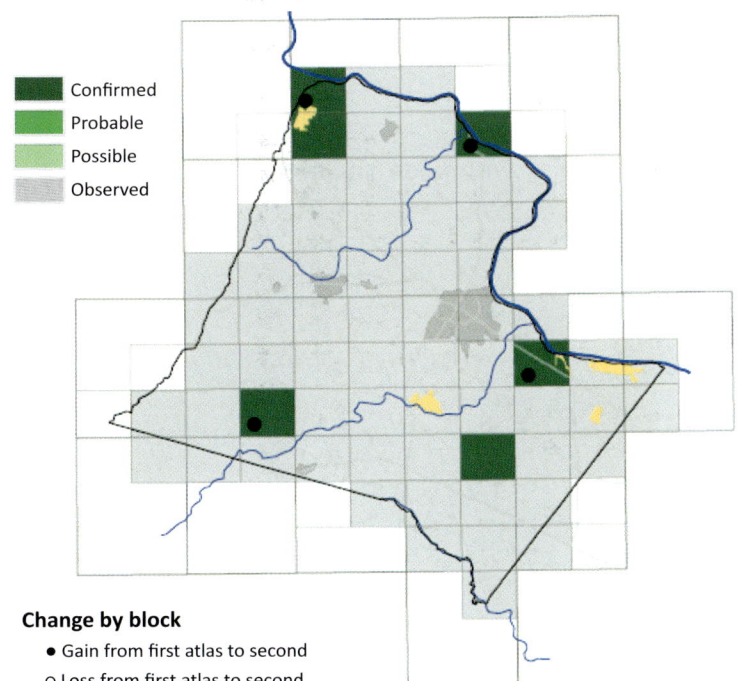

Confirmed
Probable
Possible
Observed

Change by block
• Gain from first atlas to second
○ Loss from first atlas to second

GREAT EGRET
Ardea alba

Occurrence: uncommon migrant and summer resident

Earliest spring sighting: March 13

Latest fall sighting: October 23

Photo by Gerco Hoogeweg

Great Egrets are large white wading birds, second in size only to Great Blue Herons in our area. They are beautiful birds, especially in flight, with their long neck drawn in and long black legs outstretched. Their yellow bill is also distinctive. Documented in 34 atlas blocks, mainly in more coastal eastern Loudoun, Great Egrets can be found in secluded marshes, swamps, shallow ponds, and shorelines of creeks and rivers. While no sign of breeding was found during the atlas, they do breed in the coastal plain and have been documented nesting on an island in neighboring Washington County, Maryland.

The significant decline in Great Egrets and other wading birds in the late 19th and early 20th century due to hunting for plumes for the ladies' hat trade was one of the sparks behind the creation of the conservation movement and led to some of the first laws protecting birds. Great Egret populations rapidly recovered and are considered stable and even increasing in some areas.

Written by Joe Coleman

Confirmed
Probable
Possible
Observed

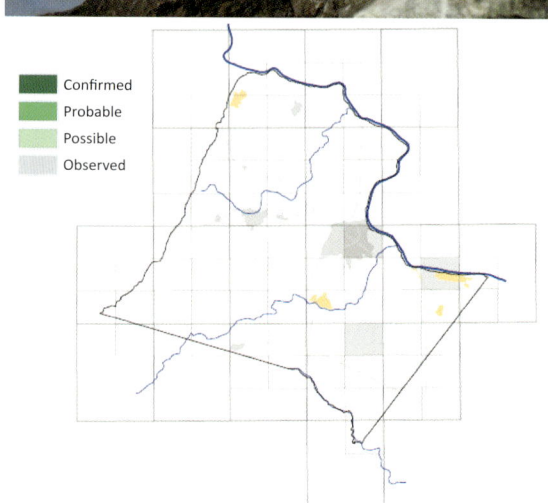

Photo by Deb Calhoun

Confirmed
Probable
Possible
Observed

SNOWY EGRET
Egretta thula

Occurrence: rare migrant and post-breeding visitor

Southerly/northerly migration periods: fewer than 5 atlas sightings, see account for details

Found year-round in saltmarshes and mudflats along the coast, Snowy Egrets can also be found inland amid wetlands and the edges of lakes and rivers. Wanderers or migratory individuals on their way to Central American wintering grounds may rarely be seen in Loudoun. Three individuals were reported in 3 eastern atlas blocks in May and late August. These highly social birds round up fish, frogs, and invertebrates in a variety of ways, including using their feet to stir up the water or probe in the mud.

This snow-white heron has a black daggerlike bill, black legs, and yellow feet, which appear greenish-yellow during the non-breeding season. It can be distinguished from the Great Egret by its smaller, more delicate size and opposing-colored legs and feet. Breeding adults develop long showy feathers on their back, neck, and head. These plumes were valued more than gold in the late 1800s and plume-hunting nearly wiped out the species. With protection from early conservationists in the early 20th century, populations rebounded and expanded. Habitat loss is now their biggest threat.

Written by Spring Ligi

LITTLE BLUE HERON
Egretta caerulea

Occurrence: rare migrant and summer visitor

Earliest spring sighting: May 4

Latest fall sighting: September 2

Photo ©Dick Rowe

The Little Blue Heron is the only heron species with two distinct age-related color morphs: the adult has a purple-maroon head and neck and slate-blue body, while the juvenile is all-white. Juveniles can be distinguished from the similar-sized Snowy Egret by their pale, bluish bill and greenish legs and their slow, deliberate movements. They are resident throughout most of their coastal breeding range, but some northern breeders migrate to the southeastern U.S. or Central America. After nesting, adults and young disperse widely from the colony, seeking out thickly vegetated, shallow water bodies. There were 6 atlas sightings in places such as Claude Moore Park and the Dulles Greenway Wetlands, including 1 aberrant December juvenile on a Bluemont pond.

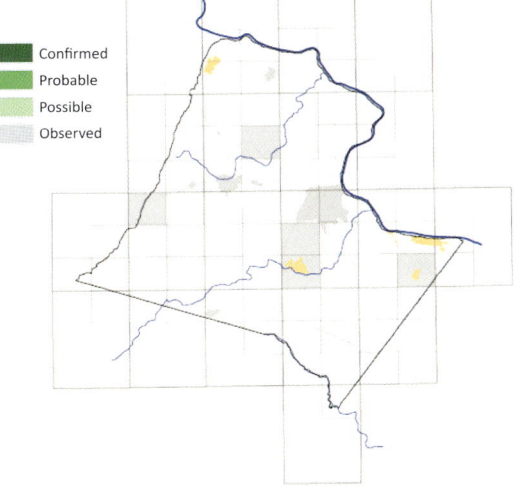

The dark adult plumage and lack of long plumes helped this species avoid the plume-hunting craze of the late 19th century. However, populations have declined in past decades due to habitat loss. This species is on the 2016 State of North America's Birds' Watch List.

Written by Spring Ligi

Photo by Laura McGranaghan

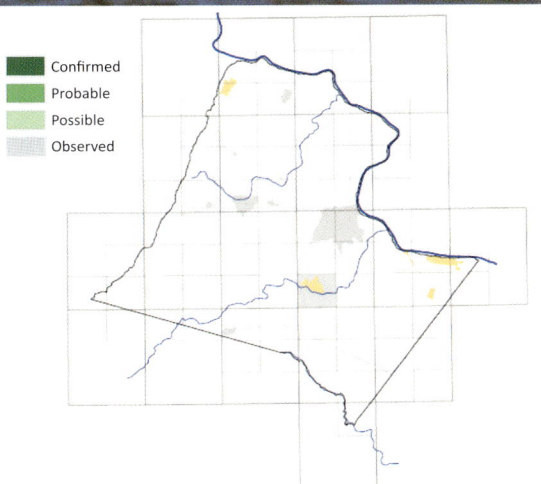

TRICOLORED HERON
Egretta tricolor

Occurrence: rare post-breeding visitor

Earliest/latest seasonal sightings: fewer than 5 atlas sightings, see account for details

One of the biggest surprises of Atlas 2 was a well-documented juvenile Tricolored Heron that spent at least 7 days at the Dulles Greenway Wetlands in September 2013, likely the first record for Loudoun. This heron is typically found in sheltered estuaries, bays, marshes, and lakes in the southeastern U.S. coastal plain, but has been known to wander north in rare instances. Formerly known as the Louisiana Heron, this solitary forager adapts its hunting approach to the situation, sometimes actively running after schools of fish, but other times waiting quietly for fish to approach before stabbing them with its sharp bill. It often breeds in large colonies with other heron and egret species.

This slender, medium-sized heron is the only dark heron (a mix of blue-gray and purple) with a sharply contrasting white belly and underwing coverts seen in flight. The white stripe down the neck is also distinctive. Juveniles have a reddish neck. According to the North American BBS, Tricolored Heron populations have declined slightly over the past 5 decades.

Written by Spring Ligi

CATTLE EGRET
Bubulcus ibis

Occurrence: vagrant

Earliest/latest seasonal sightings: fewer than 5 atlas sightings, see account for details

Unlike other white herons, this species is often found in dry pastures and fields stalking large insects flushed by grazing cattle or tractors. Cattle Egret populations expanded worldwide out of Africa in the 1800s, reaching North America by the 1950s. They are now established breeders in parts of the southern and eastern U.S. This social heron flocks year-round, forming non-breeding roosts and dense breeding colonies with native heron species. Known to wander widely, vagrants have occurred in every U.S. state besides Alaska, and as far north as Newfoundland. One Cattle Egret was observed in Loudoun in June 2012 at Dulles International Airport.

The Cattle Egret's compact build and small size are helpful in identification. This thick-necked heron has relatively short legs and a short, daggerlike yellow bill (dark in juveniles). The legs are yellow in breeding adults, but otherwise dark. The Cattle Egret's expansion into North America has slowed or stopped, likely due to loss of suitable agricultural lands and exposure to pesticides and herbicides, with population declines noted by the North American BBS.

Written by Spring Ligi

Photo by Gerco Hoogeweg

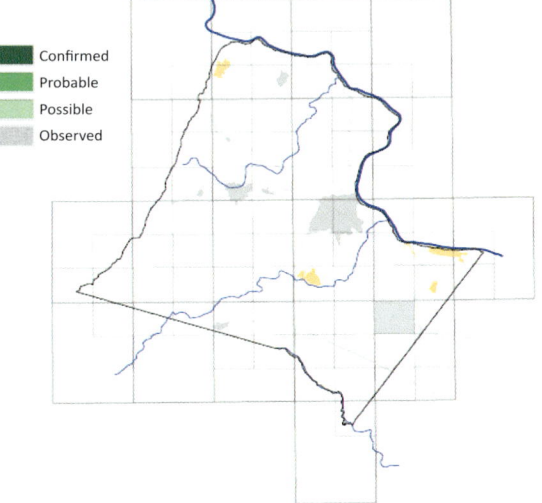

Confirmed
Probable
Possible
Observed

Photo by Gerco Hoogeweg

GREEN HERON
Butorides virescens

Occurrence: common breeder, uncommon migrant

Earliest breeding confirmation: June 5, nest with eggs (NE)

Latest breeding confirmation: August 20, recently fledged young (FL)

The Green Heron is a small, reclusive wading bird most often seen along the edges of ponds, slow-moving streams, and wetlands. The Green Heron takes its name from the dark green, lustrous feathers on its back, which contrast with its chestnut breast and neck, gray wings, and yellow legs (orange in breeding males). As the bird can appear dark from a distance, its small stature and stocky shape are often the best diagnostics. When the Green Heron is alarmed, it may raise its head crest and give its best known vocalization: a loud and emphatic *skyow.* The alarm call may be preceded by another characteristic vocalization, a low clucking or knocking call.

Green Herons adapt to a variety of wetland habitats but favor heavily vegetated water edges where they forage in the shallow water. Green Herons hunt both day and night, seeking small fish, insects, crustaceans, and amphibians. Foraging birds often crouch as they move along the shore, using their long, sharp bill to catch or spear prey. Green Herons have partially webbed feet, which enable them to swim and dive in search of fish in deeper water. They also

GREEN HERON (continued)

employ worms, twigs, and insects to lure fish closer to shore, a practice that makes the Green Heron one of the very few bird species that has mastered the use of tools.

Green Herons can be semi-colonial when nesting, although they tend to be solitary nesters in our area. Once Green Herons arrive in Loudoun in early April, the male selects a nest site, typically in a shrub or tree near water, and begins collecting nest materials, which the female then fashions into a stick nest. Both parents incubate the eggs and feed the chicks by regurgitation. Green Herons typically raise one to two broods per year. Once the breeding season has ended, Green Herons depart Loudoun by the end of September to overwinter in coastal swamps of the southern U.S., in Central America, and in upper regions of South America.

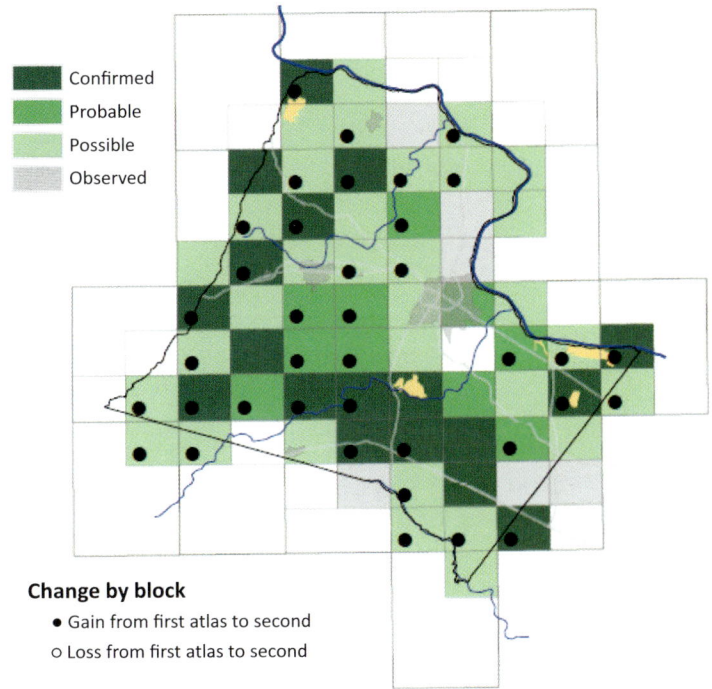

Change by block
● Gain from first atlas to second
○ Loss from first atlas to second

Breeding evidence was found in 60 blocks, with 18 confirmations. There was no data on this species from Atlas 1, which explains the significant gain in blocks. The Green Heron population is generally considered stable, although the North American BBS records a cumulative decline of 68% from 1966-2014. Habitat destruction appears to be the primary threat to this species.

Written by Christine Perdue

Photo by Gerco Hoogeweg

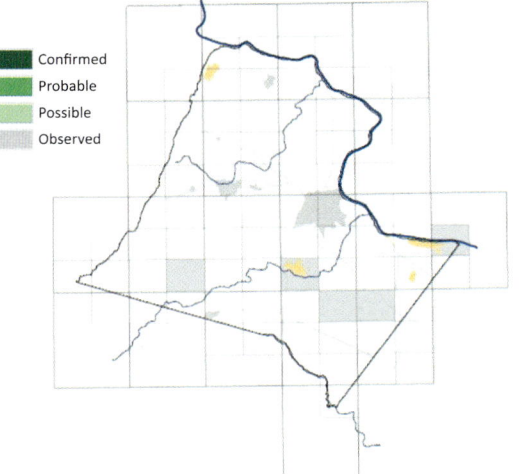

BLACK-CROWNED NIGHT-HERON
Nycticorax nycticorax

Occurrence: occasional migrant and summer visitor, rare winter visitor

Earliest spring sighting: March 31

Latest fall sighting: September 8

The most widespread heron in the world, the Black-crowned Night-Heron breeds mainly along the coastal U.S.; it was observed only 13 times in 5 atlas blocks. Two of the sightings occurred in mid-June, near the Potomac River, which hinted at the possibility of breeding or nearby post-breeding dispersal. Breeding was later confirmed post-atlas (July 2016) in Waterford 5. This species was reported on 2 of the past 20 Central Loudoun CBCs. It is a reclusive bird that conceals itself in daytime roosts among shady trees. Active mainly at night, it favors proximity to water (wetlands, marsh, streams, ponds) where, with a distinctive crouch, it stalks its fish and aquatic prey.

Black-crowned and backed, this medium-sized, stocky heron is large-headed and rarely extends its neck. It has short yellow legs, a heavy black bill, and red eyes. Pale gray upper wings, rump, and tail complement the white face, forehead, and neck. Two or three white plumes decorate its crown. Populations have decreased slightly over the past 5 decades, according to the North American BBS.

Written by Chris White

YELLOW-CROWNED NIGHT HERON
Nyctanassa violacea

Occurrence: rare migrant

Southerly/northerly migration periods: fewer than 5 atlas sightings, see account for details

Reported only once during the atlas at Bles Park (September 2011), the Yellow-crowned Night-Heron can be found inland along wooded streams and wetlands, but is more concentrated along the coastline where it breeds and forages at night or during the day for crabs and crayfish. Like the Black-crowned Night-Heron, it nests and roosts in colonies, but can also be a lone nester.

The Yellow-crowned Night-Heron has a black head with stark white cheek patches under the eyes and a yellow crown, with long yellow plumes adding a touch of elegance. Its body is mainly blue-gray with black feathering on the back and upper wings. It stands upright more than the Black-crowned does and has a longer neck and legs. The dark bill is thicker, but it has yellow legs and red eyes like the Black-crowned. The North American BBS indicates that Yellow-crowned Night-Heron populations are stable, though nesting birds can be difficult to detect during large surveys. Peculiarities of its diet are thought to be protection against toxic pesticides and chemicals.

Written by Chris White

Photo by Bill Brown

Confirmed
Probable
Possible
Observed

Photo by Bill Brown

Confirmed
Probable
Possible
Observed

WHITE IBIS
Eudocimus albus

Occurrence: rare post-breeding visitor

Earliest summer sighting: July 14

Latest summer sighting: August 8

This common bird of southeastern wetlands and estuaries is unmistakable as an adult, with its pure white plumage, black wingtips, and bright red-orange bill and legs. Occasionally a few individuals will wander north into our area in late summer, particularly the juveniles, which share the long, down-curved bill but have brown backs, the white fronts curving into a crescent over their shoulders. They fly with long necks and legs outstretched. Of the 7 atlas sightings, all but 1 were at the Dulles Greenway Wetlands, where they walk slowly and probe in shallow water for crustaceans and aquatic insects.

In their southeastern breeding grounds, they are social birds, nesting in large colonies in trees along the water's edge, changing locations nearly every year. White Ibis populations grew 4% per year from 1966 to 2015, according to the North American BBS.

Written by Mary Ann Good

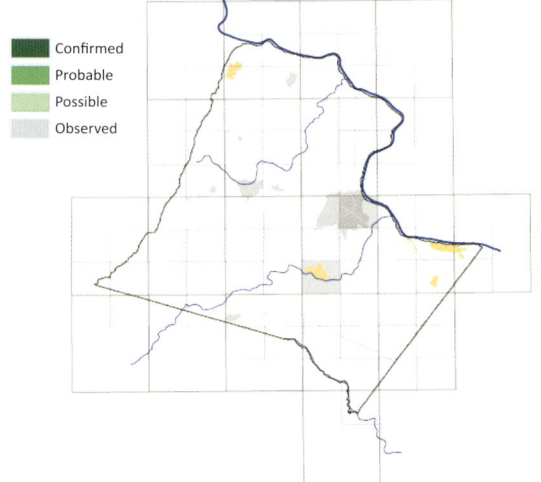

GLOSSY IBIS
Plegadis falcinellus

Occurrence: rare migrant

Southerly/northerly migration periods: fewer than 5 atlas sightings, see account for details

Photo by Bill Brown

Slightly smaller than the White Ibis, the Glossy Ibis has a similar shape and the long, down-curved bill, which is brownish. Its plumage, however, is overall dark rufous brown, with glossy blue-green wings. It shares many of the same features as the White Ibis, such as flight posture and feeding behavior; it also breeds in colonies near water, but lower in shrubs or small trees or even on the ground.

Glossy Ibises were originally an Old World species that probably invaded North America within the last few centuries and saw rapid range expansion northward on the Atlantic Coast in the second half of the 20th century. While they breed exclusively on the Atlantic Coast, individuals tend to wander widely throughout the East; however, there was only a single sighting during the atlas of a bird flying toward the Potomac River, in Sterling 3 (May 2012). The North American BBS showed the population increasing between 1966 and 2014.

Written by Mary Ann Good

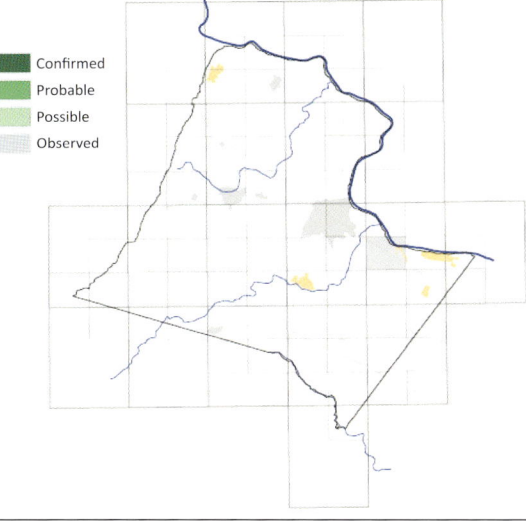

Confirmed
Probable
Possible
Observed

Photo by Dave Boltz

BLACK VULTURE
Coragyps atratus

Occurrence: common breeder, migrant, and year-round resident

Earliest breeding confirmation: April 14, nest with eggs (NE)

Latest breeding confirmation: July 18, parent entering/exiting nest site or on nest (ON)

Black Vultures can be found soaring and roosting among Turkey Vultures and are sometimes confused with Turkey Vultures. They can be differentiated by their heads which are black, not red, although this can be misleading as young Turkey Vultures have dark heads. They are darker than Turkey Vultures and have shorter tails. In flight they have broad wings, a small head, and prominent pale wingtips, versus the Turkey Vulture's pale trailing edges. The average weight of a Black Vulture is slightly greater than a Turkey Vulture, even though it's slightly smaller. Like Turkey Vultures, they do not have a syrinx (vocal organ) and communicate by hissing.

Black Vultures lack the Turkey Vulture's keen sense of smell. They soar above Turkey Vultures to keep an eye on them and follow them to carrion. Black Vultures are scavengers; their diet consists primarily of decomposing carcasses. Their digestive tract neutralizes harmful bacteria and prevents the spread of disease to other forms of wildlife and humans. On the ground groups of Black Vultures will overpower a Turkey Vulture and feed first. Unlike Turkey Vultures, they have been known to kill the newborns of larger mammals and eat from dumpsters.

BLACK VULTURE (continued)

Black Vultures are monogamous, mate for life, are extremely social, and have strong family ties. Each evening the extended family gathers in large, communal roosts. Non-family members are aggressively excluded. A pair stays together throughout the year. Their courtship display includes spiral flights high in the sky and a circle dance involving a male walking around a female with neck extended while hissing. Nesting sites include caves, hollow logs, abandoned buildings, and large tree cavities. Typically two eggs are laid and incubation is by both parents for 37-41 days. Both parents feed the young by regurgitation. Young are capable of flight in about 75 days. Parents may continue to feed them until the next breeding season.

Inhabiting forests and open areas from the eastern and southern U.S. down to South America, Black

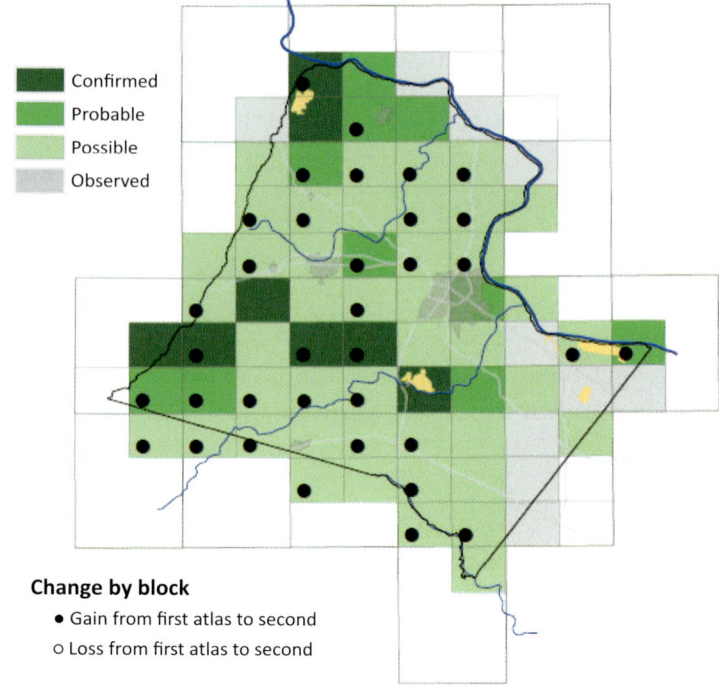

Confirmed
Probable
Possible
Observed

Change by block
- Gain from first atlas to second
- Loss from first atlas to second

Vulture populations have increased over the past 5 decades, expanding their range northward up to New England. This population increase is evident in the gain of over 30 blocks from Atlas 1 to 2. Despite using similar nesting sites, interestingly, the breeding confirmations for Black and Turkey Vultures were on opposite ends of the county (Turkey Vultures mainly to the east and south, Black Vultures to the west and north).

Written by Donna Quinn

Photo ©Dick Rowe

TURKEY VULTURE
Cathartes aura

Occurrence: abundant breeder, migrant, and year-round resident

Earliest breeding confirmations: April 20, raptor courting display (RC)

Latest breeding confirmation: July 25, recently fledged young (FL)

Often unappreciated and misunderstood, Turkey Vultures fulfill a vital role in nature's sanitary engineering department. Their dark, long-winged shapes soar high in the skies over Loudoun and most of North America, waiting to detect the scent of carrion from up to a mile away. Once located, their bald heads allow them to pick at a carcass without soiling themselves. Their digestive tracts can neutralize toxic bacteria and deadly microbes, safely disposing of what could otherwise contaminate the surroundings. Called Peace Eagles by the Cherokee Nation, these beneficial birds do not kill and seek only to remove waste.

Turkey Vultures are large, dark brown birds weighing about 4 pounds, with a wingspan of 67-70 inches. Their name derives from their featherless red head which resembles that of the Wild Turkey. They have a long tail and short, hooked, light-colored beak. From below, the trailing wing feathers are lighter, giving a two-toned appearance. Additionally, they are easily identified from similar species by their wobbly 'V' flight. The Turkey Vulture lacks a syrinx (vocal organ), and their vocalizations include hissing and grunting which are used as a warning, to announce territory, and in mating. When threatened, they vomit putrid stomach acids.

TURKEY VULTURE (continued)

Turkey Vultures are monogamous and mate for life. Pair formation involves ritualized hopping around a circle with wings partly opened. Nesting sites include caves, abandoned buildings, cliff crevices, and hollow trees. Very little nest is made. Typically two eggs are laid and both parents incubate for 34-41 days. Both parents assist in feeding, which is by regurgitation. If the young are threatened, they defend themselves by hissing and projectile vomiting. The age of first flight is about 9-10 weeks. Turkey Vultures will reuse nest sites and have strong family ties; even after young fledge, families stay together. Turkey Vultures are gregarious and roost communally in large groups. Turkey Vultures live approximately 20 years in the wild.

Loudoun's Turkey Vultures are year-round residents. However, in autumn our vultures are joined by Turkey Vultures from the northern U.S. resting on their way to wintering grounds in the southeastern U.S. and Central and South America. They are one of 14 species reported in all 73 atlas blocks. Over the past 5 decades, Turkey Vulture numbers have increased across North America, reflected in a gain of over 35 blocks from Atlas 1 to 2. The significant increase in vehicles and roads (and roadkill) is likely a contributing factor to this species' success here.

Written by Donna Quinn

Legend:
- Confirmed
- Probable
- Possible
- Observed

Change by block
- ● Gain from first atlas to second
- ○ Loss from first atlas to second

Photo by Dave Boltz

OSPREY
Pandion haliaetus

Occurrence: rare breeder, occasional summer resident and migrant

Earliest/latest breeding confirmations: fewer than 5 atlas confirmations, see account for details

On spring and summer walks near larger bodies of water in Loudoun, one may be treated to the thrilling sight of an Osprey patrolling, hovering, and plunge-diving feet first after prey below the water's surface. These magnificent raptors are a conservation success story. After near-extinction from the effects of DDT, they have rebounded after its ban in 1972, and today we once again share our waterways with these sociable fish-hawks.

The Osprey is the only bird in its family and unmistakable in appearance. It has a white crested head with yellow eyes and a dark eyeline. It is brown above; from below, the wings are mostly white with outer wing feathers mottled brown and black. In flight Osprey look slender; a kink in the wings gives their outline a distinctive 'M' shape. Females are approximately 25% larger than males. Osprey vocalizations are high-pitched whistles and chirps.

The Osprey diet consists entirely of live fish. Osprey can detect prey from 30-130 feet in the air. When prey is spotted Osprey hover momentarily then dive feet first into the water. A reversible outer toe allows them to grasp fish with two toes in front and two in back; barbed pads help secure a slippery fish while carrying it back to a favorite perch or nest

OSPREY (continued)

for eating. Bald Eagles will sometimes attempt to steal fish from Osprey.

Osprey become sexually mature at 3-4 years and typically mate for life. A pair forms through aerial flights and courtship feeding. The nest is built in open surroundings near water on top of a large tree, utility pole, or other structure including platforms built for them. Nests are made of sticks and lined with various materials, including litter. One to four eggs are laid. The male provides fish and the female stays with the young, protecting them from sun and bad weather.

Reported in 40 atlas blocks, most Osprey observed in Loudoun are migrants passing through, with sightings beginning in early March and ending by early November. However, nest building was confirmed in Seneca 3 in April 2012 on an island in

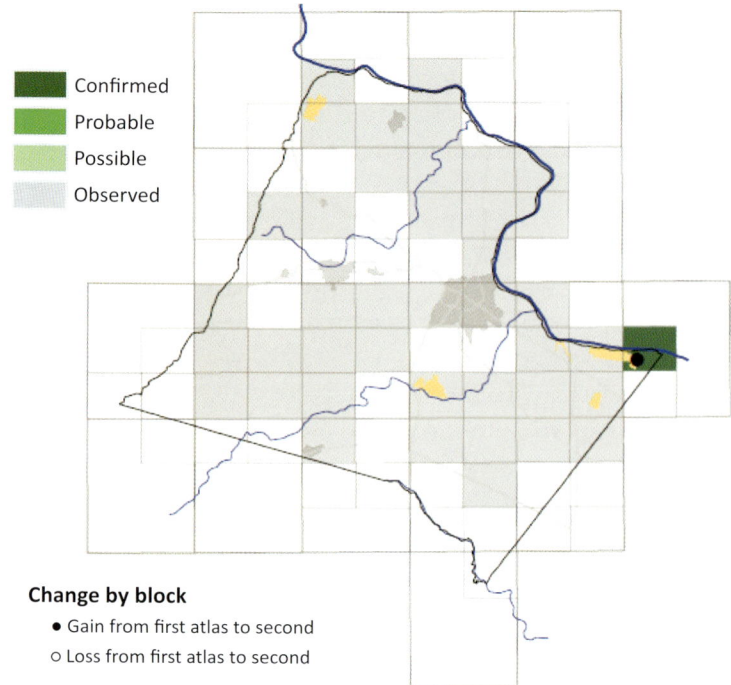

Confirmed
Probable
Possible
Observed

Change by block
● Gain from first atlas to second
○ Loss from first atlas to second

the Potomac River. Post-atlas, there was documentation of a failed breeding attempt in April 2014; breeding was later confirmed in June 2018. Both post-atlas nests were located in the Sterling area. One lone winter sighting was reported in January 2012 in Round Hill 4. Osprey typically overwinter in South and Central America and breed throughout Canada as well as the coastlines and northern parts of the U.S.

Written by Donna Quinn

Photo ©Dick Rowe

Confirmed
Probable
Possible
Observed

SWALLOW-TAILED KITE
Elanoides forficatus

Occurrence: vagrant

Earliest/latest seasonal sightings: fewer than 5 atlas sightings, see account for details

Only a handful of kites call North America home, and most of them have a very southern range. The Mississippi Kite is the only kite that regularly frequents Virginia. As such, the Swallow-tailed Kite is not expected to be seen in Loudoun, but scattered individuals are rarely found far north of their typical range. There was 1 atlas sighting at a farm in Lincoln 4 (August 2011), along with 2 post-atlas sightings in South Riding (August 2017) and Purcellville (August 2018). The U.S. population breeds in swamps, marshes, and forests along the Gulf Coast and up the East Coast through South Carolina, wintering in South America. As development converts these breeding habitats into more urban environments, the kite population has decreased. Kites have long, pointed wings and hover ("kiting") as a common flying and hunting method. This highly efficient flight allows them to hunt on the wing for insects and herpetofauna. The Swallow-tailed Kite is a small kite with a distinctive black and white pattern. It is easy to distinguish from the larger, less patterned Mississippi Kite, particularly by its deeply forked tail shape.

Written by Bryan Henson

GOLDEN EAGLE
Aquila chrysaetos

Occurrence: rare migrant and winter visitor

Earliest fall sighting: September 19

Latest winter sighting: December 28

The Golden Eagle is a raptor of impressive size, with a wingspan of 6-8 feet, legs feathered to the toes, a small head, and dark brown plumage with golden feathers on the back of its head and neck. Juvenile Golden Eagles have white patches at the base of the tail and under the wings. The female is larger than the male, and pairs are monogamous, often bonding for life. Golden Eagles primarily hunt small mammals such as rabbits and squirrels, but they will also feed on deer carrion in winter.

During Atlas 2, Golden Eagles were observed in 6 blocks in western Loudoun, with three quarters of the sightings at Snickers Gap Hawkwatch in Bluemont 1 during fall migration. They were reported on only 1 of the past 20 Central Loudoun CBCs (2011). The Golden Eagles in Virginia are part of an Eastern population, numbering roughly 5,000 birds, that breed in northeastern Canada, migrate down the central Appalachians, and winter along heavily forested slopes of the Appalachian chain. This population is thought to be stable.

Written by Christine Perdue

Photo by Liam McGranaghan (first year bird)

Confirmed
Probable
Possible
Observed

Photo by Liam McGranaghan (juvenile)

Confirmed
Probable
Possible
Observed

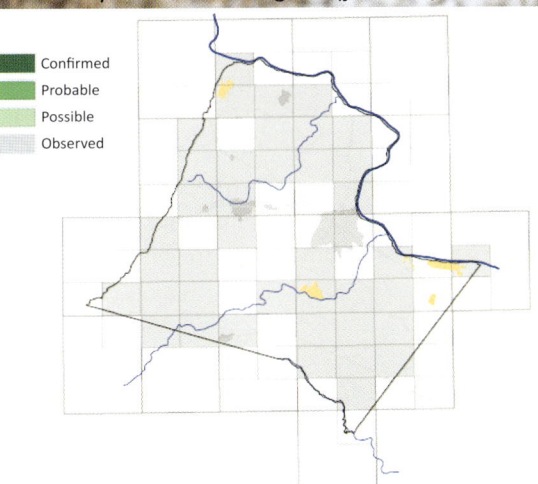

NORTHERN HARRIER
Circus hudsonius

Occurrence: occasional migrant and winter resident, rare summer visitor

Earliest summer/fall sighting: August 19

Latest spring sighting: April 27

A large hawk gliding low over open fields, the Northern Harrier is a keen hunter of small mammals and songbirds. Along with the white rump and long tail, a facial disk that is owl-like helps distinguish them from other hawks. Males are commonly called "Gray Ghosts" because of their smooth gray coloration; the female is largely brown. Their winter range is mostly the U.S. and Mexico; their summer breeding range includes the northern U.S. and Canada. Northern Harriers were found in more than half the atlas blocks. Two observations in late May and early July, along with a late June post-atlas observation, suggest the possibility of local breeding in the Waterford and Round Hill areas. In Loudoun, their favored habitat of open fields and marshes is disappearing largely due to development. Habitat loss has contributed to an overall population decline throughout their range over the past 50 years. When observing a harrier coursing over a field around dusk, stick around to watch for Short-eared Owls, which sometimes roost and hunt with harriers if present in the area.

Written by Bryan Henson

SHARP-SHINNED HAWK
Accipiter striatus

Occurrence: rare breeder, occasional year-round resident

Earliest/latest breeding confirmations: highest breeding evidence in Possible category, see account for details

The Sharp-shinned Hawk, the smallest hawk in North America, presents a challenge for breeding surveys. This jay-sized hawk prefers building its nest deep in forests near the top of conifers, and moves quickly through the trees. Despite finding Sharp-shinned Hawks in more than half the Atlas 2 blocks, the highest breeding evidence was in the Possible category, reported in 8 blocks by observing birds

Photo by Dave Boltz

during safe dates. No evidence of breeding was reported in Atlas 1. This species has been reported on every Central Loudoun CBC, with numbers ranging from 4 to 15 individuals.

Two species of accipiter are typically found in Loudoun, Sharp-shinned and Cooper's Hawks. These species are relatively easy to identify based upon size and the accipiter long tail; however, distinguishing between the two can be challenging. To distinguish a Sharp-shinned from a Cooper's Hawk, look at the head for a dark hood instead of a dark cap and a rounded shape instead of a flat shape. The tail also provides a handy distinguishing trait: The Sharp-shinned Hawk's tail is squared off, compared to the graduated tail feathers of the Cooper's Hawk. When flying, Sharp-shinned Hawks often tuck their head back into their wings while Cooper's heads extend in front of the wings.

Sharp-shinned Hawks' diet consists mostly of small songbirds up to the size of an American Robin. They are sometimes found hunting for birds at neighborhood feeders, typically in the winter. As with most hawks, the males are smaller than the females. Female Sharp-shinned Hawks overlap in size with the very similar male Cooper's Hawks. Perhaps not surprisingly, male Sharp-shinned Hawks will hunt smaller birds than females. Males decapitate the prey before bringing it to the female at the nest. The female incubates and feeds the four to five nestlings until they are ready to leave the nest and take flight. Nests are up to 2 feet in diameter and composed mostly of twigs.

Because of their evasive nature, Sharp-shinned Hawk populations are best estimated during migration. Numbers declined in the mid-20th century, likely due to use of the pesticide DDT, but have rebounded since its banning. Migratory counts, such as at the Snickers Gap Hawkwatch, indicate that the current population seems stable.

Written by Bryan Henson

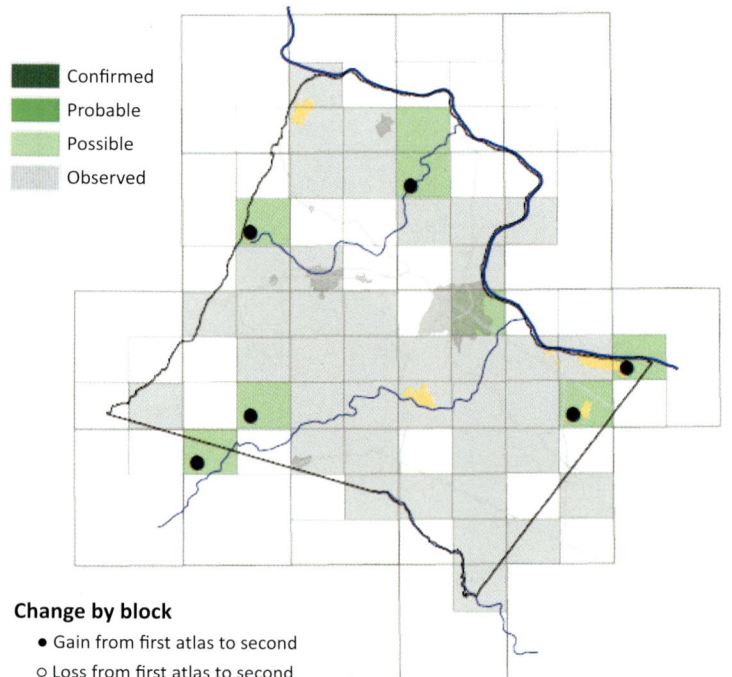

Confirmed
Probable
Possible
Observed

Change by block
- Gain from first atlas to second
○ Loss from first atlas to second

COOPER'S HAWK
Accipiter cooperii

Occurrence: uncommon breeder and year-round resident

Earliest breeding confirmation: March 13, adult carrying nesting material or nest building (NB)

Latest breeding confirmation: July 18, parent carrying food or feeding young (CF)

Photo by Gerco Hoogeweg

Cooper's Hawks seem to have adapted pretty well to human development; they are frequently seen hunting for small birds at backyard feeders despite their general preference for forest habitat. Like other accipiters, their smaller size and short wings allow them to navigate through shrubs and trees better than many of the larger hawks. Cooper's Hawks were reported in almost all Atlas 2 blocks, and breeding was confirmed in 7 blocks spread fairly evenly throughout the county. These results show a gain of 27 blocks from Atlas 1 and probably indicate a growing population in Loudoun. This species has been reported on every Central Loudoun CBC, with numbers ranging from 2 to 24 individuals. The population is considered stable across the continent according to the North American BBS.

Because of its mostly gray coloring and hawk shape, the crow-sized Cooper's Hawk can't be mistaken for many other birds except the very similar but smaller Sharp-shinned Hawk. The Cooper's Hawk has a dark cap instead of the "Sharpie's" dark hood, a flatter head, and a rounded rather than square appearance to the tail. In flight, the Cooper's Hawk is often characterized as a flying cross as opposed to the Sharp-shinned Hawk's flying 'T'. Males are notably smaller than females, leading to them being confused with the Sharpie's larger female; otherwise, the male and female are identical. Juveniles are browner overall and have thin streaks on the breast.

Cooper's Hawks are year-round residents in most of the U.S.

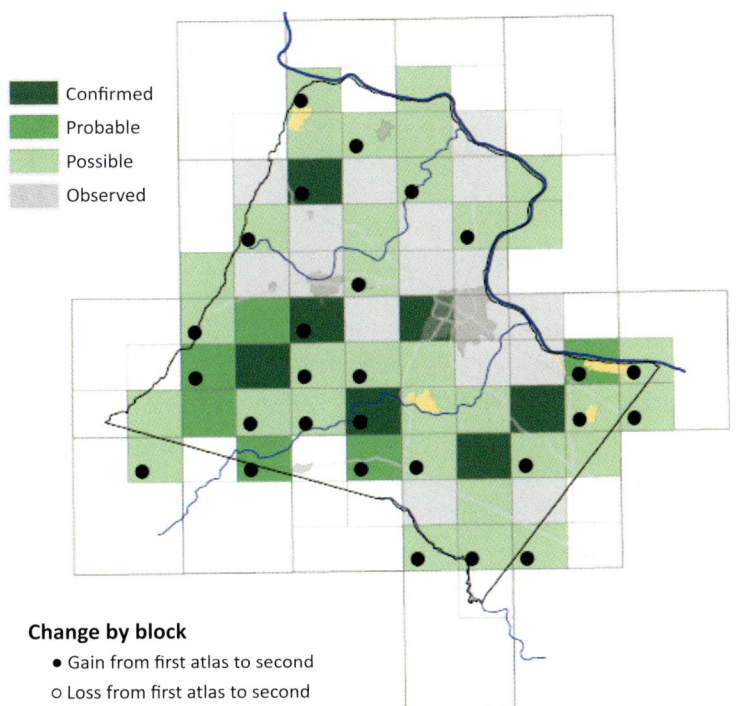

Confirmed
Probable
Possible
Observed

Change by block
● Gain from first atlas to second
○ Loss from first atlas to second

In the summer, they expand their range into the northern U.S. and southern Canada. In the winter, they expand their southern range into Mexico and Central America. They choose nest sites in a variety of tall trees, including pines and oaks, in dense woods, but are increasingly known to nest in quiet suburbs with trees. Males typically build the nest and provide food for the female and three to five young. Their prey consists mostly of small to medium-sized birds, particularly European Starlings, Mourning Doves, and American Robins. They typically kill their prey using their large (for their size) feet.

Written by Bryan Henson

NORTHERN GOSHAWK
Accipiter gentilis

Occurrence: rare fall migrant

Southerly migration period: September 30 – November 23

Northerly migration period: no atlas sightings, see account for details

Snickers Gap Hawkwatch (Bluemont 1), with more than 25 years of valuable hawk migration data along the Blue Ridge Mountains on the western edge of Loudoun, is the only place in the county where Northern Goshawks were seen during the atlas, with 7 recorded during fall migration. They generally live year-round in the northern parts of North America with some year-round presence in the western U.S. Their fall migration route takes them on rare occasions into our region. A very large accipiter, the Northern Goshawk can be identified by its shape, long tail, and the gray coloration and bold white eyebrow against a black face and cap of the adult. Its diet consists of a wider range of prey than other accipiters, including mammals and reptiles in addition to birds. It is a skilled hunter, pursuing its prey with quick, agile flight. This species' secretive nature makes population trends hard to estimate, but their preference for large, old-growth forests will probably lead to their decline in correlation with this endangered habitat.

Written by Bryan Henson

Photo by Tony LePrieur

Confirmed
Probable
Possible
Observed

Photo by Larry Meade

BALD EAGLE
Haliaeetus leucocephalus

Occurrence: uncommon breeder, migrant, and year-round resident

Earliest breeding confirmation: December 6, adult carrying nesting material or nest building (NB)

Latest breeding confirmation: June 15, recently fledged young (FL)

This majestic species serves not only as our national emblem but also as an important example that conservation efforts do work. Adult Bald Eagles are easy to recognize with their white head and tail, dark brown body, yellow bill, and large size. Juveniles have a black bill and are also very large, exhibiting patterns of dark brown and white as they mature. Found in forested and open areas near rivers, lakes, reservoirs, and wetlands, this powerful flier eats mainly fish but also consumes birds, reptiles, amphibians, and small mammals. Bald Eagles often scavenge carrion when available or steal food from other birds.

Bald Eagles are early nesters, with aerial courtship displays and nest building documented as early as December and January in Loudoun. A Bald Eagle's nest is one of the largest of all bird nests, typically 5 to 6 feet in diameter and 2 to 4 feet tall (Buehler 2000). A nest may take up to 3 months to build and may be reused and expanded each breeding season. After fledging at 10-12 weeks, juveniles spend their first 4 years exploring, capable of flying hundreds of miles

BALD EAGLE (continued)

per day, until they reach sexual maturity and return to the general area where they were born.

Since Bald Eagles are known to forage far from the nest site, the breeding codes for this species were limited to confirmations. Seven active nests were confirmed throughout Loudoun, including a well-documented perennial nest at the privately owned Dulles Greenway Wetlands. Evidence of breeding was reported for this nest during every year of the atlas.

In addition to the 7 blocks with confirmed nests, Bald Eagles were observed (no evidence of breeding) throughout the year in an impressive 52 blocks. These results provide a striking contrast to the results from Atlas 1, which did not document any Bald Eagles in Loudoun. Bald Eagles were found on the past 15 Central Loudoun CBCs, with numbers ranging from 5

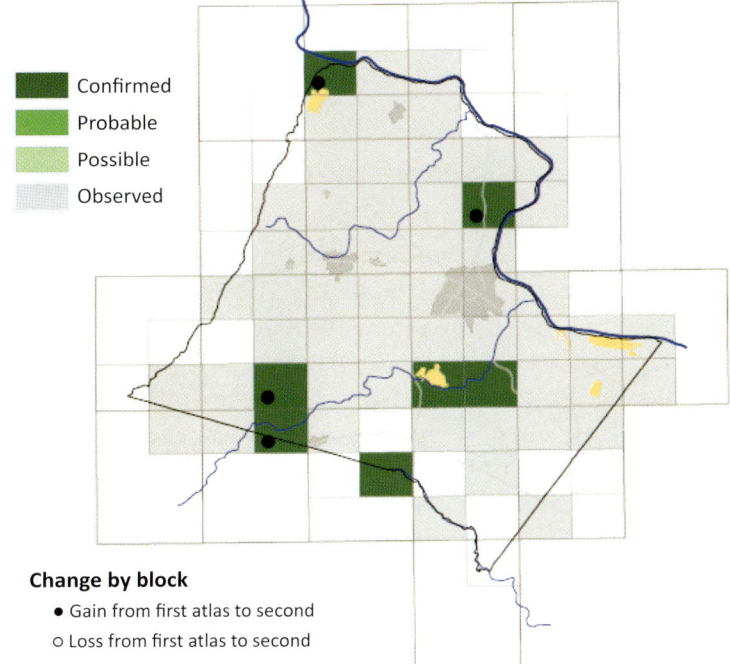

Confirmed
Probable
Possible
Observed

Change by block
● Gain from first atlas to second
○ Loss from first atlas to second

to 38 individuals. The remarkable recovery of this species can be directly attributed to the banning of DDT and placement of this species on the Endangered Species Act in 1978 (USFWS 2015). Populations have rebounded so successfully that the species was removed from the Endangered Species list in 2007. This success story provides a powerful reminder that humans can play a critical role in both the recovery and demise of a species.

Written by Spring Ligi

Photo by Bill Brown

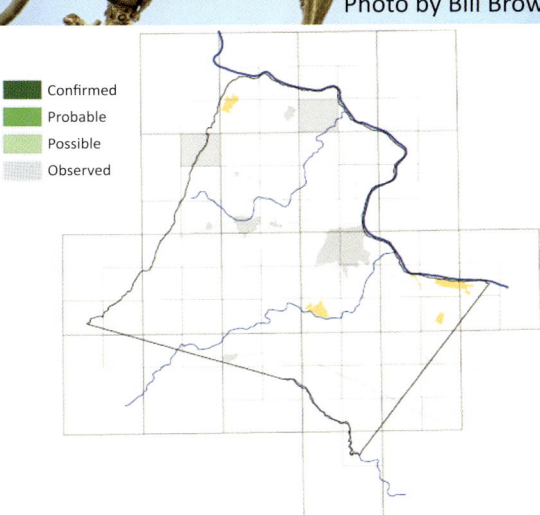

Confirmed
Probable
Possible
Observed

MISSISSIPPI KITE
Ictinia mississippiensis

Occurrence: rare migrant and summer visitor

Earliest/latest seasonal sightings: fewer than 5 atlas sightings, see account for details

Spotting a Mississippi Kite is a rare but increasing possibility in our region. There were just 2 non-breeding Loudoun sightings during the atlas period. But in July 2018 (post-atlas), a nest with young was reported in the Ashburn area. This corresponds with a jump in observations and breeding in neighboring counties to the east and south in recent years, part of an apparent northerly expansion. The species frequents hardwood bottomlands, windbreaks, parks, and even urban areas in the Southeast and Midwest. Nests are built in stands of trees, often in communal groups. They migrate a great distance, wintering in central South America. The Mississippi Kite has long, pointed wings with black wingtips, a long black tail, slender gray body, and white head, presenting a distinctive silhouette and pattern as it soars overhead. An opportunistic feeder, the Mississippi Kite captures and often devours insects, bats, and small birds on the wing, or surprises frogs, snakes, and other small prey on the ground. Populations of this superb aerialist have held steady over the past half-century, perhaps benefitting to a degree from human development and farming practices.

Written by Bruce Hill

Photo by Ian Richardson

RED-SHOULDERED HAWK
Buteo lineatus

Occurrence: common breeder and year-round resident

Earliest breeding confirmation: January 2, raptor courting display (RC)

Latest breeding confirmation: August 4, recently fledged young (FL)

Red-shouldered Hawks are frequently found by their loud *kee-yer kee-yer kee-yer* call. Perhaps in an attempt to warn other birds of the hawk's presence, Blue Jays mimic this call so effectively that it can trick even experienced birders. Red-shouldered Hawks can typically be found in deciduous and mixed woods with tall trees and relatively open understory, often near water. They are sometimes found in wooded suburban neighborhoods and parks. Their diet consists of frogs, toads, snakes, small mammals, and some smaller birds including sparrows and doves.

Both the male and female construct a 2-foot-wide stick nest, often just off the main trunk of a deciduous tree. They'll add branches and leaves to line the nest until the three to four young fledge (approximately 5-7 weeks after hatching). Incubation is mostly by the female, with the male bringing her food to feed the nestlings. Young are fed by the parents for another 8-10 weeks after fledging. The adults return to the same nesting site year after year.

Like other members of the Buteo genus, an identifying characteristic is a relatively short tail, which for the Red-shouldered Hawk is distinctively striped in black and white. Their rufous barred chest makes them easy to pick out at a distance compared to the mostly white chest of a Red-tailed Hawk. Their black and white checkered outer wings also help separate them from other hawks. While flying high overhead, translucent crescents near their wingtips are distinctive.

During Atlas 2, breeding was confirmed throughout Loudoun in more than half of the blocks. This represents a significant gain over Atlas 1, though the higher level of coverage and effort per block in Atlas 2 likely plays a factor. This population increase is supported by data from the North American BBS and Central Loudoun CBC. Between 1997 and 2006 the Central Loudoun CBC averaged 40 Red-shouldered Hawks, compared to an average of 103 individuals between 2007 and 2016. In Loudoun, as in much of the eastern U.S., Red-shouldered Hawks are year-round residents. Their range extends a little farther north to the edge of Canada in the summer and a little farther south to Mexico in the winter.

Written by Bryan Henson

Confirmed
Probable
Possible
Observed

Change by block
- Gain from first atlas to second
- Loss from first atlas to second

Photo by Liam McGranaghan

BROAD-WINGED HAWK
Buteo platypterus

Occurrence: rare breeder, occasional summer resident and migrant

Earliest/latest breeding confirmations: highest breeding evidence in Probable category, see account for details

One of the most amazing sights of North America's fall migration is thousands of Broad-winged Hawks streaming and circling along mountain ridges and coastlines down to Central and northern South America to their wintering grounds. Snickers Gap Hawkwatch, located along the Loudoun and Clarke County border, provides a great opportunity to observe migrating Broad-winged Hawks, with typically 10,000 or more individuals passing through each fall. 2011 was a banner year with a season total of 37,520; 13,952 were recorded in a single day!

Broad-winged Hawks live and nest in forested areas, preferring the edges and near water. Males or females may give a high-pitched 2- to 4-second whistle (*pe-heeeeeeee*) while circling above the forest canopy. Nests are generally located low in a variety of different tree types, often at the first split in the tree. They may reuse nests from previous years or rebuild old crow, squirrel, or hawk nests. The female incubates the one to five eggs and feeds the nestlings food brought by the male. A pair usually raises one brood per season. Pairs may stay together for multiple breeding seasons and keep at least a half-mile distance from other pairs' nests.

Broad-winged Hawks typically nest far from areas of human disturbance, which likely plays a factor in the lack of breeding confirmations. Though no evidence of breeding was documented in Atlas 1, possible breeding was reported in a handful of blocks in western Loudoun in Atlas 2, with 1 probable breeding sighting (territorial behavior) in Bluemont 1. There were observations with no evidence of breeding (likely migrants passing through) in 26 blocks throughout Loudoun. There was 1 rare December sighting in Purcellville 4. The population is considered stable and may even be increasing.

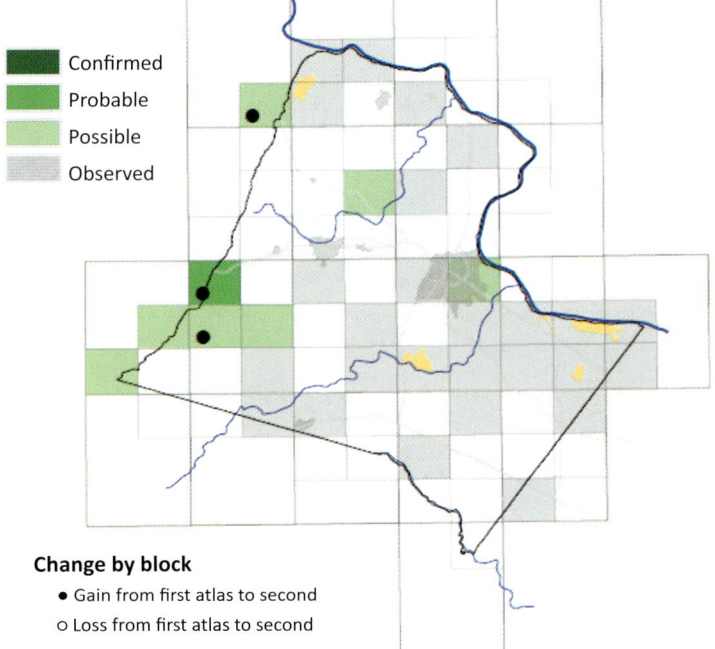

Confirmed
Probable
Possible
Observed

Change by block
● Gain from first atlas to second
○ Loss from first atlas to second

Their diet is highly varied including insects, amphibians, small mammals, and even some small, often young, birds. Generally they are a perch hunter, hanging out on a tree limb waiting for an opportunity to snatch prey from the ground.

The Broad-winged Hawk, as a member of the *Buteo* genus, has the characteristic short tail. They can be distinguished from other Buteos by their small size, broad wings, thick black and white tail bands, and the dark outline around all but the leading edge of the otherwise mostly white under-wings.

Written by Bryan Henson

Photo by Bob Schamerhorn

RED-TAILED HAWK
Buteo jamaicensis

Occurrence: common breeder and year-round resident

Earliest breeding confirmation: February 7, raptor courting display (RC)

Latest breeding confirmation: August 18, recently fledged young (FL)

As hawks that like to hunt in open fields, Red-tailed Hawks are conspicuous and can be spotted regularly in trees and on wires along Loudoun's roadways. Their wild-sounding *keeeeer* cries are both diagnostic and iconic; often, the call is substituted for that of a Bald Eagle or other large raptor in TV shows and movies.

When perched, they are easy to spot with their bold white chest spanned with a wide, variably dark "belly band." From behind, patches of white that form the shape of a 'V' help identify them. Dark patagial (shoulder) bars and the eponymous short, red tail (on the adult; but brown and banded on the juvenile) are commonly used identification characteristics while they soar. They frequently soar over open fields, slowly circling on their broad, rounded Buteo wings.

In Loudoun, as throughout the U.S. and Mexico, they are year-round residents. Their breeding range extends far into Canada and their winter range into parts of Central America. Throughout this large range, they prefer open habitats.

During Atlas 2, there was some level of breeding documented in all but a handful of blocks, and breeding was confirmed in almost half the blocks. These results provide notable gains from the Atlas 1 dataset. This apparent population increase is supported by data from the 1966-2015 North American BBS. Red-tailed Hawks have been reported on every Central Loudoun CBC, with numbers ranging widely from 28 to 141 hawks per count.

Red-tailed Hawks create a large stick nest, built by both members of the pair, near the tops of tall trees. This provides a perch to aggressively watch over their territory and hunt. They prey mostly on small mammals, including squirrels, mice, rats, and rabbits. As one of the largest raptors in North America, they will sometimes eat birds as large as quail and pheasants. During courtship, the male may dive repeatedly in an impressive aerial display, then extend his legs to "tag" the female from above. Sometimes they clasp talons and spiral toward the ground before pulling away. The male may catch prey and pass it to the female in mid-air. Once paired and the nest is built, the female lays one to five eggs. The young fledge almost 2½ months after incubation starts. A pair of Red-tailed Hawks raise one brood per season and typically stay together until death.

Written by Bryan Henson

Confirmed
Probable
Possible
Observed

Change by block
- ● Gain from first atlas to second
- ○ Loss from first atlas to second

ROUGH-LEGGED HAWK
Buteo lagopus

Photo by Liam McGranaghan

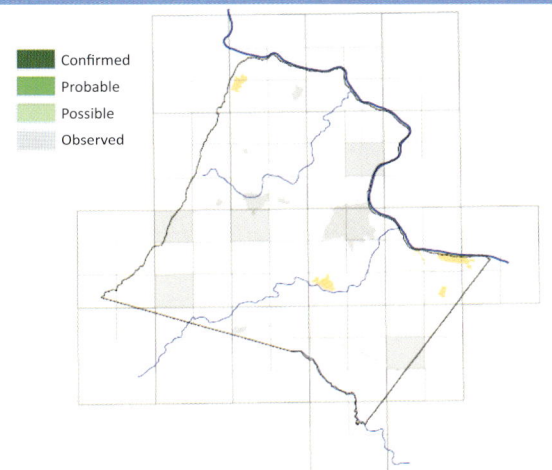

Confirmed
Probable
Possible
Observed

Occurrence: rare migrant and winter visitor

Earliest fall sighting: November 8

Latest winter sighting: February 21

The species name for Rough-legged Hawk, *lagopus*, is the genus name for ptarmigan, one of their major food sources (along with lemmings) on the open tundra of northern North America where they breed. There are dark and light morphs, the latter being somewhat more common in our area. Their distinctive white, brown, and black plumage allows them to blend into that Arctic environment. A pale tail with a dark tip, patches of black near the "wrists," and a black belly make identification straightforward compared to other eastern hawks. The dark morph is just that, mostly dark. Of the 7 atlas observations, 3 were in open fields (where they prey on voles, mice, and shrews) during the winter, including 1 at Dulles International Airport. Another 3 observations were at Snickers Gap Hawkwatch in November, migrating to their winter range, which encompasses most of the U.S. besides the Southeast. Rough-legged Hawks were reported on 5 of the past 20 Central Loudoun CBCs. Little is known about Rough-legged Hawk population trends and therefore their conservation, but overall numbers appear stable.

Written by Bryan Henson

BARN OWL
Tyto alba

Occurrence: occasional breeder and year-round resident

Earliest breeding confirmation: May 15, recently fledged young (FL)

Latest breeding confirmation: June 30, recently fledged young (FL)

The Barn Owl's ghostly appearance, eerie screeching call, and tendency to be discovered in spooky places have made it the subject of much superstition. However, the presence of a Barn Owl is a good omen indeed, especially for farmers, as they are skilled hunters of small rodents. Barn Owls are medium-sized owls, pale in color with a heart-shaped face. They are year-round residents across most of the

Photo by Liam McGranaghan

U.S. and throughout the world. During Atlas 2, Barn Owls were reported 29 times in 16 blocks. Breeding evidence was limited to the more rural western and northern parts of Loudoun. This species was found on 14 of the past 20 Central Loudoun CBCs (typically 1 or 2 individuals per count).

Barn Owls hunt at night flying low over open areas. They have excellent vision in low light and hearing so sensitive they can strike prey in complete darkness. Their diet includes small mammals such as voles, mice, and shrews which they eat whole. About twice a day a pellet is regurgitated containing prey's body parts that cannot be digested.

BARN OWL (continued)

Barn Owls are monogamous and stay together for life. A male attracts a female with display flights, including a "moth" flight in which he hovers in front of her, and once paired, brings her gifts of food. Nesting sites include barn lofts, church steeples, tree cavities, caves, and cliff ledges. The female prepares a simple nest of shredded, regurgitated pellets arranged in a cup. Three to eight eggs are laid, one every other day. The female incubates the eggs, which hatch in the sequence they were laid. In times of food scarcity, older owlets are stronger and dominate; younger hatchlings typically do not survive. Fledging occurs at 55-65 days, but young return to sleep at or near the nest for several more weeks. A pair may raise one to three broods per year, but mortality is high and most young do not survive the first year. In fact, adults rarely live longer than 3-4 years, and thus a pair is likely to breed only once or twice (Connecticut DEEP 1999).

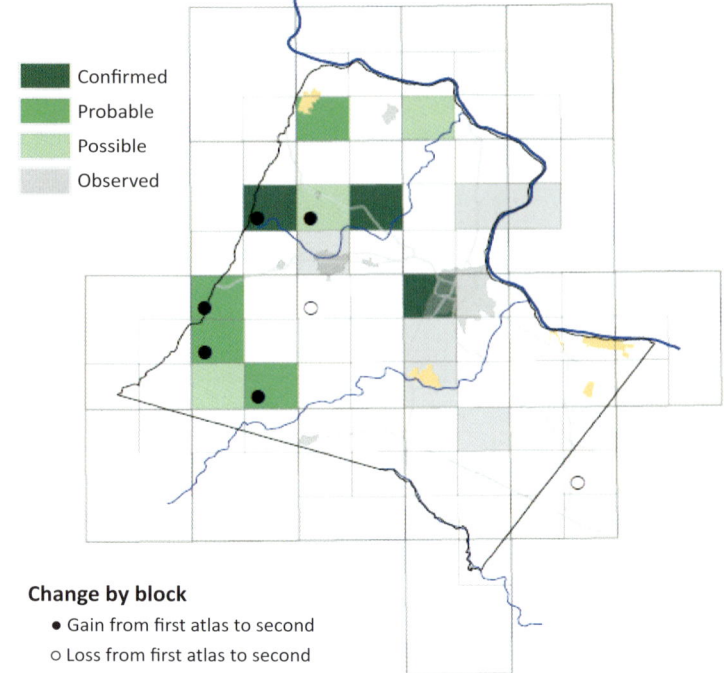

Confirmed
Probable
Possible
Observed

Change by block
● Gain from first atlas to second
○ Loss from first atlas to second

To survive and breed, a pair of Barn Owls need to eat about 5,000 prey items a year, making them a powerful ally in natural pest control. However, in Loudoun as well as elsewhere, Barn Owl numbers are declining due to loss of foraging habitat and suitable nesting sites, and the use of rodent poisons.

Written by Donna Quinn

Photo by Liam McGranaghan (gray phase)

EASTERN SCREECH-OWL
Megascops asio

Occurrence: uncommon breeder and year-round resident

Earliest breeding confirmation: June 11, nest with young (NY)

Latest breeding confirmation: June 26, recently fledged young (FL)

The Eastern Screech-Owl is distinguished by its small size (6-10 inches in length), short ear tufts, and yellow eyes. Two color morphs, rufous and gray, are found in Loudoun. Variations in color are linked to region and climate, with the rufous morphs being more common in the deciduous forests of the southern U.S. In the mid-Atlantic area, rufous morphs may form half of the population.

The plaintive calls of the Eastern Screech-Owl, most often heard at dawn and dusk, include an eerie, descending *whinny*, usually invoked for territorial defense, and a monotone trill. Both sexes sing and may perform duets of the monotone trill. These calls gave the bird its early nickname of "Shivering Owl."

So long as there is sufficient tree cover to provide the cavities needed for nesting and roosting, screech-owls adapt to a broad range of habitats. They may be found in mixed woods, parks, farmlands, and suburban landscapes. They are nocturnal hunters and especially active at dusk and before dawn. Their diet is the most varied of any North American owl, consisting of small birds, mammals, insects, amphibians, reptiles, and invertebrates.

EASTERN SCREECH-OWL (continued)

Eastern Screech-Owls are monogamous and mate for life. They rely on secondary cavities for nesting and may be found in old woodpecker holes, natural tree cavities, and nest boxes. Screech-owls do not build a nest but deposit their eggs at the base of the cavity. Both males and females feed the chicks, which remain dependent on the adults for 2 months after fledging.

Breeding evidence for Eastern Screech-Owls was found in 12 blocks, with confirmation in 2, primarily in northern and western Loudoun. There were no breeding confirmations in Atlas 1. Screech-owls were found on all but 1 of the past 20 Central Loudoun CBCs. Due to the difficulty of surveying nocturnal species such as owls in the bird atlas format, these data may not represent a complete view of the screech-owls' breeding status in Loudoun. The Eastern Screech-Owl's adaptability, tolerance of urban and

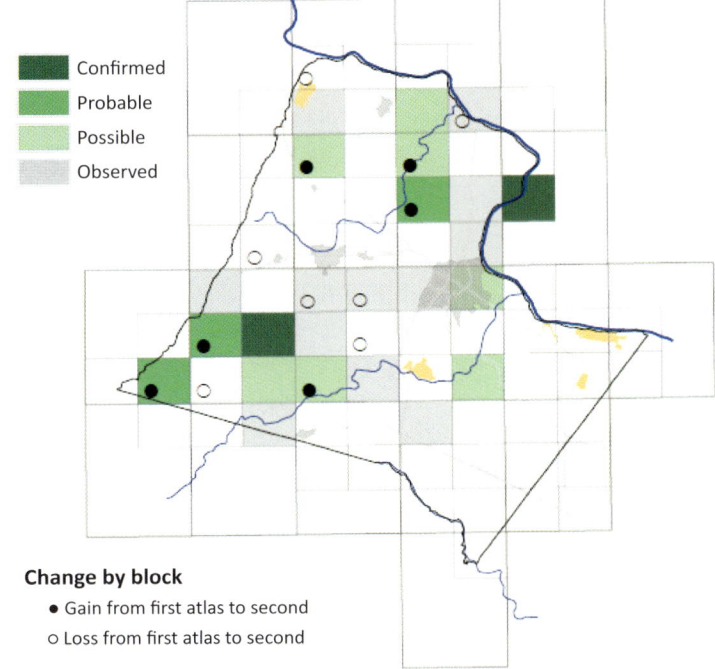

Change by block
- ● Gain from first atlas to second
- ○ Loss from first atlas to second

Legend:
- Confirmed
- Probable
- Possible
- Observed

suburban habitats, and varied diet have contributed to the species' stable population levels. Threats come from the West Nile virus, to which the species is especially susceptible, rodenticides, and vehicle collisions. Screech-owls are also predated by a range of other birds, mammals, and snakes; of these, Barred Owls may pose the greatest threat, as they tend to occupy the same habitats.

Written by Christine Perdue

Photo by Liam McGranaghan

GREAT HORNED OWL
Bubo virginianus

Occurrence: uncommon breeder and year-round resident

Earliest breeding confirmation: April 1, nest with young (NY)

Latest breeding confirmation: May 21, recently fledged young (FL)

The Great Horned Owl was confirmed as breeding in 6 atlas blocks, with breeding evidence documented in an additional 24 blocks throughout Loudoun. This bulky, tufted owl shows possible population gains from Atlas 1. Found on all of the past 20 Central Loudoun CBCs, it averages 5 individuals per count. This average falls between that of Loudoun's other fairly common owls, the Barred Owl (11 per count) and Eastern Screech-Owl (4 per count).

An early breeder, the male's territorial calling – a series of three to eight loud, deep, and rhythmic hoots – mostly heard near dawn and dusk, begins in November. Duetting pairs can be heard before their first eggs are laid. The female's voice is higher, even though she is larger, and is sometimes compared to a mourning dove. Once mated, pairs are monogamous and aggressively defend their territory. The abandoned nests of other species, like the Red-tailed Hawk, are preferred. Nesting owls can most easily be found sitting on their one to four eggs in the bulky nest before spring foliage leafs out. One possible explanation for such early nesting is to give young time to learn hunting skills before the next winter.

GREAT HORNED OWL (continued)

The Great Horned Owl uses a wide variety of wooded habitats, usually with some open land nearby. It is a nocturnal hunter, pursuing its wide range of prey, including mammals up to the size of rabbits, with ferocity. In flight, the wings are broad, long, and pointed. Their ear tufts are usually flattened and their head tucked in, making a powerful and substantial impression. Their large head, with its staring yellow eyes and ear tufts, has been compared to that of a cat. The tawny-orange facial disk is rimmed with black, and the "eyebrow"-like feathering and the fore-neck are white. The belly is cross-barred, and the back is mottled gray.

This long-lived owl is found year-round throughout North America and much of South America. Birds more than 20 years old have been found, some close to 30 (Lutmerding and Love 2015). Their chances of a

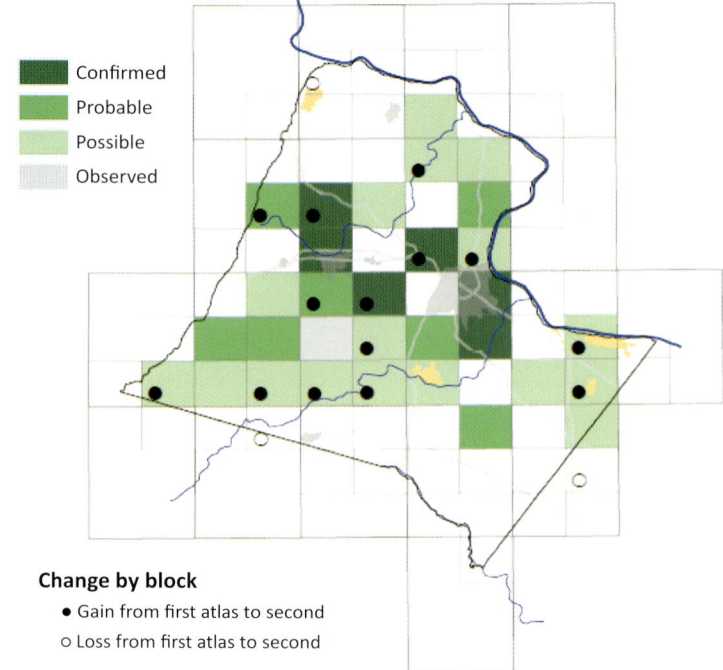

Change by block
- Gain from first atlas to second
- Loss from first atlas to second

long life improve dramatically once the hatch year is past. Half or more of the yearlings don't survive, usually due to starvation. Secondary poisoning from contaminated prey also poses a threat, but the DDT ban has helped this species, along with many others. They were heavily hunted until this was prohibited in the mid-20th century.

Written by Chris White

Photo by Tony LePrieur

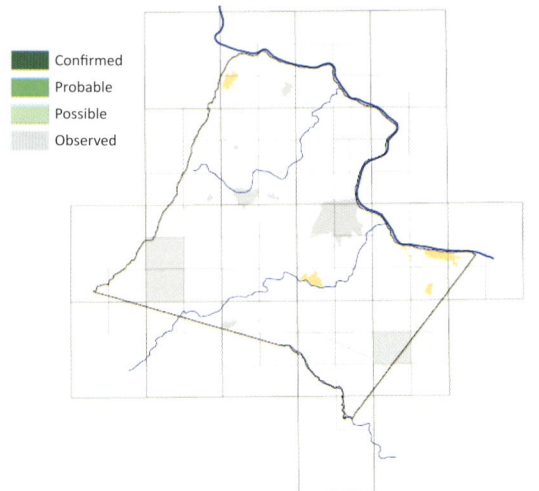

SNOWY OWL
Bubo scandiacus

Occurrence: rare irruptive winter visitor

Earliest winter sighting: December 4

Latest winter sighting: February 15

During the winter of 2013-2014 Loudoun residents were treated to 5 Snowy Owl sightings in 3 different atlas blocks, revealing a rare glimpse of life in the Arctic. Snowy Owls took the birding community by storm, gracing airports, agricultural fields, and shorelines in our region – habitats that mimic the wide-open Arctic tundra where they breed. This heavy, majestic owl typically overwinters in southern Canada and the northern U.S., but every few years a small irruption will occur, when Snowy Owls appear farther south in greater numbers than usual. The reasons for such irruptions are not fully understood, but may be attributed to an extreme abundance of lemmings, a major component of their diet, yielding an exceptional nesting season. The irruption of 2013-2014 was the largest in perhaps a century, with owls reported as far south as Florida. Adult males are all white while females and immature males have black markings. Snowy Owls are listed on the 2016 State of North America's Birds' Watch List as a bird at risk of extinction without conservation action.

Written by McKenzie and Spring Ligi

BARRED OWL
Strix varia

Occurrence: uncommon breeder and year-round resident

Earliest breeding confirmation: March 24, parent entering/exiting nest site or on nest (ON)

Latest breeding confirmation: July 23, recently fledged young (FL)

Photo by Linda Millington

The Barred Owl is the member of this iconic family most frequently encountered in Loudoun, either by sight or by hearing its familiar, two-part *Who cooks for you? Who cooks for you-all?* booming from near or far. They are also easy to bypass, sitting quietly during the day on a tree limb. Barred Owls hunt mostly at night, using their sharp eyes and ears to search for their prey, consisting of almost any type of small animal. They usually swallow the prey whole, then regurgitate the indigestible parts as a compact pellet. They prefer mixed stands of mature forest, often in lowlands near water. Barred Owls don't migrate, and are generally sedentary. The Great Horned Owl is their greatest predatory threat.

The Barred Owl is a study in browns, with a brown mottled back, bold brown vertical stripes on its creamy belly, and horizontal barring on its throat. It has large, dark eyes on the gray facial disc, in contrast to the yellow eyes of most Eastern owls, and lacks the ear tufts of some of its cousins.

Barred Owls make a variety of other loud territorial, courtship, and contact vocalizations, especially after dark. You may hear their paired duetting or a variety of cackles, hoots, whinnies, and "monkey calls" known as caterwauling. Studies have shown that they routinely use up to 10 different calls, each for a different purpose (*National Geographic* 2003). Barred Owls usually nest in an abandoned cavity, rarely enhancing the interior before laying their single clutch of two to three eggs. They sometimes nest in an abandoned stick nest or a nest box. The female incubates the eggs, and the male brings food to the female and then the nestlings. The young remain in or near the nest about 6 weeks before first flight, during which time they make a distinctive loud hissing sound when disturbed or begging for food. They often leave the nest long before they have fledged. They climb about the nest tree or even nearby trees, calling loudly to be fed.

Breeding evidence for Barred Owls was found in nearly two-thirds of the 73 atlas blocks. They were found on all of the past 20 Central Loudoun CBCs. Their numbers are doing well—populations increased 1.5% between 1966 and 2014, according to the North American BBS. Originally birds of the East, during the 20th century they expanded northwestward and down into northern California.

Written by Mary Ann Good

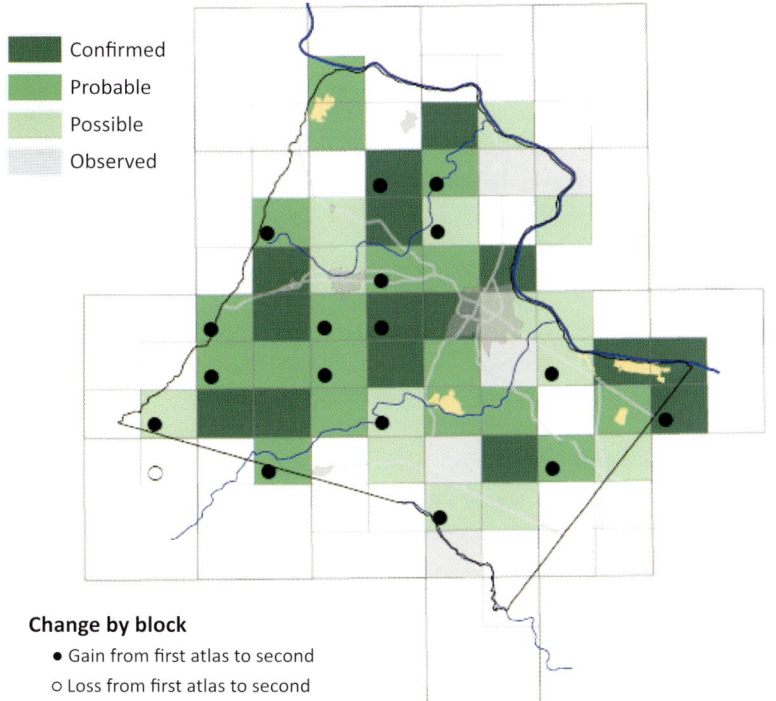

- Confirmed
- Probable
- Possible
- Observed

Change by block
- ● Gain from first atlas to second
- ○ Loss from first atlas to second

LONG-EARED OWL
Asio otus

Occurrence: rare winter visitor

Earliest/latest seasonal sightings: fewer than 5 atlas sightings, see account for details

The Long-eared Owl is slender and erect, of medium size, with mottled black and brown plumage, a rufous facial disk, yellow eyes, and tall, vertical ear tufts. Its vocalizations, heard mainly during the breeding season, include a monosyllabic *whoo*, barks, and screams. Long-eared Owls are strictly nocturnal hunters, foraging over open meadows and grasslands in search of small mammals such as mice and voles, but require dense vegetation near their hunting grounds to roost and nest. They may form communal winter roosts, camouflaged within stands of thick conifers.

This owl's secrecy, camouflage, and nomadic habits make it challenging to survey. There were 2 atlas observations, both in Leesburg 5 in the 2009 and 2012 Central Loudoun CBCs. The available data indicate that Long-eared Owls have experienced steep declines regionally, especially where habitat loss and development have eliminated the combination of open ground and dense vegetation essential to their survival.

Written by Christine Perdue

Photo by Tony LePrieur

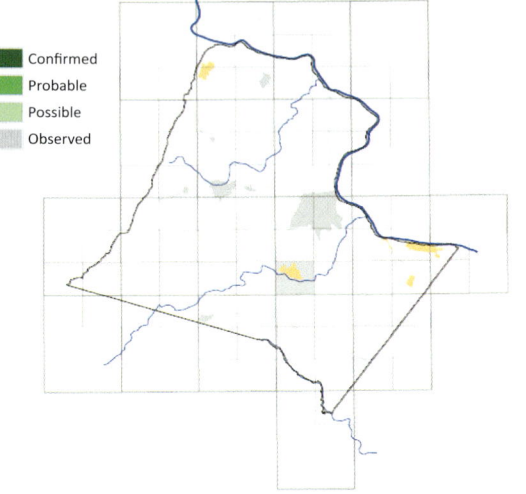

Confirmed
Probable
Possible
Observed

SHORT-EARED OWL
Asio flammeus

Occurrence: rare winter visitor

Earliest winter sighting: December 3

Latest winter sighting: February 4

Usually found at dawn or dusk hunting voles and field mice, this owl also courses low over open areas of grassland at any time of day or night, quartering the field like its competitor the Northern Harrier. It breeds across the northern U.S. and Canada, wintering throughout the remainder of the U.S. It was found in 3 of the 5 atlas years in the Round Hill and Lucketts areas, but was reported on just 3 of the past 20 Central Loudoun CBCs.

The Short-eared Owl is a medium-sized owl, though females can be 20% larger than males. Large-headed, the ear tufts for which it is named are in the center of the forehead but are not often seen. The plumage on its back is mottled brown and buff. Its belly is whitish with vertical streaking. Populations have been in decline due to habitat loss, especially through conversion of grassland to other uses and reforestation. For proper management and success, this bird is thought to require large tracts of open grassland, in excess of 240 acres.

Written by Chris White

Photo by Dave Boltz

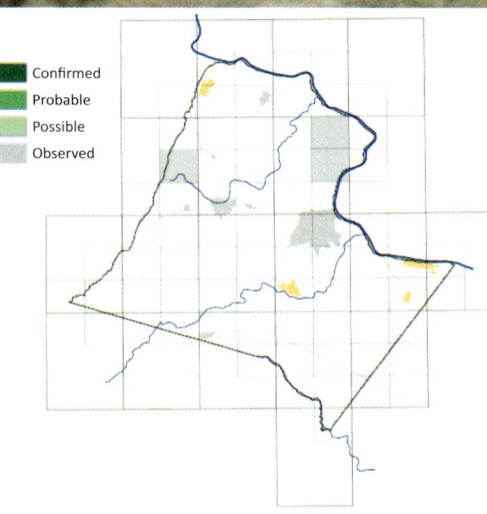

Confirmed
Probable
Possible
Observed

NORTHERN SAW-WHET OWL
Aegolius acadicus

Occurrence: rare winter visitor

Earliest/latest seasonal sightings: fewer than 5 atlas sightings, see account for details

Easily overlooked, this tiny but fierce owl was found only once during the atlas, near Rust Sanctuary (Leesburg 1) on the 2013 Central Loudoun CBC. Northern Saw-whet Owls breed in forests across northern North America and winter in habitats with dense cover across much of the U.S. Every 4 years or so the population irrupts, heading south in greater numbers than usual. By day they may be found roosting in thick conifers, typically hidden near the trunk just above eye level. At night they hunt for mice, often waiting on a low perch then swooping down to catch their prey. They are preyed upon by larger raptors, including Great Horned Owls, Cooper's Hawks, and Eastern Screech-Owls.

The tuft-less Northern Saw-whet Owl weighs slightly more than a Hairy Woodpecker and sports mottled brown and white plumage with fine white streaks on the head and a white 'V' between the yellow eyes. Their secretive nature makes population trends difficult to determine. Numbers are likely stable, though have probably declined in past decades due to habitat loss.

Written by Spring Ligi

Photo by Liam McGranaghan

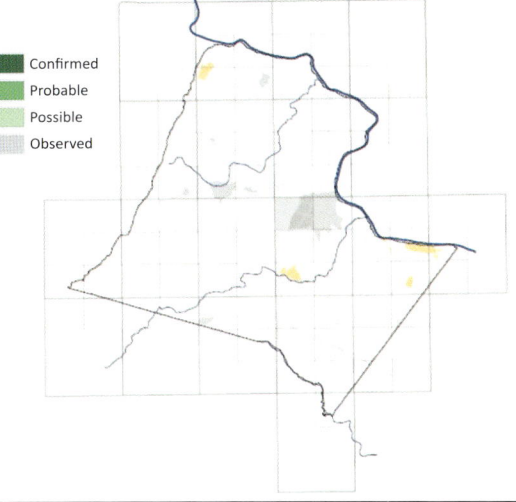

Confirmed
Probable
Possible
Observed

Photo by Linda Millington

BELTED KINGFISHER
Megaceryle alcyon

Occurrence: uncommon breeder and year-round resident

Earliest breeding confirmation: April 21, parent entering/exiting nest site or on nest (ON)

Latest breeding confirmation: July 5, recently fledged young (FL)

Belted Kingfishers can be found patrolling the banks of our streams, rivers, lakes, and ponds, flying purposefully and proclaiming their presence with a harsh, rattling call. They have a distinctive stout profile with a large head, large bill, spiky crest, and relatively short tail. Their upperparts are slate-blue, and their white chest has a broad blue band. Belted Kingfishers are one of the few bird species in which the female is more brightly colored than the male — she sports an additional rust-colored belt across her chest.

Belted Kingfishers may often be seen perched along the water's edge or on an overhead wire; they will plunge headfirst into the water with closed eyes to capture prey in their strong bills. Their diet includes small fish, crayfish, tadpoles, and aquatic insects.

Kingfishers are typically solitary except when mating. Males court females with gifts of food. The pair excavates a tunnel in a vertical dirt streambank generally 3-6 feet long, sloping upward to prevent rain from accumulating. A

BELTED KINGFISHER (continued)

kingfisher's toes have sharp claws and are designed for excavation. Two toes are fused and act like a shovel, while the middle toe is longer and used to dig. The tunnel ends in an unlined nest chamber 8-12 inches in diameter. Five to eight eggs are laid; both parents incubate and feed the young. Young kingfishers have acidic stomachs that help digest bones, scales, and shells, but once mature they begin regurgitating pellets of indigestible parts. Young leave the nesting chamber at 27-29 days and continue to be fed by the parents for another 3 weeks. Kingfishers raise one brood per year.

Though widespread throughout the U.S., Canada, and Central America, populations have declined over the past 5 decades, according to the North American BBS. The apparent significant gain in blocks from Atlas 1 to Atlas 2 is likely influenced by the higher level of coverage in Atlas 2 and not a true population spurt. The Belted Kingfisher has been reported on every Central Loudoun CBC, with numbers ranging from 12 to 37 individuals per count. Belted Kingfishers are indicators of good water quality. To remain a treasured part of Loudoun's ecosystem, they must have clean, unclouded water to see prey and suitable undisturbed earthen banks for nesting.

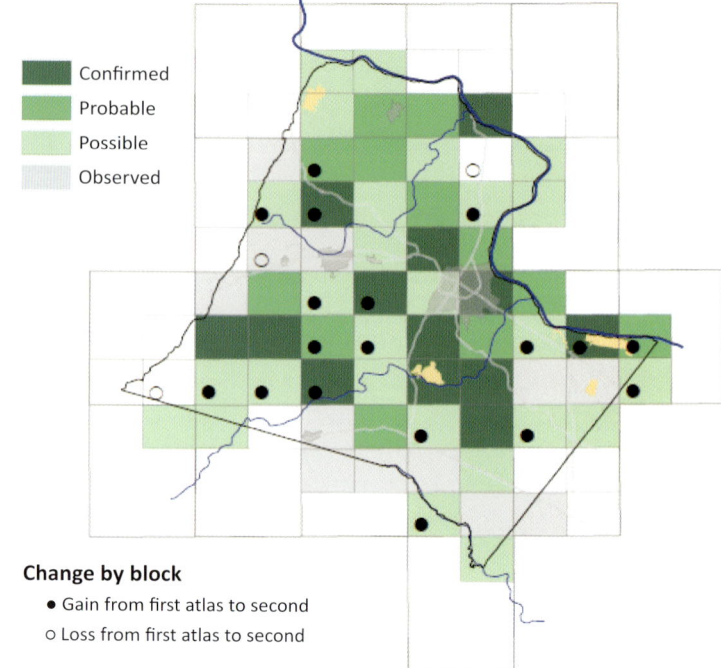

■ Confirmed
■ Probable
■ Possible
□ Observed

Change by block
● Gain from first atlas to second
○ Loss from first atlas to second

Written by Donna Quinn

Photo by Dave Boltz

RED-HEADED WOODPECKER
Melanerpes erythrocephalus

Occurrence: uncommon breeder and year-round resident

Earliest breeding confirmation: May 23, parent entering/exiting nest site or on nest (ON)

Latest breeding confirmation: September 16, recently fledged young (FL)

The strikingly handsome Red-headed Woodpecker is Loudoun's most uncommon and sought-after woodpecker. When seen seeking a meal of insects and grubs on a tree trunk, its patterning of entirely crimson-red head, black upper back, and snowy-white lower back are unmistakable. In flight, the large, stark black and white patches earned it the epithet "flying checkerboard." It frequently announces its presence with a raspy *queeah* or *queerp*.

This species is unique among Loudoun's seven woodpecker species in other ways. It is adept at catching insects in flight, and eats lots of acorns and other nuts, stowing them in crevices for later. Its diet also includes fruit. Unlike other woodpeckers, they are often colonial nesters and may remain year after year at their chosen site. Red-headed Woodpeckers favor open woodlands with clear understory, especially large standing snags in beaver swamps and other wetlands. While the chestnut blight and Dutch elm disease outbreaks of the 20th century removed an important food source for these once abundant birds, they did create lots of dead trees for their cavity nests. With the systematic removal of dead trees, these woodpeckers have seen drastic declines. Although they are aggressive

RED-HEADED WOODPECKER (continued)

defenders of their traditional nest sites, European Starlings often succeed in eviction and takeover. They are listed as "Near Threatened" on the IUCN Red List; the North American BBS shows a 70% decline from 1966 to 2014. Courtship consists of much head-bobbing and "hide and seek" around tree trunks, as well as calling and drumming. The male excavates the cavity with an oblong, 2-inch hole for the three to seven eggs, the female incubates them for 12-14 days, and the young emerge about 2 weeks later. The juvenile has a blackish head until adulthood. The pair may raise a second brood.

This uncommon woodpecker had the second-highest percentage of breeding confirmations (to Red-bellied) of the woodpeckers in Atlas 2, likely due to its striking visibility and popularity. Breeding and even its presence were less in evidence in the more-developed

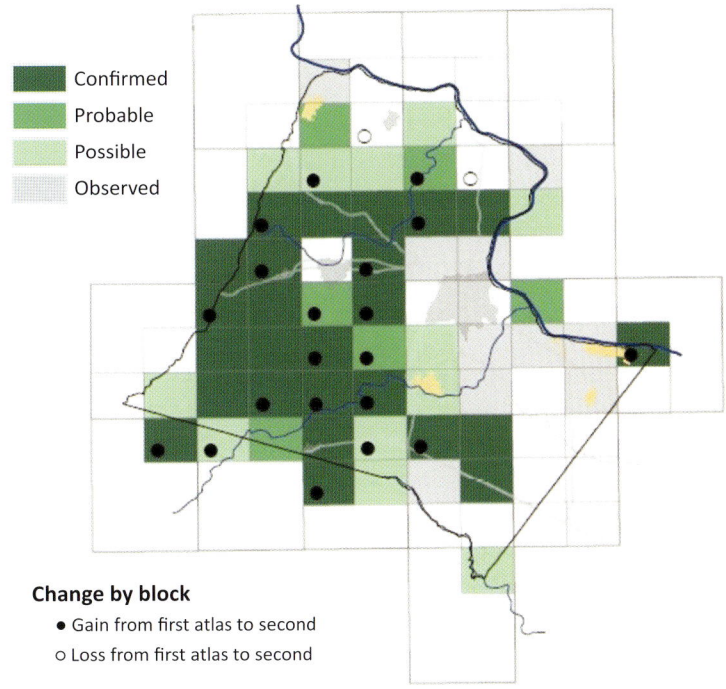

Change by block
- Gain from first atlas to second
- Loss from first atlas to second

east of the county. The apparent gain in blocks from Atlas 1 is likely due to the increased level of effort in Atlas 2 and not reflective of a true population spurt. Loudoun may see more Red-headed Woodpeckers in winter, when more northern birds may migrate southward (National Geographic 2003), though this species is still reported in smaller numbers than any other woodpecker during Central Loudoun CBCs.

Written by Mary Ann Good

Photo by Deb Calhoun

RED-BELLIED WOODPECKER
Melanerpes carolinus

Occurrence: abundant breeder and year-round resident

Earliest breeding confirmation: March 31, parent entering/exiting nest site or on nest (ON)

Latest breeding confirmation: August 31, recently fledged young (FL)

A familiar and easily recognized bird in Loudoun, the Red-bellied Woodpecker was reported more often than any other woodpecker species during Atlas 2 and was confirmed as breeding in more blocks than any other woodpecker. It was one of only 14 atlas species reported in all 73 blocks. Though its principal habitat in Virginia is oak-hickory forests, this generalist readily nests in suburban and residential areas where there are mature trees. Apparently comfortable around human activity, this woodpecker is frequently found at backyard feeders, where it will eat seeds, fruit, peanuts, suet, meat, and other offerings. It eats an equally broad spectrum of naturally available food – principally arboreal arthropods and mast from hickory and oak trees, but also fruit, sap drawn from sapsucker wells, bird eggs, and even nestling birds.

This medium-sized woodpecker has a black and white barred back with a white breast. Belying its name, its belly has simply a pale pinkish wash that is often not observed. Much more noticeable is the vibrant red on its head, which on the male covers the nape of its neck and its crown, and on the female covers only the nape. Both sexes have white cheeks and heavy bills. Like many woodpeckers, the Red-bellied has a deeply undulating flight pattern.

RED-BELLIED WOODPECKER (continued)

The Red-bellied Woodpecker's breeding range covers most of the eastern U.S., from the Atlantic Coast west as far as Kansas and Nebraska. It is thought to be non-migratory over most of its range. Males defend their feeding and nesting territory year-round, while females compete for territory each spring. At the beginning of the breeding season, the birds engage in a charming pairing-off ritual. The male perches at a potential nest site and calls to a potential mate. If the female is attracted, she will fly over and perch next to the male, and the two will tap in unison, signaling a match for the season. The two will finish excavating a nest hole together, and will share responsibility for incubating the eggs, brooding the hatchlings, and feeding the young both before and after they fledge.

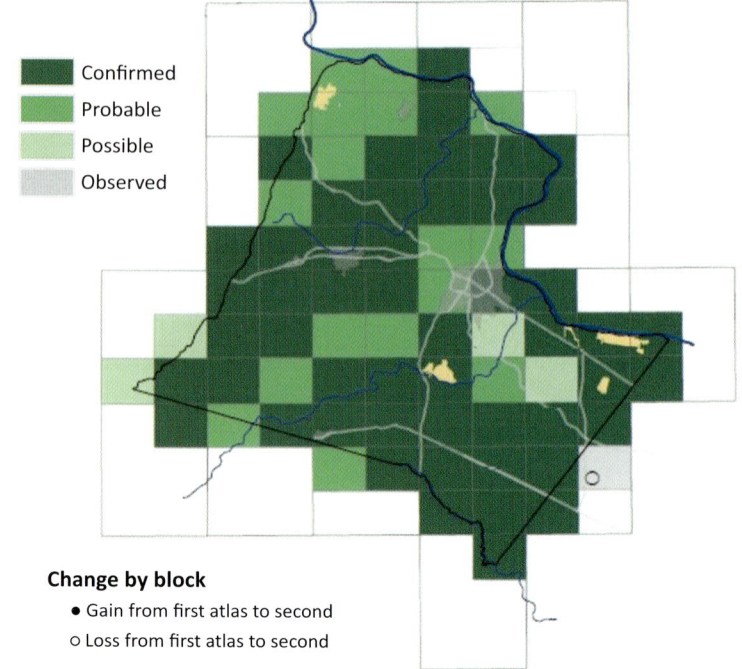

Confirmed
Probable
Possible
Observed

Change by block
• Gain from first atlas to second
○ Loss from first atlas to second

The population of Red-bellied Woodpeckers has increased in recent decades, according to the North American BBS, and their breeding range has extended further north over the past 100 years. This increase is also reflected in the Central Loudoun CBC data. Between 1997 and 2006, the count averaged 179 individuals, compared to an average of 237 individuals between 2007 and 2016.

Written by Bill Brown

Photo by Lisa McKew

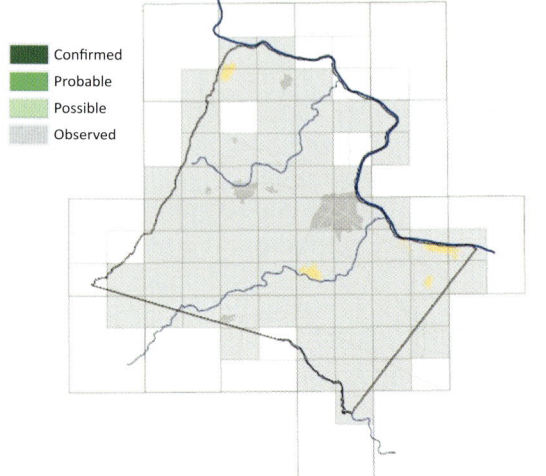

Confirmed
Probable
Possible
Observed

YELLOW-BELLIED SAPSUCKER
Sphyrapicus varius

Occurrence: uncommon migrant and winter resident

Earliest fall sighting: September 21

Latest spring sighting: May 15

The Yellow-bellied Sapsucker is a medium-size woodpecker with a red forehead and crown, a white rump, and a broad white bar across its wings. The male has a bright red throat, while the female's throat is white. Both sexes show the yellow wash on their undersides for which the bird is named. The Yellow-bellied Sapsucker is the only seasonally occurring woodpecker in Loudoun, where it is found in diverse woodlands. Numbers range from 17 to 98 individuals on the Central Loudoun CBCs. Loudoun lies at the northern edge of its winter range, which extends south through Central America. This woodpecker breeds across the boreal forest of North America and south along the Appalachian highlands.

The Yellow-bellied Sapsucker drills rows of shallow holes around living tree trunks and feeds on the sap that accumulates in them, as well as on insects drawn to the sap. Other birds, including the Ruby-throated Hummingbird, also routinely feed at these sapsucker wells. Over the past 5 decades, Yellow-bellied Sapsucker numbers have increased slightly throughout their range (USGS 2014).

Written by Bill Brown

DOWNY WOODPECKER
Dryobates pubescens

Occurrence: abundant breeder and year-round resident

Earliest breeding confirmation: April 15, parent entering/exiting nest site or on nest (ON)

Latest breeding confirmation: August 11, recently fledged young (FL)

The Downy Woodpecker is the smallest North American woodpecker and one of the most abundant in Loudoun; it was one of 14 species reported in all 73 atlas blocks. The bird measures about 6¾ inches in length and has a distinctively patterned white and black plumage. The adult male has a red patch on the back of its crown; the female

Photo by Katherine Daniels

lacks that adornment. The Downy's typical call, made by both male and female, is a whinny that descends in pitch over about 2 seconds. Like most woodpeckers, the Downy's flight undulates up and down in a wave-shaped pattern.

It makes its home in woodlands and suburban parks and readily comes to backyard feeders for suet, black-oil sunflower seeds, peanuts, or peanut butter. The Downy's continental distribution stretches from Florida up to the tree line of Canada and Alaska, absent only from the desert Southwest. It is a non-migratory species, present throughout its distribution all year long.

Away from feeders, Downy Woodpeckers eat mainly insects and other arthropods, which they glean from tree bark, shrubs, and woody plant stems. About 25% of their diet, however, is plant material – berries, nuts, and grains. They are often found feeding in mixed flocks with Carolina Chickadees, Tufted Titmice, and White-breasted Nuthatches. Male and female Downies tend to have different feeding niches, with females more often foraging on tree trunks and larger branches while males are found on smaller branches.

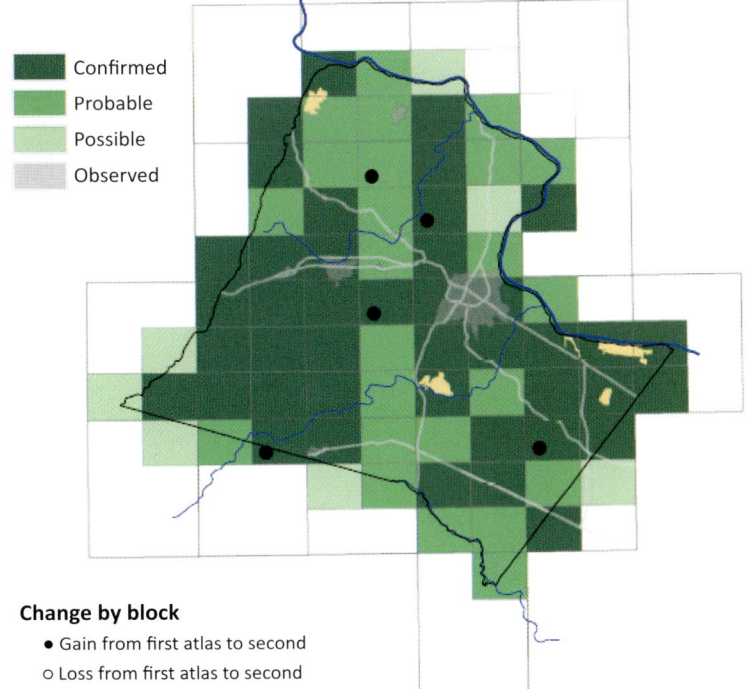

Confirmed
Probable
Possible
Observed

Change by block
- Gain from first atlas to second
- Loss from first atlas to second

Both the male and female help to excavate a nest cavity, usually in a dead branch of a living or dead tree. Excavation takes 16 days on average. After the nest is complete, the female lays between three and eight eggs, usually one a day. The male and female both participate in incubation, which lasts about 12 days. The chicks fledge within 18 to 21 days after hatching. Parental care of the young extends at least 3 weeks after fledging, during which time parents feed young, lead them to food sources, and warn of predators.

The Downy Woodpecker exhibited breeding behavior in all 73 blocks, with breeding confirmed in 42 blocks. An average of 170 individuals are reported on annual Central Loudoun CBCs. According to the North American BBS, the Downy Woodpecker's global population has remained stable over the past 5 decades.

Written by Bill Brown

HAIRY WOODPECKER
Dryobates villosus

Occurrence: uncommon breeder and year-round resident

Earliest breeding confirmation: April 17, parent entering/exiting nest site or on nest (ON)

Latest breeding confirmation: July 25, recently fledged young (FL)

The Hairy Woodpecker is nearly identical to the Downy Woodpecker in its black and white patterned plumage and facial markings. The Hairy Woodpecker, however, measures 9¼ inches – noticeably larger than the Downy. The two species can also be distinguished by relative bill sizes, the Hairy's being much longer and heavier in proportion to its head

Photo by Deb Calhoun

than the Downy's. Careful observation will show that the Downy Woodpecker's outer tail feathers are white with black bars or spots, while the Hairy's are solid white. The two species can also be distinguished by their calls. The Downy gives a high whinny that descends in pitch, while the Hairy gives a lower, more steadily pitched rattle.

The Hairy Woodpecker is primarily a resident, non-migratory bird in Loudoun and throughout its range, which extends across North America from Alaska to Florida and into Mexico and Central America. Its principal habitat is mature forest, but it can also be found in wooded suburban and urban settings; by contrast, the Downy Woodpecker favors lighter woods. It readily comes to feeders that provide suet or sunflower seeds. Away from feeders, insects make up over 75% of its diet year-round, while fruit, berries, and seeds account for the rest. It forages primarily on the trunks and heavier branches of trees.

Hairy Woodpeckers excavate nest holes in both living and dead trees. A typical clutch consists of three to six eggs. Both parents assist in incubating the eggs and brooding the young. The young fledge 28 to 30 days after hatching and remain with their parents for at least 3 weeks more.

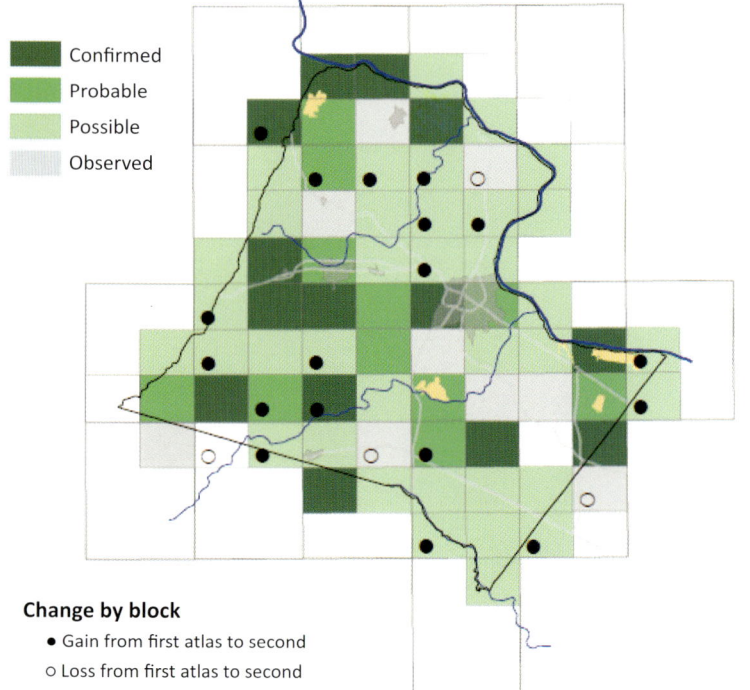

Confirmed
Probable
Possible
Observed

Change by block
- Gain from first atlas to second
- Loss from first atlas to second

In Loudoun, the Hairy is one of the least frequently encountered woodpeckers. For instance, in Atlas 2 the Hairy Woodpecker was confirmed breeding in 15 blocks, and was a probable breeder in 24 more, while the Downy was confirmed in 42 blocks and probable in 24. During Central Loudoun CBCs, the Hairy Woodpecker is always reported fewer times than any woodpecker except the Red-headed.

The Hairy Woodpecker population is considered relatively stable, but in some areas it is threatened by forest fragmentation and competition for nest holes with European Starlings. The apparent gain in 18 blocks from Atlas 1 is likely influenced by the more thorough coverage and higher level of effort per block in Atlas 2 rather than a true population spurt.

Written by Bill Brown

NORTHERN FLICKER
Colaptes auratus

Occurrence: common breeder and year-round resident

Earliest breeding confirmation: April 16, parent entering/exiting nest site or on nest (ON)

Latest breeding confirmation: August 22, recently fledged young (FL)

Photo by Bill Brown

Larger than any Loudoun woodpecker other than Pileated, the Northern Flicker sports highly distinctive plumage. Rather than the predominately black and white patterns of most woodpeckers in our area, the flicker is a rich tan, marked with black bars on the back and large black spots on its paler underparts. The bird is adorned with a large black crescent on its breast and a red crescent on its nape; the male has a black moustachial stripe. In flight it flashes a characteristic white rump and the bright yellow wing linings for which the subspecies is named "yellow-shafted." In the western "red-shafted" subspecies, the wing linings and mustache are red. Flickers have several characteristic vocalizations—a loud, long *wick wick wick wick wick*, a single *kyeer*, and the soft *flicka flicka flicka* for which they are named.

Northern Flickers are present in Loudoun – and in most of the Lower 48 – throughout the year. Populations breeding in the northern part of their range, which includes Alaska and most of Canada, migrate south in winter. It is likely, therefore, that both resident and migratory populations are present in Loudoun during the winter. The Northern Flicker is primarily a ground-foraging bird; its diet is principally ants during the breeding season. It eats more ants than any other North American bird. In the winter, it eats fruits such as poison ivy, flowering dogwood, and sumac. It often forages in small flocks on open ground that is bare or covered with short grass and near to woodlots.

Adult flickers usually excavate nest holes in dead or diseased tree trunks or large branches, but sometimes use pre-existing cavities. The nest itself is a layer of woodchips resulting from the excavation; no twigs or grasses are brought in. Males and females share in nest excavation, as well as in incubating the eggs and brooding and feeding the young.

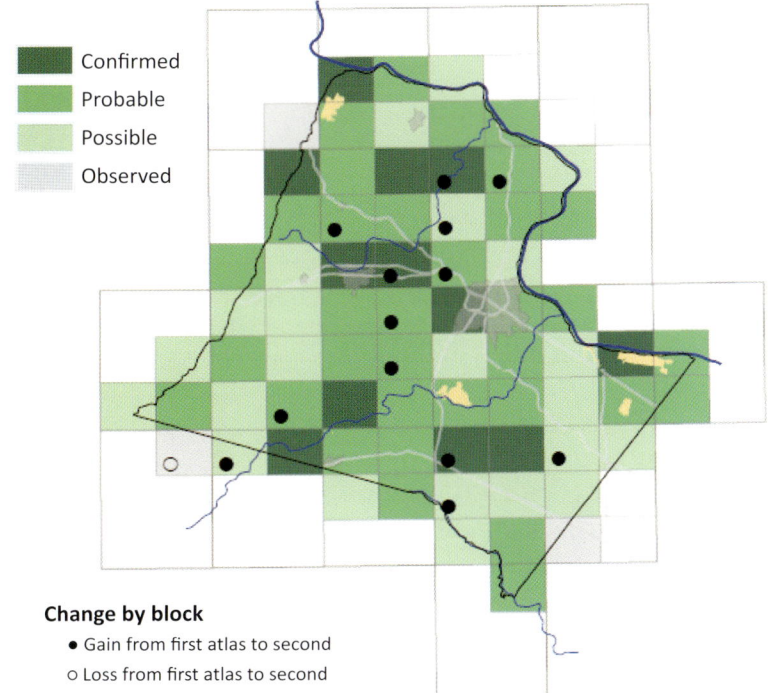

Confirmed
Probable
Possible
Observed

Change by block
- Gain from first atlas to second
○ Loss from first atlas to second

Although the Northern Flicker is not recognized as a threatened species, a long-term population decline has been documented. Hypothesized reasons for the decline include competition for nest cavities with European Starlings, reduced availability of snags in which to nest, and use of pesticides on golf courses, agricultural fields, and suburban lawns. The apparent gain in 40 blocks from Atlas 1 is likely influenced by the more thorough coverage and higher level of effort per block in Atlas 2. Central Loudoun CBC numbers range from 61 to 230 individuals per count.

Written by Bill Brown

PILEATED WOODPECKER
Dryocopus pileatus

Occurrence: uncommon breeder and year-round resident

Earliest breeding confirmation: April 9, parent entering/exiting nest site or on nest (ON)

Latest breeding confirmation: August 27, recently fledged young (FL)

The Pileated Woodpecker, about the size of a crow, is by far the largest woodpecker found in Loudoun. It is easily recognized by its size, its distinctive peaked red crest, and its heavy bill. It also draws attention to itself by its loud and prolonged *wuk-wuk-wuk-wuk* call, given year-round, often during flight.

Photo by Liam McGranaghan

This woodpecker is resident throughout the eastern U.S. and along the northern Pacific Coast, especially in mature forests, although in the East it is increasingly found in young forests and even partially wooded suburbs and backyards. It needs large-diameter trees to excavate nest cavities, while dead or dying trees are the principal source of its preferred food, carpenter ants. The bird chisels distinctive large, rectangular holes in decaying wood in search of ant nests and beetle larvae. In addition to insects, it will eat fruits and berries as available. It occasionally comes to backyard feeders to eat suet, seeds, and nuts.

The Pileated Woodpecker is not known to migrate. In fact, males and females, which typically mate for life, defend their breeding territory throughout the year. When one member of a pair dies, the remaining bird normally stays in the territory and takes a new mate there.

During the breeding season, both sexes are actively involved in excavating the nest, incubating the eggs, brooding the young, and feeding the young before and after fledging. The average clutch size is four eggs, and the incubation period is 15 to 18 days. During incubation, the eggs are attended by either parent nearly 100% of the time. The hatchlings remain in the nest for 24 to 30 days. For several months after fledging, the young continue to follow one or both parents, depending on them to provide food and show them how to forage. Juveniles leave their parents in the fall and can mate in the spring if they acquire a territory.

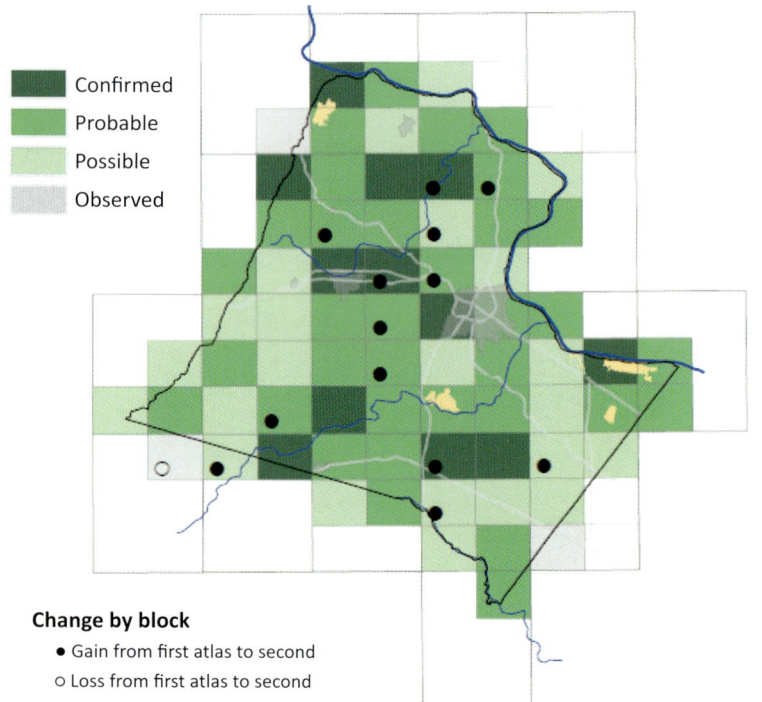

Confirmed
Probable
Possible
Observed

Change by block
- Gain from first atlas to second
- Loss from first atlas to second

The Pileated Woodpecker showed evidence of breeding in 69 of the 73 atlas blocks. This is a gain of 13 blocks from Atlas 1. According to the North American BBS, its global population increased steadily from 1966 to 2014. Central Loudoun CBC numbers range from 19 to 90 individuals per count.

Written by Bill Brown

AMERICAN KESTREL
Falco sparverius

Occurrence: uncommon breeder, migrant, and year-round resident

Earliest breeding confirmation: May 23, parent entering/exiting nest site or on nest (ON)

Latest breeding confirmation: July 11, parent carrying food or feeding young (CF)

The American Kestrel is North America's smallest and most colorful falcon. The male is distinguished by his slate-colored crown and wings, russet back and tail, and black-spotted wings and breast. The female is larger than the male but shows more subdued coloration. Both sexes display a pair of vertical malar stripes, forming a black "mustache" in contrast to their white cheeks and throat.

Photo by Liam McGranaghan

The kestrel's preferred habitat is open country, and it is typically found in fields, meadows, pastures, and parks. Kestrels are often observed perching on utility wires or poles, bobbing their tails and scanning the ground for prey. They sometimes hover a few feet above the ground before striking. Their diet consists chiefly of insects, invertebrates, rodents, and small mammals, although an earlier common name of Sparrow Hawk reflects the occasional addition of small songbirds to the diet. Kestrels may cache food during periods of abundance.

Kestrels are quite vocal on their territories and can be recognized by their loud and rhythmic calls of *killy-killy-killy*. Courtship behaviors include aerial displays, food offerings, and "flutter glides" by the male. Kestrels are cavity nesters and favor old woodpecker holes, natural tree cavities, nest boxes, and holes in buildings. The female deposits the eggs on the surface of the cavity, using little or no nesting materials. Incubation through fledging requires two months. Kestrels typically raise only one brood per season.

Although Loudoun has a resident kestrel population, it is augmented in fall and winter by migrants from further north. Kestrels molt before they migrate and are usually solitary migrants. The great majority overwinter in the southern parts of the U.S.

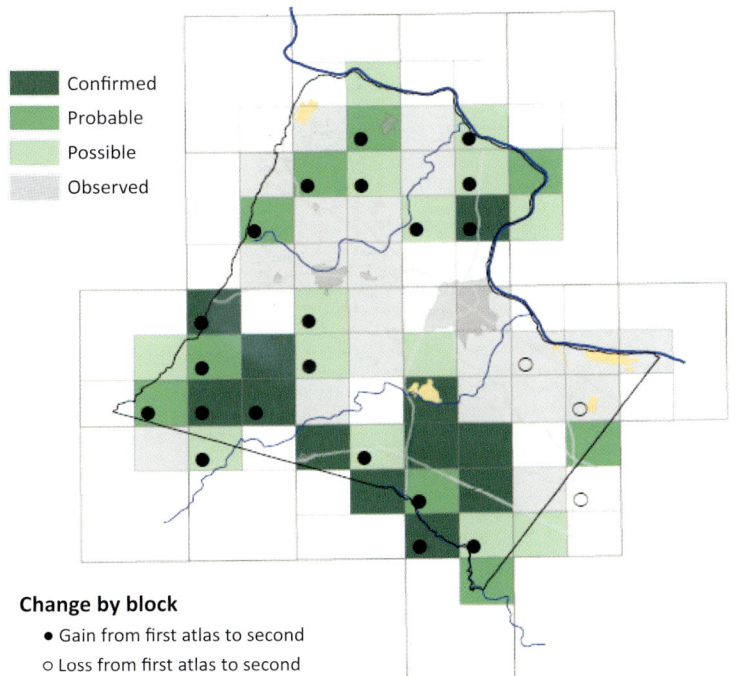

Confirmed
Probable
Possible
Observed

Change by block
- Gain from first atlas to second
- ○ Loss from first atlas to second

American Kestrels were found in 57 blocks, with breeding evidence reported in 35 blocks and confirmed in 12. During Atlas 1, breeding was confirmed in 8 blocks. While there were significant gains from Atlas 1 in the more rural parts of the county (due in part to increased coverage and effort per block in Atlas 2), breeding evidence sharply declined in Loudoun's eastern and central blocks. Data from the Central Loudoun CBC reflect a similar long-term decline in the kestrel population from 1997-2016. The observations from central and eastern Loudoun are consistent with an overall decline among kestrels in the mid-Atlantic region; habitat loss, land management changes, rodenticides, and predation are possible factors. The use of nest boxes may aid the kestrels' long-term survival.

Written by Christine Perdue

MERLIN

Falco columbarius

Occurrence: occasional migrant and winter visitor

Earliest summer/fall sighting: August 19

Latest spring sighting: May 1

This infrequently seen falcon passes through our region between its breeding range, mainly in Canada, and its wintering grounds in Central America, but also may overwinter here. Merlins have been reported on about half of the Central Loudoun CBCs, and of the 35 atlas sightings, 17 were at the Snickers Gap Hawkwatch (Bluemont 1) during fall migration. This raptor of forest edges and grasslands is an active hunter, flying low and fast from its perch to take birds and dragonflies in mid-air; it rarely soars, and does not hover like the kestrel does.

A dark, pigeon-sized falcon, the back, crown, and upper wing coverts of the adult male are bluish gray, while the slightly larger female is dark brown. The undersides are whitish, heavily streaked with brown. The characteristic mustache of the falcon is fainter than in others. It has long, pointed wings and a distinctive square tail. Merlin populations are now stable, thanks to a ban on the pesticide DDT in the early 1970s and their ability to adapt to life in urban areas.

Written by Chris White

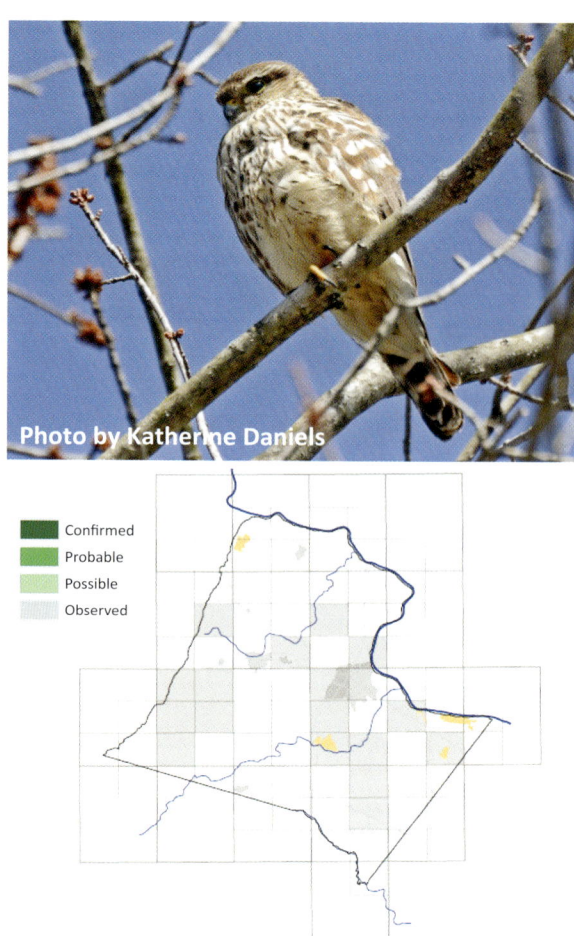

Photo by Katherine Daniels

- Confirmed
- Probable
- Possible
- Observed

Photo by Bob Schamerhorn

- Confirmed
- Probable
- Possible
- Observed

PEREGRINE FALCON

Falco peregrinus

Occurrence: rare migrant and winter visitor

Earliest summer/fall sighting: August 25

Latest spring sighting: March 6

This medium-sized, powerfully built falcon is a superb aerial hunter, chasing and catching birds of many species, some larger than itself, in spectacular dives and tail chases. Pigeons, starlings, small ducks, shorebirds, and even bats are potential prey. Peregrines are bluish-gray above, barred below, with a distinctive dark facial mask and "sideburns." They have long, pointed wings, a robust body, and fly with strong, even wingbeats intermixed with glides.

This iconic species was seen 13 times during Atlas 2, with 10 of those sightings at Snickers Gap Hawkwatch during fall migration. Peregrines were reported on the 2011 and 2014 Central Loudoun CBCs. Historically an uncommon but widespread species, they suffered greatly from the use of DDT, and were nearly extirpated throughout most of the lower 48 states. They have since recovered nicely, and now use man-made structures like tall buildings and bridges, as well as cliffs and snags, as nest sites. They are most frequently seen along the coasts. A few nest in our broader region, but they have not been known to nest in Loudoun.

Written by Bruce Hill

GREAT CRESTED FLYCATCHER
Myiarchus crinitus

Occurrence: common breeder and migrant

Earliest breeding confirmation: May 8, parent entering/exiting nest site or on nest (ON)

Latest breeding confirmation: August 11, recently fledged young (FL)

Photo by Dave Boltz

The Great Crested Flycatcher occupies the high canopy of deciduous trees and is often not observed until its emphatic *wheep!* signals the bird's presence. This colorful flycatcher is easily identified by its cinnamon-russet tail and wingtips and lemon-yellow belly. It has a gray head and a brownish, erect crown.

The Great Crested Flycatcher prefers edge habitats and can be found in open woodlands, orchards, along wooded streams or ponds, and in mature shade trees. It feeds in the treetops, occupying a niche distinct from other flycatcher species. The Great Crested is also unique among Loudoun's flycatchers in its nesting behaviors. It is a cavity nester that favors old woodpecker holes and natural openings in hardwoods but will also use suitable nest boxes. Inside the cavity, the Great Crested makes a small cup for its eggs amid an accumulation of leaves, twigs and bits of trash. A shed snakeskin is often incorporated into the nest.

The Great Crested Flycatcher can be observed in Loudoun from mid-April to late September. Its breeding season in Loudoun ends around July 31, and the birds begin migration to their wintering grounds in September. This species is typically a solitary migrant, overwintering in eastern and southern Mexico, Central America, and the northwestern edge of South America.

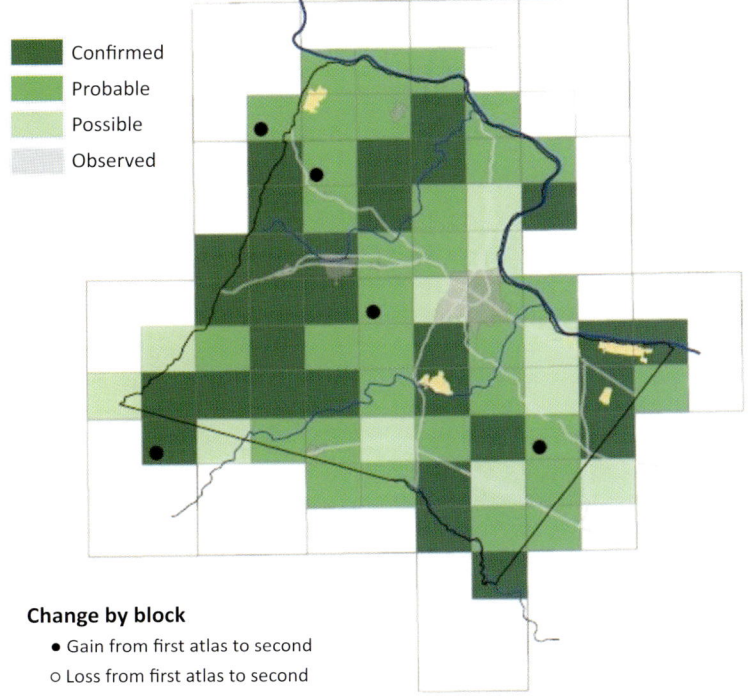

Confirmed
Probable
Possible
Observed

Change by block
- Gain from first atlas to second
- Loss from first atlas to second

Evidence of breeding was observed in all 73 blocks, with breeding confirmed in 29 blocks. The greatest number of confirmations occurred in western and southwestern Loudoun, where the tree density is typically greater than in the east. The number of blocks with breeding evidence represents a net gain of 5 blocks from Atlas 1. However, Cornell's NestWatch website (2017) indicates that the Great Crested's numbers are declining in some parts of Virginia. This may be a function of competition for nesting sites and loss of wooded habitat. More widespread use of nest boxes may help to address population decline in this species.

Written by Christine Perdue

WESTERN KINGBIRD
Tyrannus verticalis

Occurrence: rare migrant

Southerly/northerly migration periods: fewer than 5 atlas sightings, see account for details

In the same genus as the Eastern Kingbird, and about the same size, the Western Kingbird has completely different coloration: a lemon-yellow belly; pale gray breast, head, and back; dark wings; and black tail. Like its cousin, it feeds in open areas with scattered trees by sallying from a perch to catch flying insects, but it will also swoop to the ground to capture terrestrial insects such as crickets.

The Western Kingbird breeds across western North America from the Great Plains to the Pacific and from southern Canada into Mexico. It winters mostly in Central America, but is known to wander widely during migration; a few individuals show up every fall and even fewer in the spring along the East Coast from Newfoundland to Florida. This species was reported twice during the atlas, once in September along the Potomac River in Algonkian Park and once in December at the Dulles Greenway Wetlands. Populations appear stable throughout their range, which has expanded eastward during the 20th century as people planted trees across the prairies.

Written by Bill Brown

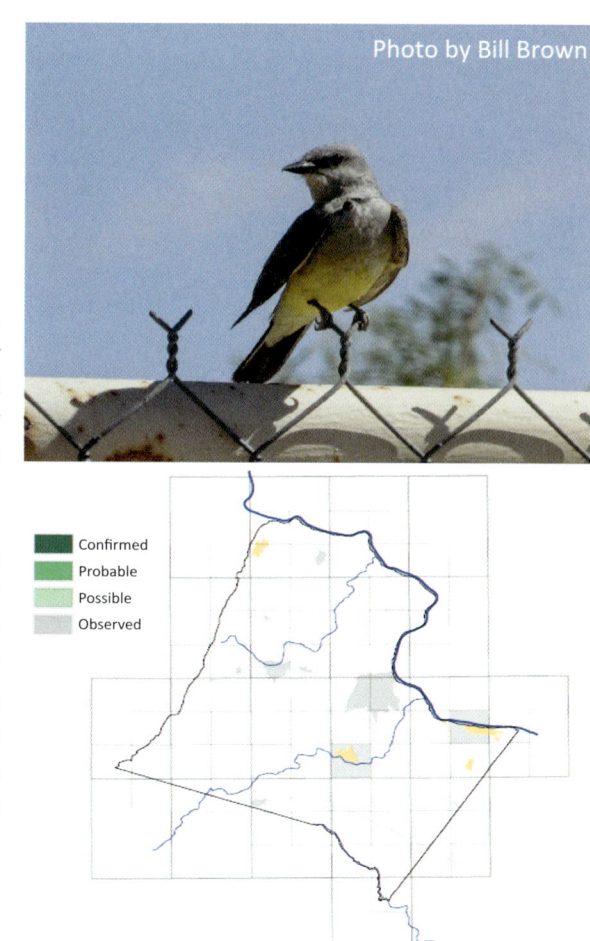
Photo by Bill Brown

Confirmed
Probable
Possible
Observed

Photo by Gerco Hoogeweg

EASTERN KINGBIRD
Tyrannus tyrannus

Occurrence: common breeder and migrant

Earliest breeding confirmation: May 7, adult carrying nesting material or nest building (NB)

Latest breeding confirmation: August 10, recently fledged young (FL)

The Eastern Kingbird is a conspicuous bird, hard to miss when present in its preferred overgrown fields, woodland edges, and hedgerow habitats. It often perches in highly visible locations, like the tops of trees, utility wires, or fence rows. Its flight with rapid, jittery wingbeats is also distinctive. It is crisply patterned in black and white, sporting a black cap and face, dark gray back, and dark wings without barring. Its white undersides are in sharp contrast, and its dark tail is distinctively tipped in white. It is about the size of a cardinal, but bulkier.

Eastern Kingbirds typically arrive in Loudoun in April. Males arrive first, followed several days later by the females. They are loyal to a good territory, and a mated pair may return to the same location throughout their life. The female builds the nest and incubates her two to five eggs alone; she will often chase away the male during this phase. But once the eggs hatch, both parents assume feeding duties, and continue to feed their offspring for as long as 7 weeks, well into their fledgling stage. This long cycle generally limits Eastern Kingbirds to one brood per season.

EASTERN KINGBIRD (continued)

Their local diet consists primarily of medium to large insects. They will often sally out to snatch prey items in-flight from a favorite perch, but also flutter or hover over grasses or brush to find other prey. Interestingly, once they leave our area in late August and September, they aggregate and migrate in loose flocks. Upon arriving in the Amazon region, they remain in flocks and adjust their diet to eat mainly fruit.

Vocalizations are variable, typically a harsh *kt-zee* or *zeer*, sometimes given once, other times strung together in a sputtering, electrical discharge-sounding chatter. If you hear a kingbird's calls, look up – they are highly territorial, as their scientific name infers, and will aggressively and relentlessly dive at and harass trespassing crows, hawks, and other large birds considered a threat.

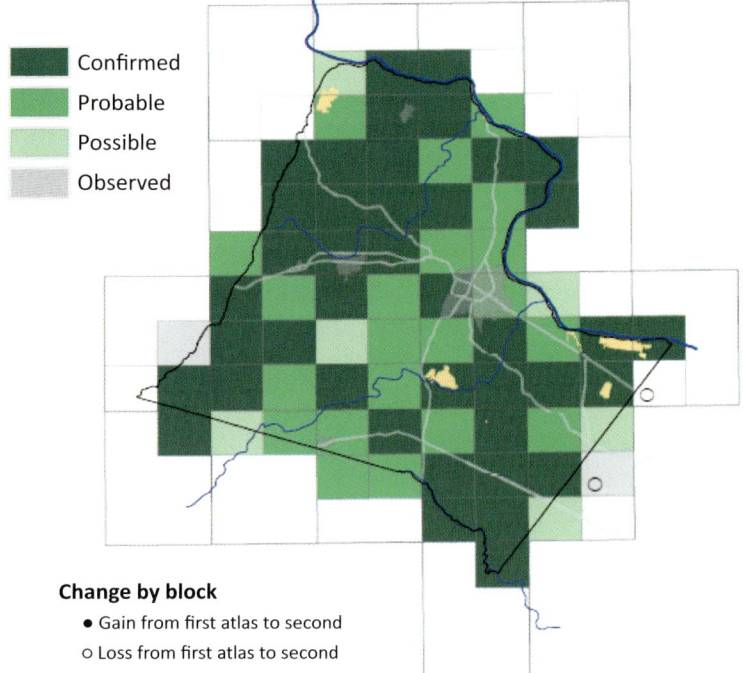

Confirmed
Probable
Possible
Observed

Change by block
- Gain from first atlas to second
○ Loss from first atlas to second

Though reported as breeding in virtually every atlas block and still numerous and widespread across much of the U.S. and Canada (26 million in 2016 according to the PIF Landbird Plan), Eastern Kingbird populations have declined almost 50% over the last 50 years. Habitat loss is the major cause. They are also often hit by cars as they forage near roads, though the overall population impact of such mortality is probably minor.

Written by Bruce Hill

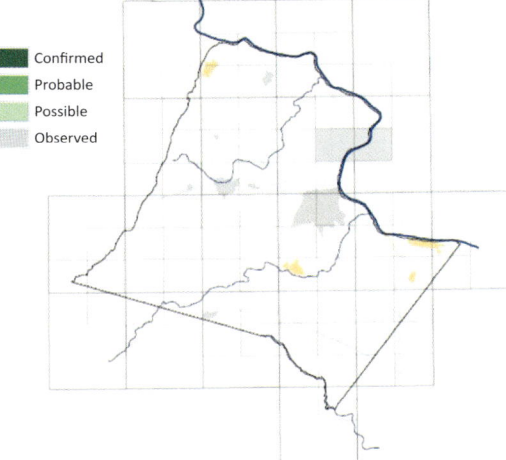

Photo by Bill Brown

Confirmed
Probable
Possible
Observed

SCISSOR-TAILED FLYCATCHER
Tyrannus forficatus

Occurrence: rare migrant

Southerly/northerly migration periods: fewer than 5 atlas sightings, see account for details

Scissor-tailed Flycatchers breed in the south-central U.S., but in rare instances wander widely on their way to and from their tropical wintering grounds in Central America, showing up almost anywhere in North America. One such wanderer made its way to Loudoun in late June 2011, observed by a group of atlasers at the future White's Ford Regional Park. In mid-June 2012, another was found nearby during a Virginia Society of Ornithology foray. This species prefers grassland or farmland with scattered trees, typically perching in the open on fence posts or utility wires.

Though they have a uniquely long, deeply forked tail, Scissor-tailed Flycatchers are closely related to kingbirds and share their aggressive nature when it comes to protecting the nest. Their tails help them maneuver expertly in mid-air, catching insects on the wing. Adults are pale gray with blackish wings and salmon-pink flanks; juveniles have shorter tails and lack the salmon flanks. Numbers have declined over the past 50 years, according to the North American BBS, due in part to habitat loss and herbicide use.

Written by Spring Ligi

OLIVE-SIDED FLYCATCHER

Contopus cooperi

Occurrence: rare migrant

Southerly migration period: September 6 – 24

Northerly migration period: fewer than 5 atlas sightings, see account for details

This distinctive flycatcher is often found perched conspicuously on the very top of a snag, or high dead branch, where it may be heard singing its burry *quick, three beers*. It is brownish or olive gray on its back, extending to form a "vest" in front, over an otherwise dull white throat, breast, and belly; it sports conspicuous white tufts on its flanks. It preys on flying insects, sallying from its solitary perch to which it returns. Reported only twice during Atlas 2 on its north-bound migration (late April and mid-May), it was found more often on its south-bound flight in September, but remains a local rarity.

The Olive-sided Flycatcher is a boreal nester, preferring burned-over forest and relatively open areas. It has seen a significant population decline over the past 30 years throughout its range, listed as "Near Threatened" by the IUCN and considered an at-risk species. Habitat loss is thought to be a major contributor to its decline.

Written by Chris White

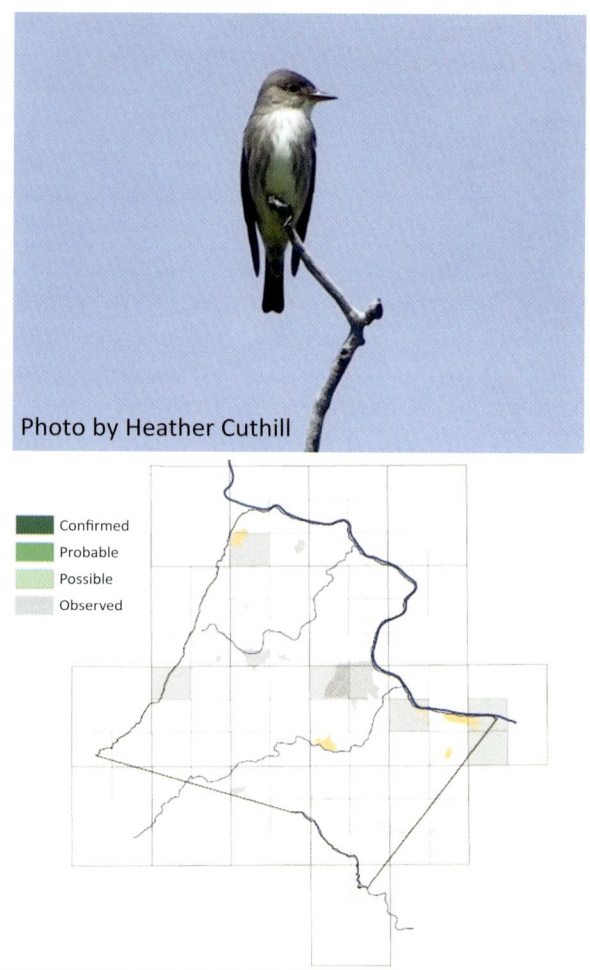

Photo by Heather Cuthill

Confirmed
Probable
Possible
Observed

EASTERN WOOD-PEWEE

Contopus virens

Occurrence: common breeder and migrant

Earliest breeding confirmation: May 23, parent entering/exiting nest site or on nest (ON)

Latest breeding confirmation: August 25, recently fledged young (FL)

An oft-repeated, whistled *Pee-a-wee…Pee-weee* is frequently the first indication that an Eastern Wood-Pewee is nearby. It announces itself tirelessly, singing plaintively from before dawn, throughout the day, and often into the late evening. Look and listen for this species in forests, parks, and the edges of woodlots throughout our area, in both suburban and rural locales. Interestingly, Cornell's All About Birds website (2017) notes that they usually avoid streams. Listen carefully, and you may even hear multiple pewees at once, each declaring ownership of adjoining territories.

Photo by Gerco Hoogeweg

Eastern Wood-Pewees are slim and gray, with a long-winged, long-tailed overall appearance. The dark wings show obvious pale wingbars. Their underparts are off-white, showing little or no yellow. They have a plain gray face and no eyering, creating a somewhat blank expression. The lack of an eyering can be helpful in distinguishing them from most other flycatchers. Their lower mandible is typically orange or yellow. They are slightly larger than the Empidonax species encountered in Loudoun, but similar in size to the Eastern Phoebe. Sexes are indistinguishable in the field.

EASTERN WOOD-PEWEE (continued)

Pewees exhibit prototypical flycatcher behavior, sitting upright on exposed perches in forest clearings and edges. When not singing, they sally out frequently to snatch flying insects, often returning to a favorite perch. They are known to sally out after bugs more than once a minute while feeding young. They are confiding birds, not overly concerned with nearby humans while they go about their business. While the birds themselves can be easy to locate, their lichen-covered nests are typically well camouflaged, easily mistaken for a knot on the branch. Males bring food to the nest while the females incubate the eggs and guard young nestlings.

Eastern Wood-Pewees are one of the later spring migrants, with arrival peaking around May 10; most are gone by early October. They winter in South America using a variety of forest types and overgrown habitats. While not a species of significant conservation concern, their numbers have dropped by about 50% in the last 50 years, for reasons not totally clear but potentially including degradation of forest habitats in both North and South America. Still, this species was found in virtually all blocks during Atlas 2; 71 of these blocks offered evidence of breeding. You have a good chance of encountering this bird during a late spring walk in Loudoun woods.

Written by Bruce Hill

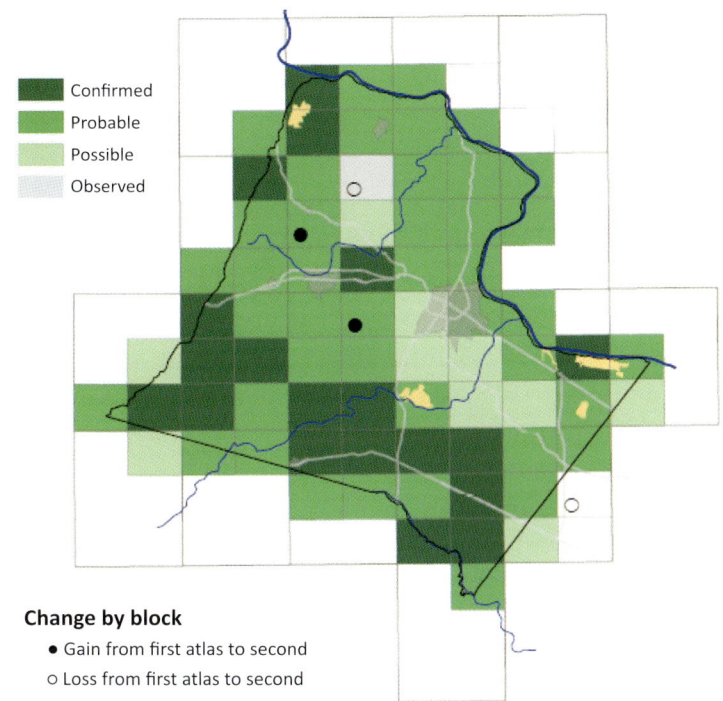

Confirmed
Probable
Possible
Observed

Change by block
● Gain from first atlas to second
○ Loss from first atlas to second

Photo by Tony LePrieur

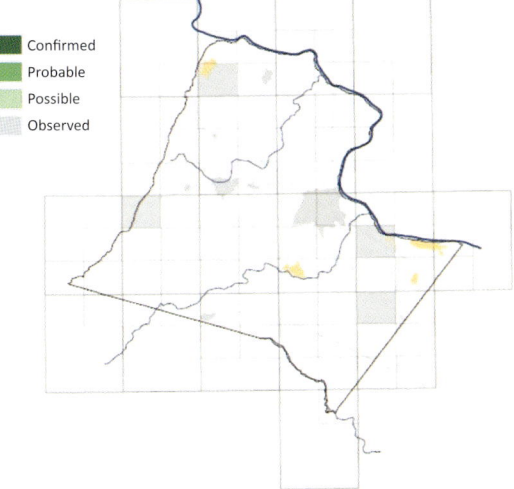

Confirmed
Probable
Possible
Observed

YELLOW-BELLIED FLYCATCHER
Empidonax flaviventris

Occurrence: rare migrant

Southerly migration period: August 31 – September 19

Northerly migration period: no atlas sightings, see account for details

Distinguished from Loudoun's other Empidonax flycatchers by its yellow underparts, the Yellow-bellied Flycatcher is yellow-olive above with a white eyering and two whitish wingbars. This small flycatcher prefers shade over sun, breeding in boreal forests and bogs where it nests on the ground. It winters in the dense rainforests and shaded coffee plantations of Central America and can be found in the understory of deciduous forests during migration. Atlas data shows this bird passing through Loudoun during a short timeframe in the fall (5 sightings in 4 blocks). The Yellow-bellied Flycatcher is a late spring migrant and though not documented as such during the atlas, there have been mid- to late May reports throughout the broader region. Numbers of spring migrants are noticeably smaller than in the fall.

Typical of flycatchers, the Yellow-bellied Flycatcher catches insects in mid-air or gleans them from foliage, often watching for prey from a low to mid-level perch. Population trends appear stable but habitat loss, especially on the wintering grounds, poses a threat.

Written by Spring Ligi

ACADIAN FLYCATCHER
Empidonax virescens

Occurrence: common breeder and migrant

Earliest breeding confirmation: June 9, parent entering/exiting nest site or on nest (ON)

Latest breeding confirmation: August 25, recently fledged young (FL)

In woods throughout Loudoun in spring and early summer, especially near rivers or streams, the emphatic, two-part *pit-SEET* of the Acadian Flycatcher is hard to miss. Spotting the source of the song can be more difficult. This bird sits very still at heights from eye level up to 50 feet in the forest, vocalizing frequently throughout the day, but doing little else to betray its presence. A patient observer may be able to hone in on the song and spot this

Photo ©Dick Rowe

small flycatcher when it raises its head to call or darts out to catch a flying insect, returning to the same perch. Acadians also glean insects from leaves.

Like other Empidonax flycatchers, the Acadian is hard to identify by appearance alone. While small, it is slightly larger with more greenish on its back and crown than the other Empid species. It appears bulkier than the similar but slimmer Willow Flycatcher. It has two distinct wingbars and a strong white eyering. Its underside is pale with a slight greenish tint. It has a long tail, and a longer wing projection than most other Empids. Both sexes are similar. Its overall greenish coloration blends extremely well with the deciduous woodlands it favors. Habitat and song can help greatly in identification.

Atlas data shows Acadians tend to arrive earlier (late April) and stay longer (late September) in our area than the Willow Flycatcher. This common breeder was reported in 66 of the 73 blocks; 63 blocks had evidence of breeding. It builds a shallow nest with dangling streamers in the outer branches of a tree, well off the ground and often over water, and lays one to four eggs. Like other flycatchers, Acadians can suffer cowbird parasitism, but seem better at avoiding becoming unwitting hosts than other species in the same woods (Audubon 2017). Nests in smaller, fragmented woodlands are more likely to be targeted by cowbirds than those in larger wooded tracts.

Given its preference for lowland deciduous forests, the Acadian Flycatcher has the most southerly distribution of the eastern Empids. Loudoun is close to the northern edge of its breeding range. Acadians winter in lower Central America and northern South America, retaining a preference for woodland habitats. Although this species has declined modestly over the past 50 years, its population remains stable, with an estimated global breeding population of around 5 million birds (Rosenberg et al. 2016).

Written by Bruce Hill

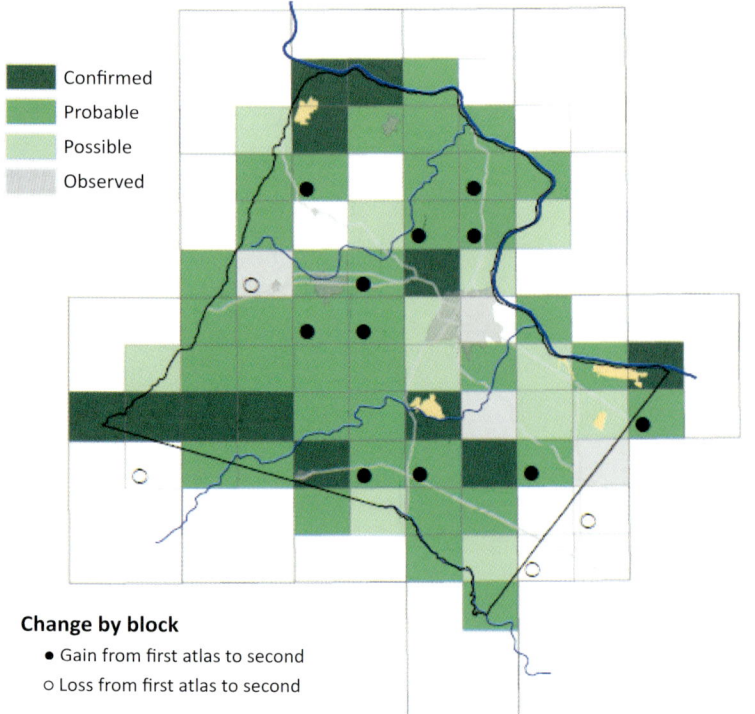

Confirmed
Probable
Possible
Observed

Change by block
- Gain from first atlas to second
- Loss from first atlas to second

ALDER FLYCATCHER
Empidonax alnorum

Occurrence: rare migrant

Southerly/northerly migration periods: fewer than 5 atlas sightings, see account for details

Photo ©Dick Rowe

Flycatchers often pose identification problems and the Alder Flycatcher is no exception. This species is so similar to the Willow Flycatcher that it was considered the same species until the 1970s. Both species are brownish-olive with two white wingbars. Song provides the key to proper identification. Alder Flycatchers sing a burry *rree-beer* while Willow Flycatchers sing a wheezy *fitz-bew*. Flycatchers, unlike many other birds, hatch knowing their song; they don't learn it from their parents.

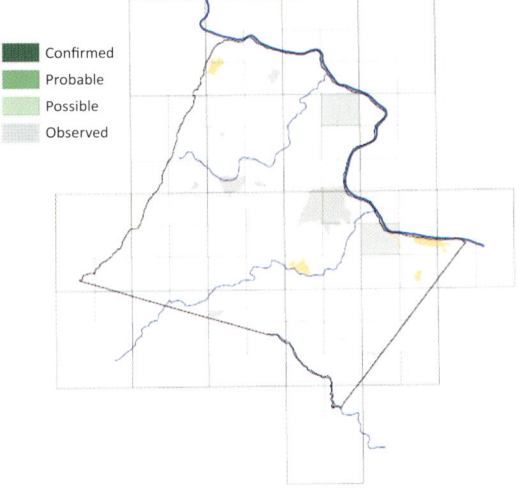

Alder Flycatchers prefer wet thickets of alder, maple, and birch as well as wood margins, hedgerows, and scrub where they consume mainly insects. They breed in Alaska and Canada's boreal forest (well north of where most Willow Flycatchers breed) and winter in the tropics of South America. Loudoun provides stop-over habitat during migration, with reports of Alder Flycatchers at Bles Park in May 2010 and 2011 and the Waterford area in June 2012. According to the North American BBS, numbers are stable in the U.S., but declined by about 44% in Canada over the past 5 decades.

Written by Spring Ligi

Photo ©Dick Rowe

WILLOW FLYCATCHER
Empidonax traillii

Occurrence: uncommon breeder and migrant

Earliest breeding confirmation: June 15, parent carrying food or feeding young (CF)

Latest breeding confirmation: July 18, parent carrying food or feeding young (CF)

The Willow Flycatcher favors relatively open field and wetland habitats interspersed with second growth or small trees, especially willows, in which it nests. It is a bird that likes open spaces away from human activity; most of the atlas observations came from the less developed western half of the county, with multiple reports from places like the Dulles Greenway Wetlands, Waterford, and Bluemont. Breeding indicators such as singing males, territorial behavior, and food carrying were noted in 34 blocks and approximately 70% of the total occurrences.

One of the confusingly similar group of Empidonax flycatchers, the Willow is a small and relatively slim bird, brown to olive green above, whitish below, with a slight yellowish wash on its belly, white wingbars, and a long tail. It shows little or no eyering, less so than most other Empid species. Males and females are similar in appearance, and like most flycatchers have an upright posture. Their behavior is also typical of other flycatchers, feeding on a variety of insects plucked out of the air or from the leaves of trees and shrubs. They can often be spotted on a prominent perch,

WILLOW FYCATCHER (continued)

singing (females are known to sing occasionally, too) or sallying out to catch flying insects and returning to the same spot. They are often heard before they are seen, especially in May and June, giving a distinctive, rolling *fitz-bew* vocalization. This two-note song, first buzzy note rising, second lower, is typically repeated every 5-10 seconds. Their song is the best way to distinguish them from other Empid flycatchers.

The Willow Flycatcher is one of two Empids that nest with regularity in Loudoun (the other being the Acadian Flycatcher). Willows arrive fairly late in spring, typically mid-May, and quickly establish their territories. Females build the nest, but both parents help feed the young. By early September, they depart for the warmer climes of Central and northern South America. Like many species, the Willow Flycatcher's breeding range appears to be shifting farther north, likely in response to climate change. It may eventually become less frequent in Loudoun, which is at the southern edge of its historic nesting region. The Willow Flycatchers seen in Loudoun are part of a healthy eastern population, but a subspecies in the western U.S., the Southwestern Willow Flycatcher, is federally listed as endangered.

Written by Bruce Hill

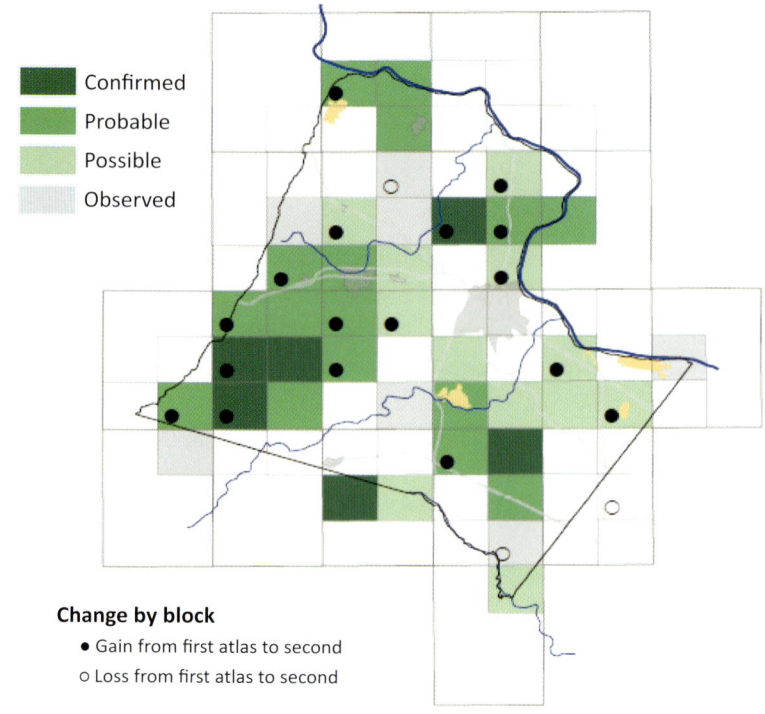

Confirmed
Probable
Possible
Observed

Change by block
- Gain from first atlas to second
- Loss from first atlas to second

Photo by Dave Boltz

Confirmed
Probable
Possible
Observed

LEAST FLYCATCHER
Empidonax minimus

Occurrence: occasional migrant

Southerly migration period: September 6 – 22

Northerly migration period: fewer than 5 atlas sightings, see account for details

The Least Flycatcher is the most likely non-breeding Empidonax flycatcher encountered in Loudoun. This species was noted 11 times during the atlas, mostly in September and May during peak migration. One late July sighting may have been an early-dispersing bird from nearby Appalachian breeding habitat. This species prefers mixed or deciduous forests across the northern U.S. and Canada, often nesting in close proximity to one another. They winter in Mexico and Central America. The Least Flycatcher is gray above, with a white eyering, two white wingbars, a grayish chest, and a light yellow wash on its belly. About the size of a chickadee, it has a large-headed, long-tailed appearance. Its short *che-bek* call is the best clue to identification. They are aggressive for their size, often chasing much larger birds. According to the IUCN, they remain globally common, with a breeding population of about 33 million, but declined by over 53% between 1970 and 2014. Trends point downward, largely due to habitat loss and forest fragmentation.

Written by Bruce Hill

EASTERN PHOEBE
Sayornis phoebe

Occurrence: common breeder and migrant, occasional winter resident

Earliest breeding confirmation: April 1, adult carrying nesting material or nest building (NB)

Latest breeding confirmation: August 27, recently fledged young (FL)

The Eastern Phoebe is one of the first migrants to return in spring, arriving in early March, and remains until late fall, with the occasional individual lingering into winter months. It favors open wooded areas like parks, yards, or forest edges, often near water. This robust flycatcher is about the size of a bluebird although less plump, and is brownish gray above, with its darker crown a distinctive feature. Its

Photo ©Dick Rowe

underside is off-white, with grayish flanks. Perhaps its most distinctive feature is its habit of pumping its tail while sitting on low but prominent perches, from where it flies out to snatch a wide variety of flying insects. It will also less frequently eat berries or seeds.

The Eastern Phoebe calls its own name: an emphatic and raspy *fee-bee*, sometimes with slight variations (*fee-bee...fee-blee*). This vocalization is usually given repeatedly, with 1- to 2-second intervals between phrases. It is heard most regularly in the spring, when the male arrives to establish a territory. Females arrive a couple weeks later than the males, and they vocalize much less frequently once nesting begins. Nests are built and young raised under cover – beneath bridges or in culverts, under natural rock overhangs, or in sheds, garages, or under building eaves. They may use suitable nest boxes.

Only the female builds the nest, a sturdy design of mud, grasses, and moss. These durable nests are sometimes reused in subsequent years. Their long nesting period often allows them to raise two broods per year. Their propensity to set up housekeeping near humans makes them one of our better known flycatchers, and also one whose breeding is relatively easy to confirm; of the 72 blocks where they were observed, breeding was confirmed in 62. A significant number of these confirmations consisted of nest building, birds on nests, or nests with young.

The hardiest of the flycatchers in our region, Loudoun is at the northern edge of this species' year-round range. It was observed in small numbers on 17 of the past 20 Central Loudoun CBCs. It is a widespread breeder throughout the eastern U.S. and Canada, wintering in the southern U.S. and Mexico. Eastern Phoebe populations are stable, with numbers estimated at 33 million (PIF 2016). Their affinity for nesting in man-made structures may help to counteract other negative pressures on these familiar and engaging birds.

Written by Bruce Hill

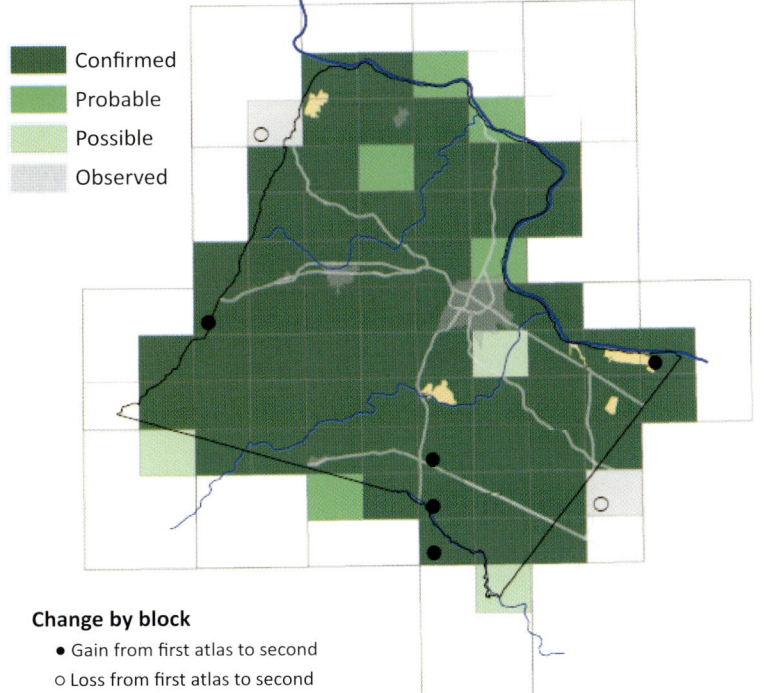

- Confirmed
- Probable
- Possible
- Observed

Change by block
- ● Gain from first atlas to second
- ○ Loss from first atlas to second

LOGGERHEAD SHRIKE
Lanius ludovicianus

Photo by Dave Boltz

Occurrence: rare breeder and year-round resident

Earliest/latest breeding confirmations: fewer than 5 atlas sightings, see account for details

A threatened species, the Loggerhead Shrike was confirmed as breeding in just 1 atlas block, Leesburg 5, in May 2009. The only other documented breeding evidence was a pair found in the same block and year (probable breeding). This represents a notable loss of 7 blocks from Atlas 1. The species prefers open country with scattered trees and shrubs. It is disappearing along with the farm-land, pastures, parks, and hedgerows where it finds the insects, small rodents, and birds on which it feeds, as well as cover for breeding. It perches on trees and shrubs, poles, fences, and utility wires from where it swoops down onto its prey. It is known as the "butcher bird" because it impales the prey on sharp objects like thorns to cache for later.

The shrike's position in the passerine order is unsettled. It is a unique combination of passerine and predator. It has the large, slightly hooked bill of the predator, set in a large head relative to its body size, giving rise to another nick-name, "block-head." But it lacks the talons and strong feet the raptor uses on its prey. Similar to, but slightly smaller than, the Northern Shrike, the Loggerhead has medium- to dark-gray upperparts which contrast with the pale gray to whitish underparts. The bird's bill is black, and it sports a black mask, running back from the bill over the eyes. The wings and tail are black; the former sport white patches, the latter white edging.

An early breeder, the Loggerhead Shrike often builds its nest in thorny trees or shrubs and raises one or two broods per year. In Loudoun, this shrike is more likely to be found during the colder months. One or two individuals were reported on just under half of the Central Loudoun CBCs up until 2012; they have not been reported since.

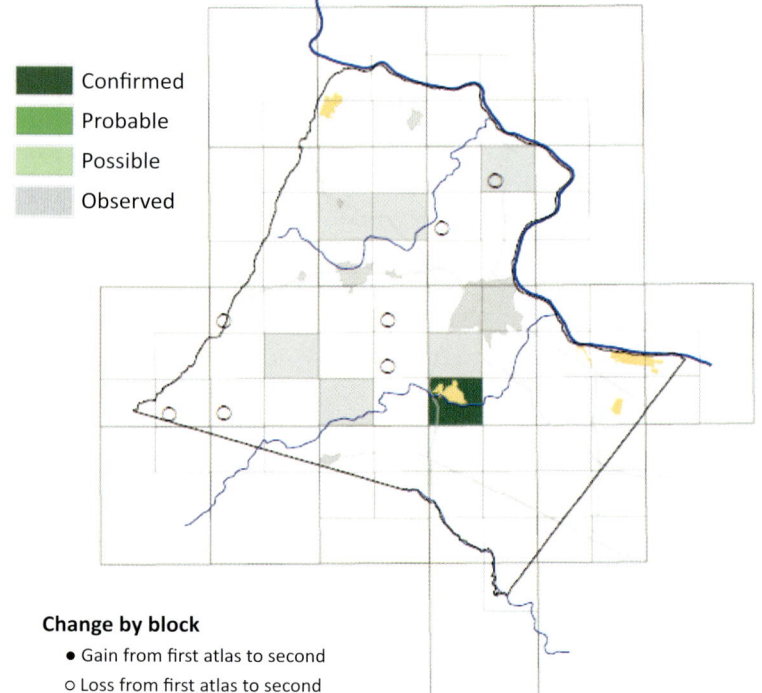

Confirmed
Probable
Possible
Observed

Change by block
● Gain from first atlas to second
○ Loss from first atlas to second

The Loggerhead Shrike's range includes much of North America, though it is much easier to observe in the southern U.S. compared to the Northeast and upper Midwest where it is becoming increasingly rare. In addition to habitat loss through changes in land use, pesticides and other biocides may negatively impact the species via its insect foods. The species is listed as endangered, threatened, or of special concern in several different states. They were shot as predators earlier in the 20th century.

Written by Chris White

NORTHERN SHRIKE
Lanius borealis

Occurrence: vagrant

Earliest/latest seasonal sightings: fewer than 5 atlas sightings, see account for details

This unexpected visitor in Loudoun was seen only once during the atlas (January 2013 at Banshee Reeks Nature Preserve), well south of its typical winter range (mainly the northern half of the U.S.). The Northern Shrike experiences irregular irruptions southward when food is scarce in its normal habitat. They prefer open fields, hedgerows, and overgrown scrublands. In summer, they nest in low trees or shrubs in the upper reaches of Canada and Alaska. Populations appear stable but should be monitored closely.

Like its cousin, the slightly smaller, somewhat less rare Loggerhead Shrike, the Northern Shrike feeds on rodents, small birds, and large insects. Prey may be impaled on thorns or barbed wire for later use. Northern Shrikes often sit atop an isolated tree or powerline, scanning for prey. Their distinctive black mask, wings, and tail, gray crown and back, and white underside shout "shrike" (once you rule out Northern Mockingbird). Note the hooked beak and the large-headed look. Distinguishing which species of shrike requires a good field guide.

Written by Bruce Hill

Photo by Gerco Hoogeweg

Confirmed
Probable
Possible
Observed

WHITE-EYED VIREO
Vireo griseus

Occurrence: uncommon breeder and migrant

Earliest breeding confirmation: April 25, adult carrying nesting material or nest building (NB)

Latest breeding confirmation: September 15, recently fledged young (FL)

While fairly uncommon in our area, this is exacerbated by how difficult this skulking vireo is to spot. Reported in roughly three-quarters of the atlas blocks, the White-eyed Vireo is a bird that is much more frequently heard than seen. It prefers to remain under cover in overgrown fields, thickets, and second-growth habitats where it forages deliberately for insects (caterpillars are a favorite) and the occasional berry. It will, however,

Photo by Dave Boltz

sometimes emerge from hiding to scold birders who make sufficiently annoying squeaks or pishing sounds. This small, compact bird has a gray crown and nape, yellow spectacles, thick, short bill, white eye (although dark in young birds), and white throat, chest, and belly, with yellowish flanks. Its back is olive, and its dark wings contrast with two sharply defined white wingbars. Its rather short, dark tail is edged with white (sometimes yellow). It sings loudly and frequently, a variable jumble of short, raspy notes that typically begin and end with a sharp *chik* note. Its song might be represented as *Chik-purr-e-o-chik*.

The White-eyed Vireo breeds in the eastern U.S., as far west as the Great Plains and north to the southern Great Lakes

WHITE-EYED VIREO (continued)

and Massachusetts. It is a year-round resident along the southern Atlantic and Gulf Coasts of the U.S. and into Mexico, and winters in similar scrub habitat (and mangroves) south to the Yucatan peninsula, Honduras, and Belize, as well as the Bahamas and Cuba. Found in our area from mid-April through late October, they are strictly migrants and summer residents during their relatively lengthy breeding season. This bird builds its well-concealed nest in small trees or shrubs, most often quite low to the ground. Still, they are quite susceptible to cowbird parasitism. Their three to five eggs (hopefully their own) are incubated by both parents for up to 15 days, and the young then leave the next 9-11 days after hatching. In our region, they typically raise one brood per year, though in the south they often produce two.

Confirmed
Probable
Possible
Observed

Change by block
● Gain from first atlas to second
○ Loss from first atlas to second

The White-eyed Vireo population appears relatively stable, with a breeding population of about 19 million birds (PIF 2017). Given their strong preference for deciduous scrub habitat, which is rarely well-protected (in Loudoun, think overgrown fields that are destined for development), they are locally susceptible to habitat loss, but on the whole remain quite common and have recently expanded their range slightly northward.

Written by Bruce Hill

Photo ©Dick Rowe

YELLOW-THROATED VIREO
Vireo flavifrons

Occurrence: uncommon breeder and migrant

Earliest breeding confirmation: May 11, parent entering/exiting nest site or on nest (ON)

Latest breeding confirmation: August 11, parent carrying food or feeding young (CF)

The Yellow-throated Vireo, perhaps unsurprisingly, sports a bright yellow throat and breast and yellow spectacles that contrast vividly with its olive crown, face, and nape. This colorful front end blends into clean white flanks, belly, and vent. Its dark wings show two pronounced white wingbars. Its bill is short, thick, and blunt-tipped, typical of vireos and very unlike the thin, pointed bills of most warblers. Its bill, as well as its unstreaked flanks, are helpful field marks that can help distinguish the Yellow-throated Vireo from its near-doppelganger, the Pine Warbler.

This most colorful of the vireos breeds almost entirely within the eastern U.S., with less than 1% of its population nesting further north in southeastern Canada. It prefers deciduous or mixed forest edges and riparian woodlands, particularly those with mature oaks, and shows a very strong preference for unbroken forest tracts of 250 acres or more. It feeds slowly and deliberately in the mid- and upper canopy, eating a variety of insects and occasionally also small fruits. Such habits can make it difficult to observe, but territorial males often betray their presence by singing persistently, a low-pitched, husky two or three notes that rise and fall, sometimes described as *Three-A? Three-a* (or in Canada, *Three-eh!*).

YELLOW-THROATED VIREO (continued)

This bird builds a cup-shaped nest in the forked outer branches of tall trees, typically 20-40 feet off the ground. Incubation takes about 15 days. Once the young hatch, they are fed by both parents until fledging, again in about 15 days. Interestingly, the parents will typically split up the young birds and each will care separately for their part of the brood after leaving the nest. Outside of the breeding season, the Yellow-throated Vireo can be quite solitary, migrating alone and aggressively excluding others of its own species from its winter feeding territory. It will however often associate in mixed flocks that include various other species. It winters in the Bahamas, Cuba, the Mexican Yucatan, Central America, and far-northern South America (primarily Colombia).

The Yellow-throated Vireo population has been generally stable over the past 50 years, with declines in the Northeast offset by growth in the upper Midwest. This may be at least partially explained by forest fragmentation in some regions. In Loudoun, it was reported as a potential breeding species in 31 blocks, spread widely throughout the county, and was confirmed in 4 blocks. It is found in our area from mid-April through September.

Written by Bruce Hill

Confirmed
Probable
Possible
Observed

Change by block
● Gain from first atlas to second
○ Loss from first atlas to second

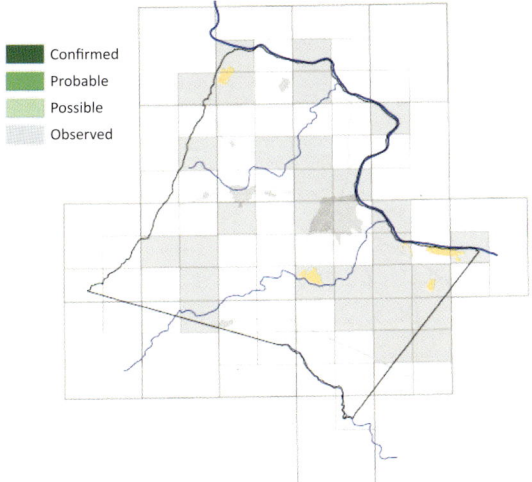

Photo by Dave Boltz

Confirmed
Probable
Possible
Observed

BLUE-HEADED VIREO
Vireo solitarius

Occurrence: occasional migrant

Southerly migration period: September 2 – October 31

Northerly migration period: April 9 – May 11

This relatively large, handsome vireo has obvious white spectacles, a blue-gray head, white throat and breast, double wingbars, and yellowish flanks. Its song is similar to the Red-eyed Vireo, with slower, higher, and sweeter phrases. Males sing frequently even during migration. The Blue-headed Vireo prefers to forage in the mid- to upper canopy, moving slowly and methodically among the branches and occasionally sallying out after flying insects.

Found in 40% of the atlas blocks, the Blue-headed Vireo is a non-breeder in Loudoun, but nests close by in the cooler forests of the Virginia and West Virginia mountains, and from Pennsylvania north across much of Canada. This species' nests often fall victim to nest predators like raccoons, Blue Jays, and squirrels, and suffer from cowbird parasitism. However, populations have increased in recent decades, perhaps as eastern forests have regenerated to provide more suitable breeding habitat. The species winters in Mexico and parts of upper Central America, though many birds overwinter in the southeastern and Gulf Coast states.

Written by Bruce Hill

PHILADELPHIA VIREO
Vireo philadelphicus

Occurrence: rare migrant

Southerly migration period: September 2 – October 2

Northerly migration period: fewer than 5 atlas sightings, see account for details

This small, fairly plain vireo breeds far to our north, mostly in Canada, nesting primarily in deciduous woodlands. It passes through our area in small numbers during migration. They are easily overlooked, as their song is similar to the common Red-eyed Vireo, and their habit of feeding high in treetops makes them difficult to identify. There were only 6 atlas reports, all but 1 in the fall. Smaller and shorter-tailed and -billed than the Red-eyed Vireo, this species has a black eye stripe and white eyebrow, gray crown, yellow-washed chest, olive-green back and wings, and no wingbars. The Philadelphia Vireo moves about actively as it searches for food, sometimes hanging upside down chickadee-like from the tips of twigs as it hunts for caterpillars or other prey. In fall, it frequently eats berries as it prepares for southward migration. It winters primarily in Mexico and Central America. While overall breeding populations are relatively small (about 4 million), its numbers have remained stable or increased slightly over the last 50 years.

Photo by ©Dick Rowe

Confirmed
Probable
Possible
Observed

Written by Bruce Hill

Photo by ©Dick Rowe

WARBLING VIREO
Vireo gilvus

Occurrence: occasional breeder, uncommon migrant

Earliest breeding confirmation: May 7, adult carrying nesting material or nest building (NB)

Latest breeding confirmation: June 8, parent entering/exiting nest site or on nest (ON)

The Warbling Vireo is a medium-sized, plain vireo, lacking distinctive markings such as spectacles or wingbars. It is most often discovered from its song which is complex, made up of an undulating pattern of warbling notes with a sweet yet slightly burry quality. Like other vireos it sings a lot, even when nesting. When seen, the Warbling Vireo can be confused with its rarer cousin, the Philadelphia Vireo, but its unique song dispels doubts.

The species breeds regularly in Loudoun, but generally in small numbers since Loudoun lies toward the southern edge of its large North American breeding range. It was confirmed as breeding in 2 atlas blocks, both in the riverside habitat the species favors. It can also be present around ponds and lakes. In our area, the Warbling Vireo is more often found during migration, arriving in mid-April and leaving in late September. Twice as many migrants were reported in the spring as the fall, though this may be because the species sings during spring migration, making it easier to detect. The Warbling Vireo is insectivorous and can be found gleaning its food in the upperparts of broad-leaf trees, both on woodland edges and interiors, where they also build their cup-shaped nest. Both sexes, but mainly the female, help

WARBLING VIREO (continued)

raise their young to the fledging stage.

Apart from its song, this bird is among the dullest of the vireos. It is a gray bird with brownish or olive-greenish tones in its upperparts, especially after molts. The underparts are whitish, sometimes with a yellowish wash, which may contribute to confusion with the Philadelphia Vireo, whose underparts are brighter yellow. The Warbling Vireo's facial pattern is also less well defined, having a faint gray eyeline and pale lures, and the tail is longer.

According to the North American BBS, Warbling Vireo numbers have increased slightly over the past 5 decades. These results are supported by a net gain of 6 atlas blocks from Atlas 1 to 2. Herbicide use, human changes in riverside habitat, and replacement of deciduous trees with conifers may negatively impact the Warbling Vireo. Changing land use patterns are also thought to benefit both nest predators and parasitic Brown-headed Cowbirds, which can lower breeding productivity. Preserving habitat throughout their Mexican/Central American wintering range is important since this area is significantly smaller than their breeding range.

Written by Chris White

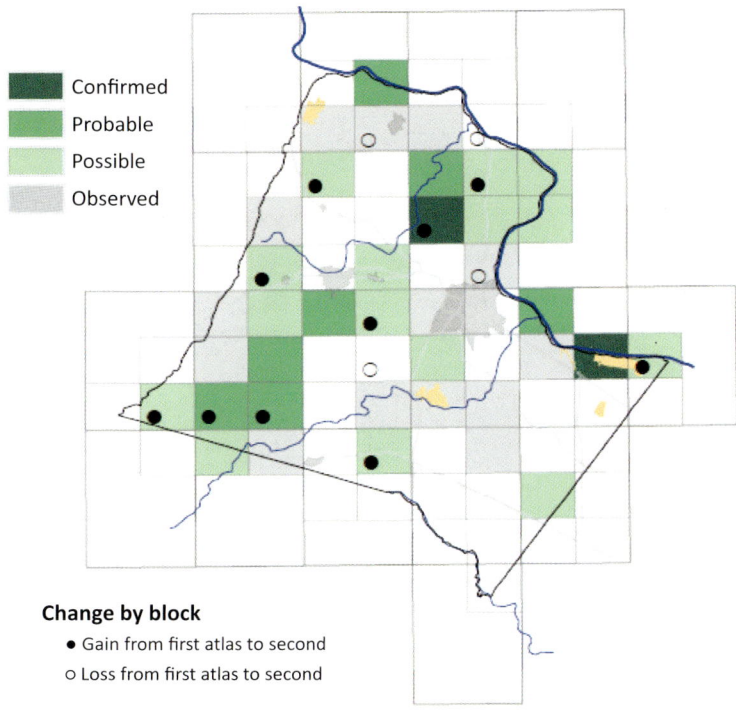

Confirmed
Probable
Possible
Observed

Change by block
● Gain from first atlas to second
○ Loss from first atlas to second

Photo by ©Dick Rowe

RED-EYED VIREO
Vireo olivaceus

Occurrence: common breeder and migrant

Earliest breeding confirmation: June 13, recently fledged young (FL)

Latest breeding confirmation: August 27, parent carrying food or feeding young (CF)

The Red-eyed Vireo is a common bird throughout its huge range, stretching across the entire eastern half of the U.S. and throughout the boreal forests of Canada from the Atlantic to Pacific. The 2016 PIF Landbird Conservation Plan estimated the population at 130 million, making it one of the most numerous breeding birds of the eastern forests. By late spring, it can seem as if most of them have settled in Loudoun. They sing tirelessly, a sing-song repetition of several short phrases given throughout the day. While their forest habitat can make them hard to see, a patient observer can often spot them moving slowly through the mid- and upper canopy in search of caterpillars and other insect prey, which comprises most of their spring and summer diet. They rely more heavily on berries later in the fall, and continue to consume fruit and berries during their winters in the lowland tropics of Central and South America.

Red-eyed Vireos breed in a wide variety of wooded habitats, from parks and suburban yards to mixed woodlands. They prefer open woods with smaller understory trees, often near streams, clearings, or edges. Nests are placed in small to medium-sized shrubs or trees, typically 5-30 feet above the ground. The female builds the nest, a small cup

RED-EYED VIREO (continued)

attached at the rim between the forks of a small branch. Typically four eggs are laid. Once hatched, both parents feed the nestlings for 10-12 days until they fledge. If they are successful in raising their own young, they continue to associate in family groups for another few weeks. However, their nests are often parasitized; it is not rare to see a Red-eyed Vireo parent feeding a much larger cowbird fledgling.

Red-eyed Vireos are quite plain overall, largely olive brown above and white below. They do in fact have red eyes, which can be seen at close range but are not their most obvious feature. Their distinct facial pattern, a dark line through the eye with a white eyebrow above and a dark cap above that, is often easier to see. They are one of the larger vireos, with a long tail and a proportionally large bill.

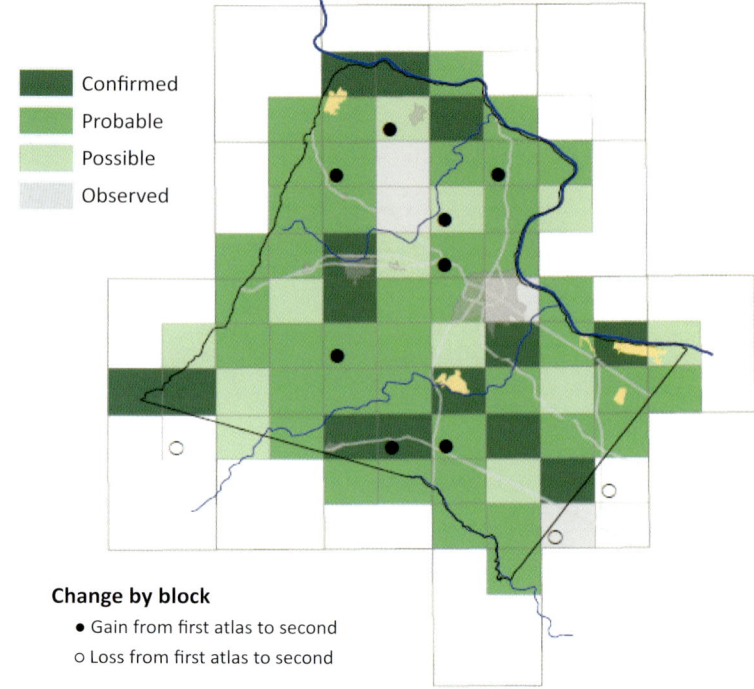

Confirmed
Probable
Possible
Observed

Change by block
● Gain from first atlas to second
○ Loss from first atlas to second

Found in Loudoun from mid-April through early October, peak migration months are May and September. If you do not see or hear a Red-eyed Vireo on your next spring or summer walk in the Loudoun woods, you must not be trying!

Written by Bruce Hill

Photo by Ian Richardson

BLUE JAY
Cyanocitta cristata

Occurrence: abundant breeder, year-round resident, and migrant

Earliest breeding confirmation: March 25, adult carrying nesting material or nest building (NB)

Latest breeding confirmation: August 26, recently fledged young (FL)

Though often seen as a bully of the bird world, upon closer inspection the aggressive and noisy Blue Jay is a truly fascinating bird. Blue Jays make a variety of sounds; the harsh *jay! jay!* call being the most familiar along with their impressive imitation of a Red-shouldered Hawk's scream. They show a softer side when singing their "whisper song," consisting of an assortment of clicks, whirrs, and whines. Larger than a robin but smaller than a crow, the Blue Jay is blue above and white below. The wings and tail are barred with black, and it sports a distinctive crest and black necklace, making it one of our more attractive birds.

Blue Jays are often found along forest edges, especially near oak trees, as well as city parks or wooded suburbs. They are a familiar sight at feeders and birdbaths. This omnivore forages in trees, shrubs, and along the ground, eating mostly nuts (especially acorns), seeds, and berries which they cache for later use. They sometimes forget to return to a cache site, assisting with the spread of oak trees and other plants. Blue Jays occasionally eat insects, birds' eggs, small rodents, baby birds, and carrion. Found year-round east of the Rocky Mountains in the U.S. and in southern Canada, populations are healthy and their range is expanding westward.

BLUE JAY (continued)

These intelligent birds have complex social systems with tight family bonds. A pair usually mates for life and remains together throughout the year. During the breeding season, a bulky nest is built of twigs, leaves, grass, rootlets, and sometimes mud about 10-25 feet above the ground. One brood of two to seven eggs is raised by both parents. Young are fed for at least a month (sometimes two) after fledging. Blue Jays use their crest to communicate with family or flock members; the higher the crest, the higher the aggression level. They lower their crests when feeding peacefully or tending to nestlings.

The Blue Jay made the top 25 list of breeding species for Atlas 2, with breeding behavior documented in 96% of the blocks (compared to 83% in Atlas 1). Though breeding and winter behavior are well studied, migration remains a mystery. Some jays remain year-round throughout their range, while others migrate in flocks. Both juveniles and adults may migrate; some migrate only every other year. It's a pattern that only the Blue Jays seem to know!

Written by Spring Ligi

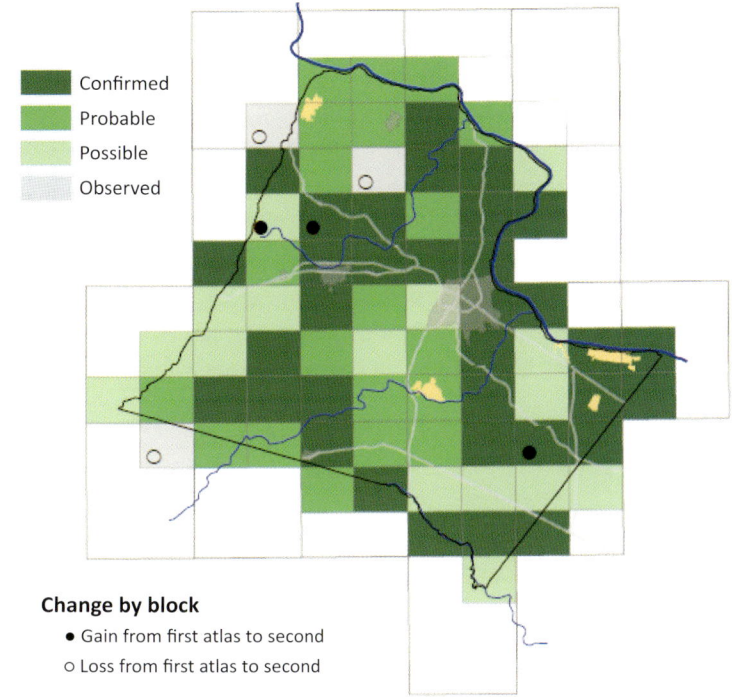

Confirmed
Probable
Possible
Observed

Change by block
● Gain from first atlas to second
○ Loss from first atlas to second

Photo ©Dick Rowe

AMERICAN CROW
Corvus brachyrhynchos

Occurrence: abundant breeder and year-round resident

Earliest breeding confirmation: March 30, adult carrying nesting material or nest building (NB)

Latest breeding confirmation: August 17, parent carrying food or feeding young (CF)

The American Crow is a bird you either love or hate. Some people are filled with admiration for its intelligence and resourcefulness while others are irritated by the noise and mess of this communal rooster. Found year-round throughout most of the U.S., this highly adaptable species will live just about anywhere except deserts. They use farmlands, woodlands, fields, marshes, parks, golf courses, yards, and town centers, just to name a few. Their adaptability extends to their diet, which ranges from seeds, berries, and insects to small mammals, fish, and carrion. Flocks can be found around dumpsters and landfills. The American Crow is crafty and quick to take advantage of new and unusual food sources. They sometimes work together to steal food from other animals or may follow adult birds to find their nests and eat their eggs or nestlings.

This familiar large, all-black bird has a slight gloss to the plumage (depending on the lighting) and a relatively long, thick bill. Their loud, distinctive *caw!* is often an easy giveaway that American Crows are in the area and differentiates them from the similar-looking Fish Crow, which produces a more nasal call.

American Crows often stay together in year-round family groups composed of a breeding pair and offspring from

AMERICAN CROW (continued)

previous seasons. The offspring sometimes assist the pair with nest building and feeding the young. The nest, often hidden in an evergreen or deciduous tree, consists of a bulky basket of sticks, twigs, and bark lined with grass, moss, and feathers. Four to six eggs are laid; the young leave the nest about 4-5 weeks after hatching. Most remain with the family group and do not breed for at least 2 years. One or two broods are raised per breeding season. In winter, they gather and sleep in communal roosts which may become very large (tens of thousands in some places). A high count of 1,664 birds was documented on the 2012 Central Loudoun CBC.

Found in nearly every type of Loudoun habitat, the American Crow's adaptability and willingness to use man-made habitats has led to its success. According to the North American BBS, populations have remained stable in recent decades. They are, however, extremely susceptible to West Nile virus, which can be disastrous to affected populations. In the end, hopefully we all can agree that, fan or not, the intelligent American Crow is worth talking about.

Written by Spring Ligi

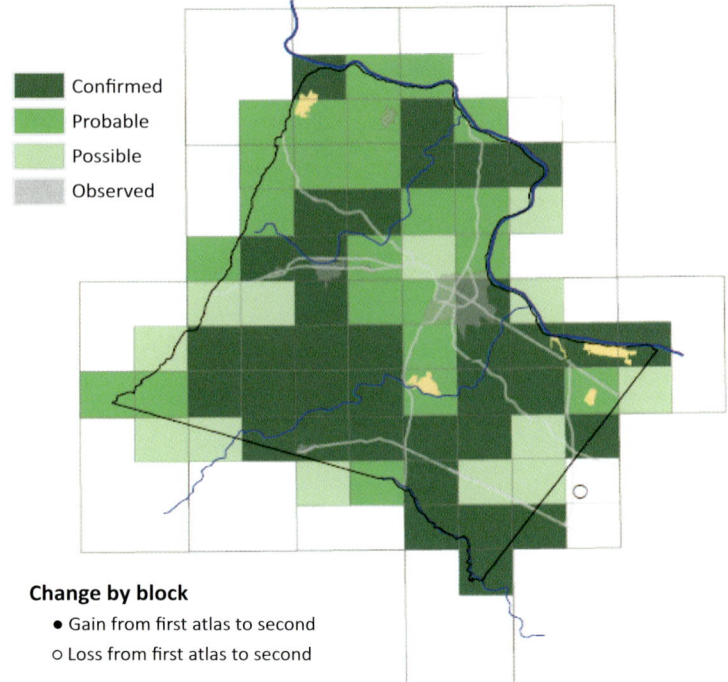

Confirmed
Probable
Possible
Observed

Change by block
● Gain from first atlas to second
○ Loss from first atlas to second

Photo ©Dick Rowe

FISH CROW
Corvus ossifragus

Occurrence: common breeder and year-round resident

Earliest breeding confirmation: April 10, adult carrying nesting material or nest building (NB)

Latest breeding confirmation: August 24, recently fledged young (FL)

While most people recognize a crow when they see one, not everyone knows there are actually two types of crows here in Loudoun. Like their cousin the American Crow, Fish Crows are entirely black with a glossy sheen, heavy bill, and sturdy legs. Though subtle differences do exist, the most reliable way to tell a Fish Crow from an American Crow is by their call. The Fish Crow produces a short, nasal *uh-uhh* with the second note lower.

Found year-round throughout coastal and tidewater regions of the Southeast, the Fish Crow uses a variety of habitats, often near water. Such habitats include beaches, estuaries, marshes, lakes, rivers, agricultural fields, suburban parks, docks, and landfills. In more inland areas, such as Loudoun, Fish Crows are usually not as abundant as American Crows. Central Loudoun CBCs have averaged 435 Fish Crows per count compared to 865 American Crows. Outside of breeding season, the two species may mix when feeding and roosting in flocks. Slightly smaller in size, the Fish Crow typically yields to the American Crow if a conflict arises.

Fish Crows are not picky eaters. Their diet includes carrion, crayfish, insects, berries, fruit, grain, trash, and more. They

FISH CROW (continued)

often raid nests of other species, eating their eggs and nestlings, and steal food from other birds. They may cache surplus food for later use.

After a courtship display flight, a breeding pair forms and holds a small territory around the nest tree. The nest is well made, taking 10 or more days to construct. It consists of a bulky platform of sticks and bark strips lined with grass, hair, feathers, and pine needles. A new nest is built each season for a single brood of two to six eggs. Young Fish Crows often play with objects that they find, revealing their intelligence and curiosity, characteristics shared among corvids.

Populations have rebounded after the West Nile virus outbreak in the early 2000s and are increasing and expanding northward and inland along major river systems. This increase is supported by a net gain in over 10 atlas blocks from Atlas 1 to 2, along with CBC data. While good news for the Fish Crow, this range expansion may spell trouble for some species whose eggs and nestlings are popular menu items for the crow.

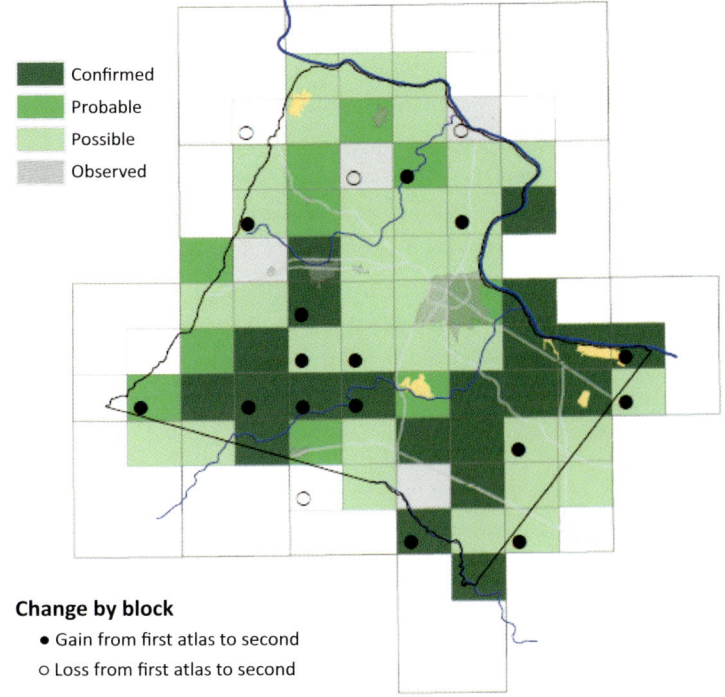

Confirmed
Probable
Possible
Observed

Change by block
● Gain from first atlas to second
○ Loss from first atlas to second

Written by Spring Ligi

Photo by Liam McGranaghan
(pair with nesting material)

COMMON RAVEN
Corvus corax

Occurrence: uncommon breeder and year-round resident

Earliest breeding confirmation: February 12, adult carrying nesting material or nest building (NB)

Latest breeding confirmation: July 10, recently fledged young (FL)

The largest corvid in the Americas, the Common Raven has a glossy sheen over black plumage, with a deep-based, massive bill and long wedge-shaped tail, together making it easily identifiable in flight. Other distinguishing features include the thick and shaggy "hackles" which cover the throat and the nasal bristles above the bill. The raven was a confirmed breeder in 7 atlas blocks. There were gains in 25 blocks over the first atlas, mainly in more mountainous and rural western Loudoun; none registered losses. The raven has also been recorded on every Central Loudoun CBC since 1991, though numbers have varied from one to a couple dozen.

Ravens are omnivorous. They are also scavengers and predators. The species was extirpated in some states because it was viewed as a pest and a threat to farm livestock as well as grain and fruit products. Pairs of ravens can be observed piling up strips of meat from carcasses before taking the whole pile elsewhere to eat. Ravens prefer hilly or mountainous territory, but can also be found on grasslands and farmland, in wooded areas, and occasionally in urban and suburban areas. Western Loudoun's Purcellville began hosting a breeding pair on the town's water tower in

COMMON RAVEN (continued)

2013, while a pair has also been in residence slightly further east outside the town of Hamilton. This early nester builds its large stick nest on cliffs, in trees, and on power-line towers, telephone poles, and other structures. Both sexes help with parental care, typically raising one brood per year.

Most often ravens are found singly or in pairs. They can be marvelous acrobats in the air and put on a spectacular performance when found in a playful mood. They will do full and half rolls using one or two wings, and even fly upside down, for fairly long times. Their deep, croaking call, along with a variety of other calls, is often the first sign of their presence.

Ravens have suffered from habitat loss. They have also been shot, trapped, and poisoned as predators and pests. This highly intelligent species seems to be on the comeback trail, moving back into areas from which it had been wiped out.

Written by Chris White

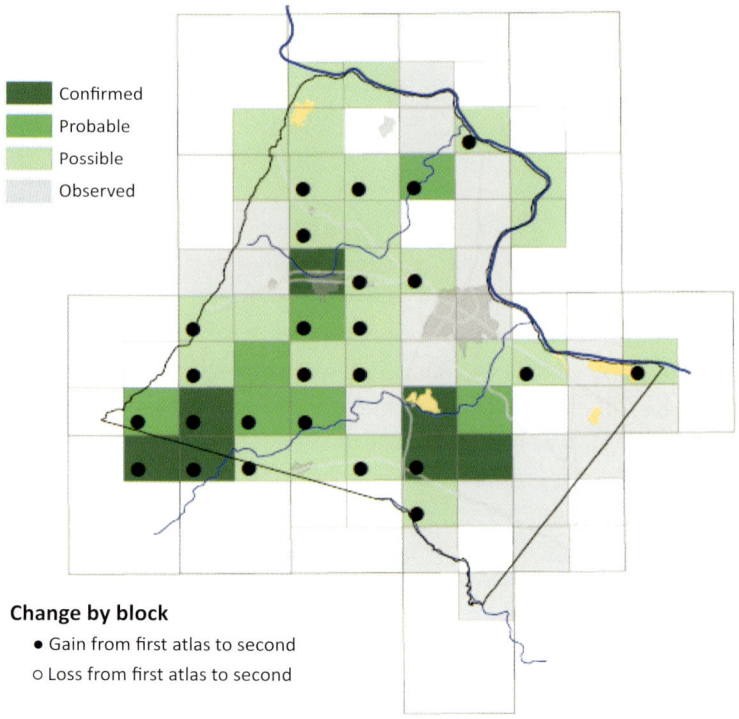

Confirmed
Probable
Possible
Observed

Change by block
- Gain from first atlas to second
○ Loss from first atlas to second

Photo ©Dick Rowe

HORNED LARK
Eremophila alpestris

Occurrence: rare breeder, occasional migrant and winter resident

Earliest/latest breeding confirmations: highest breeding evidence in Probable category, see account for details

The Horned Lark is a bird of prairies, grasslands, beaches, and fields, the kinds of wide-open spaces that can still be found in Loudoun if you know where to look. Search for them in northern and western Loudoun agricultural areas, especially in fallow fields with low ground cover or that have been recently tilled or are heavily grazed. They can also sometimes be seen along roadsides. However, as in most parts of the U.S., their preferred habitat is in steep decline. The Horned Lark's range-wide population loss of over 65% in the past 50 years is almost certainly linked to habitat loss, though it remains abundant at an estimated 97 million birds (Rosenberg et al. 2016). This species was reported on 15 of the past 20 Central Loudoun CBCs.

Named for its unique "horns," the male has bold black markings on its crown, mask, and chest set against a yellow forehead and throat. Females have a more washed-out look, and lack the male's black mask and the vibrant yellow (but may still sport a yellowish wash). The rest of both sexes' plumage is an unremarkable soft brown/tan above and white to light gray below, with tan streaks on the upper chest and flanks. They have a small, thin bill and long tail. This bird blends in well with its open ground habitat and can be surprisingly hard to spot, most often detected when

HORNED LARK (continued)

it flies or sits on fence posts to sing. Knowing its musical song can also help.

Though breeding was not confirmed during the atlas, males singing territorially and pairs together during breeding season or engaged in courtship were observed. Breeding was confirmed post-atlas (2017 and 2018) in an Ashburn area awaiting development. Females create a small depression in the ground to build their nest, which is lined with grasses and other fine materials. While raising young, the females are extremely stealthy around the nest, to avoid detection by a variety of potential predators. Horned Larks eat primarily seeds outside of breeding season, but they will eat and feed their young more nutritious insects when they can. In winter they often seek out waste grain or manure piles. These still-numerous birds inhabit much of the U.S., Canada, and northern Mexico. Though not long-distance migrants, they gather in nomadic flocks during winter, and may best be seen as they move between fields and give their tinkling contact calls.

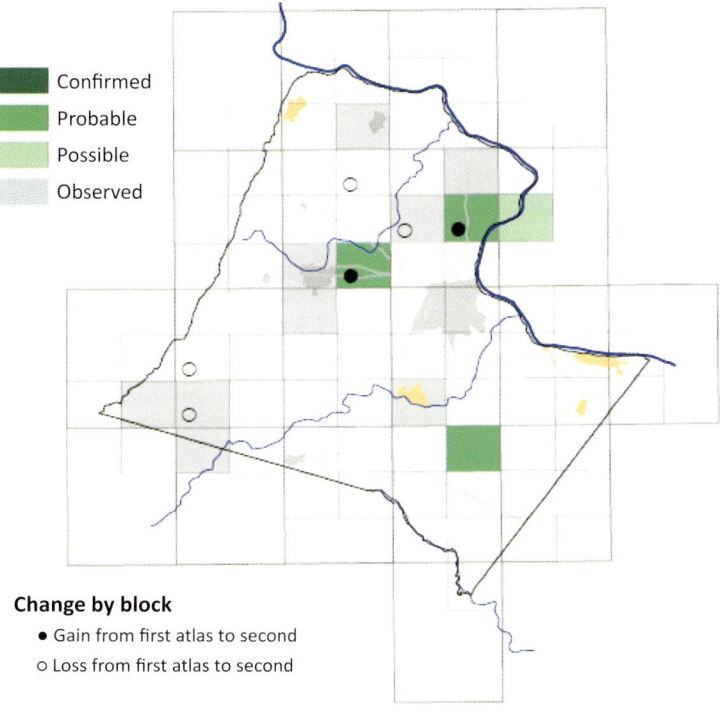

Confirmed

Probable

Possible

Observed

Change by block
- ● Gain from first atlas to second
- ○ Loss from first atlas to second

Written by Bruce Hill

Photo by Dave Boltz

PURPLE MARTIN
Progne subis

Occurrence: uncommon breeder and migrant

Earliest breeding confirmation: April 14, adult carrying nesting material or nest building (NB)

Latest breeding confirmation: July 29, recently fledged young (FL)

The relationship between Purple Martins and humans dates back to the Native Americans who hung hollow gourds around their villages to attract this insect-devouring bird. Over the years, their man-made housing has upgraded to multiple-roomed nest boxes or condominiums. In the eastern U.S., this colonial nester depends almost exclusively on these man-made nest boxes. In the West, martins tend to nest in pairs or loose colonies and often use natural cavities such as woodpecker holes in dead trees along forest edges and rivers. North America's largest swallow, adult males are glossy dark blue overall, with long brown-black wings and a short, forked tail. Females and immatures are duller above and grayish below.

The Purple Martin is a skilled flyer that forages, drinks, and even bathes on the wing. This year-round insectivore often feeds in pairs, flying low or quite high over towns, farms, parks, and semi-open habitat, especially near water where insects breed. Don't believe the old adage that martins eat "2,000 mosquitoes a day" – they actually feed on a variety of wasps, winged ants, bees, flies, beetles, and dragonflies. They are vulnerable to snaps of unseasonably cold weather lasting 3 or 4 days, which wipe out flying insect numbers and result in starvation.

PURPLE MARTIN (continued)

Purple Martins typically arrive in Loudoun in early April and depart around mid-September. The first martin to arrive at an active colony site is called a scout. Scouts are the oldest individuals in the population and can be male or female; they often return to areas where they nested before. Males sing a dawn song with throaty chirps and creaky rattles. This song may serve to attract other martins to a nesting site. Females also sing. A pair works together to build a nest of leaves, grass, twigs, and mud. They raise one or two broods of four to five nestlings.

In late summer, once the young leave the nest, Purple Martins may gather and roost in large flocks of thousands of birds as they prepare to cross the Gulf of Mexico. The flocks are so dense that they can easily be seen on weather radar! Purple Martin populations are declining for reasons not well known. This decline is supported by the net loss in blocks from Atlas 1 to Atlas 2. Possible threats include competition for nest sites with European Starlings and House Sparrows as well as pesticide use on South American wintering grounds.

Written by Spring Ligi

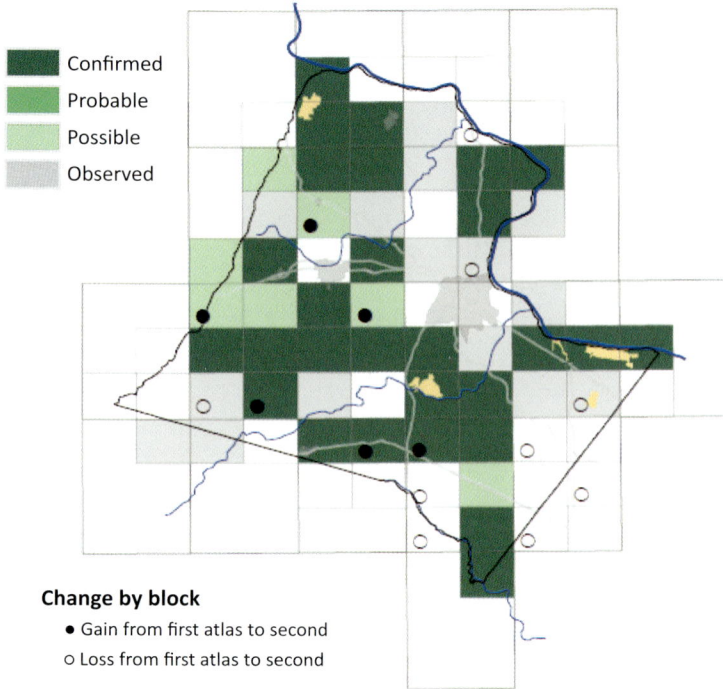

Confirmed
Probable
Possible
Observed

Change by block
- Gain from first atlas to second
- Loss from first atlas to second

Photo by Linda Millington

TREE SWALLOW
Tachycineta bicolor

Occurrence: common breeder and migrant

Earliest breeding confirmation: April 14, adult carrying nesting material or nest building (NB)

Latest breeding confirmation: July 26, recently fledged young (FL)

Brilliant aerialists, Tree Swallows return to Loudoun from their southern wintering grounds early in spring (mid-March) to stake out territories. They can be found soaring above meadows and bodies of water as well as perched on wires, shrubs, and exposed branches. Their cheerful chipping and chattering are welcome proclamations of their return and spring's arrival.

Tree Swallows are small, trim birds with metallic blue-green upperparts (males) and neat, white underparts. Their wings are pointed and tail is slightly forked. Females and juveniles are dark gray-brown on the back; the juvenile's tail is squared off. Tree Swallows catch flying insects and chase their prey with dramatic twists and dives. They will also eat berries, mainly bayberries, when insects are scarce.

Tree Swallows nest in cavities and will readily use bluebird nest boxes. Competition for nesting sites is intense and territories are aggressively defended by the resident male. Males court females by showing her potential nesting sites. Females construct a cup-shaped nest from grass and other plant materials and use feathers to line the nest. Four to seven pale eggs are laid; incubation is by the female only, lasting about 14 days. Both parents feed the nestlings and defend the nest from predators. Young leave the nest about 18 days after hatching. Tree Swallows

TREE SWALLOW (continued)

typically raise one brood per year. Their use of nest boxes allows breeding to be confirmed with relative ease; breeding confirmations were reported in over 70% of the atlas blocks.

Breeding throughout northern North America, Tree Swallows form flocks and begin migrating in July and August to their wintering grounds in Florida and Central America. This daytime migrant can be seen in Loudoun through mid-October. On rare occasion, they will turn up in colder months; there were 2 atlas sightings on November 9 and February 21.

According to the North American BBS, populations of this common bird have declined over the past 5 decades. The apparent gain in blocks from Atlas 1 to 2 is likely impacted by the higher level of coverage and effort per block in Atlas 2 and not necessarily a population increase. Limited availability of nesting sites and pesticide use pose threats to this cavity-loving insectivore. Climate change may also play a role. As temperatures have warmed since the 1960s, Tree Swallows have shifted their average date of first egg laying 9 days earlier (Winkler et al. 2011).

Written by Donna Quinn

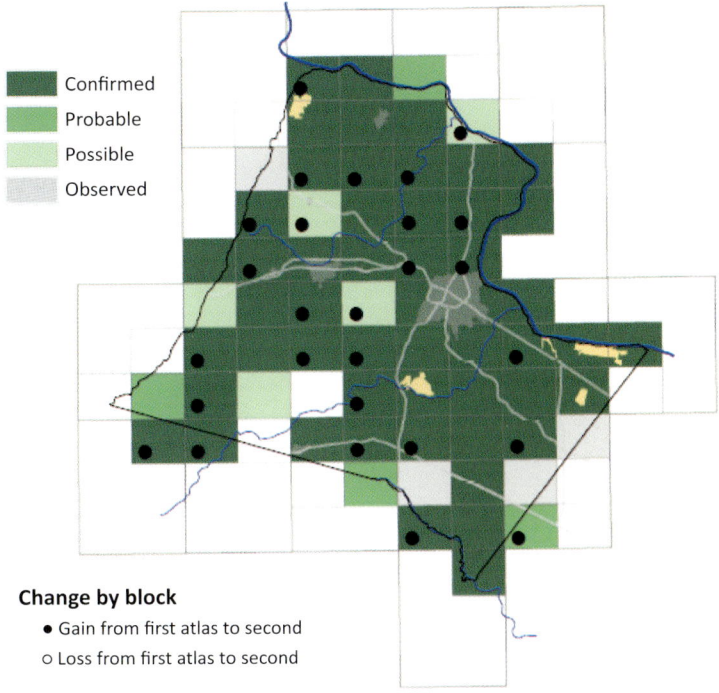

Confirmed
Probable
Possible
Observed

Change by block
- Gain from first atlas to second
○ Loss from first atlas to second

Photo ©Dick Rowe

NORTHERN ROUGH-WINGED SWALLOW
Stelgidopteryx serripennis

Occurrence: uncommon breeder and migrant

Earliest breeding confirmation: April 23, adult carrying nesting material or nest building (NB)

Latest breeding confirmation: July 30, recently fledged young (FL)

Confirmed as breeding in over a third of the atlas blocks, the Northern Rough-winged Swallow typically arrives in Loudoun in late March and departs by mid-October. Adults are plain brown above with a white belly and buffy throat and upper breast. They have square tails and white under-tail coverts that are sometimes visible in flight. Juveniles are similar to adults, but with cinnamon wingbars. Northern Rough-winged Swallows can be distinguished from Bank Swallows by their lack of a breast-band and white throat, shorter tail, and stockier build. The name "Rough-winged" comes from small hooks or points along the outermost wing feathers. The purpose of these serrations is not known, but may be linked to sound production during courtship flights (Audubon 2017).

These swallows nest singly or in small colonies of a few pairs. They nest in burrows found in clay, sand, or gravel banks typically near water. They dig their own burrow (up to 6 feet long) or use one made by kingfishers, squirrels, or Bank Swallows. Crevices found in gutters, drainpipes, walls, and bridges may also be used; in Loudoun, they often nest near man-made ponds with dams or drainage structures. The female uses grass, twigs, and occasionally fresh horse manure to form a cup nest inside the burrow or crevice and lays five to seven eggs. The male is often perched

NO. ROUGH-WINGED SWALLOW (continued)

nearby, keeping a watchful eye for intruders. Both parents feed the young, which leave the nest approximately 20 days after hatching, and raise one brood per year.

Like other swallows, Northern Rough-winged Swallows fly low over lakes, ponds, rivers, and open areas snatching small flying insects in mid-air, occasionally picking insects from the water's surface. They fly with slower, more deliberate wing-beats than other swallows. Northern Rough-winged Swallows tend to mix with other species during migration, so it's worth checking large groups of swallows for this less flashy bird. This species breeds across the U.S. and winters in the southern tip of Florida, Mexico, and Central America.

Northern Rough-winged Swallow populations declined by 18% between 1970 and 2014 (PIF 2017). The net gain of 18 blocks from Atlas 1 to Atlas 2 is likely influenced by the increased coverage and effort per block in Atlas 2. Threats to this species include pesticides that reduce the number of flying insects and climate change, which may impact the timing of when insects are available.

Written by Spring Ligi

Confirmed
Probable
Possible
Observed

Change by block
● Gain from first atlas to second
○ Loss from first atlas to second

Photo by Tony LePrieur

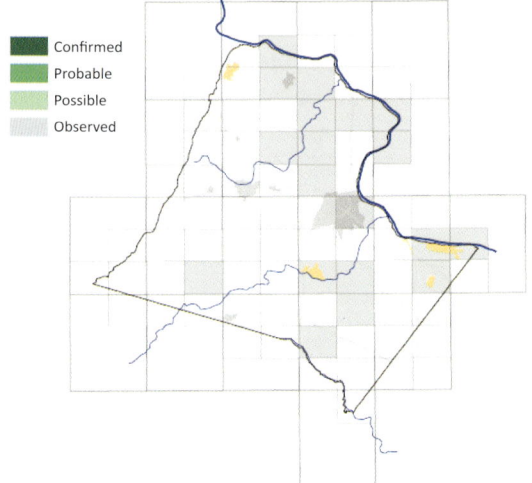

Confirmed
Probable
Possible
Observed

BANK SWALLOW
Riparia riparia

Occurrence: occasional migrant and summer visitor

Earliest spring sighting: April 7

Latest fall sighting: September 21

The Bank Swallow lives up to its name by excavating a nest cavity in the riparian banks and bluffs of rivers and streams (as well as man-made gravel quarries and cuts). Nesting has not been documented in Loudoun, which lies just outside of its breeding range, though Bank Swallows have been observed on occasion throughout the summer. Reported in roughly a quarter of the atlas blocks, Bank Swallows pass through Loudoun on their way to South American wintering grounds. This social bird is typically found in flocks, foraging for insects while expertly maneuvering over water or open ground.

The Bank Swallow is the smallest North American swallow; adults and juveniles are brown above and white below. The brown band across the chest and slightly forked tail help distinguish it from the similar Northern Rough-winged Swallow. The 2014 State of the Birds Report lists the Bank Swallow as a "common bird in steep decline." Erosion and flood control, along with road building projects, threaten this species by removing nesting sites or making them no longer suitable.

Written by Spring Ligi

CLIFF SWALLOW
Petrochelidon pyrrhonota

Occurrence: rare breeder and occasional migrant

Earliest/latest breeding confirmations: fewer than 5 atlas confirmations, see account for details

Cliff Swallows, true to their name, used to nest on the sides of cliffs, and some still do. However, many now use more widespread sites, such as bridges, barns, and other structures. The colony documented in Loudoun's northern-most block, comprised of a couple dozen nests under a bridge crossing the Potomac River, was active at least 4 of the 5 atlas years (2010-2013).

After selecting a colony site, a pair gathers mud pellets in their bills from nearby streambanks,

Photo ©Dick Rowe

lakesides, or puddles and forms a gourd-shaped nest. A nest typically contains 900-1,200 individual mud pellets lined with grass and feathers (Brown et al. 2017). Repairs are made throughout the breeding season, and nests may be reused. Both the male and female incubate the four or five eggs and feed the young.

Life in the breeding colony is far from dull. Both members of a pair frequently mate outside the pair bond. Females will lay eggs in other females' nests and carry eggs from their own nest to another's nest. When feeding the young, unsuccessful foragers watch their more successful neighbors and follow them to food sources. As the young leave their nests, they form large groups called creches. The parents recognize their young primarily by voice.

Cliff Swallows typically feed on the wing in small flocks. They forage over pastures, fields, lakes, rivers, and other open areas searching for insects, especially swarms of insects. Migrants use Loudoun as a stop-over site on their way to and from their South American breeding grounds. They migrate in flocks during the daytime, foraging as they move at a rather leisurely pace. When foraging with other swallow species, Cliff Swallows are often found higher in the air. They arrive in Loudoun around mid-April and depart in mid- to late September.

In good lighting, the adult's back, wings, and crown are a deep blue, that may be confused with the Barn Swallow. However, the Cliff Swallow has a white forehead, buff rump, and short, squared-off tail along with a chestnut-colored face. In poor lighting, they look brownish with white underparts. Populations are stable and have expanded into the southeastern U.S. in recent decades by taking advantage of man-made nesting sites. Populations in the Northeast have declined, however, likely due to the spread of invasive House Sparrows which often take over their nests.

Written by Spring Ligi

Confirmed
Probable
Possible
Observed

Change by block
- Gain from first atlas to second
- Loss from first atlas to second

BARN SWALLOW
Hirundo rustica

Occurrence: common breeder and migrant

Earliest breeding confirmation: April 21, parent carrying food or feeding young (CF)

Latest breeding confirmation: August 6, recently fledged young (FL)

Photo by Dave Boltz

Barn Swallows are a welcome and common sight, not just in Loudoun, but throughout most of the world. They benefit from our man-made structures and we benefit from their pest control. This swallow is found in a variety of open habitats including agricultural fields, suburban parks, ponds, and coastal waters. They often forage in flocks, flying with graceful aerial maneuvers over water or fields in pursuit of flies and other flying insects. They even drink and bathe on the wing. Occasionally, they can be found perched on wires near feeding and nesting sites. They have a variety of twitters and chatter, both individually and as a group, for courtship, nesting, socializing, and predator alert.

Originally nesting in caves, they now nest almost exclusively in man-made structures such as eaves and rafters of barns and sheds as well as under bridges, docks, and culverts. Unlike some swallows, they don't form dense colonies, but several pairs may nest in the same general area. After courtship, which involves aerial chases, the pair will select a nesting site and build a nest using pellets of mud mixed with grass and feathers. Nests may be reused from previous years. Males aggressively defend the nest site and may team up with other males to mob predators such as hawks and grackles.

Once the nest is built, four to five eggs are laid and both parents incubate and feed the young. One or two additional birds may help with feeding duties, typically older siblings from previous clutches but sometimes unrelated juveniles. It's no wonder the parents need extra help – they feed their nestlings up to 400 times per day! One or two broods are raised per year.

This species' close proximity to humans makes its nests easier to spot, with breeding confirmations reported in three-quarters of the atlas blocks. In addition to breeding birds, daytime migrants pass through Loudoun on their way to Central and South American wintering grounds, typically between mid-March and late September.

Barn Swallows are brightly marked in deep blue with a cinnamon throat and forehead and rufous to tawny underparts (typically paler in females and juveniles). Their long, deeply forked tail is helpful in distinguishing this species from other swallows. The hunting of Barn Swallows for the hat trade in the nineteenth century helped inspire the founding of the first Audubon Society. Populations have recovered and expanded as humans settled throughout the continent.

Written by Spring Ligi

Confirmed
Probable
Possible
Observed

Change by block
- Gain from first atlas to second
○ Loss from first atlas to second

CAROLINA CHICKADEE
Poecile carolinensis

Photo by Deb Calhoun

Occurrence: abundant breeder and year-round resident

Earliest breeding confirmation: March 23, adult carrying nesting material or nest building (NB)

Latest breeding confirmation: September 11, recently fledged young (FL)

Highly adaptable and resourceful, Carolina Chickadees can be found anywhere in Loudoun where there are trees – from forests to backyards. They are identified by their small size, round shape, and neat black cap and bib separated by a white cheek patch. Their back, wings, and tail are soft gray. Males and females look alike. Noisy and acrobatic, Carolina Chickadees are small birds with large personalities.

Birders on a walk pay close attention to the Carolina Chickadee's scolding *chick-a-dee-dee-dee* call and lovely four-note *fee-bee fee-bay* song. Outside of breeding season, they often travel in mixed flocks, and birders know finding a Carolina Chickadee can reveal other less vocal species. Their varied diet consists of seeds, fruits, and insects. They glean insects from foliage, often hanging upside down to do so.

During winter a pair remains together as part of a flock. In spring the pair breaks off to establish a territory for nesting. The nest is built in a tree cavity or nesting box. The female builds a beautiful soft nest of layered plant materials including fibers and mosses. The cup is lined with animal hair. Nests may be over 7 inches deep! Five to eight tiny white eggs with red dots are hidden deep in the nest. Finally, the female weaves a "blanket" of plant fibers to cover her eggs when she must leave the nest. Incubation is about 11 days. Young are born naked; their cozy nest helps them survive cold and damp conditions common in spring. When threatened, an adult bird on nest is known to strike the side of the box and hiss like a snake to scare off predators. Both parents feed the young; young fledge in about 18 days.

Carolina Chickadees are a favorite backyard bird. Energetic and inquisitive, they are highly entertaining to watch. Offering suet, peanut hearts, and sunflower or safflower seeds will attract them to feeders. They are polite guests, taking just one seed at a time and flying off to pry it open in a nearby tree. Populations have declined in recent decades according to the North American BBS, though they remain common throughout their southeastern U.S. range where they live year-round. The Carolina Chickadee made the top 25 list of breeding species for the atlas and was 1 of 14 species documented in all 73 blocks. Breeding was confirmed in 80% of the blocks.

Written by Donna Quinn

Confirmed
Probable
Possible
Observed

Change by block
- Gain from first atlas to second
○ Loss from first atlas to second

BLACK-CAPPED CHICKADEE
Poecile atricapillus

Photo ©Dick Rowe

Occurrence: rare winter visitor

Earliest fall sighting: October 13

Latest spring sighting: March 31

Acrobatic and active, this small, round-bodied bird has a black cap and bib separated by a broad white cheek patch. The back and wings are gray, the long tail is edged in white, and the underside is white to buff. The Black-capped Chickadee typically shows greater white in its primaries and has a slightly smaller bill and black bib than our much more common Carolina Chickadee. The Black-capped song is also shorter (two to three notes) and their calls slower. Using these subtle clues, observant western Loudoun atlasers identified this species 5 times during the winter of 2010–2011.

Resident across the northern U.S. and much of Canada and Alaska, Black-capped Chickadees are generally non-migratory. While rare here (found on only 15% of the Central Loudoun CBCs), this species breeds nearby at higher elevations. Birds that wander into our area may be moving down-slope in pursuit of food. Primarily insectivores, they switch to seeds in winter and can show up at feeders. The overall population is healthy and has increased slightly in the last 50 years.

Written by Bruce Hill

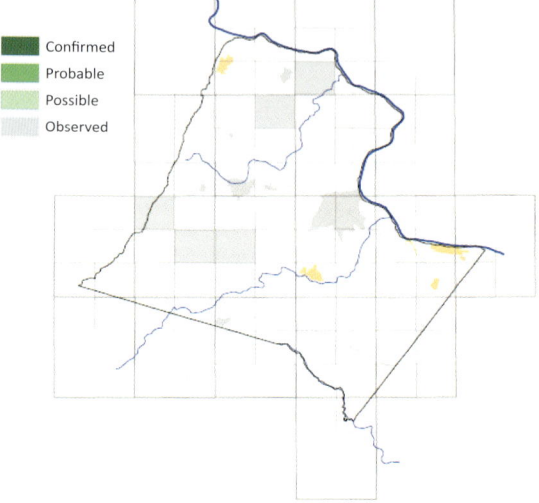
Confirmed
Probable
Possible
Observed

Photo by Dave Boltz

TUFTED TITMOUSE
Baeolophus bicolor

Occurrence: abundant breeder and year-round resident

Earliest breeding confirmation: April 20, adult carrying nesting material or nest building (NB)

Latest breeding confirmation: September 11, recently fledged young (FL)

While enjoying a leisurely spring or summertime stroll through Loudoun's deciduous and mixed forests, you're likely to be greeted by the quick and often-repeated *peter-peter-peter* song of the male Tufted Titmouse. Females occasionally sing a quieter version of the song. This vocal species can also be found in wooded suburban and urban areas, actively hopping among branches and even hanging upside down while foraging for insects, seeds, and berries. Titmice readily visit bird feeders for seeds (especially sunflower seed) and suet, boldly evicting smaller or less aggressive birds as needed. Like their chickadee cousins, they often cache the seeds for later use, taking one seed per trip. Their hardy bill is used to hammer open the seeds and nuts. The Tufted Titmouse is relatively easy to identify, with a gray crested head, large black eyes, and a black forehead. Look for gray upperparts, white underparts, and a peach wash on the sides.

Tufted Titmice cannot excavate their own cavities; they use natural holes, cavities left by woodpeckers, and nest boxes. A cup-shaped nest is built from grass, moss, leaves, and bark strips and lined with animal hair. The hair is

TUFTED TITMOUSE (continued)

sometimes pulled directly from living squirrels, opossums, woodchucks, livestock, and even humans! The male often feeds the female from courtship until the three to nine eggs hatch; nestlings are fed by both parents. After fledging, the youngsters typically remain with the parents during the winter. When they do disperse, most don't go more than a few kilometers from their birthplace. Sometimes one of the offspring will stick around to help the parents raise next year's brood.

In winter, foraging Tufted Titmice are often joined by chickadees, nuthatches, kinglets, and woodpeckers. The titmice and chickadees often influence the path the flock follows (Ritchison et al. 2015) and are quick to investigate and join in the mobbing of predators such as crows, owls, hawks, and snakes. In recent decades, Tufted Titmouse populations have been

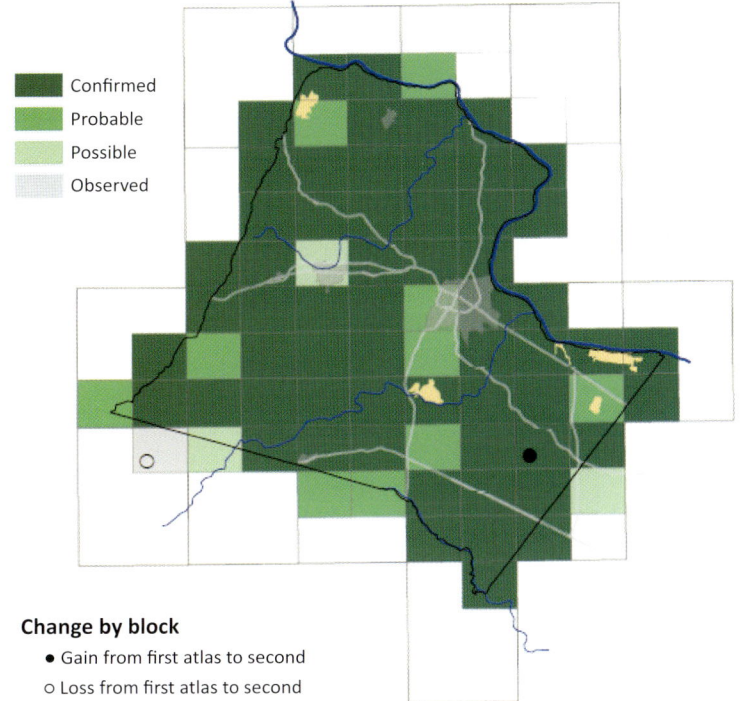

Confirmed
Probable
Possible
Observed

Change by block
- Gain from first atlas to second
- Loss from first atlas to second

increasing throughout their eastern U.S. range. They were 1 of 14 species reported in all 73 atlas blocks, with breeding confirmations in over 80% of the blocks. This population increase is also supported by Central Loudoun CBC data. Their range is expanding northward into southern Canada, likely due to global warming along with the growing popularity of bird feeders. This cavity nester benefits from leaving dead trees and branches in wooded areas.

Written by Spring Ligi

Photo by Larry Meade

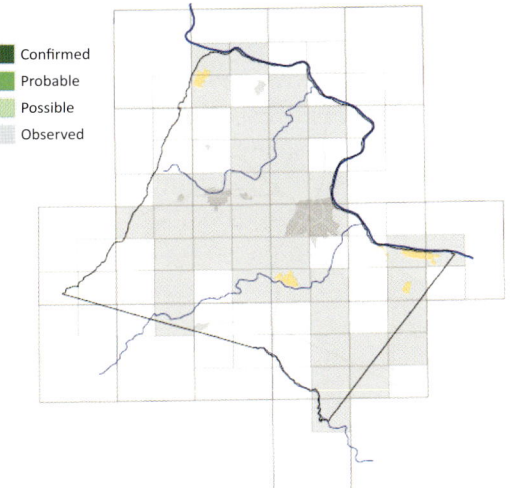

Confirmed
Probable
Possible
Observed

RED-BREASTED NUTHATCH
Sitta canadensis

Occurrence: rare irruptive migrant and winter visitor

Earliest summer/fall sighting: August 27

Latest spring sighting: May 10

Unlike the White-breasted Nuthatch which resides in Loudoun year-round, Red-breasted Nuthatches may be found here when pinecone production is poor on their boreal breeding grounds. They prefer conifers, but use a variety of wooded habitats and will visit backyard feeders. These tiny bundles of energy move quickly up and down tree trunks and branches searching for insects and seeds, including seeds they cached earlier in the year, and often join foraging flocks of chickadees and other songbirds, sounding their nasal, tin horn-like *yank-yank* call. Smaller than its familiar cousin, this compact, blue-gray bird has a short tail, almost no neck, rusty cinnamon underparts, and a strongly patterned head. It was documented in 5 or fewer atlas blocks in 2009, 2011, and 2014, but appeared in 10-15 blocks in 2010 and 2013 and over 20 blocks in 2012. Red-breasted Nuthatches have been reported on just over half of the Central Loudoun CBCs. Populations have increased throughout most of their range over the past 5 decades. This endearing bird benefits from dead trees left standing in forests.

Written by Spring Ligi

WHITE-BREASTED NUTHATCH

Sitta carolinensis

Photo by Dave Boltz

Occurrence: common breeder and year-round resident

Earliest breeding confirmation: March 16, adult carrying nesting material or nest building (NB)

Latest breeding confirmation: August 11, recently fledged young (FL)

Unlike the Red-breasted and Brown-headed Nuthatches which are found mostly in pines, the White-breasted Nuthatch is associated with deciduous trees and is by far the most common nuthatch you will encounter in Loudoun. Found in mature forests, woodland edges, and wooded parks, pairs remain together throughout the year. In winter you can find them foraging in flocks with chickadees and titmice, a strategy that may help with locating food and predators.

Courtship begins in late winter with displays and feeding rituals. Females build the nest in a natural cavity or abandoned woodpecker hole, so it's important to retain dead or partially dead trees in their habitat. Less commonly, they'll use a birdhouse or excavate their own nest cavity. The simple cup nest of bark fibers, grasses, twigs, and hair holds five to nine eggs. Crushed insects are sometimes added to the nest, likely to repel predators. Both parents feed the young and raise one brood per breeding season; they often reuse nest holes from year to year.

This compact bird has a big head with almost no neck and a short tail. It has a black crown (gray in females), white cheeks, blue-gray upperparts, and white underparts with chestnut spots near the rear. Oftentimes its distinctive silhouette is all you need for identification, as it clings upside-down on a tree trunk or large branch with its head craned up and back. With great agility, the White-breasted Nuthatch creeps up, down, and sideways over tree trunks in search of food. Named for their eating habits, nuthatches stuff large nuts into tree crevices and hammer them with their bill to "hatch" out the seed from within. A large percentage of their diet is insects, including pests such as gypsy moths, tent caterpillars, and stinkbugs. A common feeder bird, they also enjoy suet and seeds, sometimes caching seeds in bark crevices for later use.

According to the North American BBS, populations have increased in recent decades throughout their year-round range (including much of the U.S., parts of Mexico, and southern Canada). This increase is supported by atlas and Central Loudoun CBC data. Found in virtually every atlas block, this species was confirmed as breeding in 40% of the blocks. On your next late winter or spring walk through Loudoun's deciduous woods, listen for the loud, nasal *yank-yank* of the White-breasted Nuthatch — it will likely lead you right to this captivating bird.

Written by Spring Ligi

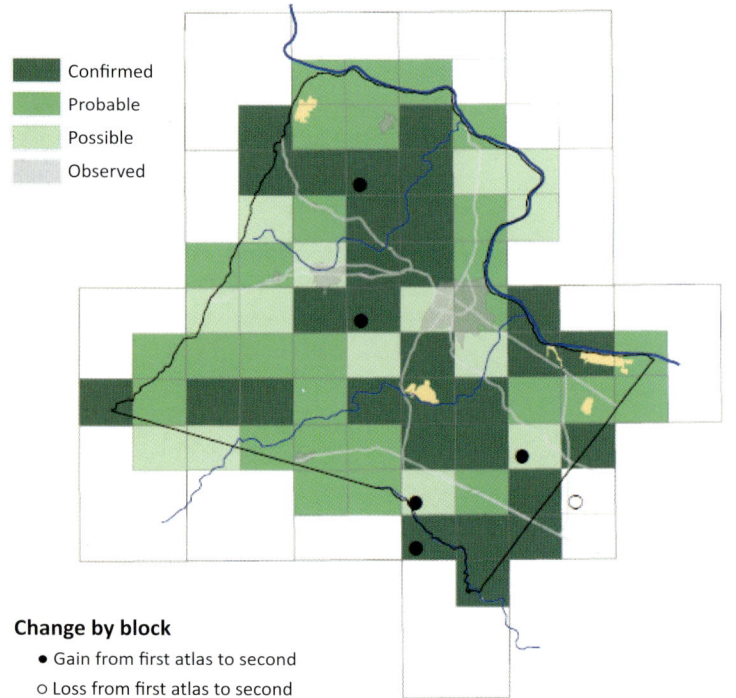

Confirmed
Probable
Possible
Observed

Change by block
- Gain from first atlas to second
○ Loss from first atlas to second

BROWN-HEADED NUTHATCH
Sitta pusilla

Occurrence: vagrant

Earliest/latest seasonal sightings: fewer than 5 atlas sightings, see account for details

A sound like a toy rubber ducky may alert birders to a Brown-headed Nuthatch actively feeding in the canopy of an open pine forest. It is a compact bird, like the Red-breasted, smaller than the familiar White-breasted Nuthatch, with a distinctive brown cap, blue-gray back, and whitish underparts. It has a chisel-like bill which it uses to dig for insects under tree bark and to crack pine seeds that it feeds on in colder months. The bird is notable for its use of tools; it has been observed using stiff pieces of bark to pry loose bark off trees to expose insect larvae and eggs.

Rarely seen this far north, the Brown-headed Nuthatch was observed only once during the atlas – on November 16, 2012 near a water retention pond at an eastern Loudoun business park. The bird's normal year-round habitat is southern pine forest, and it is more regularly found on the Eastern Shore and in the Tidewater area. Populations have declined over the past 5 decades, likely due to habitat loss.

Written by Bill Brown

Photo by Dave Boltz

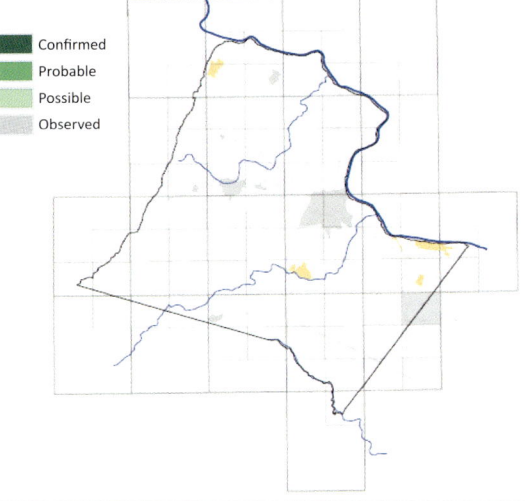

Confirmed
Probable
Possible
Observed

BROWN CREEPER
Certhia americana

Occurrence: uncommon migrant and winter resident

Earliest fall sighting: October 8

Latest spring sighting: April 15

The diminutive Brown Creeper's mottled brown and buff plumage (contrasting with its white front) camouflages it well as it forages for insects along the trunk of a tree. It is most often recognized by its distinctive foraging behavior – climbing the tree in an upward spiral, then flying downward to a nearby tree and repeating that pattern. The creeper's adaptations for this feeding behavior include long claws to cling to the tree bark, stiff tail feathers for bracing itself, and a long, decurved bill.

Although the Brown Creeper breeds principally in mature forest interiors, during migration and winter it can also be found in urban and suburban woodlots. There was one summertime sighting of a Brown Creeper, recorded as a possible breeder on August 31, 2012, at the Blue Ridge Center in northern Loudoun. This bird generally breeds from Pennsylvania north and in the Great Lakes region, as well as in the Appalachian highlands and the coniferous forests of western North America. Populations appear stable throughout its range.

Written by Bill Brown

Photo by Dave Boltz

Confirmed
Probable
Possible
Observed

HOUSE WREN
Troglodytes aedon

Occurrence: common breeder and migrant, rare winter visitor

Earliest breeding confirmation: May 8, parent carrying food or feeding young (CF)

Latest breeding confirmation: August 2, recently fledged young (FL)

This small, rust-brown wren is a common suburban resident during the breeding season in Loudoun. As a cavity nester, it often nests in bird houses and other nooks and crannies in our built environment. Its loud, boisterous jumble of a song, repeated frequently, is familiar to many, even if they don't know the singer. Aggressive and persistent, House Wrens will fight over nest sites with other wrens and with many other

Photo by Dave Boltz

cavity nesters, frequently evicting chickadees, bluebirds, Tree Swallows, or other unfortunate targets. Males often start multiple nests, allowing females to then select and complete their favorite. Nests are surprisingly large and bulky, made up primarily of jumbled twigs that often block the entrance of the cavity, apparently to deter intruders. A finer, softly lined cup nest is built within or on top of this foundation, where the female lays 3 to 10 small, speckled eggs per brood.

Besides being brown, distinctive House Wren features include subtle black barring on the wings and tail, the latter short and usually held cocked. Their pale throat tends to stand out from a darker face and belly. Their song or chattering calls are the usual giveaways that one is nearby. House Wrens are almost exclusively hunters, not gatherers, eating a broad spectrum of small to medium-sized insects and spiders. They forage busily on the ground or low in shrubs or the forest understory. When they take to the air, flight is low and direct, and they will usually not stray far from cover.

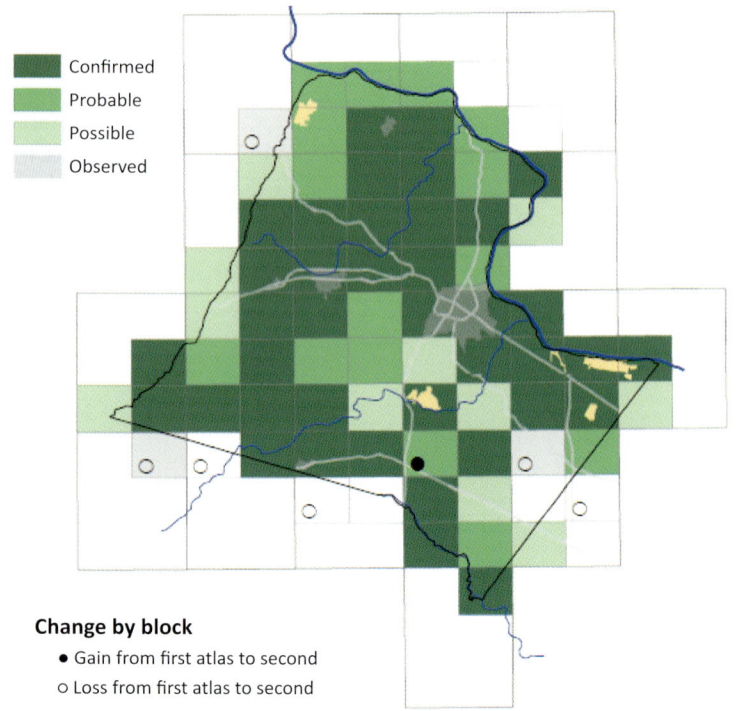

Confirmed
Probable
Possible
Observed

Change by block
- Gain from first atlas to second
○ Loss from first atlas to second

One of the most widespread birds in the Americas, this species inhabits and breeds in both North and South America. In North America, most are migratory — they breed throughout the northern two-thirds of the U.S. and into Canada, and winter in the southern U.S. and Mexico. In the tropics, many are year-round residents. But in much of South America, populations are also migratory, breeding as far south as the tip of Chile and Argentina, and returning north to find more temperate climes during the Southern Hemisphere's winter. The overall population is generally stable, but some regional declines have been observed. Their global breeding numbers are estimated at around 160 million (Rosenberg et al. 2016). In Loudoun, they were documented as confirmed breeders in 39 atlas blocks and probable breeders in most others. Typically found from early April through mid-October, there were 2 rare winter sightings (January 2012 and February 2013).

Written by Bruce Hill

WINTER WREN
Troglodytes hiemalis

Occurrence: uncommon migrant and winter resident

Earliest fall sighting: September 5

Latest spring sighting: April 17

Photo ©Dick Rowe

Seeming more mouse-like than bird-like when foraging, the tiny, all-dark Winter Wren scurries and flies low among fallen logs and dense brush, searching for a variety of insects, spiders, and berries. They often remain out of sight, but occasionally betray their presence with their jubilant long, bubbly song, delivered with ten times more power than a crowing rooster per unit weight (Cornell 2014). Found mainly throughout the eastern half of North America, they prefer evergreen or deciduous forests with a dense understory, often near water, breeding in the Northeast and upper Midwest and across Canada.

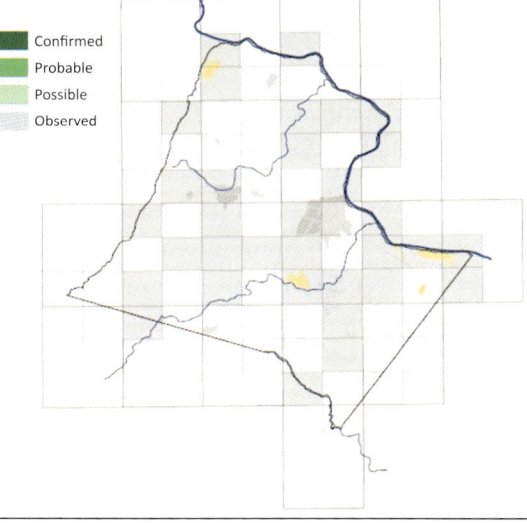

Confirmed
Probable
Possible
Observed

The Winter Wren is brown overall, with darker barring on the wings, belly, and tail, along with a tan eyebrow stripe and stubby tail that is usually cocked upright. This energetic bird was documented in 33 of the 73 atlas blocks, scattered throughout Loudoun. It has been reported on every Central Loudoun CBC, with numbers ranging from 2 to 24 individuals per count. Populations have remained fairly stable over the past 5 decades, according to the North American BBS.

Written by Spring Ligi

Photo ©Jim Clark

MARSH WREN
Cistothorus palustris

Occurrence: rare breeder and migrant

Earliest/latest breeding confirmations: highest breeding evidence in Probable category, see account for details

The Marsh Wren is a hard-to-see but vocal denizen of both salt and freshwater wetlands throughout the U.S. and southern Canada. Many, especially the more northerly inland nesters, move south during winter into the southern U.S. and Mexico; others remain as permanent residents where the weather is mild enough. In our larger region, many of these hardy birds remain year-round on the Eastern Shore of Delaware, Maryland, and Virginia; rare individuals venture this far inland.

This small wren looks a lot like a House or Winter Wren in size and posture, often holding its short tail severely cocked as it sings from marsh vegetation. But it has a distinct white eyebrow reminiscent of a Carolina Wren, bright rust highlights on shoulders, rump, and flanks, a white throat, and black and white streaking on its upper back. Its song is a series of buzzy trills, often strung together in phrases of varying pitch. This bird lives much of its life out of sight deep in marsh vegetation, only occasionally emerging to sing from a more elevated perch near dusk and dawn, and sometimes into the night. Recognizing its unique song can be important in finding them. Marsh Wrens are insectivores, gleaning spiders and insects from vegetation or occasionally taking winged insects in flight.

MARSH WREN (continued)

In spring, the male builds multiple dome-shaped nests within stands of cattails or rushes. Using his powers of song and fluttering display flights, he entices a female to select a preferred nest. She lines it with finer materials before laying 3 to 10 eggs and rearing the young over the next several weeks. A male may mate with several different females. Both sexes are aggressive in defending their territory and may destroy nests and eggs of competing Marsh Wrens and other species.

Considered a common species overall, their numbers have increased over the past 50 years. Their total breeding population is approaching 10 million (Rosenberg et al. 2016). However, habitat loss, particularly as climate change reduces coastal marshes, is a foreseeable threat. While breeding has not been confirmed in Loudoun, the Marsh Wren was seen or heard 3 times in May and late June 2013 at the Dulles Greenway Wetlands, which provides suitable habitat for the species. Based on territorial behavior it was assessed as a probable breeder. Of note, this species has been seen and heard again in several Loudoun wetland locations since the atlas period ended.

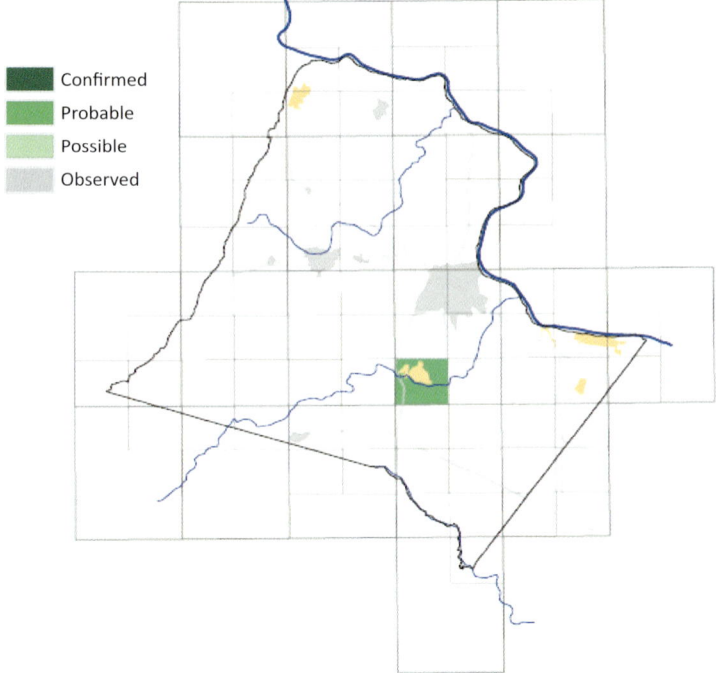

Confirmed
Probable
Possible
Observed

Written by Bruce Hill

Photo by Ian Richardson

CAROLINA WREN
Thryothorus ludovicianus

Occurrence: abundant breeder and year-round resident

Earliest breeding confirmation: April 10, nest with eggs (NE)

Latest breeding confirmation: August 30, recently fledged young (FL)

The Carolina Wren is a familiar and vocal bird, seen and heard year-round in well-vegetated residential areas, wood lots, briar patches, and other overgrown habitats with good cover. They were 1 of 14 atlas species documented in all 73 blocks. They adapt readily to human environments, nesting in planters, under decks, or even in nooks and crannies inside your garage if you leave the door open long enough.

At the time of this writing, a pair was raising nestlings in the decorative wreath on the front door of this author's neighbor. Both male and female assist in building the large, loosely woven, dome-shaped nest, incorporating a wide variety of available natural and man-made materials. Nests are placed in cavities from ground level up to about 6 feet high. After laying four to eight eggs, the incubation and nestling phases each last approximately 2 weeks. They may stay together in family groups for several more weeks after the young fledge. Carolina Wrens can raise one to three broods per year.

This species eats mainly insects, hunting on the ground and in tangled vegetation. They also consume berries and seeds in winter. Pair bonds persist throughout the year, and they are often seen or heard together in all seasons. Relatively weak fliers, they tend to stay low to the ground and make short flights between areas with protective cover.

CAROLINA WREN (continued)

The Carolina Wren has characteristic broad white eyebrows, a white throat, warm cinnamon plumage above, and a buffy wash below. It shows fine black and white barring on its tail and primary wing feathers. The decurved bill is dark gray; the tail is fairly long and typically held in a cocked position. They are noticeably larger than the other wren species found in our area (House and Winter Wrens). They possess a varied repertoire of songs, singing even in winter, with phrasing such as a loud *tea-kettle, tea-kettle, tea-kettle* (in threes), repeated over and over. Pairs frequently perform duets involving a variety of raspy and chattering calls, especially when disturbed by birders or other intruders.

They are a non-migratory species, resident throughout the eastern and midwestern U.S. down into northeastern Mexico. Stable or growing slightly in overall numbers, they appear to be extending their range northward, perhaps taking advantage of warming winters resulting from climate change. Carolina Wrens are known to suffer significant die-off during extreme cold periods, but populations recover rapidly.

Written by Bruce Hill

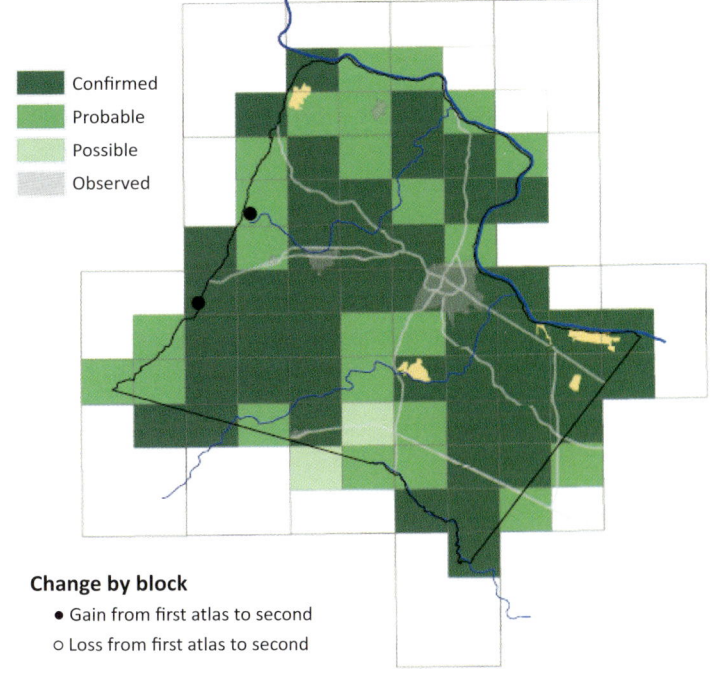

Confirmed
Probable
Possible
Observed

Change by block
- Gain from first atlas to second
- Loss from first atlas to second

Photo by Dave Boltz

BLUE-GRAY GNATCATCHER
Polioptila caerulea

Occurrence: common breeder and migrant

Earliest breeding confirmation: April 24, parent entering/exiting nest site or on nest (ON)

Latest breeding confirmation: August 11, recently fledged young (FL)

This tiny dynamo is a slim, long-tailed, and active bird, moving busily among the upper branches of deciduous trees. They are common in various woodland habitats, especially near water and forest edges. Males are bluish-gray above and white below, while the duller females' coloration is more grayish than blue. Their long tail is black with white outer feathers. Dark eyes are surrounded by a complete white eyering, and the male has a black V above its eyes, giving it a fierce (or perhaps comical) countenance. The long legs and small bill are dark gray. These birds frequently cock and flick their tails, especially while defending territory or flushing insect prey.

Their diet consists of a broad range of invertebrates, spiders, and small insects. They glean food from trees and also chase moths and other insects in flight, eating larger ones only after removing the wings and beating them against a branch to subdue (and perhaps tenderize) them. Their tiny nests are well constructed and camouflaged, with an open, cup-like structure of fine materials stuck together with spider webs and concealed with lichen. Nests are located high off the ground on a thin outer branch. A pair shares nest-building, incubation, and feeding duties, and both are aggressive defenders of their young and their territorial boundaries.

BLUE-GRAY GNATCATCHER (continued)

Blue-gray Gnatcatchers are long-distance migrants in our area, but in more temperate parts of the U.S. and much of Mexico, they are year-round residents. In Loudoun, they often appear quite early in the spring and can be found through mid-October. Look and listen for them in early April, when they are easiest to see before the trees have leafed out. They become harder to see but can still be heard throughout late spring and early summer. Most commonly heard is the varied repertoire of very thin and high-pitched, nasal calls produced by both males and females. During breeding season males will sing a rapid, jumbled song of thin, wheezy notes, including a variety of whistles, chips, and mews that often includes imitations of other species.

After breeding season, our migrant Blue-gray Gnatcatchers head south, wintering in Mexico, northern Central America, the Bahamas, and Cuba. Across their large range, this species' breeding population is estimated at 160 million (Rosenberg et al. 2016), with numbers stable or even increasing slightly in recent decades. There was a net gain in 11 blocks from Atlas 1 to Atlas 2.

Written by Bruce Hill

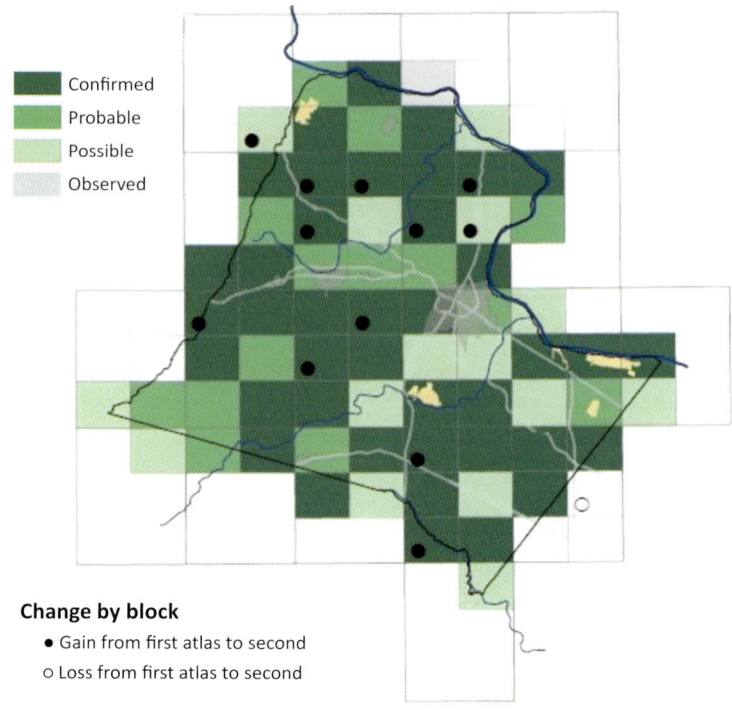

Confirmed
Probable
Possible
Observed

Change by block
- Gain from first atlas to second
○ Loss from first atlas to second

Photo by Dave Boltz

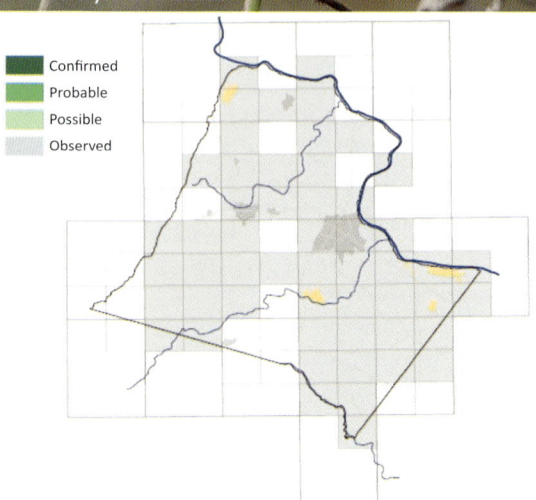

Confirmed
Probable
Possible
Observed

GOLDEN-CROWNED KINGLET
Regulus satrapa

Occurrence: uncommon migrant and winter resident

Earliest fall sighting: September 28

Latest spring sighting: April 19

The small, plump Golden-crowned Kinglet calls attention to itself by its incessant flitting from twig to twig as it feeds, as well as by its high, thin call — often delivered in three *zee-zee-zee* notes. Wintering throughout Loudoun, it can be seen foraging at all levels in both coniferous and deciduous trees, as well as in weedy vegetation. It often feeds in mixed flocks that can include the Ruby-crowned Kinglet. Although its feeding behavior is similar to the Ruby-crowned, the Golden-crowned Kinglet is readily distinguished by its strongly patterned facial markings, which include a black eye stripe, wide white eyebrow, and black stripe that encircles the yellow-orange crown for which it is named. Golden-crowneds are reported in greater numbers on Central Loudoun CBCs (averaging 52 individuals per count versus 17) than Ruby-crowneds, which are more common during migration.

This bird breeds in fir and spruce trees of the boreal forest, as well in more southerly montane forests, including the Appalachians. Though numerous, populations have declined over the past 5 decades.

Written by Bill Brown

RUBY-CROWNED KINGLET
Regulus calendula

Photo by Dave Boltz

Occurrence: uncommon migrant, occasional winter resident

Earliest fall sighting: September 16

Latest spring sighting: May 13

A tiny feathered ball of energy with little fear of people, the Ruby-crowned Kinglet brightens many a spring or fall bird walk, offering close looks at its acrobatic behavior and demonstrating its out-sized vocal abilities. They appeared in 58 atlas blocks, and are a regular on Central Loudoun CBCs. Named for the male's often-hidden red crown patch, this olive-green to gray bird has an otherwise plain head, white patch around the eye, bold white wingbar with a black bar immediately behind it, and yellow-washed underparts. It moves actively through the outer tree branches, often hanging upside down as it gleans insects under the leaves, and frequently flicks its wings.

Breeding in the northwestern U.S. and Canada, Ruby-crowned Kinglets guard their spruce-fir nesting territory with bubbly, inordinately loud, and long songs. They migrate south in fall into the central and southern U.S. and Mexico, using a variety of forest and scrub habitats, and may affiliate loosely with mixed-species flocks while feeding. Their population remains stable; they seem to handle some forest fragmentation and human disturbance fairly well.

Written by Bruce Hill

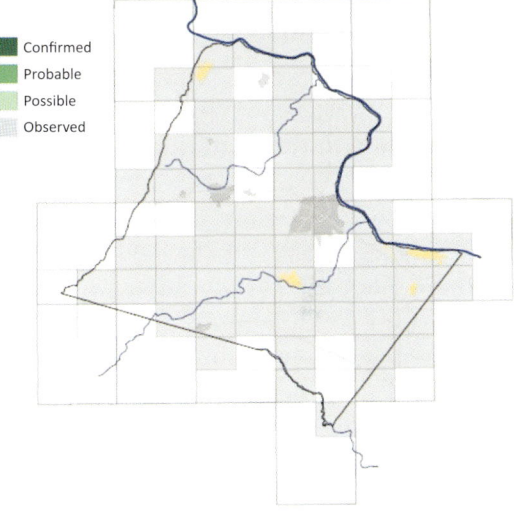

Confirmed
Probable
Possible
Observed

Photo by Linda Millington

EASTERN BLUEBIRD
Sialia sialis

Occurrence: common breeder and year-round resident

Earliest breeding confirmation: March 20, parent entering/exiting nest site or on nest (ON)

Latest breeding confirmation: September 10, recently fledged young (FL)

The Eastern Bluebird is once again a common and welcome sight in Loudoun and throughout its range, after its numbers plummeted in the middle of the last century. The male is a small, vividly colored thrush with a royal blue back and head and reddish-brown breast. Females are grayish-backed with paler blue wings and tail and an orange blush on the breast. Eastern Bluebirds are often found perched on fences or power lines along roads and in open fields, meadows, parks, and golf courses. They hunt insects by dropping to the ground and returning quickly to their perch. Their fall and winter diet includes berries as well as sumac, mistletoe, black cherry, currants, and other fruits. Fruit, mealworms, peanut hearts, and suet are their favorite feeder foods.

Although the male Eastern Bluebird attracts the female by displaying and flying in and out of the nest site with small amounts of nesting material, the female does the actual nest building. Bluebird nests are composed of loosely woven grasses and pine needles, and eggs are pale blue. Eastern Bluebirds traditionally nested in natural cavities, including

EASTERN BLUEBIRD (continued)

old woodpecker holes, but as decaying trees became harder to find, they have readily accepted nest boxes and other artificial structures. The North American, Virginia, and Michigan Bluebird Societies are good nest box design resources. Eastern Bluebirds often have two, sometimes three broods per year. Young from earlier broods disperse in summer, while young from later broods often overwinter with their parents.

The Eastern Bluebird exhibited breeding behavior in 70 of the 73 atlas blocks (96%), claiming a spot on the top 25 list of breeding species for Atlas 2. This species was documented in 80% of the blocks in Atlas 1. Populations of Eastern Bluebirds have increased significantly since the introduction of bluebird nest box campaigns and nesting box trails, after it was observed in the mid-20th century that they were losing their traditional nest holes to European Starlings and House Sparrows and to removal of decaying trees and old orchards. Loudoun Wildlife Conservancy maintains an extensive trail system of monitored bluebird nest boxes. During the first year of Atlas 2, 725 bluebird fledglings were documented in 250 nest boxes. More bluebird trails were added over the 5-year atlas period, with populations growing to 1,330 fledglings in 467 nest boxes during the final year.

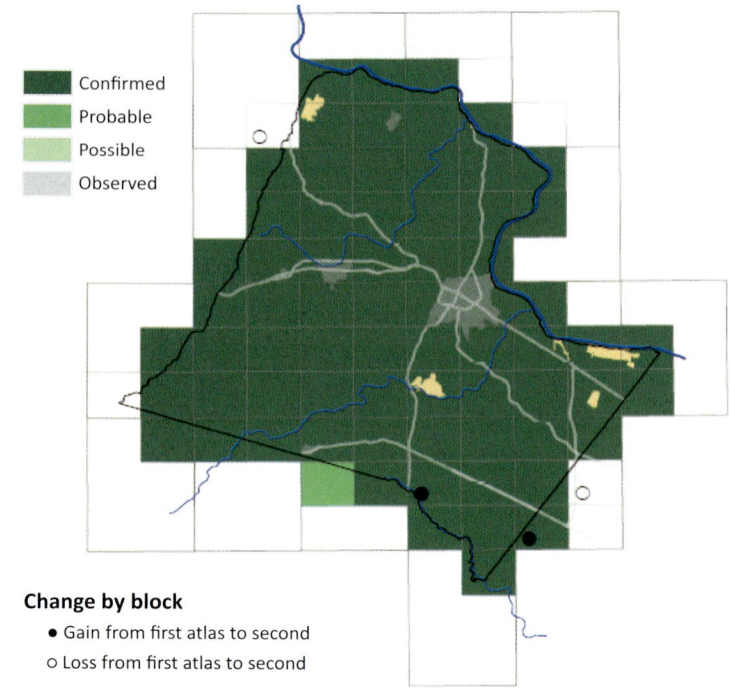

Change by block
- Gain from first atlas to second
- Loss from first atlas to second

Written by Linda Millington

Photo ©Dick Rowe

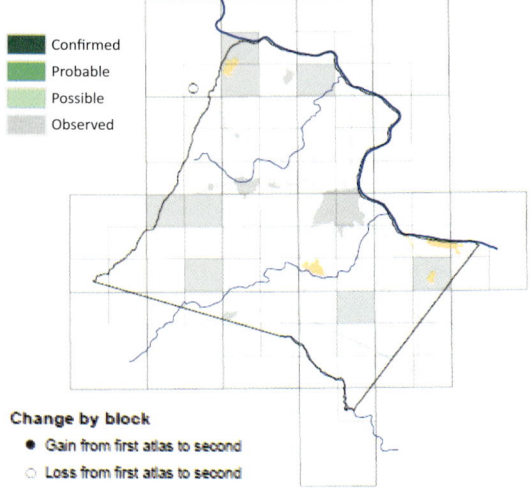

Change by block
- Gain from first atlas to second
- Loss from first atlas to second

VEERY
Catharus fuscescens

Occurrence: occasional migrant

Southerly migration period: fewer than 5 atlas sightings, see account for details

Northerly migration period: May 2 – 23

The Veery is one of the *Catharus* thrushes – a genus of birds with spotted breasts and plain brownish upperparts, usually found in the undergrowth of shady forests. About the size of a bluebird, the Veery is distinguished from other thrushes by its richer cinnamon color. Its relatively faint breast spots differentiate it from the similarly colored but boldly spotted Wood Thrush, a summer resident of Loudoun.

This ground forager was found in roughly 10% of the atlas blocks, spread throughout the county. About 75% of the sightings were during May, with just 3 during fall migration. Though absent from Loudoun in the summer, the Veery breeds in Virginia's Blue Ridge and can be found along Skyline Drive. The full breeding range extends along the Appalachians as far south as Georgia and, further north, reaches from New England across the northern states and southern Canadian provinces to the West Coast; they winter in South America. Populations are declining, likely due to habitat loss and forest fragmentation, which often results in increased cowbird parasitism.

Written by Bill Brown

GRAY-CHEEKED THRUSH

Catharus minimus

Occurrence: rare migrant

Southerly migration period: September 26 – November 3

Northerly migration period: May 7 – 18

At first glance, the Gray-cheeked Thrush might easily be mistaken for the more commonly seen Hermit or Swainson's Thrush. Like those other *Catharus* thrushes, its most striking characteristic is a heavily spotted breast. The Gray-cheeked Thrush is generally grayer than the others, lacking the reddish tinged tail of the Hermit Thrush and having gray rather than buffy facial markings like the Swainson's Thrush. Its eyering is faint and incomplete, and size is just slightly larger than the Eastern Bluebird or Swainson's Thrush.

The Gray-cheeked Thrush breeds across the northern boreal forest from Alaska through Newfoundland and winters in South America. Its preferred habitat during migration is forest with a heavy understory or shrub layer. This shy bird forages on the ground for insects and berries. It was reported only 11 times during the 5-year atlas, 6 times during spring migration and 5 times during fall migration. This species' remote breeding grounds and elusive behavior make population trends difficult to measure.

Written by Bill Brown

Photo by Deb Calhoun

Confirmed
Probable
Possible
Observed

SWAINSON'S THRUSH

Catharus ustulatus

Occurrence: uncommon migrant

Southerly migration period: September 5 – November 26

Northerly migration period: April 29 – June 5

Swainson's Thrush is one of several similar-looking thrushes of the genus *Catharus*. Birds of this genus have heavily spotted breasts and throats and unmarked upperparts and are usually found on forest ground and understory. Swainson's can be distinguished by its cool olive-gray upperparts – lacking the reddish color seen in the tail of the Hermit Thrush – and by the bold buffy eyering, more prominent than that of the Gray-cheeked Thrush or Veery. It breeds in North America's boreal forests and winters in Central and South America.

Swainson's Thrush was reported each year of the atlas, in 17 blocks spread throughout the county. These sightings were divided nearly equally between fall and spring migration, even though the southerly sightings occurred over a period more than twice as long as the northerly ones. This data is in keeping with a broader regional trend of a more protracted migration during the fall (Mack and Yong 2000). Populations of this nocturnal migrant are gradually declining – threats include habitat loss and collisions with towers and buildings.

Written by Bill Brown

Photo by Larry Meade

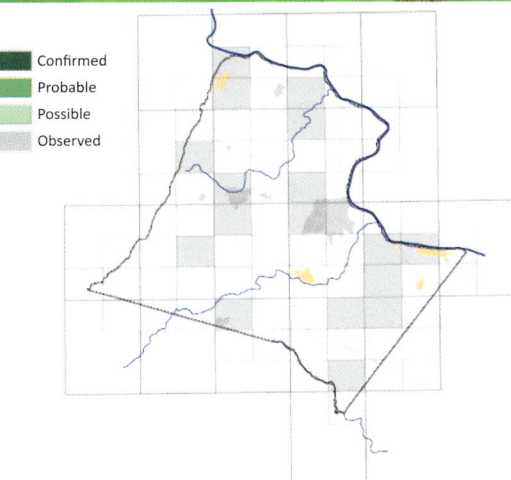

Confirmed
Probable
Possible
Observed

HERMIT THRUSH
Catharus guttatus

Occurrence: uncommon migrant and winter resident

Earliest fall sighting: September 22

Latest spring sighting: May 9

Photo by Larry Meade

Unique among *Catharus* thrushes for wintering in North America, this bird seems to be as solitary as its name indicates. It was observed in just over half of the atlas blocks, and ranges from 3 to 38 individuals per Central Loudoun CBC. The Hermit Thrush favors wooded or edge habitats. Its breeding range includes northern hardwood and boreal coniferous forests where it forages and nests at ground level in the undergrowth. This species is thought to be the only forest-dwelling thrush whose population has remained stable, or even increased, in recent years (Dellinger et al. 2012).

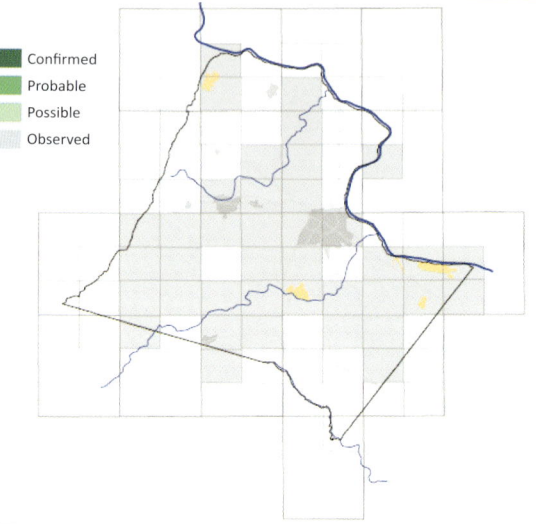

Confirmed
Probable
Possible
Observed

Smaller than the other *Catharus* thrushes, the Hermit Thrush has dull-brownish upperparts, with contrasting reddish-brown tail and wing primaries. Its breast and belly are whitish, with a dense, dark spotted pattern extending from the base of the bill and throat through the breast. The flanks are buffy or grayish. It has distinct white eyerings. The song of the Hermit Thrush, described as ethereal, or flute-like, is a treat to hear, albeit rare in our parts.

Written by Chris White

Photo ©Dick Rowe

WOOD THRUSH
Hylocichla mustelina

Occurrence: common breeder and migrant

Earliest breeding confirmation: May 13, recently fledged young (FL)

Latest breeding confirmation: August 1, parent carrying food or feeding young (CF)

The Wood Thrush is a study in elegant browns, but it is its song that makes it one of our most beloved birds. Its haunting, flutelike song floats from the forest interior, where it prefers a shrubby subcanopy and open forest floor with moist soil and plenty of decaying leaf litter in which to forage. Usually variations of *ee-o-lay*, the song has harmonized notes produced by the bird's double larynx, and ends with a higher, metallic *tii*, likened to a spoon dropping. It will also give a distinctive *whip whip* alarm or territorial defense call. A reclusive bird of mature eastern deciduous and mixed forests, the Wood Thrush is declining due to habitat fragmentation, resulting increased cowbird parasitism, deer over-browsing, and acid rain depleting its invertebrate food sources. Nevertheless, it is still fairly common from early April through early October in tracts of appropriate habitat in Loudoun, and was found in nearly every atlas block, with at least probable breeding evidence in most.

Our only summer thrush other than the bluebird and robin, the Wood Thrush has smooth reddish-brown upperparts,

WOOD THRUSH (continued)

fading to brown on the lower back and wings. Its pure white and somewhat pot-bellied front has bold blackish spots, and it sports a bold white eyering. Although retiring, it is not necessarily shy, and will often hop into view on an open branch or fallen log then go about its business of foraging through the litter for insects. Berries become an important food source in preparation for migration.

Together the male and identical female raise one to two broods per season. The female selects a spot low in a sapling or shrub, builds the nest of leaves, dead grass, and twigs, and incubates the three to four eggs. Pairs are monogamous, and new pairs form each year. The Wood Thrush leaves its breeding range in the eastern half of the U.S. and barely into southern Canada in mid-fall for its wintering grounds in low elevations of southern Mexico and Central America.

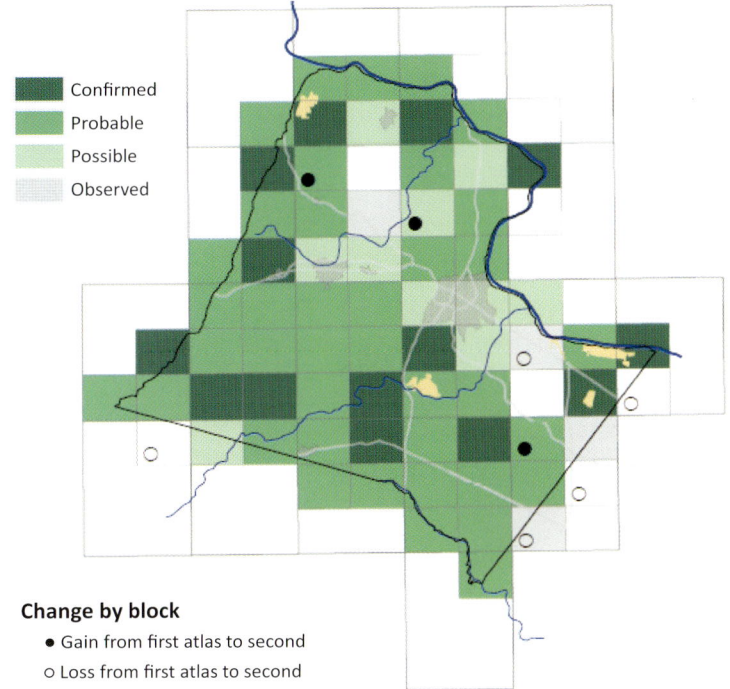

Confirmed
Probable
Possible
Observed

Change by block
● Gain from first atlas to second
○ Loss from first atlas to second

This beloved songster has been on the PIF Watch List for over a decade. It has experienced strong population declines throughout most of its range, particularly the Atlantic Coast and New England, where most common. According to the North American BBS, populations declined by almost 2% per year between 1966 and 2015, resulting in a cumulative decline of 62%.

Written by Mary Ann Good

Photo by Ian Richardson

AMERICAN ROBIN
Turdus migratorius

Occurrence: abundant breeder, common year-round resident

Earliest breeding confirmation: April 9, adult carrying nesting material or nest building (NB)

Latest breeding confirmation: September 15, recently fledged young (FL)

Perhaps our most recognizable bird, American Robins are commonly seen hopping on lawns in search of earthworms and other insects. Early birds, their cheerful *cheer up, cheerily* rich caroling is often heard before the sun rises as well as throughout the day. *Tuk* calls announce location, and a sharp whinny is given when alarmed. A medium-sized, dark bird with a round orange belly, partial white eyering, and perky stance, robins are a friendly presence in our daily lives.

While the sight of the first robin is said to announce the arrival of spring, they are actually year-round residents in Loudoun and throughout nearly all of the lower 48 states. Insects, earthworms, snails, and spiders make up the majority of their summer diet. Young are fed mostly insects and worms. In winter robins form flocks and spend more time in wooded areas. Because of this, we are less likely to see them. Winter diet consists heavily of berries and fruit. Robins are reported on every Central Loudoun CBC, averaging over 1,100 individuals per count.

AMERICAN ROBIN (continued)

Males attract females by singing and shaking their wings; he will defend his territory by singing and fighting other males. Females do most of the nest building using materials such as twigs, roots, and feathers to form a cup. The nest is reinforced with mud then lined with grass. Nests are built on horizontal branches and other structures. Usually four eggs, "robin's egg blue," are laid. Incubation is by the female for 12-14 days. Both parents feed the young; young fledge about 14 days after hatching. Robins typically have two, sometimes three, broods per year. Mortality is high, however, and only 25% of young will live until their first November (Vanderhoff et al. 2016).

Well documented as breeding throughout Loudoun, robins use both man-made and natural habitats including parks, fields, and woodlands. Their adaptability has likely led to their success. According to the North American BBS, populations have remained stable or increased over the past 5 decades. Since robins spend much of their time in our lawns, they are particularly susceptible to pesticide poisoning. Help keep them safe by not using chemicals on your lawn. While robins do not visit bird feeders, we can provide food sources for them by planting fruit-bearing trees and shrubs such as serviceberry, elderberry, dogwood, and crabapple. Robins also enjoy bathing and enthusiastically use birdbaths.

Written by Donna Quinn

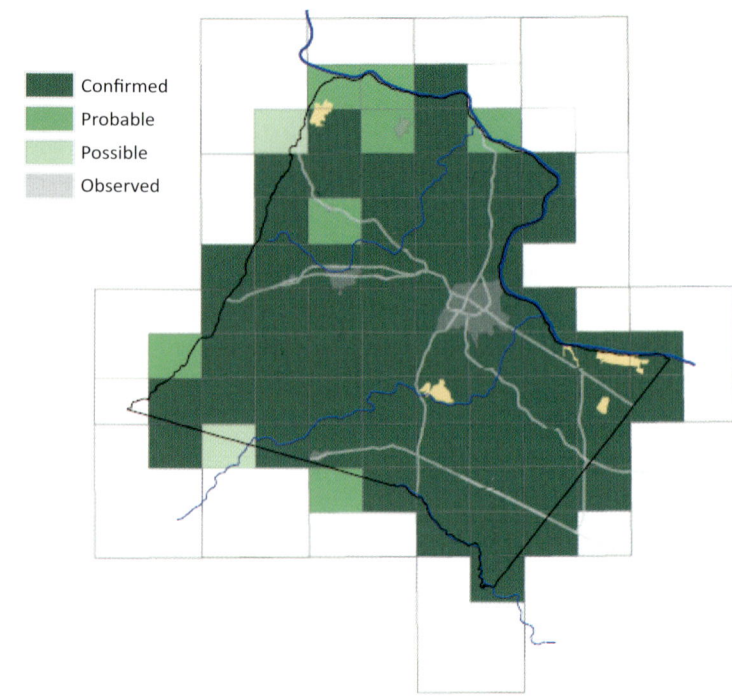

Confirmed
Probable
Possible
Observed

Photo by Dave Boltz

GRAY CATBIRD
Dumetella carolinensis

Occurrence: abundant breeder and migrant, rare winter visitor

Earliest breeding confirmation: May 4, adult carrying nesting material or nest building (NB)

Latest breeding confirmation: September 15, recently fledged young (FL)

The Gray Catbird, found in all 73 atlas blocks and confirmed as breeding in the majority of blocks, is abundant like its fellow mimid, the Northern Mockingbird. Unlike the mockingbird, the catbird is secretive, skulking low in the thickets and shrubbery where it builds its open cup nest, often no more than 6 feet from the ground. The bird's generic name *Dumettella* means "small thicket." The density of catbird populations has been found to increase linearly with the density of shrubbery. They also keep close to the ground in flight and avoid flying through open spaces. They do not favor areas dominated by conifers, or grazing land.

Named for their *mew* call (resembling a cat's), Gray Catbirds have as extensive a repertoire as mockingbirds do. However, they do not put on public displays of their prowess but will sing and chatter almost continuously from the depths of the undergrowth and lower story where they lurk. Catbird songs are made up of combinations of syllable-like sounds delivered in rapid sequence; the order seems random, the tempo uneven. They can produce more than 100 different sounds, including whistles, squeaks, harsh chattering, and some mimicry, but much less than the

GRAY CATBIRD (continued)

mockingbird. The two sides of their syrinx can produce sounds independently of each other (Smith et al. 2011), helping to produce the impression of larger numbers than are present.

Catbirds are monogamous and have been found in some places to maintain the pair bond from one year to the next. They are one of the few species that can recognize the Brown-headed Cowbird's eggs and eject them from their nests. They eat insects, caterpillars, and small moths, as well as fruit, sometimes to the annoyance of growers. No other North American bird has the uniform dark gray plumage sported by the Gray Catbird, which it accents with a black cap, black tail, and chestnut-colored undertail coverts. They arrive in Loudoun in mid-April and most leave by late October. They typically overwinter along the Gulf Coast and in Central America and the Caribbean, though on rare occasions

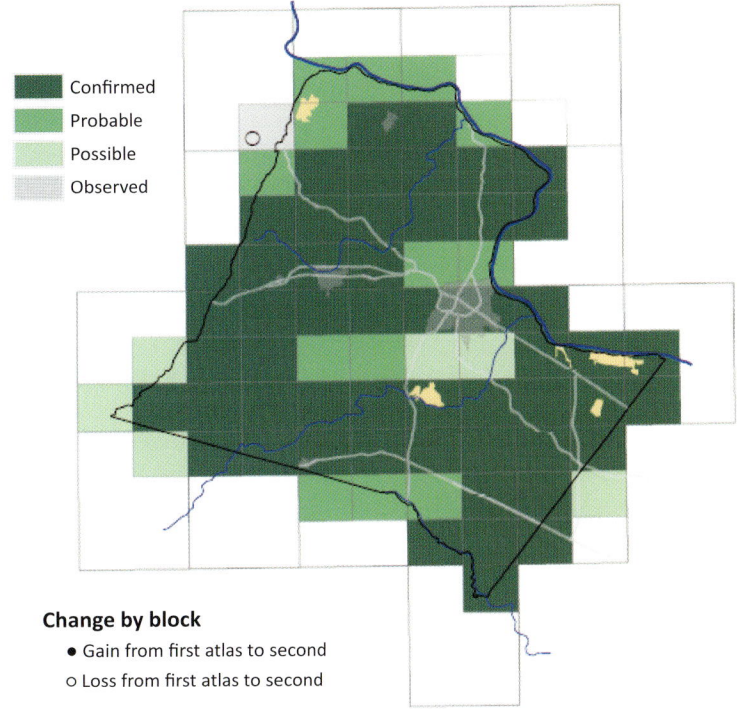

Confirmed
Probable
Possible
Observed

Change by block
● Gain from first atlas to second
○ Loss from first atlas to second

they turn up here, reported in low numbers on roughly half of the Central Loudoun CBCs. Overall, populations appear stable throughout their North American range. Because the catbird prefers successional habitats, it may benefit from human activities like the regeneration of cutovers, planting shrubbery, or adding edge habitat in forests by road or utility construction. Elimination of fence rows counteracts this and reduces available habitat.

Written by Chris White

Photo by Ian Richardson

BROWN THRASHER
Toxostoma rufum

Occurrence: common breeder and migrant, rare winter visitor

Earliest breeding confirmation: April 17, nest with eggs (NE)

Latest breeding confirmation: August 26, recently fledged young (FL)

Confirmed as a breeder in 44 atlas blocks, there are only a handful of areas where this early spring arriver was not recorded. Like its fellow mimids the Gray Catbird and Northern Mockingbird, the Brown Thrasher is a prolific songster. It shares with the catbird a preference for deep undergrowth and hedgerows where it skulks. Like the mockingbird, it can be found exuberantly singing its distinctively patterned songs from treetops and exposed perches, with its tail held down. Indeed, at one time the mockingbird was given credit for many of the thrashers' songs. The bird has one of the largest documented repertoires of song types – more than 1,100 – which it sings in long sessions with short pauses between the pairs of repeat phrases. In contrast, mockingbirds typically repeat phrases three or more times. The Brown Thrasher can also mimic other species, including the titmouse and cardinal.

This thrasher builds its bulky cup nest on the ground or in the middle of the dense, thorny shrubbery and undergrowth it prefers. Monogamous for the breeding season, the thrasher's courtship behavior includes an intimate

BROWN THRASHER (continued)

whisper song which is in sharp contrast to the ebullience of its territorial singing and counter-singing. Special care is needed when searching for this bird's nests because it will abandon them. It is a frequent parasitizing target of the Brown-headed Cowbird. It can recognize and remove those eggs, though not as efficiently as the Gray Catbird.

The Brown Thrasher arrives in Loudoun in late March, and most leave by mid-November or earlier for wintering grounds in the southeastern U.S. (where some live year-round). However, there were 4 winter atlas records, and one or two individuals are reported on roughly half of the Central Loudoun CBCs.

Despite its name the upperparts of the Brown Thrasher are more of a rich reddish-brown color. It is a medium-sized bird with a long tail and long legs. The underparts are white to buffy with extensive black streaking. Two wingbars are formed from the black and white feather patterns on the wing coverts. A yellow-eyed bird, its bill is long and slender with a slight decurvature. Though not listed as threatened or endangered in any part of its range, numbers have been declining in recent decades. The shrubby edge habitat it prefers is in decline as old fields revert to forest, manicured suburban areas grow, and farming is transformed.

Written by Chris White

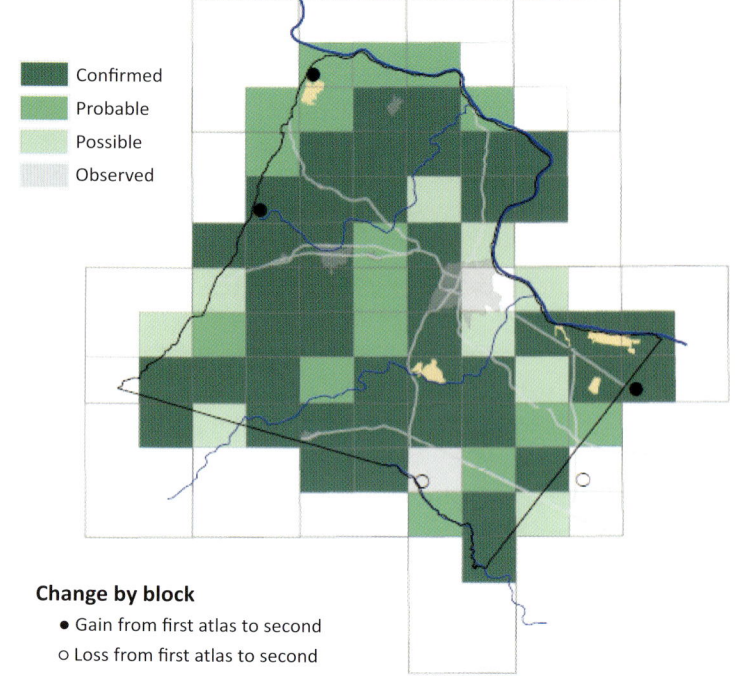

Confirmed
Probable
Possible
Observed

Change by block
● Gain from first atlas to second
○ Loss from first atlas to second

Photo by Ian Richardson

NORTHERN MOCKINGBIRD
Mimus polyglottus

Occurrence: abundant breeder and year-round resident

Earliest breeding confirmation: April 1, adult carrying nesting material or nest building (NB)

Latest breeding confirmation: September 2, recently fledged young (FL)

The Northern Mockingbird is found throughout Loudoun (and much of the U.S.) in urban, suburban, and rural areas, and was confirmed as breeding in 75% of the atlas blocks. This bird prefers open grassy areas with shrubby vegetation and thickets. It can readily be found showcasing its vocal repertoire from some high or exposed perch, like trees, utility wires, fences, or on a sign in a local park adjacent to its nesting area. Both sexes sing. The male can develop an impressive musical inventory of over 150 songs. These change during its adulthood, and the number may increase with age. In addition to imitating the songs and calls of other birds, it will imitate the sounds of non-bird species as well as machinery and other mechanical sounds. Unpaired males will also sing at night.

Mockingbirds typically raise multiple broods during the breeding season, and do not reuse the same nest. Sometimes the male builds three nests for the first brood before any eggs are laid. Nests are built in trees and shrubs, and human

NORTHERN MOCKINGBIRD (continued)

artifacts and cast-offs (paper, plastic, duct tape, shredded cigarette filters) are employed almost as promiscuously as are the elements of its musical repertoire. Mockingbirds are monogamous, and likely to be found in pairs. They aggressively defend both their nesting sites and territories and often chase after and attack predators like crows.

About the size of the American Robin but less bulky and with a longer tail, the mockingbird's upperparts are smooth gray, and the underparts are whitish. The long black tail is edged with white outer feathers, and the black wings have conspicuous white wingbars and white patches at the base of the primaries. These white featherings are prominent in aggressive and courtship displays. Mockingbirds are omnivorous and will eat insects, whether found on the ground or hawked in flight, as well as berries and even flowers.

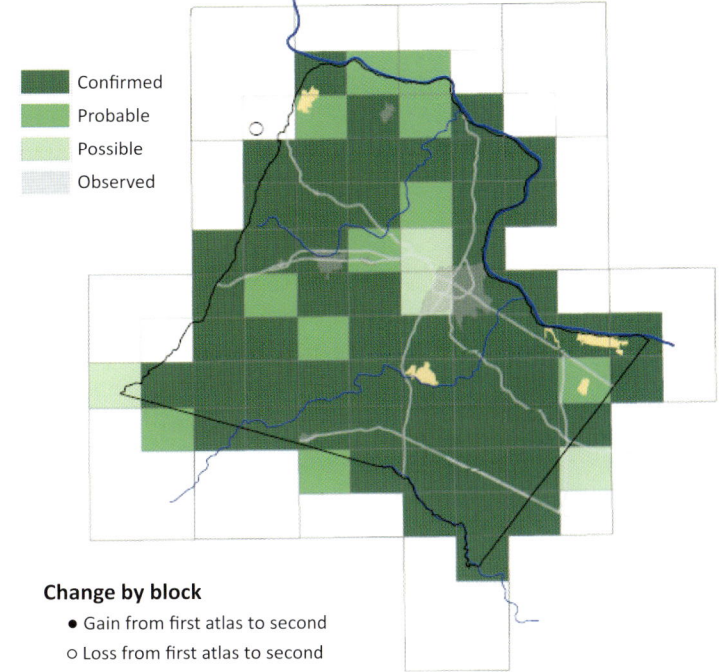

Confirmed
Probable
Possible
Observed

Change by block
- Gain from first atlas to second
- ○ Loss from first atlas to second

With an affinity for human settlements, mockingbirds are also exposed to the resulting contaminants, including lead and pesticides. The reforestation of agricultural land may be contributing to population declines in some areas. Populations were hardest hit in the 1800s when they were captured and sold as pets. Thanks to the International Migratory Bird Treaty Act, this practice was banned and populations have since rebounded and expanded northward.

Written by Chris White

Photo by Katherine Daniels

EUROPEAN STARLING
Sturnus vulgaris

Occurrence: abundant breeder and year-round resident

Earliest breeding confirmation: March 22, adult carrying nesting material or nest building (NB)

Latest breeding confirmation: August 31, recently fledged young (FL)

From about 100 birds imported to New York in the 1890s, the invasive European Starling population has exploded, now well-established in every U.S. state and much of Canada and Mexico. In Loudoun, they were found in almost every atlas block. Like disagreeable neighbors, starlings can be quarrelsome, noisy, messy, and not averse to "borrowing" from others. Almost any natural or artificial cavity is a potential starling nest site, and any birdhouse with a large enough opening is subject to a hostile takeover, whether already occupied or not. They have adapted to man-made habitats arguably better than any other bird species, nesting under house eaves and siding, in traffic light poles, under bridges, in almost any sheltered cavity you can imagine.

These qualities make them a highly successful invasive species, and interesting birds if you can get past the negatives. Large flocks, called murmurations, provide impressive visual displays as they fly in tight formation, changing direction in unison to avoid predators and often appearing like shifting smoke on the horizon. As individuals, starlings are

EUROPEAN STARLING (continued)

inquisitive and bold, opportunistically searching out food and nesting opportunities with great persistence. They are excellent mimics; captive birds have been taught various words and sounds, and their normal chatter includes whistles, rattles, and passable imitations of other birds and even man-made noises.

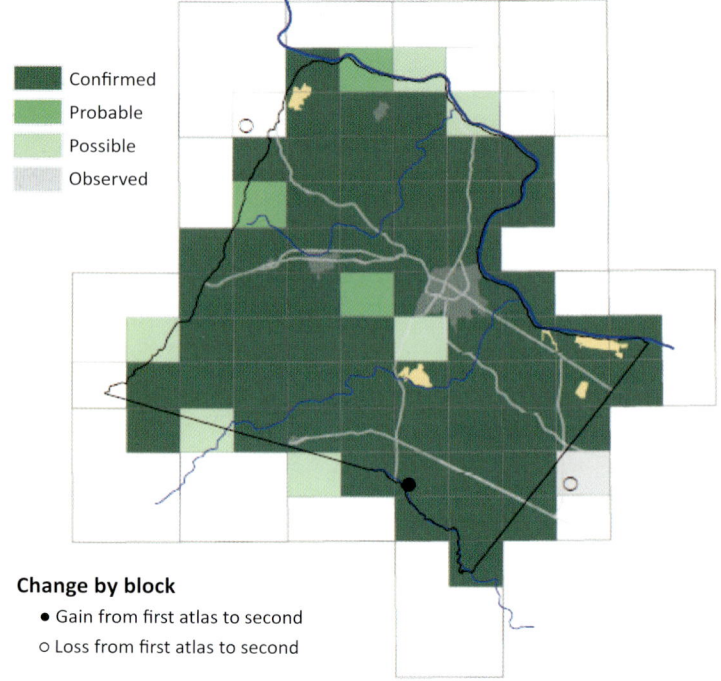

- Confirmed
- Probable
- Possible
- Observed

Change by block
- ● Gain from first atlas to second
- ○ Loss from first atlas to second

European Starlings have a pointed, dagger-like bill, yellow in breeding season, darker in winter. Adults are iridescent black with glossy purple and green highlights in breeding plumage. The gloss fades revealing white spots on their otherwise black/brown back and underside the rest of the year. Juveniles are pale brown and generally unmarked. They are about the size of a blackbird, but have a stubby tail and short but broad, pointed wings. Flight is fast and direct when moving about individually, but they are highly maneuverable when needed. European Starlings aggregate in large flocks outside of breeding season and range widely in search of feeding opportunities. More northerly populations, especially the juveniles, will often migrate short distances southward or downslope toward the coasts as winter approaches. They feed primarily on the ground, moving rapidly in groups. Their diet consists of almost anything they come across, but insects and invertebrates are preferred. The North American population consists of over 150 million individuals (PIF 2016). Perhaps fortunately, this represents a decline of 50% in the last 50 years (Sauer et al. 2017).

Written by Bruce Hill

Photo by Ian Richardson

CEDAR WAXWING
Bombycilla cedrorum

Occurrence: uncommon breeder and year-round resident

Earliest breeding confirmation: May 13, adult carrying nesting material or nest building (NB)

Latest breeding confirmation: August 1, recently fledged young (FL)

Regarded as one of North America's most handsome birds, because of its beautiful and finely detailed plumage, the Cedar Waxwing is also unique as a true fruit-eater. The species' breeding and migration behaviors are intimately tied to the availability of its primary food source. Sleek looking and crested, the Cedar Waxwing's upperparts are smooth cinnamon-brown on the crown and neck with a darker olive back. The rump and upper-tail areas are slate-gray, the underparts and belly pale yellow. Small-billed, the head features a black mask edged in white. Red-colored feathering on the wings appears like waxen droplets. The tail is squared off with a yellow terminal band.

Constantly foraging for fruit, in flocks, Cedar Waxwings do not maintain territories, and rarely return to a previous year's nest site. They do not have a distinctive song, but instead communicate with calls, one a buzzy, high-pitched trill and the other a *tsee* call of high-pitched, hissy whistling sounds. Their calls are thought to be related to courtship and other behavior patterns. Cedar Waxwings are monogamous during their breeding season; these social birds often

CEDAR WAXWING (continued)

nest in loose colonies. Courting males and females exchange a fruit, insect, or other item, passing it back and forth until the female eats it. The birds nest at the edge of wooded areas or in isolated trees and shrubs in old fields. Their nests are usually found by streams and ponds, where they hunt for the insects which provide the first food for their hatchlings and supplement their fruit intake. They tend to avoid forest interiors.

During fall and winter the birds thrive on a fruit diet. They completely digest the fruits' pulp and expel the seeds, acting as dispersers of their own food sources. Waxwings compete with mockingbirds and robins for fruits and use flocking tactics to overwhelm opposition. Cedar Waxwing populations have remained stable and increased in some areas over the last 30 years. This increase is supported by a net gain in 20 blocks from Atlas 1 to Atlas 2 and may be due to

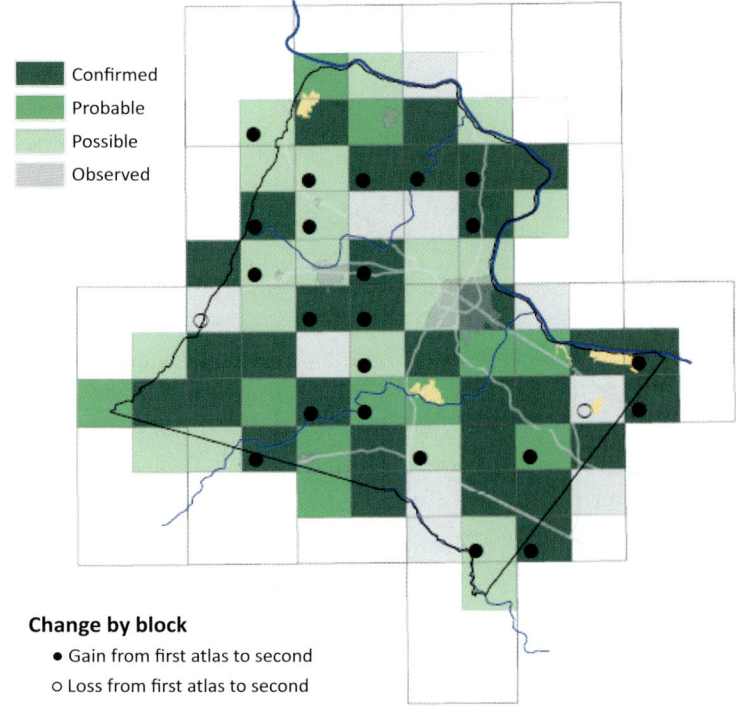

Confirmed
Probable
Possible
Observed

Change by block
- Gain from first atlas to second
○ Loss from first atlas to second

man-made changes to habitat; they are increasingly found in suburbs with cedar trees and ornamental fruit bearers. Cowbirds attempt to parasitize Cedar Waxwing nests, but hatchlings do not survive on their host's fruit diet. Surprisingly for an uncommon species, the Cedar Waxwing was reported in every atlas block, a distinction held by only 14 of the 262 atlas species.

Written by Chris White

Photo by Ian Richardson

HOUSE SPARROW
Passer domesticus

Occurrence: abundant breeder and year-round resident

Earliest breeding confirmation: February 18, adult carrying nesting material or nest building (NB)

Latest breeding confirmation: September 11, recently fledged young (FL)

Arguably, no U.S. species is more intertwined with humans than the non-native House Sparrow. A group of 100 House Sparrows from England was released into New York City in 1851, tasked with controlling a caterpillar pest that was killing elm trees. Introductions into San Francisco and Salt Lake City in the early 1870s enabled this tough, adaptable bird to become a common year-round resident throughout North America (except Alaska and northern Canada). This species was reported in nearly every atlas block and confirmed as breeding in all but a handful. In urban areas where food and nesting sites can be challenging to find, they fill a niche not used by native birds. In more agricultural areas, however, this aggressive sparrow competes with native birds for limited nesting cavities. They are known to evict Eastern Bluebirds, Purple Martins, and Tree Swallows from their nests to the point of affecting local populations.

House Sparrows are not related to our native sparrows; they are chunkier with a larger, rounded head and stouter bill. Breeding males have a gray crown, chestnut neck, white cheek, and black bib. The male's bib darkens during the

HOUSE SPARROW (continued)

breeding season; males with larger patches of black tend to be older and more dominant. Non-breeding males lack the black bib and chestnut neck, while females are buffy brown overall with striped backs. Males sing one or a series of *cheep* or *chirrup* notes throughout much of the year. After losing a mate, females may sing to attract a new one.

House Sparrows are found almost anywhere, scrounging for crumbs along city streets or suburban parks, dining on seeds at bird feeders, foraging for grain around farm buildings, snagging insects to feed their young, or dust-bathing along dirt roads. The only places they avoid are uninhabited forests and grasslands. They nest in holes of buildings, street lights, signs, traffic lights, rain gutters, tree cavities, and nest boxes. Both parents stuff the hole with nesting material and incubate and feed the three to six young. They often

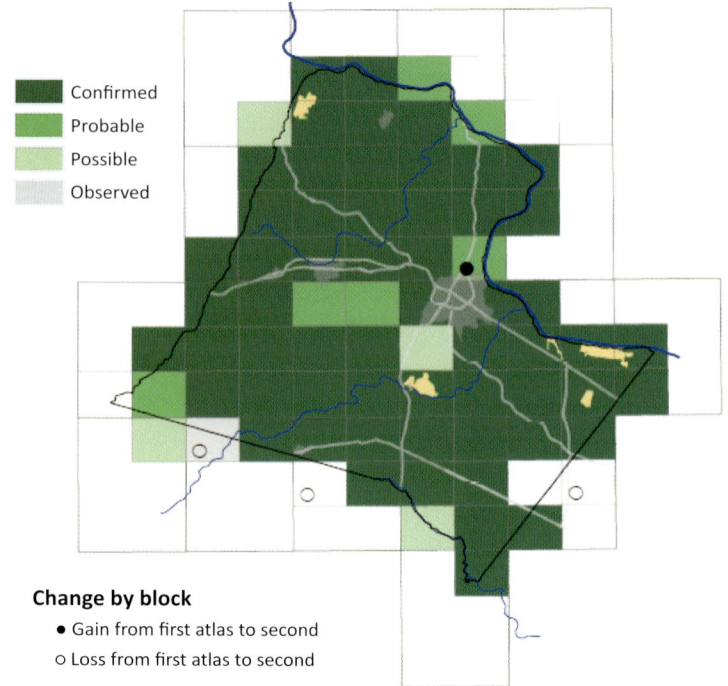

Confirmed
Probable
Possible
Observed

Change by block
- Gain from first atlas to second
- Loss from first atlas to second

breed in small colonies, raising two to three broods per year. Once the young leave the nest they flock with other juveniles. Ironically, this Old World sparrow from Europe is red-listed as a species of high conservation concern throughout its native range. Though still numerous in North America, populations have gradually declined over the past 5 decades, due in part to the industrialization of farms.

Written by Spring Ligi

Photo by Laura McGranaghan

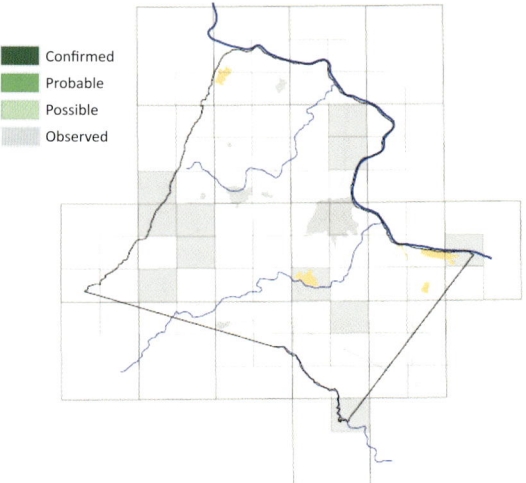

Confirmed
Probable
Possible
Observed

AMERICAN PIPIT
Anthus rubescens

Occurrence: occasional winter visitor, rare migrant

Earliest fall sighting: October 3

Latest spring sighting: May 9

This winter visitor may be spotted in small flocks on plowed fields or open grassy areas in Loudoun and throughout the southern U.S. Shorelines are another favorite feeding ground; their former name "Water Pipit" reflects this. Their diet consists largely of insects, but seeds play a significant role during winter. This species is grayish-brown above and a streaky buff to light orange below, with long legs and dark eyes that stand out on an otherwise blank face. It may look like a small thrush at first glance, but note that it habitually bobs its tail. The flight call, a sharp *pi-pit*, and white outer tail feathers are also helpful in identifying this species.

The American Pipit breeds on the northern tundra of Canada and Alaska. They were documented in 15% of the atlas blocks and approximately 75% of the Central Loudoun CBCs. While possibly declining, and threatened by the effects of climate change on their Arctic breeding grounds, they remain numerous with a global population of about 20 million birds (PIF 2016).

Written by Bruce Hill

HOUSE FINCH
Haemorhous mexicanus

Occurrence: abundant breeder and year-round resident

Earliest breeding confirmation: March 25, adult carrying nesting material or nest building (NB)

Latest breeding confirmation: September 11, recently fledged young (FL)

Photo by Ian Richardson

Native to the southwestern U.S. and Mexico, this cheerful songster was introduced to the East Coast in 1940 when a few dozen were released by illegal cage-bird dealers who feared prosecution. Over the next 50 years, these finches successfully colonized the eastern U.S. Their habitat expanded from western deserts to almost any kind of man-made habitat, including city parks, backyards, shopping centers, farms, and woodland edges. Most House Finches in Loudoun reside here year-round, though more northern populations may move south for the winter.

Adult males have rosy red around their face and upper breast, with a streaky brown back and belly. The red coloration is influenced by diet; the more carotenoid-rich foods eaten, the redder the male. Females prefer the reddest males, perhaps increasing the odds that their mate will be a good provider for their young. Juveniles and females are streaky brown overall. House Finches eat mainly vegetable matter, including seeds, buds, berries, and fruits. In fact, they stand out in the bird world for feeding their nestlings regurgitated seeds instead of animal foods. They make themselves comfortable at bird feeders, lingering to crack open and eat the sunflower seeds before flying away.

This gregarious bird is often found in flocks. Pairs typically form while in their winter flocks, though some pairs stay together year-round. They nest in a variety of trees (especially conifers), hanging planters, ivy growing on buildings, and old nests of other birds. Both parents feed the nestlings; the male may continue feeding the young for a couple weeks after they leave the nest while the female begins a second clutch. Pairs can raise three or more broods per breeding season. Males sing year-round, a long and lively warbling comprised of short notes that often end with an upward or downward slur. Females may sing a shorter, simpler version during the breeding season.

According to the North American BBS, populations have increased in recent decades and appear to be spreading. Their success is likely due to their affinity for man-made habitats. Found in 66 of the 73 atlas blocks, many of the breeding confirmations were located in blocks with urban and suburban areas. These adaptable birds are not invincible though. Conjunctivitis, a contagious infection that causes respiratory problems and swollen eyes, has taken a toll on populations in some areas, leaving affected individuals vulnerable to predators and starvation and reminding us to keep our feeders clean!

Written by Spring Ligi

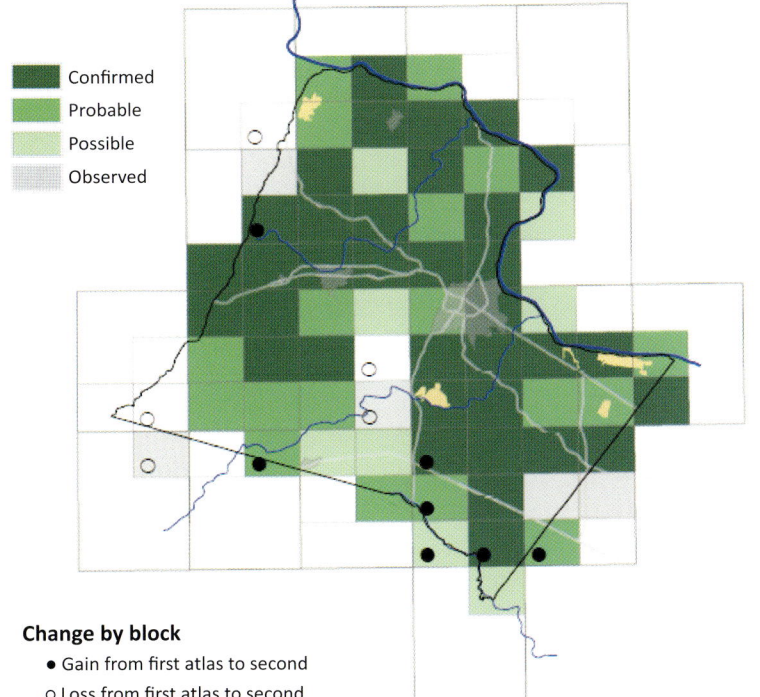

Confirmed
Probable
Possible
Observed

Change by block
- Gain from first atlas to second
○ Loss from first atlas to second

PURPLE FINCH
Haemorhous purpureus

Occurrence: occasional irruptive migrant and winter visitor

Earliest fall sighting: September 26

Latest summer sighting: May 15

Photo by Dave Boltz

These seasonal Loudoun visitors are easily mistaken for their less vivid counterpart, the House Finch. Purple Finches have more defined markings, and their heavy, seed-cracking bill is larger. Males show a richer, reddish-purple wash on their nape, head, and chest. Females are brown and heavily streaked, with distinct facial markings, including white eyebrows and dark brown cheek patches. They were reported every year of the atlas, in just under half the blocks, and on roughly three-quarters of the Central Loudoun CBCs. Some Purple Finch populations reside permanently in conifer forests of the northeastern U.S. and Pacific Coast, including nearby highlands in Virginia, West Virginia, and Maryland, likely accounting for 2 atlas sightings in June. Other populations migrate into the Canadian boreal forest to breed; outside of breeding season, they travel widely throughout the U.S. following food sources. Though conifer seeds are a staple, their diet is varied; they are fond of black oil sunflower seeds at feeders. Their population has declined over 50% since 1966 (Sauer et al. 2017), perhaps in part from competition with the expanding House Finch.

Written by Bruce Hill

Confirmed
Probable
Possible
Observed

Photo by Bill Brown

Confirmed
Probable
Possible
Observed

COMMON REDPOLL
Acanthis flammea

Occurrence: rare irruptive migrant and winter visitor

Earliest winter sighting: December 28

Latest spring sighting: April 9

A visitor from the far north, this diminutive finch makes rare irruptions into our region in years when limited food supplies push them south of their normal wintering grounds. When they appear, they tend to travel in flocks of several to several hundred individuals. This author hosted about 125 Common Redpolls at his feeders in the late 1980s, going through several ten-pound bags of thistle seed in a few short weeks. They were reported 5 times in 3 atlas years and found on 3 of the past 20 Central Loudoun CBCs.

The Common Redpoll has a small yellow bill, red forehead, and streaked back and flanks; most exhibit a black patch on their lores and chin. Males have a rosy wash on their cheeks and upper breast. They feed actively on seeds in weedy fields and open woodland, seemingly never sitting still as flocks forage on the ground or in low vegetation. Redpolls breed in the high Arctic tundra and forests of northern Alaska and Canada. They remain a widespread and abundant species, though climate changes in the Arctic could be of concern.

Written by Bruce Hill

RED CROSSBILL
Loxia curvirostra

Photo by Dave Boltz

Occurrence: rare irruptive migrant and winter visitor

Earliest/latest seasonal sightings: fewer than 5 atlas sightings, see account for details

The Red Crossbill is a permanent resident and nester in northern and montane conifererous forests, but outside of breeding season, small numbers can irrupt southward into our region. Two late fall 2012 sightings were recorded in Loudoun. As the name indicates, crossbills possess a unique bill, adapted to extract seeds from cones, especially those of spruce, firs, pines, and hemlocks. They can be highly nomadic, wandering extensively while seeking out areas with abundant food sources. Red Crossbills are red to orange (male) or greenish (female), with darker black/brown wings and tail and a uniquely twisted and crossed bill. They are slightly larger and stockier than House Finches. Calls include multiple sharp *kip* notes, given while feeding and in flight. Typically found in small groups in the vicinity of conifers, they can occasionally be spotted consuming grit along roadsides. The global population is considered stable, though it has suffered declines in some areas. Red Crossbills exhibit significant geographic variations in diet, bill size, weight, and calls; some subspecies may be designated full species in the future.

Written by Bruce Hill

Confirmed
Probable
Possible
Observed

WHITE-WINGED CROSSBILL
Loxia leucoptera

Photo by Dave Boltz

Occurrence: rare irruptive migrant and winter visitor

Earliest/latest seasonal sightings: fewer than 5 atlas sightings, see account for details

The White-winged Crossbill is one of two crossbill species that can appear in our area, albeit rarely. The only atlas sighting was a flock of 14 reported from Snicker's Gap Hawkwatch in November 2012. While similar in appearance to the Red Crossbill, the White-winged male is often a more vibrant red, and has two bold white wingbars on pure black wings. Females are greenish, with mottled gray streaking on the mantle, chest, and flanks. Their song is a dry trill, and their call is a rapid *chit-chit-chit*. A fun fact: 75% of individuals are righties (with the lower mandible of their thick, curved bill crossing to the right), the rest are lefties (Benkman 2012).

White-winged Crossbills nest in the far northerly latitudes of the U.S. and Canada, where their preferred food source is spruce and tamarack cones. These nomads breed whenever and wherever food is abundant, and have been known to nest successfully in all 12 months of the year. Their overall global population is estimated at 50 million and numbers appear stable, but accurate counts are difficult due to their nomadic nature.

Written by Bruce Hill

Confirmed
Probable
Possible
Observed

PINE SISKIN
Spinus pinus

Occurrence: occasional irruptive migrant and winter visitor

Earliest fall sighting: October 12

Latest spring sighting: May 19

Pine Siskins were observed in 24 of the 73 atlas blocks before returning to their breeding grounds in the coniferous forests of the north. Their presence has been recorded in roughly half of the Central Loudoun CBCs. An irruptive species, with its irregularity thought to relate to its food supply, this is a bird that can seem abundant in a particular location one year and pop up somewhere else the next. When they do appear, small flocks can often be found at thistle feeders in company with American Goldfinches and in weedy fields and pine stands.

The Pine Siskin is a small, slender bird with a notched tail and narrow, finely pointed bill. The head and body are brown and streaked overall; the underparts are whitish with streaking across the breast and flanks. The wings have varying amounts of yellow along the feather edges, with buffy to white wingbars. This species is considered a "common bird in steep decline" (PIF 2017).

Written by Chris White

Photo ©Dick Rowe

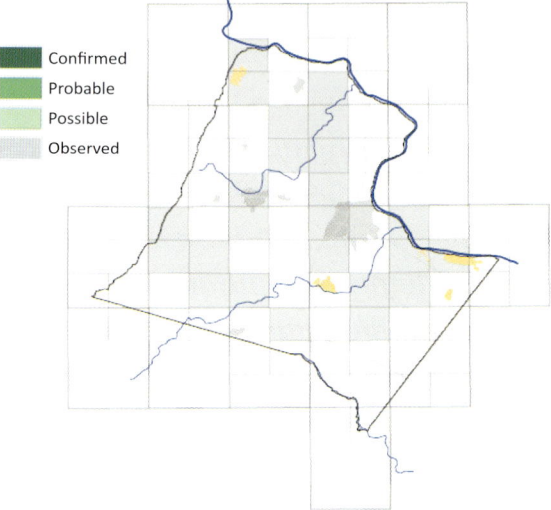

Confirmed
Probable
Possible
Observed

Photo by Ian Richardson

AMERICAN GOLDFINCH
Spinus tristis

Occurrence: abundant breeder and year-round resident

Earliest breeding confirmation: May 31, adult carrying nesting material or nest building (NB)

Latest breeding confirmation: October 12, recently fledged young (FL)

As the dog days of mid-summer approach and many of our breeding birds quiet down, the American Goldfinch draws attention with its *po-ta-to-chip* call, often given when flying in a bouncy, roller coaster-like pattern. Though the male does sing in the spring, a long series of varying warbles and twitters, this late breeder is thought to hold off on nesting until thistle is in peak abundance (mid-June through mid-September in Loudoun). Their nests are lined with thistle down, and young are fed regurgitated thistle seeds. Ideal goldfinch habitat includes weedy fields and floodplains with thistle and a few shrubs or trees for shelter and nesting. They are also found in suburban parks and backyards, readily visiting feeders for niger and sunflower seeds. Goldfinches have a special ability to eat while hanging upside-down from a thistle, dandelion, or other seedhead, allowing access to food sources unavailable to other birds. Throughout the non-breeding season they can be found foraging nomadically in flocks; loose colonies may form when nesting.

Their short breeding season allows time for only one brood per year, though experienced females may leave their

AMERICAN GOLDFINCH (continued)

mate to finish raising the first brood while they start a second brood with a new mate. The female lays four to six eggs in a tightly woven, open cup nest. The parasitic Brown-headed Cowbird does not pose a threat to this species – the cowbird chicks can't survive on their all-seed diet. Not the most aggressive of songsters, the American Goldfinch does not join other songbirds in mobbing predators.

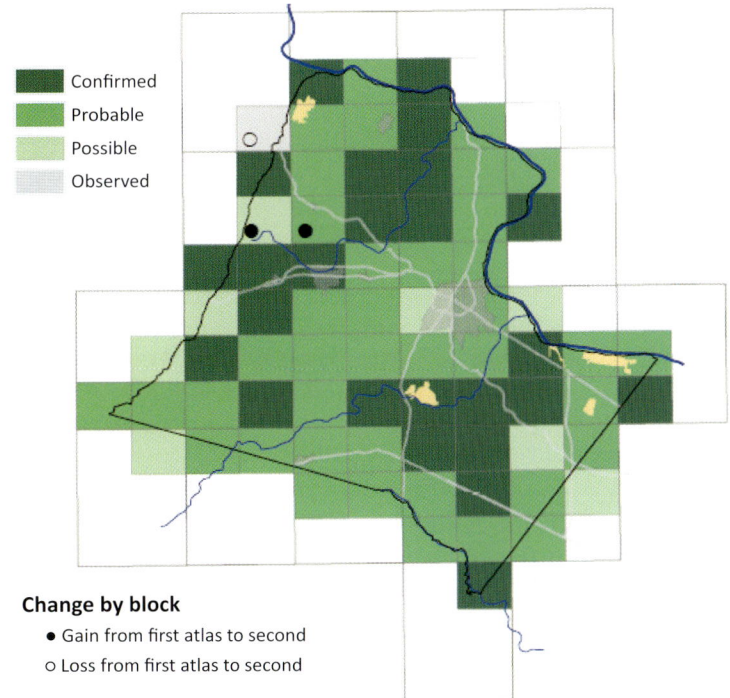

Confirmed
Probable
Possible
Observed

Change by block
● Gain from first atlas to second
○ Loss from first atlas to second

Breeding males are easy to identify with their cheerful yellow body, black forehead, and black wings with white markings. Females and juveniles, with less and variable amounts of yellow, are identifiable by their blackish-brown wings with white wingbars and lack of streaking. Breeding males dress down for the winter, making identification more of a challenge. They are the only finch to molt twice a year, in late winter and late summer. The American Goldfinch is widespread and common throughout its North American range, though populations have declined slightly in recent decades. Populations in Loudoun are non-migratory; individuals in the northernmost part of their range (southern Canada and the northern U.S.) migrate south for the winter. This golden beauty made the top 25 list of breeding species for the atlas and was 1 of 14 species documented in all 73 blocks.

Written by Spring Ligi

Photo by Heather Cuthill

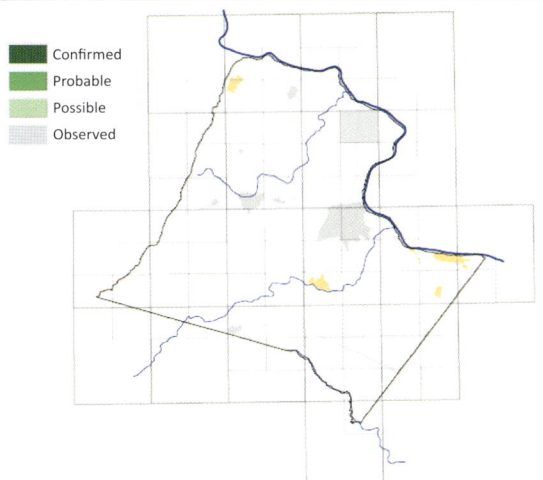

Confirmed
Probable
Possible
Observed

LAPLAND LONGSPUR
Calcarius lapponicus

Occurrence: rare winter visitor

Earliest/latest seasonal sightings: fewer than 5 atlas sightings, see account for details

This songbird of the high Arctic breeds in wet tundra with continual daylight and winters in open fields (prairies, pastures, grassy beaches) across much of the U.S. and southern Canada, though the majority winter on the Great Plains. Lapland Longspurs are known for forming huge flocks, but in Loudoun there was only a flock of 7 observed flying over Waterford 2 in December 2012. This species was reported on 3 of the past 20 Central Loudoun CBCs. It forages on the ground, eating mostly seeds and insects. The name "longspur" refers to an elongated claw on the hind toe.

Breeding males have a distinctive black face, crown, and throat, a broad white brow-line, and chestnut nape. Males in non-breeding plumage and females appear similar, streaky overall with chestnut on the wings and cheeks outlined in black. The Lapland Longspur is common throughout its remote breeding range. Potential disturbance in the Arctic National Wildlife Refuge may pose a threat for this species.

Written by Spring Ligi

SNOW BUNTING
Plectrophenax nivalis

Photo by Lucy Rowe

Occurrence: rare winter visitor

Earliest/latest seasonal sightings: fewer than 5 atlas sightings, see account for details

Snow Buntings are birds of the high Arctic, nesting in rock crevices on the tundra. They winter in open fields and along the shores of lakes and oceans across Canada and into the northern U.S. They are sometimes called "Snowflakes" as flocks of Snow Buntings may conjure the image of snowflakes swirling through the air and settling on a winter field. Though Loudoun is south of their typical wintering range, in 2013 a flock of 47 birds was documented for the atlas in Waterford 4. Single Snow Buntings were reported on the 2011 and 2012 Central Loudoun CBCs, both at the County Landfill in Leesburg 5.

Snow Buntings forage on the ground for insects and seeds, occasionally jumping up to reach seeds from taller stems. Breeding males are a striking white with a black back. Females and non-breeding males have white underparts with rusty patches on the head, "ear," and shoulders (more pronounced in females) along with a dark, streaky back. This species is listed on the 2014 State of the Birds Report as a "common bird in steep decline."

Written by Spring Ligi

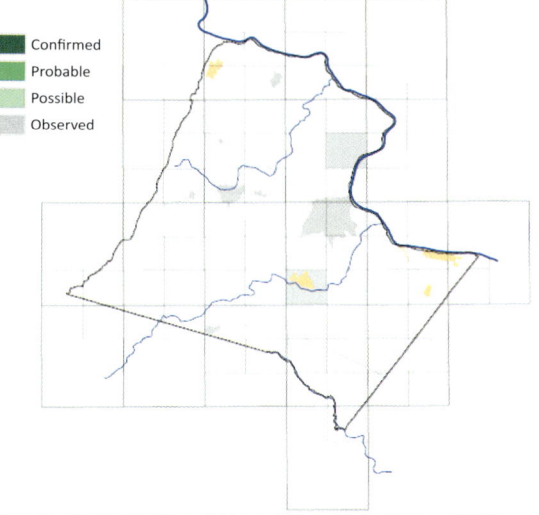

Confirmed
Probable
Possible
Observed

Photo by Larry Meade

EASTERN TOWHEE
Pipilo erythrophthalmus

Occurrence: common breeder and migrant, occasional winter resident

Earliest breeding confirmation: May 13, adult carrying nesting material or nest building (NB)

Latest breeding confirmation: September 8, parent carrying food or feeding young (CF)

The Eastern Towhee is a widespread avian resident of Loudoun. This species frequents forest edges, backyard gardens, and beneath feeders as it scratches around noisily for food in the leaf litter. Its call (*che-wink*) and song (*drink-your-tea!*), both with an upwards inflection, are familiar to most birders. While they spend most of their time under cover in low brush and overgrown areas, they are quite curious and will frequently perch up on a high branch when singing or investigating a disturbance.

Distinctively marked and colored, male Eastern Towhees have a black head, throat, and back, rufous flanks, and a white belly. Females are similarly patterned, but the head and upperparts are a rich brown instead of black. Both sexes show white spotting on the outer edges of their wings and tails, which can be conspicuous in flight. They have large, conical bills and red eyes. Larger than the other sparrow-like birds in our area, they are approximately the size of a cardinal, but more robust. Towhees are omnivorous, regularly eating insects, spiders, berries, fruit, and flower

EASTERN TOWHEE (continued)

buds as well as a variety of seed types, large and small. They nest on the ground or in low shrubs, typically no more than 4 feet high. They can raise between one and three broods per year. While more numerous in our area during the breeding season and in migration, many overwinter, and they are regularly found on the Central Loudoun CBC. They can actually be easier to find during winter as they rustle loudly through dry leaf litter.

This species resides almost exclusively in the eastern half of the U.S., but very small numbers reach up into southern-most Canada during the breeding season. The more northerly birds, including those in our area, typically migrate short distances south after breeding, while in the southern states, many remain permanent residents. Though their population has declined by nearly 50% in the past 50 years (Sauer et al. 2017), Eastern Towhees remain quite common

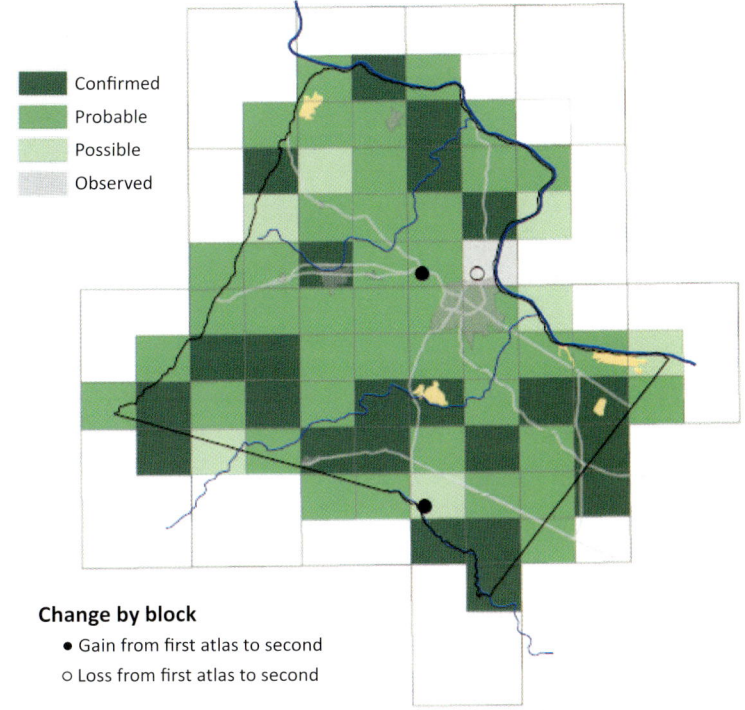

Change by block
- ● Gain from first atlas to second
- ○ Loss from first atlas to second

throughout their range. Overall numbers appear to rise and fall as land use and farming practices change and their preferred scrubby edge habitat waxes and wanes. They were observed in all 73 atlas blocks and identified as probable or confirmed breeders in 65. The Eastern Towhee made the top 25 list of breeding species in both Atlases 1 and 2.

Written by Bruce Hill

Photo by Gerco Hoogeweg

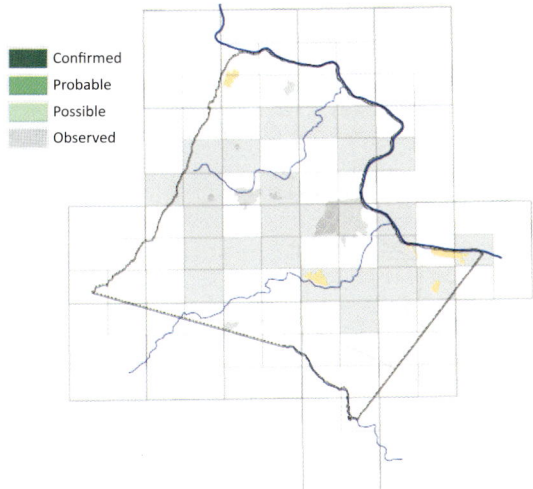

AMERICAN TREE SPARROW
Spizelloides arborea

Occurrence: occasional migrant and winter visitor

Earliest fall sighting: November 14

Latest spring sighting: March 25

The American Tree Sparrow is proof that birds don't always live up to their names; it prefers the ground over trees for foraging and nesting. This sparrow migrates to its far northern breeding grounds in early spring and returns in late fall. It winters throughout southern Canada and the northern half of the U.S; females tend to winter farther south than males. Its preferred habitat includes weedy old fields, marshes, and groves of small trees. In the winter months it may occasionally show up at bird feeders.

The American Tree Sparrow is distinguished by its rufous-crowned gray head and nape. A rufous stripe runs behind the eye. The throat and breast are gray with a dark central spot. The sides and flanks are buff, and tail feathers are edged in white. Loss of weedy old field habitat and wider changes in land use are thought to be among the major causes of a significant population decline. This sparrow was found in just over 30% of the atlas blocks and reported on nearly every Central Loudoun CBC.

Written by Chris White

CHIPPING SPARROW
Spizella passerina

Occurrence: abundant breeder and migrant, rare winter resident

Earliest breeding confirmation: April 24, adult carrying nesting material or nest building (NB)

Latest breeding confirmation: September 7, recently fledged young (FL)

Photo by Gerco Hoogeweg

Pugnacious and with little fear of people, this small bird casts a big shadow as one of the more numerous and readily observable breeding species in Loudoun. In urbanized areas with street trees, throughout the suburbs, and across a wide range of rural and natural habitats, the "Chippie" was logged as either a confirmed or probable breeder in virtually every atlas block. With its rufous cap, black eye stripe, dark bill, crisply patterned brown wings, and clean gray face and underside, this tiny, active sparrow makes a good first impression as it searches for food under trees, along roadsides, and around bird feeders and flowerbeds. Size alone is often enough to separate it from other larger sparrows that regularly frequent feeders and suburban yards. The male's rapid mechanical trill is sung repeatedly from trees and rooftops in spring, beginning in early April in Loudoun as they arrive to stake out and defend territories.

This confiding open forest species was quick to adapt to city life, and was reportedly the most common sparrow in urban areas before it lost this distinction to the invasive House Sparrow. It was known to use horse hair as a preferred nesting material, but other animal hair, grasses, and weeds will also do. Chipping Sparrows breed throughout most of the lower 48 and much of Canada. They build their small, open nest in various types of trees and occasionally on the ground. They lay three to four eggs, and in our area usually raise two broods per season. Cowbird parasitism is a frequent problem for this species.

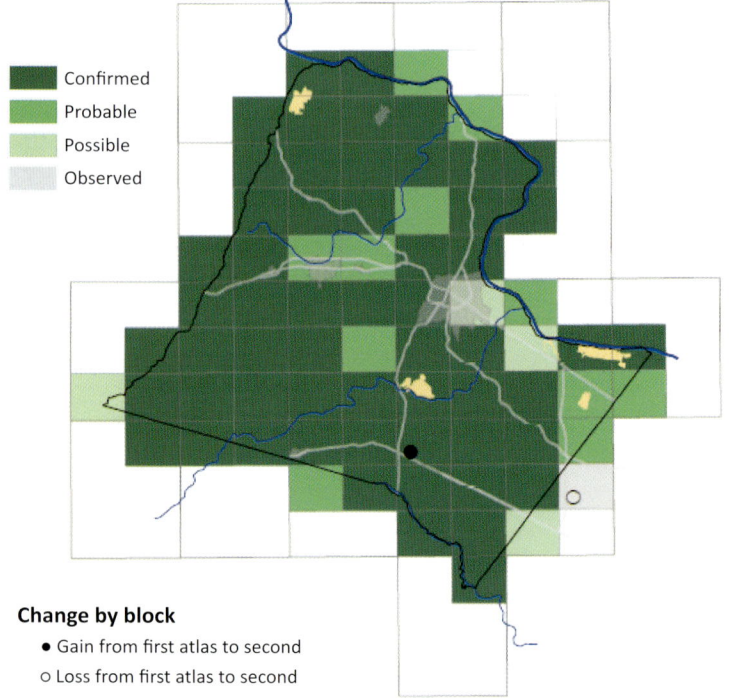

Confirmed
Probable
Possible
Observed

Change by block
- Gain from first atlas to second
○ Loss from first atlas to second

The Chipping Sparrow feeds largely on insects in summer, switching in winter primarily to seeds. It most often forages on the ground, looking under leaves and debris for prey, but will also hunt in bushes and trees and even occasionally chase down flying insects on the wing. This species migrates and feeds mostly in flocks outside their nesting period. They winter primarily in the southern U.S. and Mexico. However, their numbers have been increasing on recent Christmas Bird Counts in our region, and a few may be overwintering more successfully as climate change moderates our temperatures. This widespread habitat generalist remains numerous, with an estimated population of 210 million individuals (2016 PIF Landbird Plan), and their numbers seem to be holding steady over time.

Written by Bruce Hill

CLAY-COLORED SPARROW
Spizella pallida

Occurrence: vagrant

Earliest/latest seasonal sightings: fewer than 5 atlas sightings, see account for details

This crisply patterned sparrow from the U.S. interior is rarely seen in our area, but vagrants occasionally make an appearance along the coasts, especially during fall migration. Three atlas sightings, two in the vicinity of Banshee Reeks Nature Preserve and the Dulles Greenway Wetlands, were recorded over 2 years. Their overall pale appearance, light gray collar, and clean tan and gray markings are distinctive. Their unique and repetitive song, two to eight short, low *buzz* notes, is often the first and best clue to their presence.

They remain a common bird in southern Canada and the northern Great Plains, where they nest in field edges and shrubby areas, although like many grassland and plains species, their numbers are declining. Clay-colored Sparrows are very active birds, moving quickly among the branches of low shrubs and trees to feed on a variety of seeds and insects. During migration, they tend to form flocks, which sometimes include a mix of other sparrow species. They winter primarily in northern to central Mexico, especially in desert and high-plains habitats.

Written by Bruce Hill

Photo by Dave Boltz

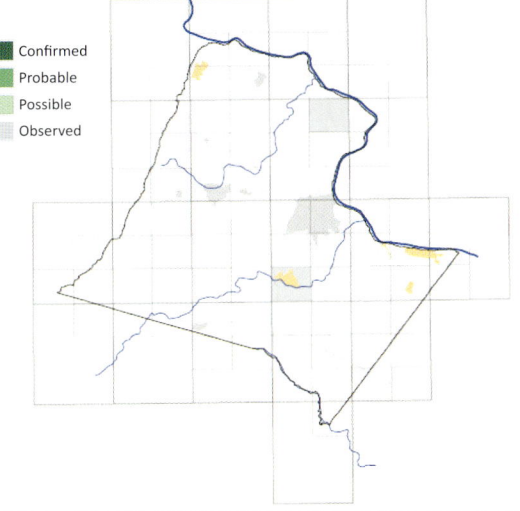

Confirmed
Probable
Possible
Observed

Photo by Lisa McKew

FIELD SPARROW
Spizella pusilla

Occurrence: common breeder and migrant, uncommon winter resident

Earliest breeding confirmation: May 2, parent entering/exiting nest site or on nest (ON)

Latest breeding confirmation: September 9, parent carrying food or feeding young (CF)

The Field Sparrow is perhaps best known for the male's sweet, trilling song that accelerates like a bouncing ping pong ball. This song is a welcome and familiar summer sound in brushy overgrown fields, forest edges, hedgerows, and roadsides. Their pink bill, white eyering, rusty crown and cheek patch, and otherwise clear grayish face and underparts are distinctive field marks. Juveniles lack the rusty markings. Field Sparrows forage on the ground or in low vegetation, eating mainly small grass seeds in the winter along with insects in the summer. They are creative and resourceful foragers, flying to the top of a grass stalk and letting their weight carry the stem to the ground where they can harvest the seeds.

Two to three broods are raised per season. Early spring nests are usually built on the ground in a clump of grass or at the base of a bush. As grasses grow and bushes and trees leaf out, subsequent nests are built higher (1-10 feet off the ground) to deter predators. Parents may perform a broken-wing display to distract predators from the nest. They often abandon nests parasitized by Brown-headed Cowbirds. Adults usually return to the same breeding area each

FIELD SPARROW (continued)

year (offspring do not), with males returning a couple weeks prior to females to establish a territory. Apparently not big on romance, an unmated male wins over a mate by striking at the female, sometimes sending her to the ground.

Field Sparrows form flocks during migration and winter months, sometimes mixing with other species such as White-throated and Song Sparrows. With their smaller size and less aggressive nature, Field Sparrows hold a subordinate ranking within the flock. They have to take more risks to secure their share of food; for example, being the first to return to a food source after the flock is flushed by a predator. Found mainly in the eastern and midwestern U.S., northern breeders migrate south for the winter while southern breeders are permanent residents or move short distances.

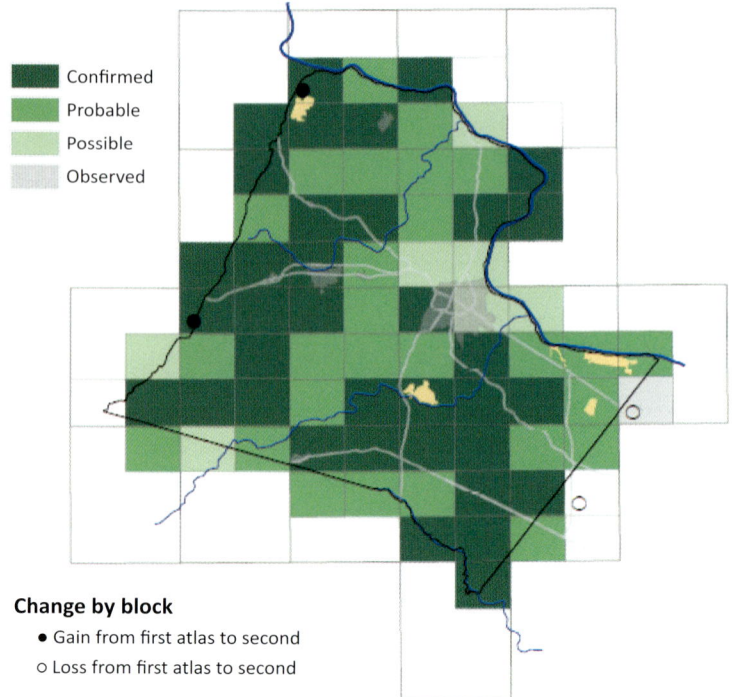

Confirmed
Probable
Possible
Observed

Change by block
● Gain from first atlas to second
○ Loss from first atlas to second

Loudoun hosts a mixture of migrants, breeders, and year-round residents. Evidence of breeding was found in practically every atlas block, with breeding confirmed in half the blocks. Field Sparrows are found on every Central Loudoun CBC. Though still common throughout their range, populations have declined sharply in recent decades. Loss of their shrubby field and grassland habitat to human development is likely a significant factor.

Written by Spring Ligi

Photo by ©Dick Rowe

VESPER SPARROW
Pooecetes gramineus

Occurrence: rare breeder and winter resident, occasional migrant

Earliest breeding confirmation: May 17, adult carrying nesting material or nest building (NB)

Latest breeding confirmation: June 11, parent carrying food or feeding young (CF)

The Vesper Sparrow is a relatively unfamiliar bird in Loudoun. With only 22 atlas records and 7 indicating confirmed or probable breeding, it is the least frequently reported of the known breeding sparrows in our county. However, stay alert, as it can appear just about any time of year, with those 22 records spread over every month except February and March and throughout the county. Most breeding evidence came from western parts of Loudoun. The Vesper Sparrow was reported on one Central Loudoun CBC (2013).

This is a crisply defined, brown-bodied bird with heavy black and white streaking above and below. Look particularly for the thin white eyering and white outer tail feathers that distinguish it from most other sparrows. It may also show a chestnut-colored shoulder patch, though this is not always reliable or easy to see. It has a small, conical bill. Relatively large-bodied and chunky, it is larger than the Song or Savannah Sparrows it superficially resembles. Its complex song typically begins with several clear notes and ends with a jumbled mix, somewhat reminiscent of but distinct from that of the Song Sparrow.

VESPER SPARROW (continued)

Vesper Sparrows favor sparsely vegetated grasslands, prairies, and fields, especially those with the occasional taller weed or fencepost to perch on and sing from. They have a reputation for being easy to see as they perch or go about their business out in the open, quite unlike most furtive grassland species. Their breeding stronghold encompasses much of the upper Midwest and the mountain West, while their wintering habitat stretches along the southern tier of the U.S. and well into Mexico. Much less common during breeding season in the East, the southern limit of their range just grazes our area. In winter, look for them feeding in mixed flocks with other sparrows.

This ground feeder eats a variety of insects and seeds, favoring insects in warmer months when they are readily available, and seeds during winter. It builds its nest on the ground beneath a clump of grass or other vegetation. Nesting females

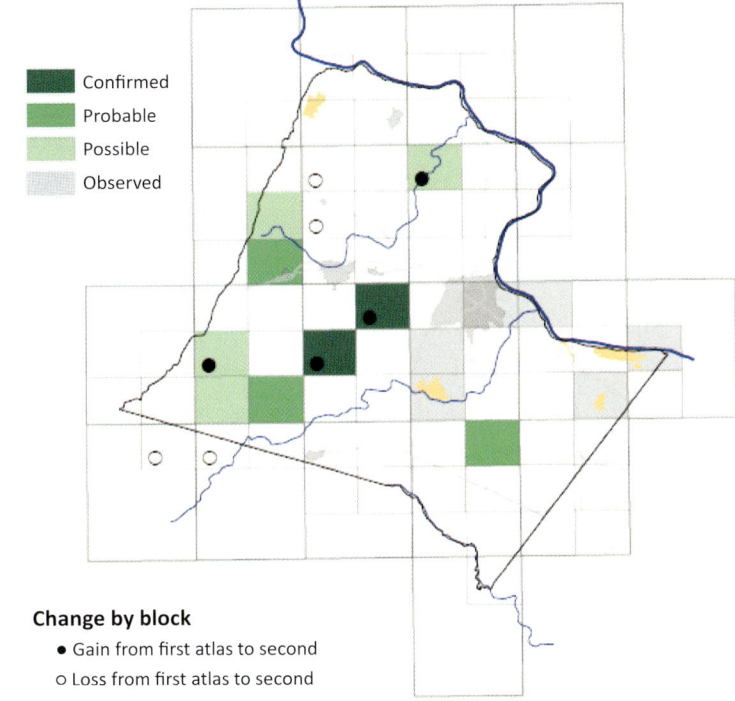

Confirmed
Probable
Possible
Observed

Change by block
● Gain from first atlas to second
○ Loss from first atlas to second

sometimes use fluttering distraction displays to draw away predators. They can raise from one to three broods per year. Still a common bird overall, with a population in excess of 30 million (PIF 2017), they declined by over 30% between 1970 and 2014 (Sauer et al. 2017), largely attributable to habitat loss, early haying and mowing of their nesting fields, and changing agricultural practices.

Written by Bruce Hill

Photo by Dave Boltz

SAVANNAH SPARROW
Passerculus sandwichensis

Occurrence: occasional breeder and winter visitor, uncommon migrant

Earliest breeding confirmation: June 16, recently fledged young (FL)

Latest breeding confirmation: June 27, parent carrying food or feeding young (CF)

More often observed in Loudoun as a migrant passing through, the Savannah Sparrow sometimes overwinters here, as Central Loudoun CBC records attest, and was confirmed as breeding in 2 atlas blocks with probable and possible evidence in 7 additional blocks. It favors open habitat, such as grassy meadows and cultivated fields and pastures, as in western Loudoun where the majority of breeding evidence was documented. This bird can also be found along roadsides gleaning for insects or seeds, depending on the season. It tends to avoid areas with significant tree cover and keeps close to the ground, walking while foraging and running or jumping between foraging sites. When flushed from its nest, or disturbed, it crouches down low, looking like a rodent. Sometimes it will fly up and away from the disturber in a distinctive stair-step pattern.

During spring migration, males arrive first to establish a territory. They sing a buzzy, insect-like song from shrubs or fence posts. This sparrow is a ground nester which covers its nest site as camouflage and protection from predators,

SAVANNAH SPARROW (continued)

which are numerous. They include Sharp-shinned Hawks and Northern Harriers, corvids and grackles, as well as snakes and mammals. White-tailed deer, and even cows, have been found eating Savannah Sparrow eggs and fledglings. The nest, composed of coarse and thin grasses, holds two to six eggs. After the breeding season, flocks are formed as they prepare for fall migration.

This medium-sized sparrow is distinguished by its short, square tail, small head, and well-marked facial pattern with a yellow spot before the eye. The amount of yellow displayed can vary considerably. It is heavily streaked with brown on its whitish underparts, except for the throat, central belly, and undertail areas which are white. Though widespread and abundant throughout much of their North and Central American range, populations have declined over the past 50 years, likely due to changes in land use and agricultural

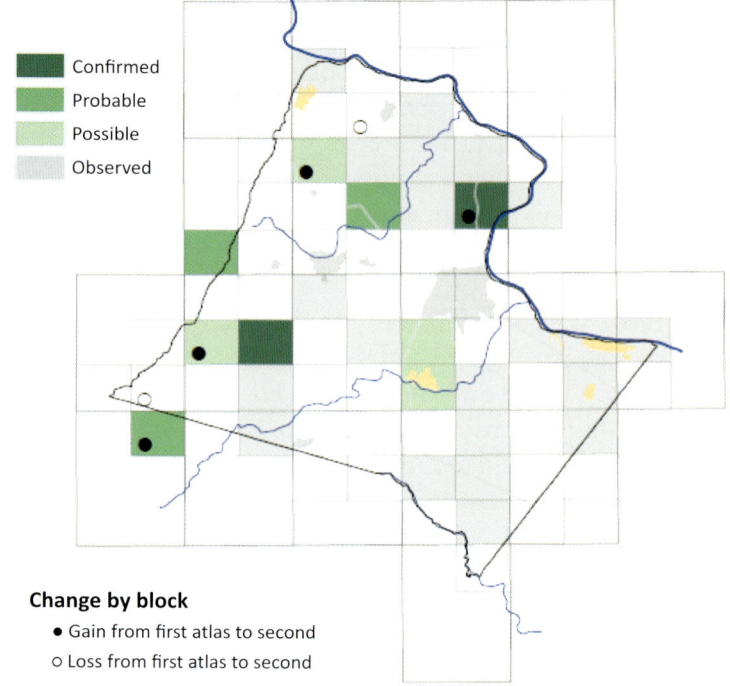

■ Confirmed
■ Probable
■ Possible
□ Observed

Change by block
● Gain from first atlas to second
○ Loss from first atlas to second

practices. Urbanization and reversion of marginal farm lands to woods and forest may have had negative effects. Similarly, agricultural harvesting and mowing practices can have dramatic consequences for the birds' breeding productivity. If the timing of mowing and harvesting does not consider breeding activities, then otherwise favorable habitat can turn into a population sink for the Savannah Sparrow and other open-habitat ground nesters.

Written by Chris White

Photo by Linda Millington

GRASSHOPPER SPARROW
Ammodramus savannarum

Occurrence: uncommon breeder and migrant

Earliest breeding confirmation: May 4, parent entering/exiting nest site or on nest (ON)

Latest breeding confirmation: September 4, recently fledged young (FL)

The Grasshopper Sparrow is a classic bird of open grasslands. Its name reflects both its diet and its distinctive, insect-like song. It is small and mostly brownish, with an unmarked buffy breast and a streaked back. The dark crown with a pale middle stripe stands out on an otherwise light-colored and fairly plain bird. The head is large and flat-crowned, the tail short, and the wings short and rounded. Its flight can appear fluttery and weak at times.

This species can be seen or heard throughout much of Loudoun from mid-April through mid-October, singing frequently from a perch on a plant stalk or fencepost. If flushed, Grasshopper Sparrows will typically fly low and duck quickly into cover. They prefer drier, open grassy or scrubby fields, where they forage on the ground for insect prey. Nests are placed on the ground in a well-concealed location, often covered by a dome of overhanging grasses.

This species is found primarily in rural areas, but also in surprising numbers where appropriate remnants of habitat remain in developed or developing parts of Loudoun. For example, the Arcola region, a now largely developed area,

GRASSHOPPER SPARROW (continued)

had approximately as many reported observations of this species as the more rural Purcellville and Waterford regions. More broadly, they can be found during the breeding season across much of the eastern U.S. and Great Plains. After breeding, they migrate south for the winter, primarily to open fields in the coastal states of the southeastern U.S., southern portions of the southwestern states, Mexico, Central America, and the Caribbean. Rarely, Grasshopper Sparrows will linger in Loudoun into the winter. There were two reports of this species in Point of Rocks 5 in late January 2011.

In Atlas 2, this species was observed in 59 blocks; 56 of those showed evidence of breeding (compared to 41 blocks in Atlas 1). This species is uncommon in Loudoun, but relatively easy to find in the right habitat. Nonetheless, as a grassland species, its options clearly diminish as development expands.

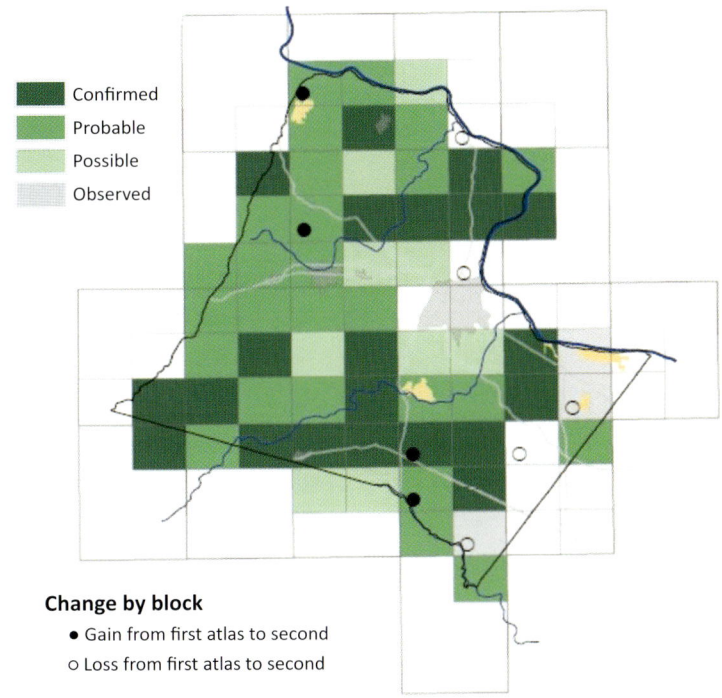

Confirmed
Probable
Possible
Observed

Change by block
● Gain from first atlas to second
○ Loss from first atlas to second

According to the North American BBS, Grasshopper Sparrow populations declined across their full range by almost 3% per year between 1966 and 2014, resulting in a cumulative decline of 75%; this may be attributed to habitat loss, fragmentation, and degradation. This species is considered a "common bird in steep decline" (PIF 2016).

Written by Bruce Hill

Photo by Dave Boltz

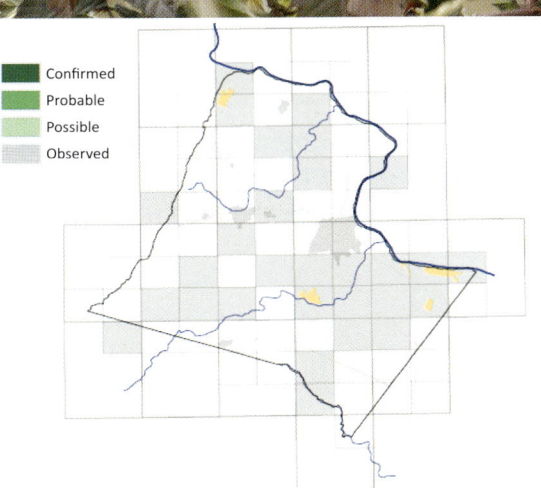

Confirmed
Probable
Possible
Observed

FOX SPARROW
Passerella iliaca

Occurrence: uncommon migrant and winter resident

Earliest seasonal sighting: October 12

Latest seasonal sighting: May 15

The Fox Sparrow is shy in behavior and relatively large in size. It has a gray nape and upper face and rich rufous/chestnut streaking, backed with gray on the mantle and rump and white on the breast and flanks. Its size and coloring distinguish it from the Song Sparrow, which also bears a central chest spot. The bill is mostly yellow, versus the Song Sparrow's grayish or pinkish bill. Its whistled song, heard on remote northern breeding grounds and occasionally here, is distinguished for its richness. Fox Sparrows were documented throughout Loudoun in 40% of the atlas blocks. Look for them in thick cover, hiding out in thickets and underbrush on the edge of woods or streams. It forages in the leaf litter for insects or other food with a distinctive double scratching motion and also appears at feeders. Sought after by sparrow lovers on Central Loudoun CBCs, it averages 8 individuals per count. Not impacted by human activity as much as some species, Fox Sparrows are fairly numerous throughout their North American range, but populations have declined in recent decades.

Written by Chris White

SONG SPARROW
Melospiza melodia

Occurrence: abundant breeder and year-round resident

Earliest breeding confirmation: April 9, adult carrying nesting material or nest building (NB)

Latest breeding confirmation: September 2, recently fledged young (FL)

Photo by Gerco Hoogeweg

The Song Sparrow is among the most widespread of songbirds in North America. In Loudoun it is found any time of year in every type of habitat from the suburban east to the Blue Ridge mountains in the west. This ubiquitous sparrow was confirmed as breeding in 37 of the 73 atlas blocks, with evidence of probable or possible breeding in an additional 32 blocks and appearances on all Central Loudoun CBCs.

A plump, medium-sized sparrow, the Song Sparrow has a rather large head and a short tail, blunt at the tip. The streaked breast and mantle converge on a central dark spot on the breast, like that found on the larger Fox Sparrow. The streaking is clearly defined on a pale-white or gray background. A pale central stripe on the crown is bordered by darker bands. Legs and feet can range from medium to dark brown. Interestingly, Song Sparrows show large differences in size and coloration throughout their vast range, varying from small, pale birds in the desert Southwest to large, dark birds in the Aleutian Islands. Song Sparrows have a distinctive, cheerful song made up of three parts; it begins with usually three identical notes and passes through trills to a buzzy conclusion.

Song Sparrows can be found foraging on or near the ground for the fruit, seeds, and insects that make up their food sources. They are nearly as at home among busy human establishments as in the countryside. They employ the double hop and the double scratch as they move through undergrowth and grasses or shrubs. They will also glean insects from tree bark, and work downward in bushes with their tail bobbing. They also dip their tail as they fly.

Their nest is built low down in grasses or shrubs, often on the ground. Females build a sturdy open cup nest and disguise it well for protection from Cooper's Hawks and other predators. They are a frequent target of the Brown-headed Cowbird. Song Sparrows often raise two or more clutches in a breeding season.

This sparrow has not been a subject of conservation concern thanks to their relative abundance, wide distribution, and ease of association with humans and their activities. However, populations declined by approximately 30% over the past 5 decades, according to the North American BBS. The domestic cat poses a danger in more urban settings.

Written by Chris White

Confirmed
Probable
Possible
Observed

Change by block
- Gain from first atlas to second
- Loss from first atlas to second

LINCOLN'S SPARROW
Melospiza lincolnii

Photo by Dave Boltz

Occurrence: occasional migrant, rare winter visitor

Earliest fall sighting: September 12

Latest spring sighting: May 14

A medium-sized, crisply patterned sparrow, this "little brown job" occasionally passes through Loudoun in route between breeding grounds in Canada and the western U.S. and a wintering range in the southern U.S. and Mexico. Look for them in shrubby fields and forest edges where they may associate with more numerous species like Song or Swamp Sparrows during migration. All atlas sightings except 1 in mid-February were of migrants.

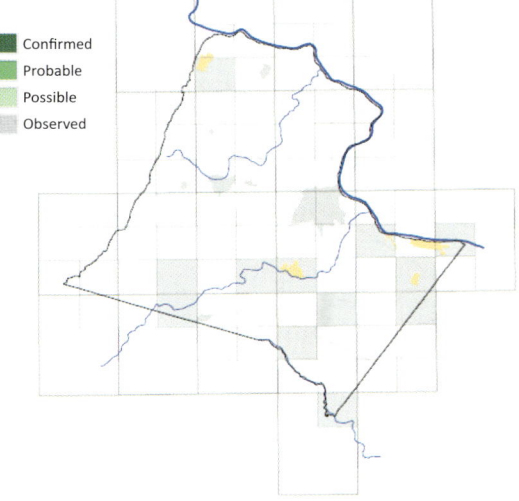

■	Confirmed
■	Probable
■	Possible
■	Observed

A gray face; buffy eyering, mustache stripe, and chest; small bill; and fine dark streaking are characteristics of this species. These secretive, ground-feeding birds can be difficult to see, but like other sparrows, may sit up briefly on an exposed perch in response to pishing or other disturbance. They eat primarily insects in summer, but switch to seeds and sometimes visit feeders in winter or if insects are scarce. The Lincoln's Sparrow is a stable and common bird throughout its range, with a population estimate of about 70 million (PIF 2017). However, they may be vulnerable to grazing or climate impacts on their wetland breeding habitat.

Written by Bruce Hill

Photo by Dave Boltz

SWAMP SPARROW
Melospiza georgiana

Occurrence: rare breeder, uncommon migrant and winter resident

Earliest/latest breeding confirmations: fewer than 5 atlas confirmations, see account for details

Swamp Sparrows generally arrive in late September and remain in Loudoun through mid-May. However, a family was documented over multiple August atlas surveys (2009) in an area of lowland with a standing water spring and heavy grass in Sterling 6, confirming breeding for this species in Loudoun. Probable breeding was documented a month earlier in nearby Seneca 3, which borders the Potomac River in eastern Loudoun. While exciting, these sightings are not altogether surprising since there are well-documented breeding records for this species across the river in Frederick, Montgomery, and Prince George's Counties (Maryland) where it is considered, in low numbers, a year-round bird. The majority of Swamp Sparrows breed throughout Canada and the northeastern U.S.

Though uncommon and elusive, the Swamp Sparrow can be found in its favored wetland, swamp, and marsh habitat. Its presence is often signaled by its song, a distinctive slow, liquid trill, or a mechanical *chink*. A medium-sized sparrow, its upperparts are a rusty brown streaked with black, its wings are chestnut colored, and its face and neck are gray with a dark eyeline. A gray chest band, which can be unstreaked or faintly streaked, blends into rusty flanks; the

SWAMP SPARROW (continued)

throat and belly are whitish. The breeding adult sports a chestnut cap.

Water, whether as river or pond, marsh, swamp, or bog, seems to be required by the breeding Swamp Sparrow. It both builds its nest near water and forages among rushes and sedges for insects during the breeding season. At other times its food sources include seeds and fruits. The bird walks on the ground to forage, scratching among leaves. It also climbs up and down reeds and sedges, and wades at the edge of open water picking insects from mud and the water's surface. It has even been observed submerging its head in water. Nests can be elevated or on the ground, but are generally located in dense grass, reeds, or occasionally shrubs. The nest is a bulky cup, coarsely made on the outside, finely woven on the inside. Sometimes the nest can be roofed. One or two broods of four to five young are raised per year. Swamp Sparrow populations have remained stable in recent decades. However, the wetland habitats in which the bird thrives have been under threat from human activity of different kinds. Preservation of such habitats is critical to the future of the species.

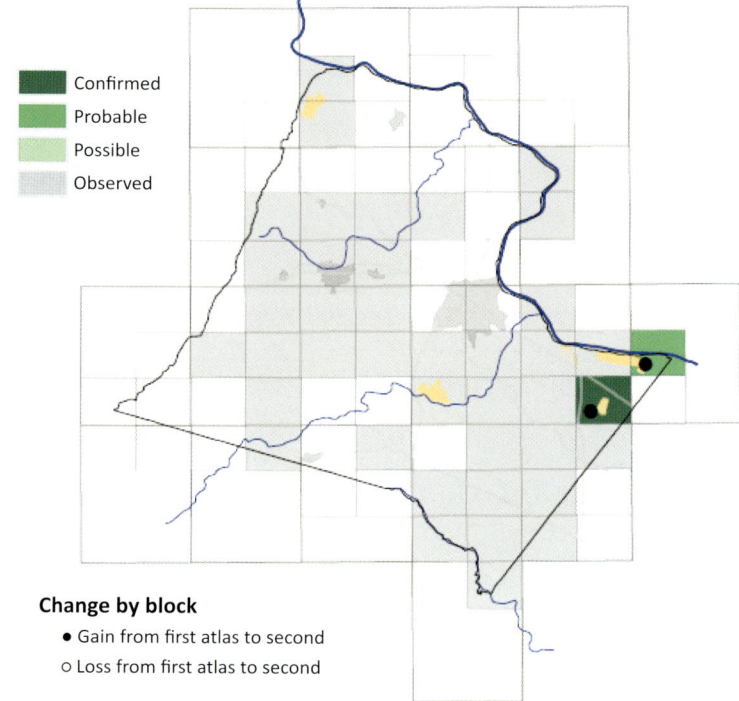

Change by block
- ● Gain from first atlas to second
- ○ Loss from first atlas to second

Written by Chris White

Photo by Nicole Suddoth

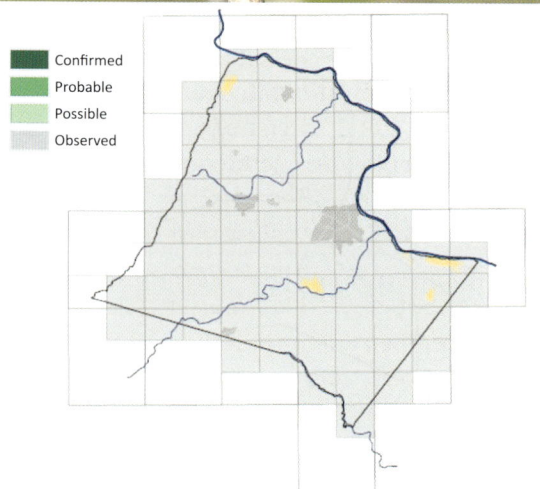

WHITE-THROATED SPARROW
Zonotrichia albicollis

Occurrence: abundant migrant and winter resident

Earliest fall sighting: September 26

Latest spring sighting: May 12

A welcome sign of fall for Loudoun residents, the White-throated Sparrow arrives in silence only to depart in the spring with a flourish of song, a wavering whistle of *Old Sam Peabody-peabody-peabody.* Generally found here through mid-May, there were 2 atypical atlas sightings on June 6 and 13, 2012. Aptly named, this sparrow has a distinct white throat and head stripes along with yellow lores and a black eye stripe. White-throated Sparrows forage in flocks with established pecking orders, commonly visiting bird feeders and occupying various habitats including thickets, overgrown fields, and parks. They hop along, scratching the ground in search of seeds, buds, and blossoms. This ground nester breeds in open forested areas across Canada and the northeastern and north-central U.S. Populations are stable throughout their range, with a slight decline in recent decades. White-throated Sparrows come in two color forms, displaying either a white or tan-striped crown. Males of both color types prefer the more aggressive white-striped females, while females of both color types prefer the more nurturing tan-striped males (Kaufman 2017).

Written by Spring Ligi

WHITE-CROWNED SPARROW
Zonotrichia leucophrys

Occurrence: uncommon migrant and winter resident

Earliest fall sighting: October 2

Latest spring sighting: May 15

Photo by Gerco Hoogeweg

White-crowned Sparrows show up in mid-fall in Loudoun and much of the contiguous U.S., after breeding in various semi-open habitats in Canada, Alaska, and higher elevations of the northwestern U.S. Range-wide, populations appear stable. An adult bird's sharp black-and-white head pattern, pale beak, and clean gray breast, as well as its relatively large size and long tail, are distinctive. Immatures lack the bold black-and-white head markings, instead showing gray and reddish stripes on their face and crown. Documented in just over half the atlas blocks and on every Central Loudoun CBC, watch for singles or small flocks of this species in brushy roadside borders and overgrown fields, often in the company of other more common sparrows. They will sometimes pop up onto an open perch for longer than other species, allowing good looks. They may also frequent backyards, foraging for seeds on the ground. With luck, you might hear them sing as spring begins to take hold — a sweet jumble of whistled and then buzzy notes, quite different from other resident sparrow species.

Written by Bruce Hill

Photo by Lisa McKew

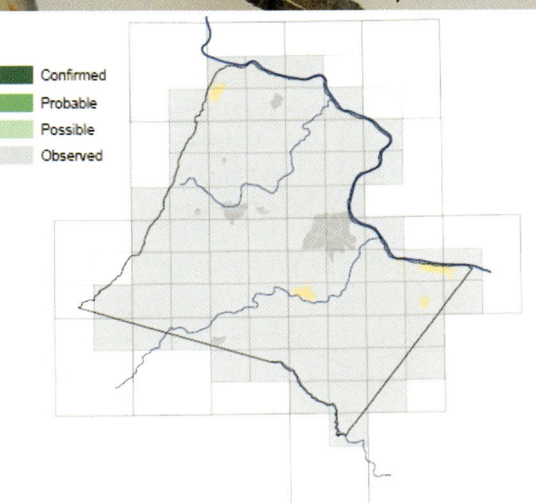

DARK-EYED JUNCO
Junco hyemalis

Occurrence: abundant migrant and winter resident

Earliest fall sighting: October 9

Latest spring sighting: May 11

We sometimes call Dark-eyed Juncos snowbirds because they abound in Loudoun during the season of cold weather and snow. A medium-sized sparrow, they are dark gray or brown above and white below, as though reflecting the gray winter sky over snow-covered ground. They are easily identified in flight by their flashing white outer tail feathers.

Juncos can be found pretty much anywhere throughout North America in winter, though populations have declined slightly in recent decades. Central Loudoun CBCs average over 1,000 juncos per count. They are ground feeders and can be seen hopping and scratching in grass, leaf litter, as well as snow. Their diet consists of seeds, berries, and insects, and they readily help themselves to leftovers below bird feeders. They communicate in sharp *tic* chips. In early spring they begin to trill, a song like the Chipping Sparrow's, but slower and more musical, a sign they will soon leave us. As the weather becomes milder they migrate to forests at higher elevations to breed and are not seen again until autumn's chill is upon us.

Written by Donna Quinn

YELLOW-BREASTED CHAT
Icteria virens

Photo by Linda Millington

Occurrence: uncommon breeder and migrant

Earliest breeding confirmation: June 9, distraction display (DD)

Latest breeding confirmation: July 25, parent carrying food or feeding young (CF)

A bright yellow throat and breast with olive-green upperparts provide a good argument that the Yellow-breasted Chat is a warbler. But its large size, 7 inches long, heavier weight, and unique vocalizations made a compelling enough case for the American Ornithological Society to move the chat into its own family in 2017. With a long tail, white spectacles, and white mustache, this bird is unique and rarely confused with any other. The Yellow-breasted Chat's lower belly and undertail are clean white. Males can sometimes be separated from females via their darker (black versus gray) lores.

It's more common to hear than see the Yellow-breasted Chat because of its preference for dense environments. Their vocal repertoire includes whistles, croaks, gurgles, and chatter that is more like a Brown Thrasher or Northern Mockingbird than a warbler's song. They are even known to sing at night like mockingbirds. Their fluttering descending display flight witnessed during the breeding season is also distinctive.

On both their breeding grounds, which include most of the U.S. and Mexico, and their wintering grounds in southern Mexico and most of Central America, they choose low shrubby habitats such as power cuts and hedgerows, often near water. Nests for their three to six eggs are composed of stems, leaves, and grasses and are found 1 to 8 feet from the ground and measure 5 to 6 inches in diameter. The Yellow-breasted Chat feeds mostly on spiders and insects, but will also eat available fruits. They will often grip insect prey with their feet, which is uncommon in songbirds and more common in raptors.

Because of their secretive nature, atlasers confirmed breeding in only 5 blocks, but possible and probable breeding evidence was gathered throughout the county. Yellow-breasted Chats are generally found in Loudoun from late April through mid-September. A couple confused individuals were reported in late October and on 1 of the past 20 Central Loudoun CBCs. With a global population of around 13 million (PIF 2017), North American numbers have declined by about 37% over the past 5 decades (Sauer et al. 2017). Their preferred habitat is something that is disappearing in Loudoun with the succession of scrubby fields into forests and fields getting developed into housing.

Written by Bryan Henson

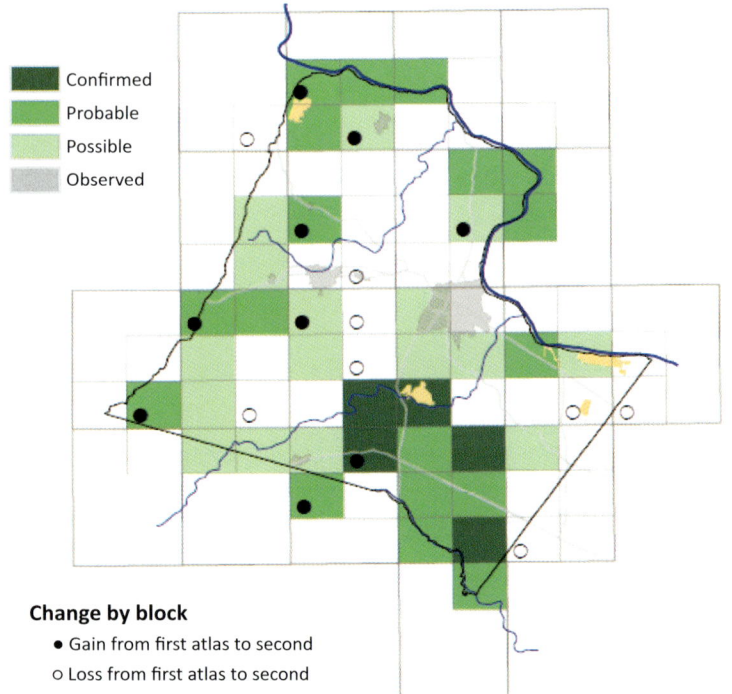

Confirmed
Probable
Possible
Observed

Change by block
- Gain from first atlas to second
○ Loss from first atlas to second

YELLOW-HEADED BLACKBIRD
Xanthocephalus xanthocephalus

Photo by Dave Boltz (with cowbirds)

Occurrence: vagrant

Earliest/latest seasonal sightings: fewer than 5 atlas sightings, see account for details

Experienced birders can attest that sorting through a large flock of birds, though tedious, can be very rewarding. In March 2010 at a feeder near Banshee Reeks Nature Preserve, a Yellow-headed Blackbird was found mixed in with a flock of Red-winged Blackbirds and grackles. Typically found in the Midwest and West, this striking vagrant with its golden-yellow head and chest (duller in females and immatures), black body, and white wing patches was indeed a treat (and not hard to pick out!).

Yellow-headed Blackbirds breed in freshwater wetlands, with one male having up to eight females nesting in his territory. Populations from as far north as Canada's prairies migrate to the Southwest and Mexico where they form "rolling" winter flocks in farm fields, with birds at the back of the flock continuously flying to the front to feed on seeds and insects. Males tend to winter farther north than females. Populations are thought to be relatively stable throughout their range, though population size varies from year to year based on wetland conditions and the amount of rainfall.

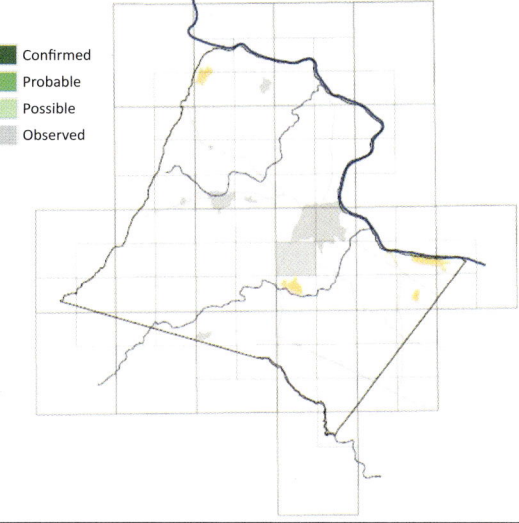

Confirmed
Probable
Possible
Observed

Written by Spring Ligi

Photo ©Dick Rowe

BOBOLINK
Dolichonyx oryzivorus

Occurrence: occasional breeder and migrant

Earliest breeding confirmation: June 24, distraction display (DD)

Latest breeding confirmation: July 28, parent carrying food or feeding young (CF)

The male Bobolink, in full breeding plumage, provides one of the most spectacular displays found among songbirds, whether perched or flying low to the ground giving voice to its effervescent courtship and territorial song. The plumage of the breeding male is solid black below but lighter above. Parts of the head, wings, and tail are black. The shoulders, lower back, and rump are white varying to a pale gray. The nape is a distinctive yellowish buff. In flight display, the white on the upperparts and rump flares and dazzles. By mid-August the display plumage molts away, and both sexes are found in an equally attractive plumage which mixes yellow with darker or dusky streaks on the flanks and buffy olive above streaked with black. The top of the head is distinctively patterned with buffy and blackish stripes, along with a black eyeline, unstreaked nape, and pale bill.

Found in Loudoun from early April through mid-September, Bobolinks were confirmed as breeding in 4 atlas blocks in the rural southwest and north where the meadow and hayfield habitat they seek can still be found. Loudoun falls along the southern edge of this ground nester's breeding range. Males mate with several females in a breeding

BOBOLINK (continued)

season, and clutches laid by a single female often represent multiple fathers. The different fathers, along with young from the previous year, may assist the female in varying degrees with feeding the young. The Bobolink's diet is comprised of insects and spiders which it finds while walking on the ground.

The Bobolink endures one of the longest migrations of any songbird in the New World, traveling in flocks from its northern U.S. and southern Canadian breeding grounds through Florida and across the Gulf of Mexico to its South American wintering grounds. On its journey the bird faces threats of being poisoned or shot as a pest by rice-growers, or trapped and sold as a pet or food source. In its breeding habitat, untimely mowing turns breeding efforts into a population sink.

Bobolinks are included on the 2016 State of North America's Birds' Watch List. Habitat loss ranks among the most serious of the threats faced throughout its breeding range, due not only to disappearance from the inventory, but also to changes in farming technology and methods. Here education can provide significant relief, though other consequences of human activity also need to be addressed.

Written by Chris White

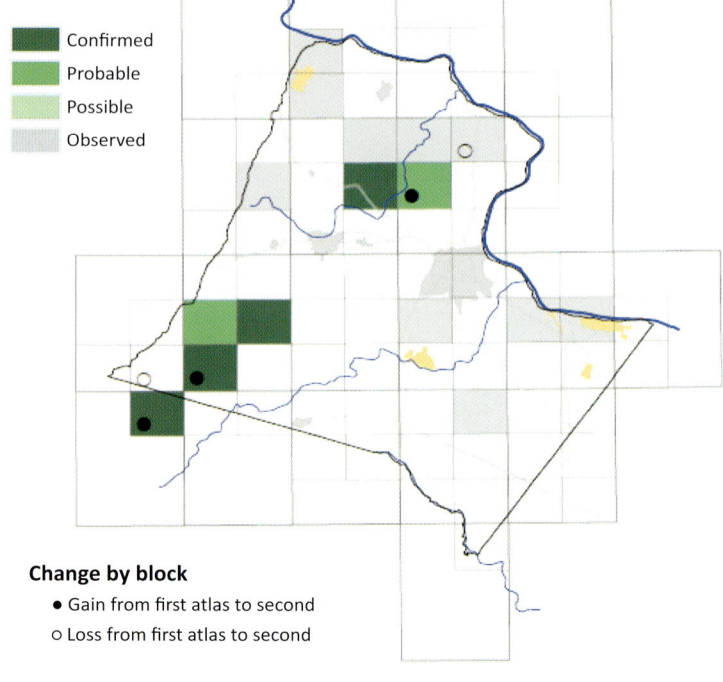

- ■ Confirmed
- ■ Probable
- ■ Possible
- ■ Observed

Change by block
- ● Gain from first atlas to second
- ○ Loss from first atlas to second

Photo ©Dick Rowe

EASTERN MEADOWLARK
Sturnella magna

Occurrence: uncommon breeder and migrant, occasional winter resident

Earliest breeding confirmation: May 4, parent entering/exiting nest site or on nest (ON)

Latest breeding confirmation: September 1, recently fledged young (FL)

The Eastern Meadowlark was confirmed as breeding in 22 of the 73 atlas blocks, all in the southwestern and northern parts of the county. This rural, relatively open country, with fields, grasslands, and meadows, still provides this species with appropriate habitat for nesting, shelter, and food. Here, the meadowlark's flute-like whistled song, trilled from fence post and utility wire, still greets the spring; it is sometimes described as *spring-o-the-year*. Comparisons from Atlas 1 to 2 reveal a striking decline and loss of blocks in Loudoun's eastern suburban and transition areas, where the meadowlark is sadly no longer breeding. This sometimes year-round resident, sometimes short-distant migrant is a regular on Central Loudoun CBCs in low numbers, averaging only 8 individuals per count.

Readily recognized for its bright yellow breast with a wide black V, the overall cryptic plumage is well suited for camouflaging this ground-nesting and -feeding member of the blackbird family. Both sexes look similar; the female is slightly smaller. The upper body is a patterned mixture of buff, brown, and black streaks and bars; the flanks and

EASTERN MEADOWLARK (continued)

undertail are white. The outer tail feathers are mostly white and exposed in flight, and there is a light line above the eye. The long, slender bill forms an almost straight line with the top of the head when opened wide in song with head thrown back.

Nests are built by the female in pastures or meadowland. Her construction of dried grasses and forbs is well disguised and can also be woven into the surrounding vegetation. The structure may be partially arched or even covered and holds three to five eggs. Both parents feed the young, and they raise one or two broods per breeding season. The strong bill probes for insects, worms, and grubs, able to be opened underground to take the food found. Grasshoppers, caterpillars, and crickets are also on the menu.

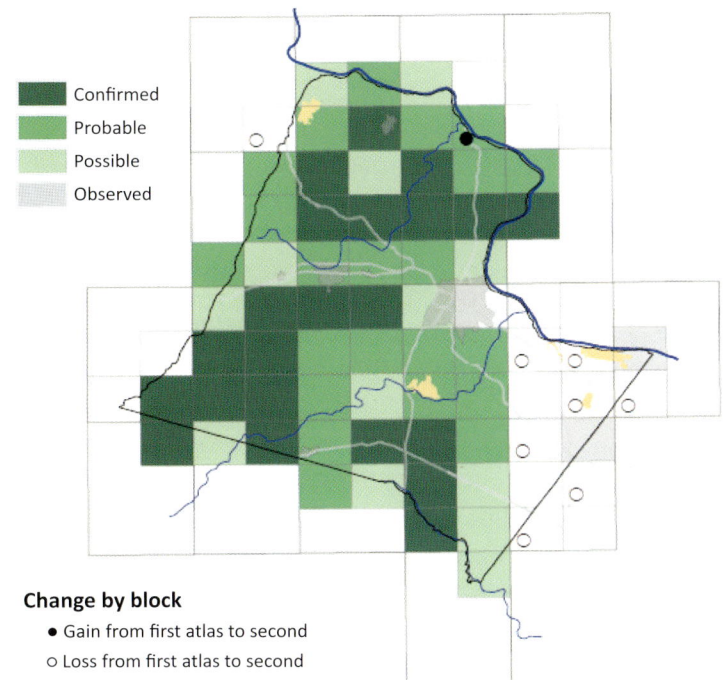

- ■ Confirmed
- ■ Probable
- ■ Possible
- ▒ Observed

Change by block
- ● Gain from first atlas to second
- ○ Loss from first atlas to second

The meadowlark is very sensitive to human activities and presence throughout its eastern North American range and is considered a "common bird in steep decline" (NABCI 2014). Changes in farming practices, early mowing of grass and hay crops, and transformation of abandoned farm land to emerging woods have all taken their toll. Protection of habitat along with education about land use practices and timing of seasonal activities like mowing can provide crucial assistance in supporting the life cycle of this beloved grassland bird.

Written by Chris White

Photo ©Dick Rowe

ORCHARD ORIOLE
Icterus spurius

Occurrence: uncommon breeder and migrant

Earliest breeding confirmation: April 26, adult carrying nesting material or nest building (NB)

Latest breeding confirmation: August 11, recently fledged young (FL)

Orchard Orioles arrive in Loudoun in late April to early May, after spending the winter in mixed-species flocks in Mexico through northern South America. After such a long journey, this oriole spends a relatively short time on its breeding grounds, with adult males departing around late July. Females and fledglings stay behind and flock together, feeding on insects and fruit before beginning their fall migration. To find an Orchard Oriole, scan the treetops of open woodlands along river edges, orchards, pastures with scattered trees, and parks. Or listen for the male's sweet whistled song, similar to robins, but interspersed with distinctive churrs and chatters. The smallest of North America's orioles, adult males are black above and rich chestnut below. Females are yellow-green with two white wingbars; immature males appear similar but have black around the pointed bill and throat.

In good habitat Orchard Orioles are semi-colonial breeders; in less suitable habitat they tend to be solitary. They are relatively unterritorial and may nest in the same tree as more aggressive species such as Baltimore Orioles and Eastern Kingbirds, who help ward off predators and parasitic Brown-headed Cowbirds. The female builds a hanging, pouch-like

ORCHARD ORIOLE (continued)

nest woven from long blades of grass. A single brood of four to six eggs is generally raised, though double-brooding has been documented in this species (Ligi and Omland 2007). Unlike the strictly single-brooded Baltimore Oriole that molts on its breeding grounds, Orchard Orioles migrate and then molt after or just before reaching their wintering grounds (Scharf and Kren 2010). This delay in molt may provide Orchard Orioles with more energy and time to raise a second brood in a breeding season.

Orchard Orioles showed evidence of breeding in 59 of the 73 atlas blocks, and were observed as a migrant in 5 additional blocks. There was 1 rare winter sighting at Claude Moore Park in Sterling 6 (January 2013). Comparisons to Atlas 1 reveal a net gain of 20 blocks throughout Loudoun. The more thorough coverage and higher level of effort per block in Atlas 2 are likely influential factors in the

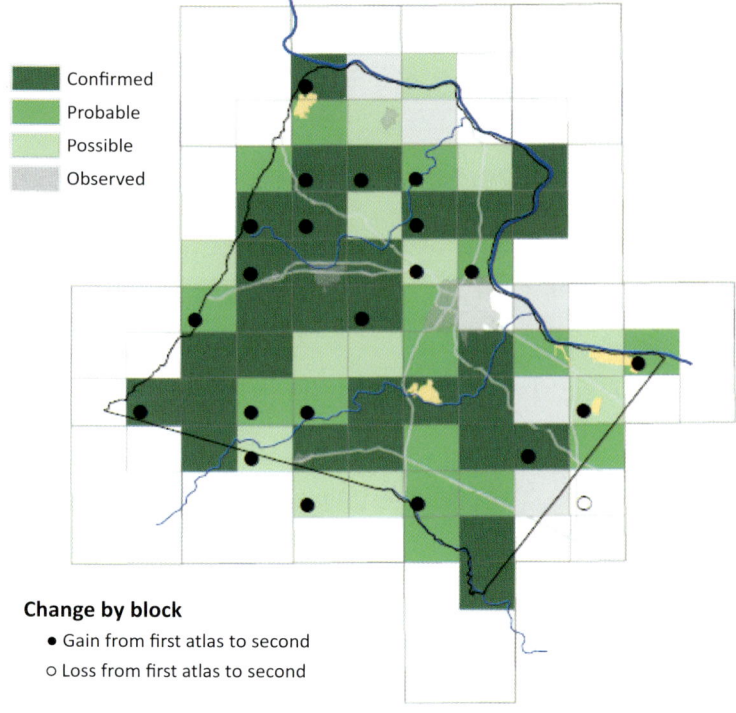

Confirmed
Probable
Possible
Observed

Change by block
- Gain from first atlas to second
- Loss from first atlas to second

apparent growth of this species in Loudoun. According to the North American BBS, the Orchard Oriole population decreased by 35% between 1966 and 2014. Loss of habitat, particularly along rivers, and a general increase in cowbird parasitism are some of the threats this species faces in Loudoun and throughout its range.

Written by Spring Ligi

Photo by Dave Boltz

BALTIMORE ORIOLE
Icterus galbula

Occurrence: uncommon breeder and migrant

Earliest breeding confirmation: May 4, adult carrying nesting material or nest building (NB)

Latest breeding confirmation: August 22, recently fledged young (FL)

Known for the adult male's bold orange and black plumage and the female's extraordinary pendant nest, this member of the blackbird family departs its Central and South American wintering grounds to arrive in Loudoun around late April. Some Baltimore Orioles continue as far north as Canada to breed, while others make Loudoun their summer home. They become quiet and harder to find in late July, when nesting is mostly complete and molting has begun, but migrants can be found passing through Loudoun until late September. Evidence of breeding was documented in roughly three-quarters of the atlas blocks. There was 1 rare winter sighting in Middleburg 2 (February 2012). Post-atlas, at least three birds have been reported at Loudoun feeders for extended winter visits.

To observe a Baltimore Oriole, look high in deciduous treetops where they can be found acrobatically foraging through the foliage. During summer, they consume and feed their young a variety of protein-rich insects. In spring and fall, they feed on berries, fruit, and flower nectar for an energy boost necessary for migration. This oriole has adapted relatively well to human settlement and visits backyard fruit or sugar-water feeders. They inhabit open woodlands,

BALTIMORE ORIOLE (continued)

forest edges, orchards, parks, and stands of trees along rivers.

Their characteristic chatter or rich whistling song is often your first clue that an oriole is around. A welcome sign of spring, males sing a short, disjointed series of paired notes, repeated two to seven times, to establish and defend their relatively small territory. Females sing shorter songs. Males and females give a staccato chatter call when chasing an intruder from their nest space. This call alerts and attracts neighboring orioles, leading to scenes such as a crow being mobbed by multiple orioles as it flies over a field. This oriole's smaller and less aggressive, chestnut-colored cousin, the Orchard Oriole, often nests nearby to benefit from this alarm system.

The relatively drab, orange-yellow and dark-winged female skillfully weaves a distinctive hanging pouch nest about 20 to 30 feet above the ground, made from slender plant fibers, bark strips, grass, and moss. Both parents raise one brood of four to five nestlings per year. Baltimore Oriole populations have declined in recent decades due to habitat loss and degradation throughout their breeding and wintering ranges, providing an opportunity for nations to work together to develop a conservation plan for this and other neotropical migrants.

Written by Spring Ligi

Confirmed
Probable
Possible
Observed

Change by block
- Gain from first atlas to second
- Loss from first atlas to second

Photo by Larry Meade

RED-WINGED BLACKBIRD
Agelaius phoeniceus

Occurrence: common breeder and year-round resident

Earliest breeding confirmation: April 29, parent entering/exiting nest site or on nest (ON)

Latest breeding confirmation: August 6, recently fledged young (FL)

If you are looking for a boisterous, social bird with commitment issues, the Red-winged Blackbird fills the bill. This familiar bird is known for its musical *oak-a-leeee* song, heard all day long in marshes and wetlands during the breeding season. The glossy black male sings from exposed perches (often atop cattails or dead trees) while displaying striking red and yellow shoulder patches – all to defend a territory and impress the ladies. Females are altogether different than males, with their streaky brown, almost sparrow-like body and skulking behavior. Both males and females communicate with a distinctive *check* call.

Red-winged Blackbirds are highly polygamous; each male mates with five or six females. As many as 15 females have been found in a single male's territory! However, males aren't the only ones having all the fun...females add to the drama by mating with multiple neighboring males. Females build a cup nest low among marsh vegetation, in bushes close to water, or in dense grassy fields. Both parents feed insects to the three to four young and aggressively defend the nest, bolding attacking larger birds. They may reach speeds up to 30 miles per hour when chasing away intruders.

162

RED-WINGED BLACKBIRD (continued)

Outside the breeding season, this ground feeder flocks with other blackbirds, grackles, cowbirds, and starlings to eat seeds and waste grain in farm fields, pastures, and grasslands. Flocks can become very large, with thousands of birds roosting together at night and moving around during the day to feed; they are harder to find in the winter due to this tendency. Red-wings are attracted to feeders with suet and sunflower seeds spilling onto the ground, especially during migration. Though they are year-round residents throughout most of their North American range, northern populations migrate up to 800 miles south to overwinter in the southern U.S. and Mexico.

Loudoun hosts a combination of year-round residents and migrants that pass through in the spring and fall. Red-wings are found on every Central Loudoun CBC, some years numbering in the thousands. The male's conspicuous breeding behavior led to confirmations

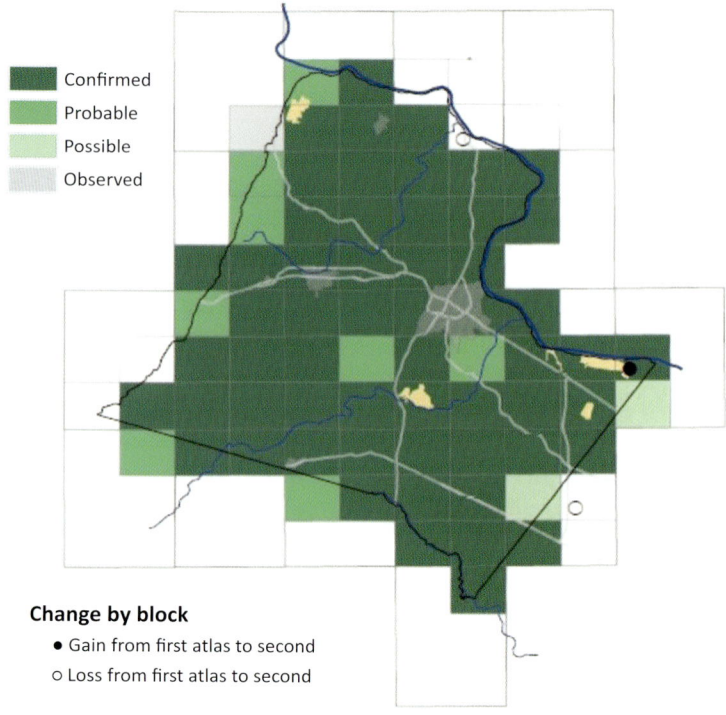

Confirmed
Probable
Possible
Observed

Change by block
- Gain from first atlas to second
- Loss from first atlas to second

in over three-quarters of the atlas blocks. Though one of the most abundant birds across North America, surveys show that populations are declining. The global breeding population of approximately 130 million is down from 190 million in 1974 (PIF 2017). Likely reasons for their decline include increases in the efficiency and expansion of modern agriculture along with climate change.

Written by Spring Ligi

Photo by Gerco Hoogeweg

BROWN-HEADED COWBIRD
Molothrus ater

Occurrence: common breeder, uncommon in winter, year-round resident

Earliest breeding confirmation: April 15, nest with eggs (NE)

Latest breeding confirmation: August 12, recently fledged young (FL)

The Brown-headed Cowbird leads a fascinating life as the most widespread brood parasite in North America. Females do not build a nest, but instead invest all their energy into producing up to 40 large eggs a season which they lay in the nests of over 140 bird species. Most individual females specialize on a particular host species, often removing a host egg before depositing one of their own. Cowbird eggs hatch earlier, giving the young a jumpstart on receiving food from their unsuspecting foster parents. The nestlings develop at a faster rate and sometimes push the host's eggs and nestlings out of the nest. Common host species include Red-winged Blackbirds, Song Sparrows, and Eastern Towhees. Though the majority of hosts are none the wiser, some birds have evolved a way to fight back. Species such as Cedar Waxwings, Gray Catbirds, and Blue Jays can recognize and eject cowbird eggs from their nests. The Yellow Warbler, too small to push the eggs out, instead builds a new nest on top of the old one to prevent incubation.

Brown-headed Cowbirds are considered a significant cause of songbird decline in North America. Originally associated

BROWN-HEADED COWBIRD (continued)

with bison herds on the Great Plains, this species can now be found snatching insects flushed by cattle or horses in Loudoun's pastures. Populations increased and spread in the 1800s as forests were cleared for development, providing new host species to exploit. Cowbirds prefer open habitat such as farm fields, meadows, woodland edges, and suburban lawns. Though still common across North America, populations have declined slightly in recent decades.

Cowbirds are year-round residents in Loudoun, though some more northern and western populations migrate short distances. Found on nearly every Central Loudoun CBC, numbers fluctuate widely from year to year with sightings sometimes hit or miss given their flocking behavior with other blackbirds, grackles, and starlings. The male's subtle brown head and short, stout bill help distinguish it from other blackbirds;

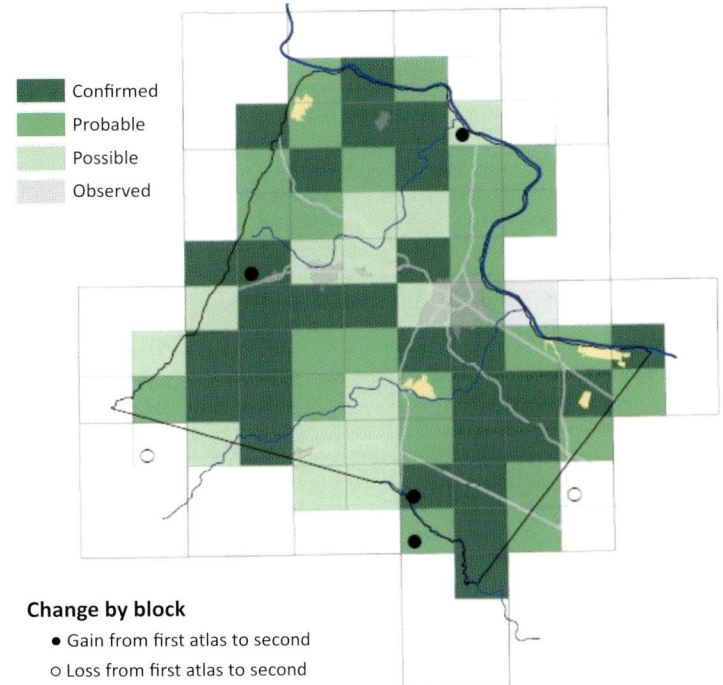

Confirmed
Probable
Possible
Observed

Change by block
● Gain from first atlas to second
○ Loss from first atlas to second

females are all brown instead of glossy black. This social bird produces a variety of clicks and high-pitched whistles and sings a flowing gurgling song, which is intriguing since the young don't learn these vocalizations from their parents. With no nest of their own, atlas breeding confirmations were limited to bittersweet (and sometimes comical) sightings of fledglings being fed by the host parent, who in some cases was half the size of the fledgling!

Written by Spring Ligi

Photo by Dave Boltz

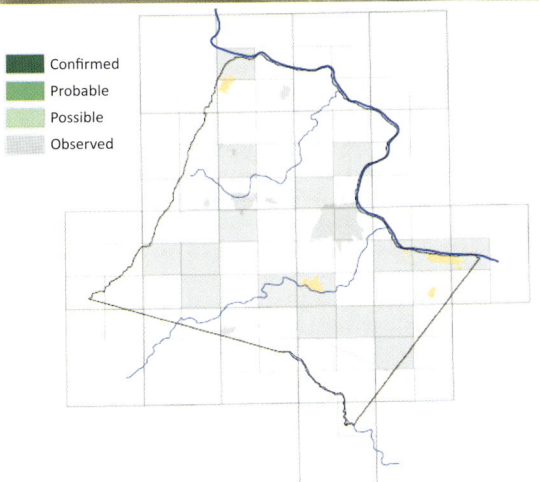

Confirmed
Probable
Possible
Observed

RUSTY BLACKBIRD
Euphagus carolinus

Occurrence: occasional migrant and winter visitor

Earliest fall sighting: October 15

Latest spring sighting: April 16

Listed as "Vulnerable" on the IUCN Red List, the Rusty Blackbird holds the unfortunate distinction of being one of North America's most rapidly declining migratory birds. Populations have declined by an estimated 85-95% over the past 40 years. Scientists now have a greater understanding of this species, but the principal cause for their continuing decline remains unclear. Degradation and loss of Canadian breeding and southeastern U.S. wintering habitats, mercury contamination, and global warming are leading hypotheses. Central Loudoun CBCs averaged 45 Rusty Blackbirds in the 1997-2006 counts, in contrast to only 3 Rusties in the 2007-2016 counts. Reported in just under a quarter of the atlas blocks, this water-loving blackbird with a pale-yellow iris may be found wading or perched in wooded wetlands, marshes, and pond edges or flocking with other blackbirds in dry fields where they consume seed and grain. They breed in bogs and wet woods of boreal forest, farther north than our other blackbirds. Aptly named, their song calls to mind the creaking of a rusty gate and their non-breeding plumage sports rusty-colored feather edges.

Written by Spring Ligi

BREWER'S BLACKBIRD
Euphagus cyanocephalus

Occurrence: vagrant

Earliest/latest seasonal sightings: fewer than 5 atlas sightings, see account for details

Though rare in Loudoun, the Brewer's Blackbird is commonly found across western North America in a variety of habitats ranging from grassland, marshes, and woodland edges to farmland, suburban yards, and city streets. This ground forager may be found in flocks with grackles, Red-winged Blackbirds, cowbirds, and starlings. The Brewer's Blackbird was reported only twice during the atlas (April and November 2010) and once on a Central Loudoun CBC. Appearing very similar to the Rusty Blackbird, the breeding male Brewer's Blackbird is a glossier black mixed with iridescent blue and green. Males of both species have a prominent yellow eye. Females are plain brown and lack the male's bright eye or the female Red-winged Blackbird's streaks. Though they've adapted well to human development and expanded their range eastward, the Brewer's Blackbird is listed as a "common bird in steep decline" in the 2014 State of the Birds Report. Often associated with livestock, they generally cause only minor damage to crops (unlike some of their cousins) and have an appetite for insect pests that likely benefits farmers.

Written by Spring Ligi

Confirmed
Probable
Possible
Observed

COMMON GRACKLE
Quiscalus quiscula

Occurrence: common breeder, uncommon in winter, year-round resident

Earliest breeding confirmation: April 15, adult carrying nesting material or nest building (NB)

Latest breeding confirmation: August 6, recently fledged young (FL)

The Common Grackle is a familiar bird to Loudoun residents, easily dismissed or considered a pest. But once you get to know this bird, it may surprise you. Did you know that grackles practice anting, a behavior where they spread their wings on the ground to encourage ants to crawl on their feathers and skin? One explanation for this mysterious behavior, observed in over 200 other bird species, is that the ants secrete a liquid which rids the bird of parasites. Or did you know that Common Grackles can mimic other birds and human noises? Though not in the same league as mockingbirds, impressive none-the-less. They also make a variety of squeaks, whistles, and croaks; their song, sung by both males and females, resembles a rusty gate. If you're still not intrigued by the Common Grackle's antics, here's some food for thought. This opportunistic omnivore eats anything and everything – seeds, fruit, insects, fish, mice, birds, and garbage, just to name a few. They steal food from other birds and may dominate backyard feeders.

Common Grackles stand out in mixed winter flocks with cowbirds, starlings, and other blackbirds – look for the tallest

COMMON GRACKLE (continued)

and longest-tailed blackbirds. Upon closer inspection you'll notice a glossy bluish head, iridescent body, hefty bill, and bright golden eye. Females and immatures are less glossy; immatures have a dark eye. Found on almost every Central Loudoun CBC, year-to-year numbers fluctuate widely from thousands to single digits due to their flocking nature. Grackles are year-round residents throughout Loudoun and much of their eastern and midwestern North American range. They prefer open habitats ranging from forest edges, grassland, and marshes to farmland, suburban parks, and lawns. Well documented during the atlas, this social bird breeds in loose colonies of 10-30 pairs (sometimes much larger), with their bulky cup nests camouflaged among dense trees or shrubs near open areas or water. Grackles typically raise one or two broods of four to five young.

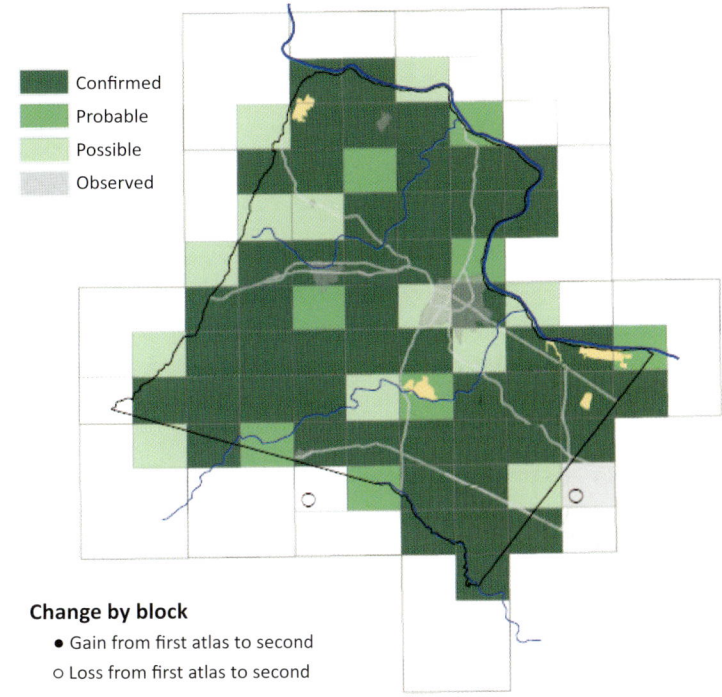

Confirmed
Probable
Possible
Observed

Change by block
- Gain from first atlas to second
- Loss from first atlas to second

Here's a fact that may surprise you: The Common Grackle is listed on the 2014 State of the Birds Report as a "common bird in steep decline." Likely reasons for their decline include extermination in large numbers as an agricultural pest and shrinking habitat as eastern forests, cleared for agriculture in the eighteenth and nineteenth centuries, have grown back. Perhaps the next time you see a grackle, you'll give pause to recall the finer points of this interesting bird.

Written by Spring Ligi

Photo by Bob Schamerhorn

OVENBIRD
Seiurus aurocapilla

Occurrence: uncommon breeder and migrant

Earliest breeding confirmation: May 12, distraction display (DD)

Latest breeding confirmation: July 27, recently fledged young (FL)

This unique warbler behaves much like a thrush, walking and bobbing along the woodland floor searching for insects and other invertebrates in the leaf litter, or singing from a low perch in the deep forest. It even looks like one, with heavy black spotting on its white chest and flanks and an olive-brown face, back, wings, and tail. The head is distinctively marked, with an orange crown between two black stripes and a white eyering. The pink legs are relatively long, and the bill is often at least partially pink. Its ringing song, *tea-cher, tea-Cher, Tea-Cher, TEA-CHER, TEA-CHER*, starts softly and gets louder, and can be heard from quite a distance. At times, you may hear multiple birds singing as they respond to one another from their respective territories.

Ovenbirds breed in large, unbroken broadleaf or mixed woodlands in the eastern and central U.S. and Canada. They tend to disappear where their preferred closed-canopy forests become fragmented (again, much like the Wood Thrush). Even 250- to 2,000-acre patches may lose Ovenbirds as breeders if there are not larger unbroken tracts nearby (Porneluzi et al. 2011). Finding them in eastern Loudoun has become more difficult as forests have succumbed

OVENBIRD (continued)

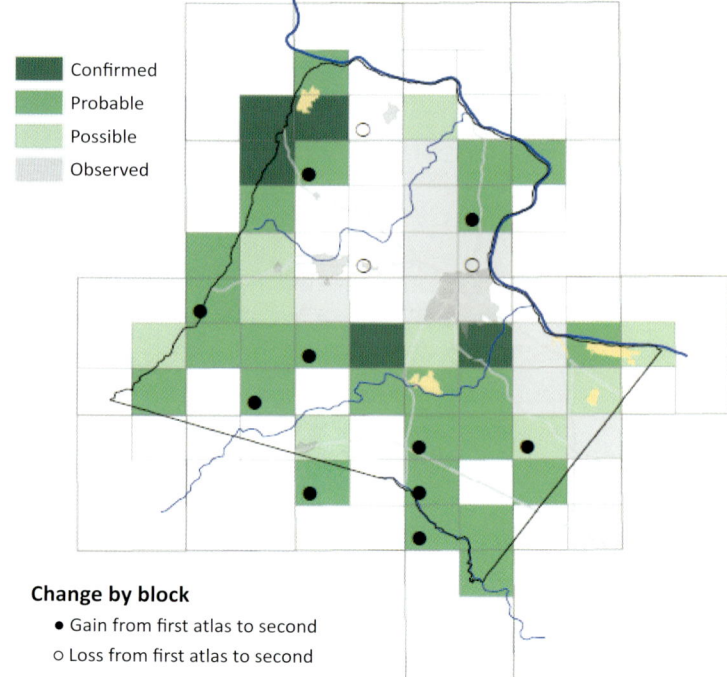

to development. The apparent gain in blocks from Atlas 1 to 2 is likely influenced by the increased coverage and effort-hours per block in Atlas 2.

The name Ovenbird comes from the shape of their nest, carefully woven of grasses and leaves with a domed roof over the side entrance hole (picture a primitive oven). Built on the ground in a well-hidden location, the female often drops more leaves on top of the nest for added camouflage. The female broods the eggs and chicks, but both parents provide food. The female will remain with the chicks until a threat is right on top of her, then will often perform a distraction display to lead the danger away. Once fledged, young are split among the two parents for continuing supervision.

Legend for map:
- Confirmed
- Probable
- Possible
- Observed

Change by block
- ● Gain from first atlas to second
- ○ Loss from first atlas to second

Typically found in Loudoun from early April through early October, this long-distance migrant travels to Mexico and the Caribbean (eastern breeders tend to fly to Cuba and other islands, while more westerly breeders migrate to Mexico). They use a broader variety of wooded habitats in the winter. Their population remains stable overall, declining where forests are disturbed but increasing where they are regenerating. They are susceptible to predation and cowbird parasitism, especially in fragmented habitats.

Written by Bruce Hill

Photo by Dave Boltz

WORM-EATING WARBLER
Helmitheros vermivorum

Occurrence: occasional breeder and migrant

Earliest breeding confirmation: May 7, adult carrying nesting material or nest building (NB)

Latest breeding confirmation: July 12, parent carrying food or feeding young (CF)

This small, brown warbler is generally nondescript, enlivened by a crisply patterned head with four dark brown stripes running through the eyes and along the crown. Its flesh-colored bill is relatively thick and large compared to most warblers. The upperparts are a mousy brown, paler and often a rich buff color below, with some olive highlights in its wings and short, squared-off tail. The song is a rapid, insect-like trill, not as musical as the similarly paced trills of a Chipping Sparrow or Pine Warbler. Over time, a keen listener can learn to distinguish this species by voice alone.

Despite its name, the Worm-eating Warbler will not be found in your front yard pulling up earthworms. But its diet is heavily reliant on caterpillars ("the other white meat"), along with other insects. It forages low and slow in shrubs and trees, plucking prey from dense clusters of dead or live leaves. This species breeds in large tracts of deciduous or mixed forest, almost always on dry, steep slopes and hillsides with a dense understory. Its cup-shaped nest is placed on the ground, typically lined with moss and well-concealed under available cover. Females do the incubating, and are known for sitting tight even if closely approached. If and when they do flush, they may perform a distraction display to

WORM-EATING WARBLER (continued)

lure predators, and birders, away from their nest site. Young birds leave the nest at an early age, often only 8-10 days after hatching, but will continue to stick close to their parents for a couple weeks longer.

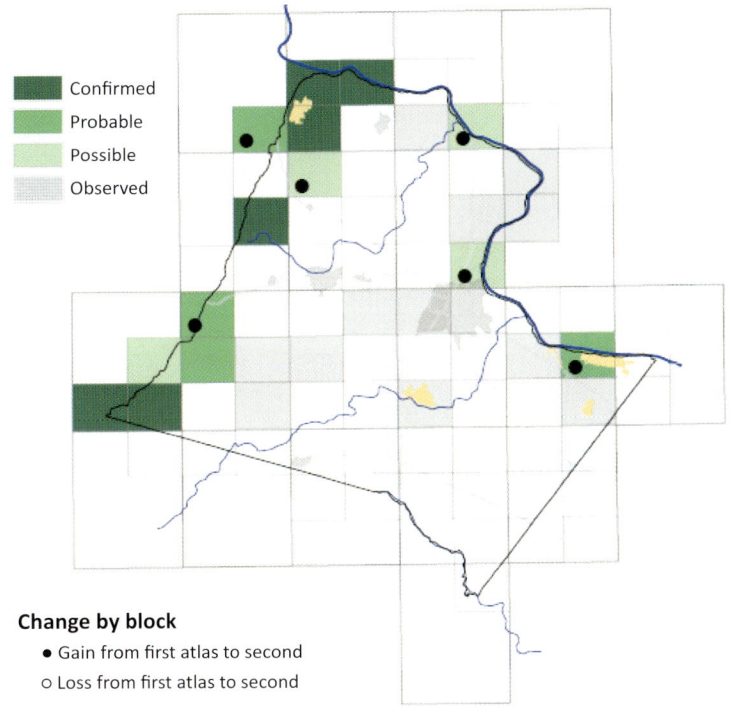

Confirmed
Probable
Possible
Observed

Change by block
- Gain from first atlas to second
○ Loss from first atlas to second

Typically found in Loudoun between late April and mid-September, the Worm-eating Warbler breeds in limited locations and small numbers where the habitat is right. Breeding was confirmed in just 6 western Loudoun atlas blocks, though the species was reported as a probable or possible breeder in an additional 8 blocks. Its core breeding habitat is to our west, in upland forests from northern Arkansas up to southern New York State. Northern populations may pass through Loudoun on their way to wintering habitat in tropical forests of the Caribbean, Mexico, and Central and South America. Migrants were observed in 12 atlas blocks. The species' population has remained fairly stable over time. But it has never been an abundant bird; the global breeding population is estimated at only about 830,000 (PIF 2017). Habitat loss and forest fragmentation are its most likely vulnerabilities.

Written by Bruce Hill

Photo ©Dick Rowe

LOUISIANA WATERTHRUSH
Parkesia motacilla

Occurrence: uncommon breeder and migrant

Earliest breeding confirmation: May 9, distraction display (DD)

Latest breeding confirmation: June 29, parent carrying food or feeding young (CF)

One of the earliest arriving neotropical migrants, Louisiana Waterthrushes appear in our area as early as late March, with reports continuing through July. After that, sightings become scarce in Loudoun, with only a couple September atlas reports. Found near flowing streams in deciduous upland forests, they breed across much of the eastern third of the U.S., absent from the southern coastal plain, Florida, and the Gulf coastal region. They migrate to wintering grounds in southern Mexico, Central America, the Caribbean, and the Bahamas, where they favor similar wooded streamside habitats. Populations appear to be generally stable, although they have never been a numerous species. The total global population is estimated to be about 360,000 (PIF 2017). The notable gain in atlas blocks from Atlas 1 to 2 is likely influenced by the increased coverage and effort per block in Atlas 2.

Males guard a long, narrow territory along their chosen stretch of stream, singing frequently. The ringing, complex song, typically about five descending clear notes, followed by a jumbled mix, carries well over the sound of running water. Within their territory, males tend to respond aggressively to imitations of their song or pishing, flying in to

LOUISIANA WATERTHRUSH (continued)

investigate the source. Their sharp *chip* alarm note also often gives them away. Once nesting is underway, they sing much less frequently, and can be harder to find. Nests are constructed in nooks or crannies on streamside banks or under fallen trees nearby. Somewhat like a robin's nest, mud and twigs are used to create a solid foundation, with finer materials lining the cup. Females are thought to build the nest. Three to six eggs are laid, though cowbird parasitism is a frequent challenge. Once hatched, both parents feed the young.

This thrush-like warbler is dark brown above, with a whitish breast and flanks showing dark streaking. Note especially the thick white eyebrow that broadens behind the eye and long pink legs; these can help distinguish the Louisiana from its close relative, the Northern Waterthrush. Overall, this bird has a long, slim look to it. It frequently bobs its tail as it walks, foraging along banks or even in shallow water. Its diet consists primarily of insects and other arthropods, but it will also eat the occasional small frog or fish. Look for this fascinating species especially in western Loudoun, where its preferred rocky streams and forested hillsides are more common.

Written by Bruce Hill

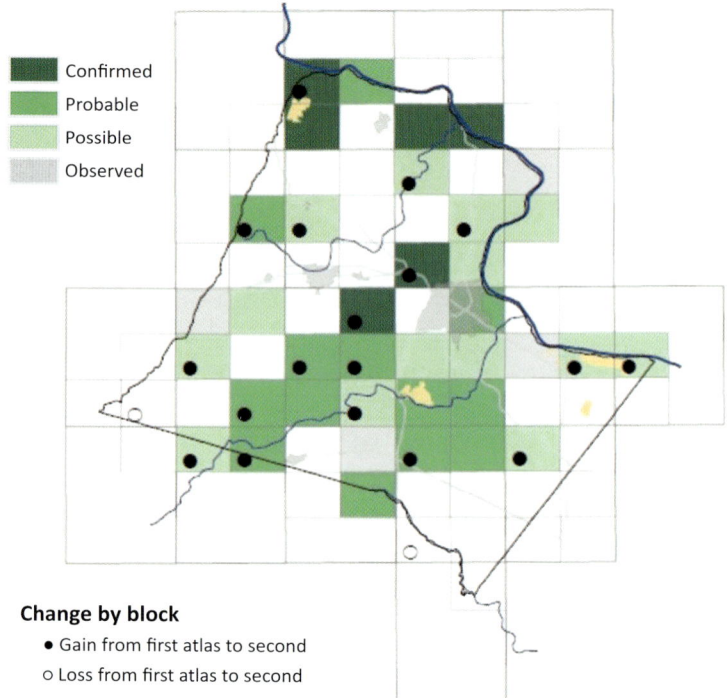

Confirmed
Probable
Possible
Observed

Change by block
● Gain from first atlas to second
○ Loss from first atlas to second

Photo ©Dick Rowe

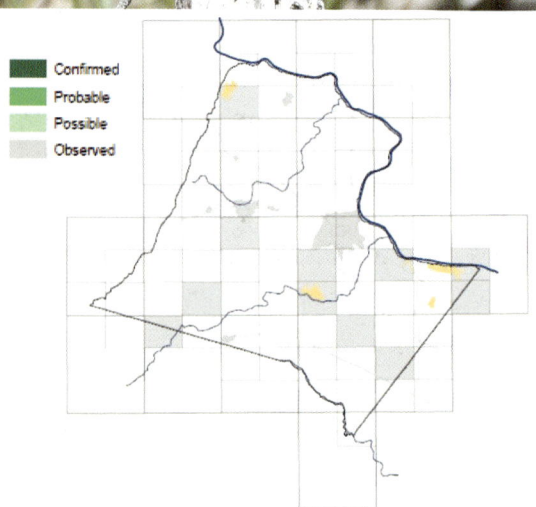

Confirmed
Probable
Possible
Observed

NORTHERN WATERTHRUSH
Parkesia noveboracensis

Occurrence: occasional migrant

Southerly migration period: no atlas sightings, see account for details

Northerly migration period: April 20 – May 22

Similar in appearance to the Loudoun-breeding Louisiana Waterthrush, the Northern's song, range, and habitat preferences set the two apart. This low-cavity nester breeds near bodies of still or sluggish water, in a broad swath from the Northeast across Canada and Alaska. Small numbers occur at higher altitudes down into Virginia and West Virginia. They winter in Mexico, Central America, and the Caribbean. This skulking species hunts for insects, arthropods, and the occasional minnow while walking along the ground or in shallow water. While the Northern is brown above and pale with dark streaks below, like the Louisiana, distinguishing features include a narrower white or buffy eyebrow, darker legs, heavier streaks on the breast, and sometimes a yellowish belly. Its song also differs: several loud, single-pitch notes followed by a more rapid series of variably pitched, evenly spaced notes. While numbers declined slightly in recent decades, their population is healthy, at about 19 million (PIF 2017). Atlas sightings were strongly skewed towards springtime, when they are vocal, and riparian and wetland habitat in central and eastern Loudoun.

Written by Bruce Hill

BLUE-WINGED WARBLER
Vermivora cyanoptera

Occurrence: occasional breeder and migrant

Earliest/latest breeding confirmations: fewer than 5 atlas confirmations, see account for details

Photo ©Dick Rowe

The small, compact Blue-winged Warbler has a bright yellow head, breast, and belly, an olive nape and back, bluish-gray wings with two broad white wingbars, and a short bluish-gray tail. A black eyeline and dark lores, directly in line with its pointed black bill, give this species a masked look. Its diagnostic, thin and burry *bee-buzz*, sung from exposed perches on tall trees or shrubs edging open field areas, is used to defend territorial boundaries from rivals. The Blue Ridge Center in May, especially along the powerline cut and "Butterfly Alley," is a great place and time to listen and look for this handsome little warbler, but it can show up just about anywhere during migration. Found in Loudoun between mid-April and mid-September, it breeds regularly (though in small numbers) only in the northwestern corner of the county, at the extreme southern edge of its summer range. Breeding was confirmed only once during the atlas (June 2009), though evidence of possible and probable breeding was recorded about a dozen times, with all but 2 records at the Blue Ridge Center. It settles in shrubby pastures, overgrown fields, and edge habitats in a band across the eastern U.S., from New Jersey and Massachusetts to Missouri and Iowa. Migration takes it through the southeastern U.S. and over the Gulf of Mexico en route to wintering locales in southwestern Mexico and the Caribbean slope of Central America.

Blue-wings eat caterpillars, grasshoppers, beetles, and other insects, often hanging upside down at the ends of branches to get at prey hidden in leaf clusters. They build their nest on the ground, under shrubs or in clumps of grass. Males stake out breeding territory and aggressively chase away other males. Pairs are thought to be monogamous, though some dalliance can occur. Their typical brood is four to seven young, though many nests are parasitized by Brown-headed Cowbirds, lowering overall success. Despite an estimated 22% decline over the last half-century, this species is not seriously threatened, with a breeding population of about 710,000 individuals (PIF 2017). They are definitely faring better than their close relative, the Golden-winged Warbler, which historically bred in relative isolation farther north. But forest clearing and farming in the past couple centuries enabled Blue-wings to expand northward, with subsequent interbreeding ("Brewster's" and "Lawrence's" are common hybrids) and a steady reduction in Golden-winged numbers. Climate change may continue to push both species northward and into further competition with one another.

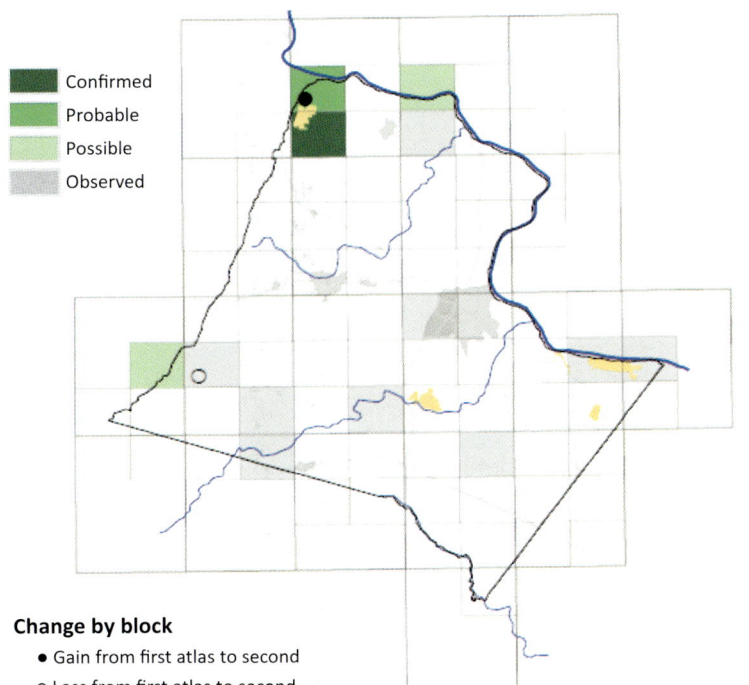

Confirmed
Probable
Possible
Observed

Change by block
- Gain from first atlas to second
- Loss from first atlas to second

Written by Bruce Hill

BLACK-AND-WHITE WARBLER
Mniotilta varia

Occurrence: occasional breeder, uncommon migrant

Earliest/latest breeding confirmations: fewer than 5 atlas confirmations, see account for details

Photo by Dave Boltz

As the name implies, this warbler species lacks the colorful plumage of many of its relatives. Still, it is a beautiful bird, with a strongly contrasting and complex black and white pattern of stripes above and below. Males are more boldly patterned, showing a black throat, triangular black cheek patches, and broad white eyebrow, while the paler females have a white throat and more grayish cheeks. Their thin, dark bill is sometimes slightly decurved. Black-and-white Warblers feed primarily by clambering up or down the trunks and larger branches of trees, gleaning insects, especially moth larvae, from the bark. But they will also venture out to pluck caterpillars from leafy branches. In migration, they are not overly discriminating about their foraging habitat, and may be spotted in just about any urban, suburban, or rural setting with deciduous trees.

Black-and-white Warblers typically arrive in Loudoun around mid-April and depart in early October. Documented throughout Loudoun, most atlas sightings were likely migrants; this species was confirmed only once as a breeder – a young fledgling was found on July 17, 2009 in Ashby Gap 6. But with a respectable number of probable and possible breeding records, Black-and-white Warblers likely nest in small numbers in Loudoun each year, particularly towards the western edge of the county.

This off-beat neotropical migrant nests on the ground, hiding its bowl-shaped nest under a rock or fallen tree on the floor of deciduous forest. Females are the primary nest builders and incubators. Breeding males may sing frequently and late into the season in aggressive defense of their territory, a distinctive *whee-za, whee-za, whee-za* lasting several seconds. Their breeding range extends from as far south as eastern Texas and Louisiana, through much of the southeastern interior and mid-Atlantic, into New England and the Great Lakes region, and across the eastern two-thirds of Canada. They are notably absent from the mountain and Pacific West. Black-and-white Warblers winter in southern Florida and Texas, throughout the Caribbean, Mexico, and Central America, and into far-northern South America. While there, they tend to stick to forested regions, but are also found in coffee plantations that maintain some tree cover.

This species has declined by about 33% over the past half-century (Sauer et al. 2017), but overall population numbers remain healthy at about 20 million. Threats to Black-and-white Warblers include forest fragmentation, pesticide poisoning, and collisions with man-made structures during their nocturnal migrations.

Written by Bruce Hill

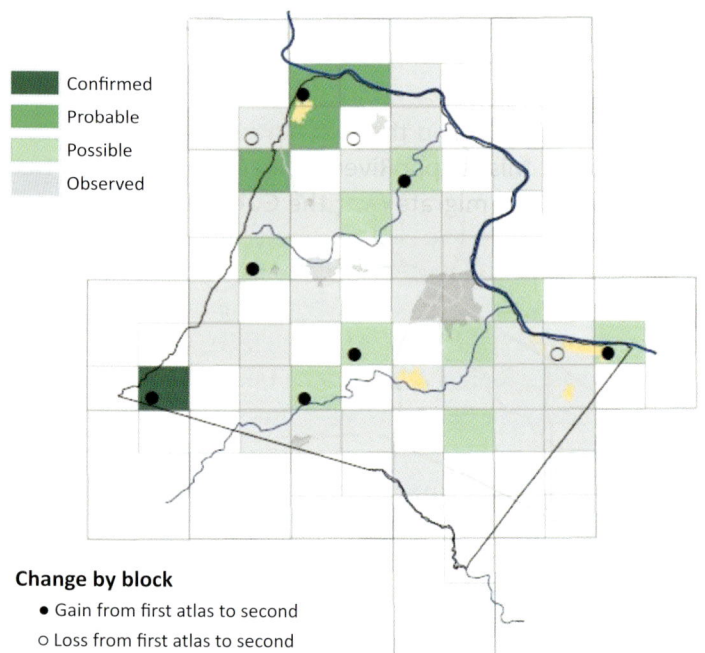

Confirmed
Probable
Possible
Observed

Change by block
- Gain from first atlas to second
- Loss from first atlas to second

PROTHONOTARY WARBLER
Protonotaria citrea

Occurrence: occasional breeder and spring migrant, rare fall migrant

Earliest breeding confirmation: May 7, adult carrying nesting material or nest building (NB)

Latest breeding confirmation: July 7, recently fledged young (FL)

Photo by Dave Boltz

The Prothonotary Warbler is a stunning bird, golden-yellow above and below, with an olive nape, gray wings (without wingbars), rump, and tail, and dark eyes set against a plain face. Only the vent area is white. Males and females are similar, with the female slightly paler. Breeding in larger tracts of wooded wetlands and along forested rivers and streams, it is one of only two warblers to use tree cavities as nest sites. Cavities over or very near water are strongly preferred. They will also use well-designed and -located nest boxes. The male typically selects several possible nest holes and shows them off; the female selects her favorite and completes the nest building. Once paired, they tend to remain monogamous, and may return to the same location year after year.

In Loudoun, floodplain forests along the Potomac River are the best place to search for this beautiful and highly sought-after species. They generally arrive in early May and depart by early September. Despite their bright coloration, they can be difficult to spot when not actively in motion. Knowing their song helps reveal their presence. Their vocalizations are not nearly as flashy as their looks; listen for a monotonous *sweet-sweet-sweet-...sweet-sweet*, with each song consisting of 4 to 14 notes. Males will sit up on a low to mid-level perch, singing every 10-15 seconds or so, before moving to another spot around the perimeter of their territory to repeat the performance. They forage in the understory and on the ground, preying on a wide selection of insects and invertebrates. Outside of the breeding season they supplement their diet with seeds and berries.

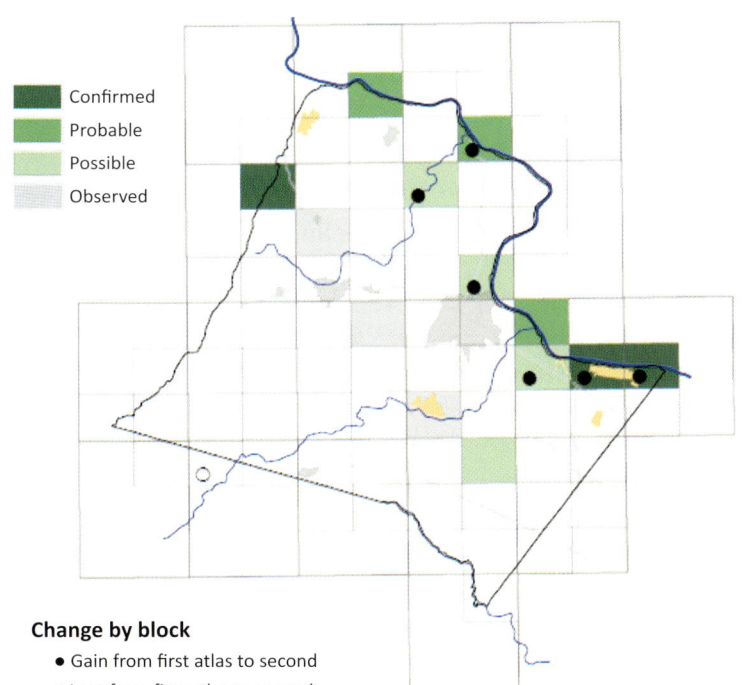

Confirmed
Probable
Possible
Observed

Change by block
- Gain from first atlas to second
○ Loss from first atlas to second

The Prothonotary is an endemic U.S. breeder, with a few reports of possible nests in Canada. They summer in suitable habitat throughout the Atlantic coastal plain and the Gulf states, as well as quite far up the Mississippi River drainage to the Great Lakes area. They migrate over the Gulf of Mexico to winter in coastal mangroves and other lowland forests in southern Mexico, Central and South America, and parts of the Caribbean. While migrating, more varied habitats are used, and one can show up almost anywhere. A watch-list bird that has suffered a 42% decline in population over the past 50 years (Sauer et al. 2017), the Prothonotary Warbler is vulnerable to habitat loss throughout its range, as bottomlands are lost in the U.S. or coastal mangroves succumb to development in Central and South America.

Written by Bruce Hill

SWAINSON'S WARBLER
Limnothlypis swainsonii

Occurrence: vagrant

Earliest/latest seasonal sightings: fewer than 5 atlas sightings, see account for details

The Swainson's Warbler is one of the most cryptic warblers, muted in appearance, skulking in behavior, and inhabiting some of the most inaccessible Southern swamps and thickets. It is extremely rare in our area, but a single well-documented atlas observation was accepted from June 2, 2013 in Harpers Ferry 4. Both sexes are brownish overall (paler underneath), with a distinctively large, pointed bill, rusty cap, whitish eyebrow, and dark eyeline. They forage by walking quickly along the forest floor, flipping leaves to uncover insects. Males patrol surprisingly large territories, usually only giving away their presence with a loud, whistled *so, so, so, so, sweet-to-hear*. Their breeding range extends from Virginia's lower coastal plain (the Great Dismal Swamp is a go-to location) through the Gulf states to eastern Texas. Winters are spent in Cuba, Jamaica, and the Yucatan Peninsula. The overall population is stable but small, with a global estimate of about 90,000 birds (PIF 2017). Their specific habitat requirements and small numbers may make them susceptible to habitat loss, severe weather events, or climate change.

Written by Bruce Hill

Photo by Mark Johnson

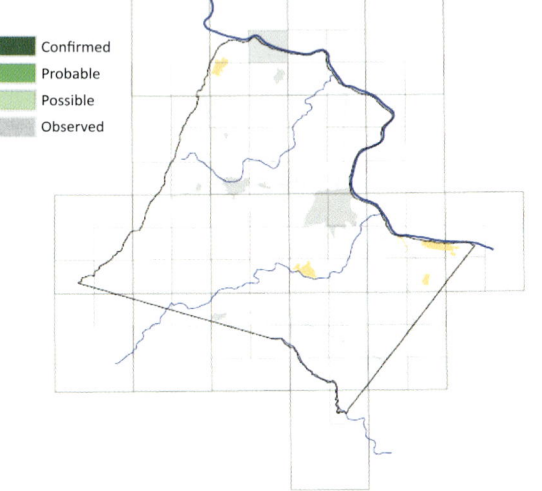

- Confirmed
- Probable
- Possible
- Observed

TENNESSEE WARBLER
Oreothlypis peregrina

Occurrence: occasional migrant

Southerly migration period: September 6 – October 12

Northerly migration period: April 6 – May 18

The small, short-tailed Tennessee Warbler is greenish-yellow above and whitish below, with a gray face and crown (male) and pale eyebrows. Females often look very similar to males, but may show less gray on the head and some yellowish wash below. This ground-nesting species breeds far from Tennessee, primarily in the boreal forests of Canada. Small numbers stop just south of the border in comparable habitat from upper Michigan to Maine. On its breeding grounds, the Tennessee Warbler's diet relies heavily on the cyclical spruce budworm. While wintering in Central and South America, its eating habits are more varied, often feeding on nectar by puncturing the base of flowers to supplement a diet of insects. During migration through the eastern and central U.S., look for them high in trees, or listen for the loud, three-part, trilled song. Over 75% of the atlas sightings were reported in the fall. Tennessee Warblers have experienced localized declines over the past 50 years, but remain numerous at about 70 million breeding birds (PIF 2017).

Written by Bruce Hill

Photo by Tony LePrieur

- Confirmed
- Probable
- Possible
- Observed

ORANGE-CROWNED WARBLER
Oreothlypis celata

Occurrence: rare migrant

Southerly/northerly migration periods: fewer than 5 atlas sightings, see account for details

This is one of the few "western" warblers that regularly wander into the East. Orange-crowned Warblers breed from Arizona to Alaska and across central Canada, using a variety of forest types. While scarce along the East Coast, some eastern Canada breeders migrate through to winter along the lower Atlantic and Gulf Coasts. They forage rapidly in trees and on the ground for invertebrates, supplemented by berries, seeds, and even sap. They are also known to feed at suet and hummingbird feeders. Their plumage is drab olive-green to dull yellow above and below; wings are unbarred. They lack any conspicuous markings, though a close look shows a thin dark eyeline, with a lighter eyebrow and broken white eyering. Males may display their orange crown during territorial displays, but otherwise this field mark is rarely seen. Though abundant in some locations, and numbering about 80 million (PIF 2017), they have declined by 34% in recent decades (Sauer et al. 2017). With only 3 fall and 2 spring atlas sightings, this bird is not to be expected on an average day...but who knows?

Written by Bruce Hill

Photo by ©Dick Rowe

Confirmed
Probable
Possible
Observed

Photo by Dave Boltz

Confirmed
Probable
Possible
Observed

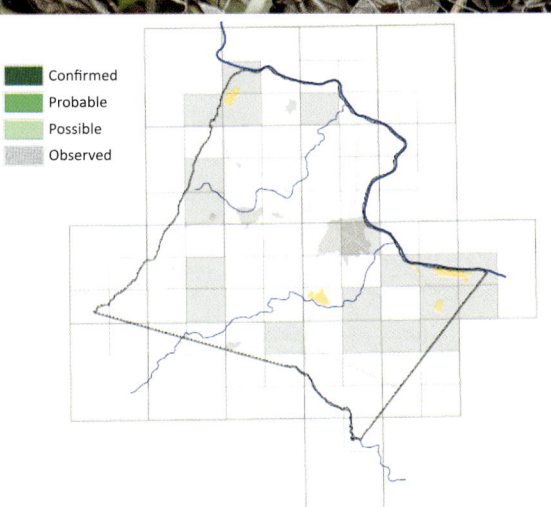

NASHVILLE WARBLER
Oreothlypis ruficapilla

Occurrence: occasional migrant

Southerly migration period: August 31 – October 11

Northerly migration period: fewer than 5 atlas sightings, see account for details

At first glance, the Connecticut-Mourning-Nashville Warbler trio all share a basic look: gray-hooded head, olive-yellow back and wing coverts, no wingbars, and plain yellow underparts. Like the Connecticut, the Nashville has a white eyering. But unlike the other two, its hood does not extend to its chin and throat, which are yellow. Its song is distinctive, a loud, two-parted combination of double-note phrases and then a trill. This species probes for insects on branch tips and flower tassels in second-growth mixed forests with a healthy understory. In Loudoun, there were 5 times more atlas sightings in the fall than the spring, along with 2 well-documented aberrant sightings in late November and January. This ground nester breeds throughout the Northeast, upper Midwest, and far-western U.S., and across much of central Canada. The bulk of the population overwinters in Mexico in various habitat types. With a population of about 32 million (PIF 2017), this species has suffered small declines over time but remains numerous. Like the Mourning, Nashville Warblers appear to benefit from human land disturbances that increase available second-growth.

Written by Bruce Hill

CONNECTICUT WARBLER

Oporornis agilis

Occurrence: rare fall migrant

Southerly migration period: fewer than 5 atlas sightings, see account for details

The Connecticut Warbler is high on many a birder's wish list, and remains a nemesis bird for some (this author included). There were only 4 atlas sightings in two years (2012, 2013), all within a 7-day span (September 9-16). This enigmatic bird migrates through Loudoun almost exclusively in fall, when it moves down the mid-Atlantic Coast prior to a multi-day, nonstop trip over the Atlantic and Caribbean to South America. In spring it heads north on a more inland track to its breeding range in south-central Canada and the extreme northern U.S. This large warbler skulks on or near the ground in dense cover, using its long legs to walk (not hop) through the leaf litter in search of insects. It has a blue-gray hood and throat, well-defined and complete white eyering, and long, flesh-colored bill. It is yellow underneath, olive-green above, with no wing markings. Male and female patterns are similar, but females are paler. This watch-listed species has declined by 62% since 1966 (Sauer et al. 2017), and remains vulnerable to habitat degradation and climate change.

Written by Bruce Hill

Photo by Mark Johnson

Confirmed
Probable
Possible
Observed

Photo by Dave Boltz

MOURNING WARBLER

Geothlypis philadelphia

Occurrence: rare migrant

Southerly/northerly migration periods: fewer than 5 atlas sightings, see account for details

This small, rotund neotropical migrant superficially resembles the Connecticut Warbler, with a dark hood and plain yellow underparts. But it is noticeably smaller and differs significantly in behavior and habitat. Visual differences include the lack of an eyering and a black chest immediately under the gray hood on males. The back is olive-brown, and the wings lack wingbars. Females appear similar, but more washed out. They like second-growth forested habitats, especially wetter areas with thick vegetation. This insect-eating ground nester breeds across southern Canada and the northeastern U.S. around the Great Lakes. Wintering habitat includes second growth and tropical scrub in southern Central and northern South America. Migration routes center on the Mississippi River drainage and along the eastern Mexican coastline, with few birds passing through our region. There was just one atlas sighting (May 22, 2010) in Banshee Reeks Nature Preserve. Overall, populations have declined, but the Mourning Warbler remains fairly common in its range at about 17 million individuals (PIF 2017). Its penchant for disturbed habitat may help the species in some regions.

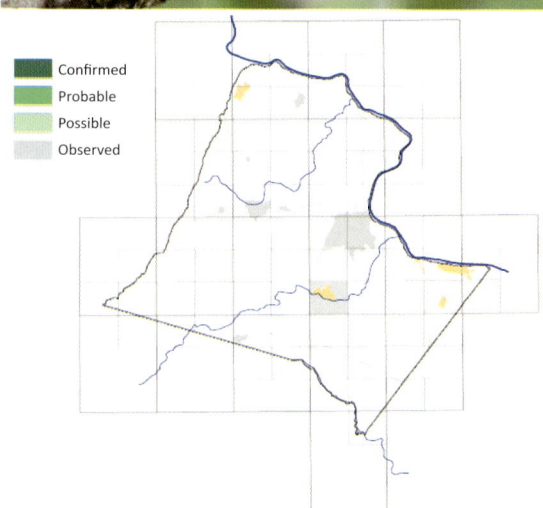

Confirmed
Probable
Possible
Observed

Written by Bruce Hill

KENTUCKY WARBLER
Geothlypis formosa

Occurrence: occasional breeder and spring migrant, rare fall migrant

Earliest breeding confirmation: June 2, distraction display (DD)

Latest breeding confirmation: July 24, recently fledged young (FL)

Arthur Cleveland Bent (an American ornithologist, 1866-1954) described the Kentucky Warbler as "a lover of deep shade and dense, damp thickets." This seems an accurate assessment, and helps explain why this bright yellow bird is much more frequently heard than seen. The Kentucky Warbler lives its life in thick deciduous forests, especially favoring wet bottomlands and ravines. It is bright yellow below, olive-green above, with a dark angular cheek patch and crown and yellow lores and eyebrows that curve like a fishhook behind the eye. It hunts for insects near the forest floor, hopping on the ground or working through low understory on long pink legs, flipping over leaves and gleaning caterpillars from the bottoms of low-hanging leaves. Its vivid colors blend remarkably well into the dark forest understory, and it can take surprising effort to spot one even when it is singing nearby. Males will sit up on slightly higher perches to sing, an oft-repeated *chery-chery-chery* at an even pitch. This song sounds similar to that of our omnipresent Carolina Wren except for the even pitch, and has a notably longer pause between each burst of song.

The Piedmont region and Loudoun are near the heart of this species' breeding range, which covers the bulk of the southeastern U.S. Typically arriving in late April and leaving in mid- to late September, it migrates south to winter in the coastal forests of southern Mexico and Central America. Kentucky Warblers thrive in unbroken woodlands with a healthy understory, but have declined where forests are fragmented or deer have eliminated most ground cover. As ground nesters, the double whammy of less camouflage for their nests and increased access by predators and brood parasites (like raccoons and cowbirds) can significantly reduce breeding success. Many woodlands in Loudoun that may have offered good habitat for this bird in the past have suffered both afflictions (too many deer; fragmentation). Kentucky Warblers were found in just 18 blocks during Atlas 2 (with breeding confirmed in 5), a net loss of 8 blocks from the first atlas, providing convincing evidence of a local decline. In fact, this bird's range-wide numbers have dropped by about 36% over the past 50 years according to the North American BBS, and it was identified as an at-risk species on the 2014 State of the Birds Watch List. Habitat loss remains a threat in both its summer and winter range.

Written by Bruce Hill

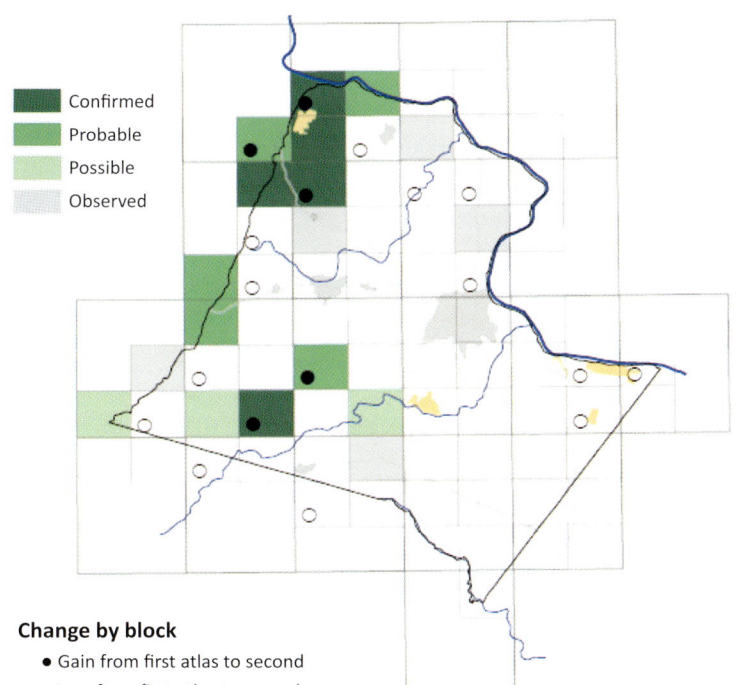

Confirmed
Probable
Possible
Observed

Change by block
- Gain from first atlas to second
- Loss from first atlas to second

COMMON YELLOWTHROAT
Geothlypis trichas

Occurrence: common breeder and migrant

Earliest breeding confirmation: May 7, adult carrying nesting material or nest building (NB)

Latest breeding confirmation: August 7, recently fledged young (FL)

The Common Yellowthroat's memorable song and unique markings make it one of Loudoun's most easily identified wood warblers. The male is brownish-olive above, with a bright yellow throat, breast, and undertail coverts. His most distinctive feature is a black "bandit" mask which wraps around his crown and eyes, bordered above by a blurred white stripe. The female's plumage is similar, but she lacks the mask and is duller overall in coloration.

Photo by Dave Boltz

The small size, lively movements, and cocked tail of Common Yellowthroats are reminiscent of wrens, and indeed an early name for the species was "Yellow-throated Wren." Their scolding behavior is also wren-like: The male will often pop up if an intruder comes near the nest and deliver a tirade of loud, insistent *tchek* calls. The vocalization for which the Common Yellowthroat is best known, however, is its cheerful song, a rhythmic *witchity-witchity-witchity-witch,* often rising in pitch towards the end.

Although this species makes rare winter appearances in Loudoun, with 1 report on February 13, 2013 and 2 documented sightings during the past 20 Central Loudoun CBCs, Common Yellowthroats typically arrive in mid-April from their wintering grounds in the southeastern U.S., Mexico, and Central America and depart Loudoun by late October. They breed across most of the U.S. and the Canadian provinces and into western Mexico. Their favored habitats are swamps, marshes, and damp meadows, but they will also nest in hedgerows and brushy thickets. The female builds a cup-shaped nest close to the ground, enclosed in a bulky construction of coarse grass or leaves and lined with finer grasses, hairs, or fibers. Two broods per season are usual. Brown-headed Cowbirds often lay eggs in their nests; the yellowthroats respond by deserting the nest or building a new nest on top of the parasitized one. Breeding evidence for Common Yellowthroats was found in 66 of the 73 atlas blocks, with breeding confirmed in 21 blocks.

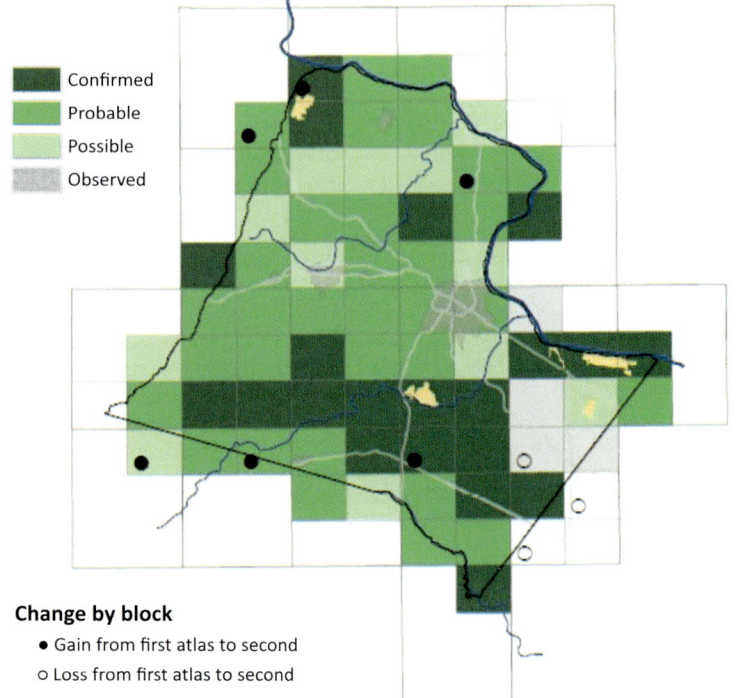

Confirmed
Probable
Possible
Observed

Change by block
- Gain from first atlas to second
- Loss from first atlas to second

Common Yellowthroats are insectivores that require dense vegetation for nesting and foraging. Consequently, elimination or degradation of their preferred habitats, particularly wetlands, constitutes the primary threat to this species in Loudoun. Although the population in Loudoun remained relatively stable from Atlas 1 to Atlas 2, data from the North American BBS indicate that populations of Common Yellowthroats declined across their range by nearly 1% per year between 1966 and 2014.

Written by Christine Perdue

HOODED WARBLER
Setophaga citrina

Occurrence: occasional breeder and migrant

Earliest/latest breeding confirmations: fewer than 5 atlas confirmations, see account for details

The Hooded Warbler's brilliant appearance belies its skulky habits. With vivid yellow cheeks and forehead surrounded (on adult males) by a stark black hood, yellow underbody, olive-green nape and wings, and bright white spots on the tail feathers, these warblers should be easy to spot. However, their strongly delivered *weeta-weeta-weet-ee-o* song frequently is the only indication of their presence. Their preferred breeding habitat, the shrubby understory of mature deciduous forests, keeps them frequently just out of sight behind a leaf and in dim light. According to a

Photo ©Dick Rowe

study in Pennsylvania, the bright white tail spots appear to be involved in helping them catch their food, a diet composed of insects, including caterpillars, moths, beetles, and spiders (Mumme 2002). The white spots may possibly startle the insects into taking flight. Hooded Warblers frequently catch their prey by "hawking" like flycatchers.

Hooded Warblers breed across much of the eastern U.S. as far north as southern New York and as far south as northern Florida. In Loudoun, atlasers detected only a single confirmation of breeding, an adult carrying food or feeding young (CF code) in the Ashby Gap 5 block on July 19, 2009. Most of the possible and probable breeding reports were also in rural western Loudoun. Pockets of suitable habitat in eastern Loudoun attracted migrants, with all but 1 of the springtime atlas sightings occurring in May on their way to more northerly breeding grounds. Hooded Warblers don't sing in the fall which, combined with their stealthy behavior and dense habitat, may explain why there were no fall atlas reports; they typically linger until mid-September.

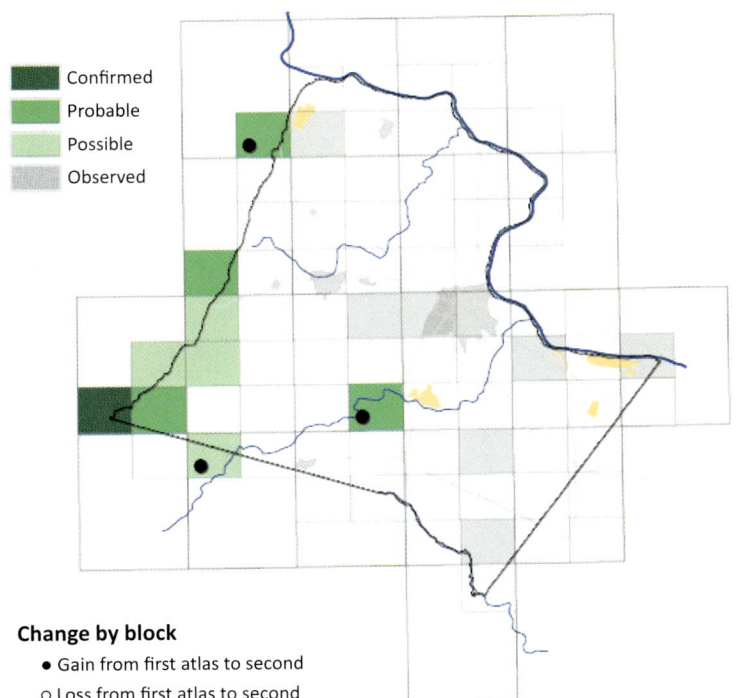

Confirmed
Probable
Possible
Observed

Change by block
• Gain from first atlas to second
○ Loss from first atlas to second

The female typically lays four eggs only a few feet from the ground in a nest she made of plant down, leaves, bark, and grasses. Hooded Warblers have strong site fidelity, often building nests in the same basic location year after year. Females are known to choose locations on the edges and near gaps in the forest. Brown-headed Cowbirds are very effective at using the Hooded Warbler as a brood host, and are one of the larger threats to the Hooded Warbler's population. Despite this, the population has grown in recent decades according to the North American BBS (supported by a gain in blocks from Atlas 1 to 2).

Wintering grounds, mostly located in eastern Central America and the Caribbean, are similar in habitat to the breeding grounds. Interestingly, the Hooded Warbler females and males overwinter in separate territories, with the females typically inhabiting younger forests.

Written by Bryan Henson

AMERICAN REDSTART
Setophaga ruticilla

Occurrence: uncommon breeder and migrant

Earliest breeding confirmation: June 14, parent carrying food or feeding young (CF)

Latest breeding confirmation: July 19, recently fledged young (FL)

Photo by Larry Meade

With a sudden flash of orange in the dappled woods, a redstart announces its presence, and perhaps scares up a meal. Like a tiny mockingbird, this species frequently employs its colorful wing and tail pattern to its advantage. The male is trick or treat-ready, with a black back, head, and chest, flame-orange flank, wing, and tail patches, and a white belly. The female, or "yellowstart," substitutes gray or olive for the black and yellow for the orange of the male, but in the same overall pattern. Extremely active, they flit quickly from place to place at all heights in the forest, chasing down insects and frequently spreading their long tail or extending their wings for effect. They often capture prey on the wing or while hovering, much like flycatchers. While mostly insectivores, they will also eat small berries, especially in fall. Their high-pitched, musical song is quite variable, but is usually accented at the end.

Widespread as breeders, American Redstarts can be found across southern Canada and large sections of the U.S., especially in the Northeast and mid-Atlantic and down the Appalachians and the Mississippi watershed. In Loudoun, all confirmed breeding reports came from the western fringe of the county. Redstarts are more likely found in the forest interior than the edges, preferring large, unfragmented tracts. Look for them between late April and early October in deciduous or mixed second-growth and riparian woodlands with a shrubby understory. They often build their open-cup nests on branches, braced against the trunk of smaller tree species like maple, alder, or willow. Females build the nests and do the egg-sitting, while males mostly show-boat and defend territory. However, both parents assume feeding duties once the eggs have hatched, and they will often split up the brood to care for separately once fledged.

These long-distance migrants spend the winter in southern Florida, throughout most of the Caribbean, and from southern Mexico down to northern South America, where they can be found in a wide variety of lowland habitats with trees, like coffee or fruit plantations, mangroves, or scrub forests. This species has suffered only small declines over the past 50 years, and remains quite abundant with a population of about 39 million (PIF 2017). But as nocturnal migrants, collisions with manmade structures like buildings, towers, or wind turbines can be deadly. And climate change may push them farther north over time.

Written by Bruce Hill

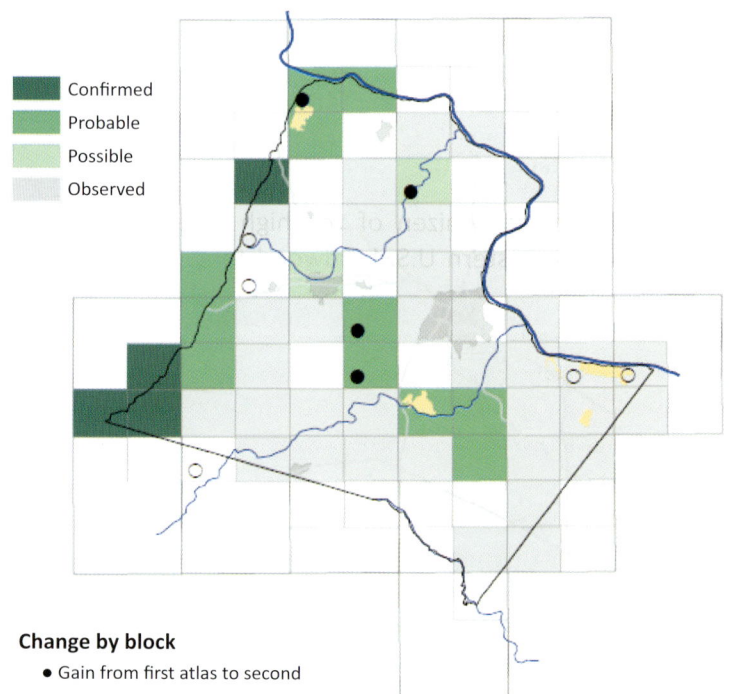

Confirmed
Probable
Possible
Observed

Change by block
- Gain from first atlas to second
○ Loss from first atlas to second

CAPE MAY WARBLER
Setophaga tigrina

Occurrence: occasional migrant

Southerly migration period: September 11 – October 6

Northerly migration period: April 25 – May 16

The male Cape May Warbler is a heavily streaked, yellow and olive-green bird with a striking chestnut and bright yellow face pattern; note also the black eyeline and broad white shoulder patch. This species is another spruce budworm specialist, its staple food during summers in Canadian and northern U.S. boreal forests. Its song is a simple, high-pitched *seet-seet-seet-seet*.

The Cape May winters in the Bahamas, the Caribbean, and along the eastern coast of Mexico, Guatemala, and Honduras. This poorly understood species has a tubular tongue unique for a warbler, used to feed extensively on nectar (and insects) in its winter haunts. Purely a migrant through Loudoun, the Cape May can show up in a variety of habitat types. Atlas observations were roughly split between spring and fall, with records in five of the seven specially protected areas. This bird is in steep decline, dropping 72% between 1966 and 2015 (Sauer et al. 2017), and is on the 2016 State of North America's Birds' Watch List. Continued boreal forest logging and budworm control efforts pose ongoing threats.

Written by Bruce Hill

Photo by Margo Dolan

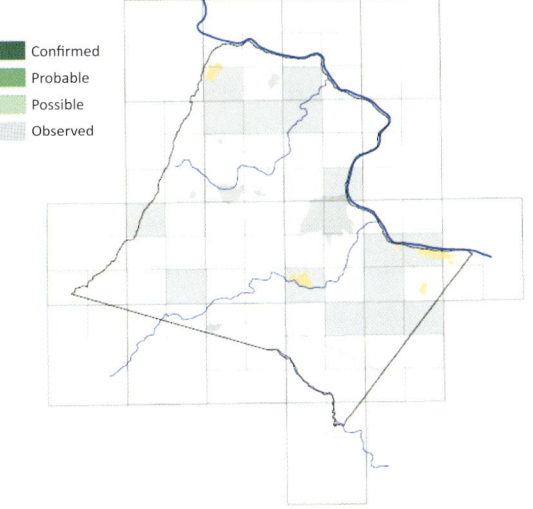

Confirmed
Probable
Possible
Observed

Photo by Dave Boltz

CERULEAN WARBLER
Setophaga cerulea

Occurrence: occasional breeder and spring migrant, rare fall migrant

Earliest/latest breeding confirmations: highest breeding evidence in Probable category, see account for details

This iconic denizen of the high treetops breeds in mature eastern U.S. hardwood forests with minimal understory, in uplands, or along stream and river valleys. They are found in small numbers in far-western and northern Loudoun, especially along ridgelines such as at the Blue Ridge Center and similar locations, beginning in late April. While breeding was not formally confirmed during the atlas period, there were enough possible and probable breeding observations between mid-May and mid-July to consider the Cerulean a regular, albeit marginal, nesting species. They typically depart the breeding grounds early, and are rarely seen past the end of August. Migrating at night over the Gulf of Mexico to overwinter at low densities in the northern Andes mountains of South America, they remain a treetop specialist, associating in mixed feeding flocks with tanagers and other canopy dwellers.

Male Ceruleans are a brilliant sky-blue above and white below, with black streaks on the back and a blue necklace and streaking on the chest and flanks. They also have a partial white collar and two obvious white wingbars. Females are a less obvious blue-green above, with a white eyebrow and partial white eyering. Their underside is often washed in a

CERULEAN WARBLER (continued)

light yellow. Overall, they are small, short-tailed, and typically sit horizontally when resting. Almost everything they do takes place high in trees, including feeding, nesting, and singing, making good looks hard to come by. Nests are constructed on the outer branches of large trees, sometimes up to 90 feet high. They eat mostly insects, especially caterpillars, taken while foraging on or fly-catching from upper-level branches. Their song is a good one to learn – several burry, ascending phrases ending in a fast trill, sung from high perches by the territorial males.

Habitat loss and degradation on their breeding and wintering grounds has dramatically reduced Cerulean Warbler numbers; they have an IUCN status of "Vulnerable," possibly heading towards an Endangered Species Act listing. Their population is down to about 570,000, following a decline of 72%

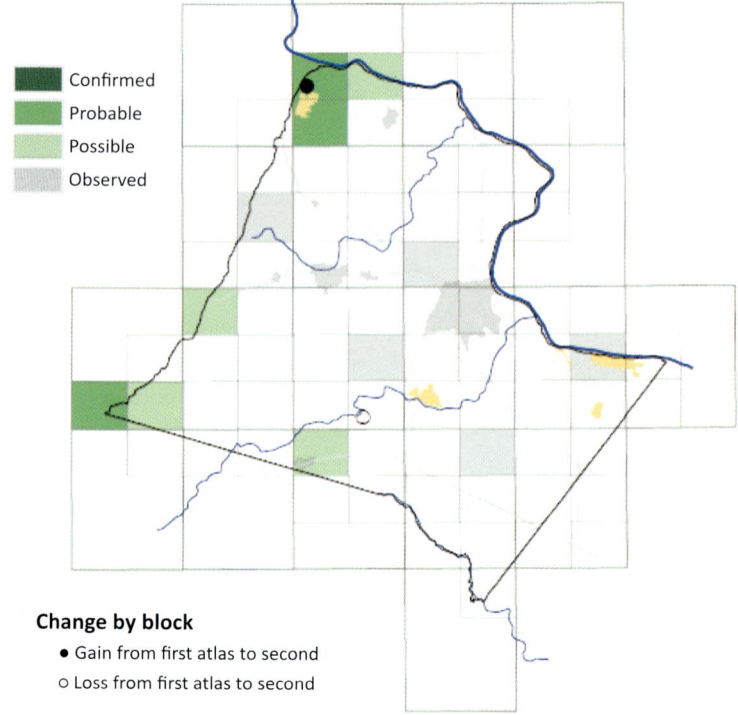

Confirmed
Probable
Possible
Observed

Change by block
● Gain from first atlas to second
○ Loss from first atlas to second

between 1970 and 2014 (PIF 2017). Conversion of coffee plantations from shade to sun varieties in their winter valley strongholds appears to be one factor in their decline (Moreno et al. 2006). And they are no longer found in much of their historical breeding habitat in the Mississippi and Ohio River valleys, possibly due to forest fragmentation and corresponding increases in cowbird parasitism.

Written by Bruce Hill

Photo by Bill Brown

NORTHERN PARULA
Setophaga americana

Occurrence: uncommon breeder and migrant

Earliest/latest breeding confirmations: highest breeding evidence in Probable category, see account for details

The Northern Parula breeds throughout most of the eastern U.S. and into southeastern Canada. It looks for mature forests near water, often settling in swamps and bogs or along rivers and streams. They show a strong predilection for trees laden with moss, lichen, or similar vegetation. They hollow out nests in this hanging vegetation, often as high as 100 feet, which can make study and breeding confirmation difficult. Where such growth is missing, they may make a hanging nest from other materials. Their absence as breeders in parts of the lower Great Lakes region may be partly owing to a lack of mossy growth there, possibly due to increased air pollution. Northern Parulas winter in the Bahamas, the northern Caribbean, and along the eastern Mexican coast. They are less particular about habitat in migration and winter, showing up in fields, scrub, woodland understory, and plantations. They often join in mixed feeding flocks outside of breeding season.

This warbler arrives fairly early in the spring (atlas sightings begin in mid-April and continue through mid-October), quickly establishing a territory and singing frequently throughout the day. The typical vocalization is quite recognizable: a fast, rising trill that drops off at the very end. Males have a blue head and nape and a yellow-green

NORTHERN PARULA (continued)

back; females are more grayish than blue. Both sexes have a plain, dark face, with a dark eye surrounded above and below by a broken white eyering, or crescents. The yellow throat and chest are separated by a dark gray and chestnut band in males; females generally lack the gray in this band. The belly and vent are white, and the dark wings have two strong white wingbars. Small, plump, and active, these birds sometimes feed in flight, fluttering around branches and plucking caterpillars and other insects from leaves. In both size and behavior, they often resemble a kinglet.

This species has actually increased significantly in recent decades, up 62% since 1970 (Sauer et al. 2017). Its population numbers about 17 million range-wide (PIF 2017). In Loudoun, the Northern Parula showed a similar trend, recorded in 17 more blocks during Atlas 2 than in Atlas 1. While there were no confirmed breeding records during the most recent atlas, over 85 probable or possible breeding reports came from 34 blocks, providing abundant reason to believe that this species is a well-established nester here.

Written by Bruce Hill

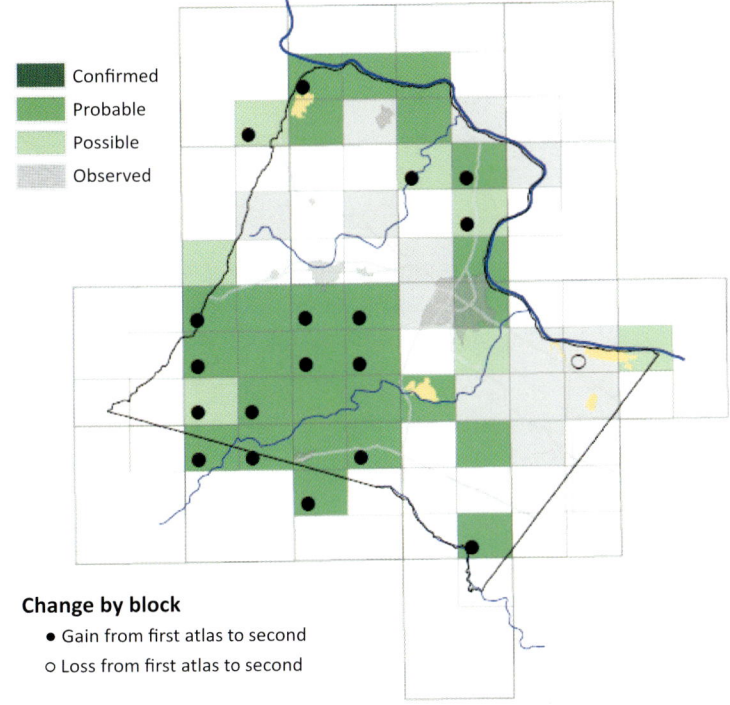

Confirmed
Probable
Possible
Observed

Change by block
- Gain from first atlas to second
- ○ Loss from first atlas to second

Photo by Dick Rowe

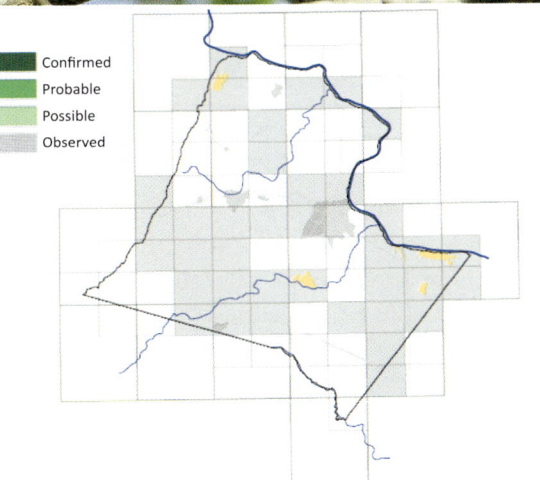

Confirmed
Probable
Possible
Observed

MAGNOLIA WARBLER
Setophaga magnolia

Occurrence: uncommon migrant

Southerly migration period: August 10 – October 13

Northerly migration period: April 26 – May 28

The gaudy male Magnolia Warbler is outfitted in black, gray, yellow, and white, with a black necklace and streaking on its yellow chest and flanks, black mask and nape, gray cap, white eyebrow, and bold white wing-patch. The female is understated, with a gray head and face, white eyering, green back, yellow underside with faint streaking, and two thin white wingbars. Look for a diagnostic under-tail pattern, white on the inner part and black towards the tip. Their song is very short, several quick phrases with an emphatic ending.

Magnolias breed in boreal forests of Canada and the northeastern U.S. They transit Loudoun in migration, using a variety of second-growth habitats, and were observed in just over half the atlas blocks. Look for them especially in fall when they migrate farther east than in spring. They are active feeders, usually seen low in trees and near branch tips, snagging caterpillars and other insects. Magnolias winter in Central America, the Caribbean, and the Bahamas. This species is numerous (39 million) and has been increasing in recent decades (PIF 2017).

Written by Bruce Hill

BAY-BREASTED WARBLER

Setophaga castanea

Occurrence: occasional migrant

Southerly migration period: September 17 – October 8

Northerly migration period: fewer than 5 atlas sightings, see account for details

Photo by Bill Brown

The breeding-plumaged Bay-breasted Warbler is a handsome sight: A relatively large warbler, males have a chestnut crown, throat, and chest, black face, cream-colored collar and flanks, and black and gray mantle and wings showing two white wingbars. Their song, a high-pitched *seetzee, seetzee, seetzee*, may be heard in spring. Females are a subtler version of the male. In fall, this species transforms into a much different-looking "confusing fall warbler." Closely related to the Blackpoll Warbler, these two species often hybridize. As summer residents of boreal forests across central Canada, Bay-breasted Warblers feed heavily on spruce budworms; spraying of these forest pests may have contributed to precipitous population declines, down about 74% over the past 50 years (Sauer et al. 2017). They also eat other insects, and fruit in winter. Look for them feeding in the mid- and upper level of woodland trees. Migration flows through the eastern U.S. and continues, sometimes across the Gulf, to northern South America, where they settle into lowland tropical forests. There were 14 atlas observations, only 3 of which were in spring.

Written by Bruce Hill

BLACKBURNIAN WARBLER

Setophaga fusca

Occurrence: occasional migrant

Southerly migration period: August 28 – October 5

Northerly migration period: May 6 – June 4

Photo ©Dick Rowe

A good look at this stunning little neotropical gem is unforgettable. The male's face and throat glows a brilliant orange, contrasting vividly with a triangular black cheek patch and crown. Black wings show broad white wingbars that merge into a white patch. The breast and flanks are yellow with dark barring; the belly is white, and the black tail has broad white outer edges. The female has similar markings, but is more yellowish with less contrast overall. They favor the upper branches of mature trees, where they forage deliberately for insects. Often hard to spot, they are best located by song, a reedy, high-pitched *zip-zip-zip-zip, titititi, tseeee*.

Favoring coniferous and mixed woodlands, Blackburnian Warblers breed in New England, the Great Lakes region, southeastern Canada, and down the spine of the Appalachians. Fall migration takes them through Mexico to winter habitat in humid montane forests of Central and South America. Look for them in woodlands and parks as they pass through Loudoun, primarily during May and September. Their population is stable at about 10 million (PIF 2017).

Written by Bruce Hill

YELLOW WARBLER
Setophaga petechia

Occurrence: uncommon breeder and migrant

Earliest breeding confirmation: May 9, adult carrying nesting material or nest building (NB)

Latest breeding confirmation: July 9, recently fledged young (FL)

Photo by Dave Boltz

The Yellow Warbler is our only truly all-yellow warbler from head to tail. They are small, round-headed, and active birds. Their dark eye stands out on an otherwise blank yellow face. Males typically have fine chestnut streaking on their yellow breast, which females lack. Relatively confiding and accessible, they hang out in second-growth trees, thickets, and shrubs, often around water. Willows are a favorite, but various other trees will do, like birch, aspen, dogwood, or even orchard fruit trees. The male's musical, whistled song, sometimes represented as *sweet, sweet, sweet, little-more-sweet*, is repeated often throughout the breeding season from visible perches atop trees or shrubs. Quite territorial, they will defend turf not only from their own kind, but from other species as well. Pairs are monogamous and often remain together from year to year. Nests are built well off the ground (10-40 feet high) in the vertical fork of a small to medium-sized tree. Females do all the nest-building and incubating, but males assist by feeding the female during incubation and bringing food to the nestlings. When cowbirds sneak eggs into the Yellow Warbler's nest, the female sometimes recognizes the deception and may build a new nest on top of the original to thwart the effort. This species' diet is primarily limited to insects, typically taken by foliage gleaning or fly-catching.

From April through early October, Yellow Warblers can be found in migration or during breeding season along streams, wetlands, and field edges throughout Loudoun. Found in 46 of the 73 atlas blocks, the notable increase from Atlas 1 to 2 is likely influenced by the higher coverage and effort per block in Atlas 2. Populations have declined moderately (about 25%) throughout their range since the 1960s (Sauer et al. 2017). They are nonetheless a very numerous and widespread species at about 90 million individuals (PIF 2017). They breed throughout Alaska, Canada, and the upper two-thirds of the lower 48 states, as well as in central Mexico and much of the Caribbean. They overwinter along the coasts of Mexico and throughout Central and northern South America, mainly in mangroves, lowland forests, and a variety of upland habitats. During migration, some Yellow Warblers fly non-stop over water from the U.S. to their winter destination, while others use the more westerly overland route. Storms over water, as well as collisions with manmade structures during their nighttime flights, pose a mortality threat.

Written by Bruce Hill

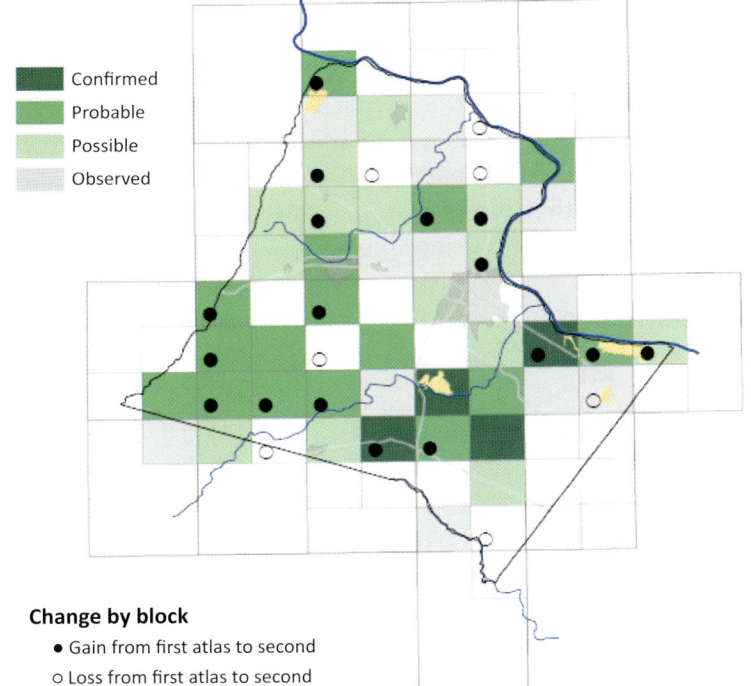

Confirmed
Probable
Possible
Observed

Change by block
- Gain from first atlas to second
- Loss from first atlas to second

CHESTNUT-SIDED WARBLER
Setophaga pensylvanica

Occurrence: uncommon migrant

Southerly migration period: August 28 – October 10

Northerly migration period: April 15 – May 23

The Chestnut-sided Warbler is a rather frequently encountered migrant warbler in Loudoun, reported in 31 of the 73 atlas blocks. Males are strikingly patterned, with a gold forehead patch, a black mask and sideburns over white cheeks and throat, chestnut flanks, and brown wings with golden-yellow wingbars and feather edging. The underside is white. Females have the same overall pattern but the colors are muted and less crisp. Their song, most typically a whistled *pleased-pleased-pleased-to-MEET-cha*, rings from the middle and upper branches of trees, where they forage deliberately for insects.

This warbler breeds in southeastern Canada and the northeastern U.S., as well as down the spine of the Appalachian mountains to northern Georgia, favoring deciduous woodlands. Some nest immediately to our west in the mountains of northwestern Virginia. They winter in tropical forests of southern Mexico and Central America, where individuals often return to the same location and mixed-species feeding flock year after year. They have declined 44% in recent decades (Sauer et al. 2017), now numbering about 19 million (PIF 2017).

Written by Bruce Hill

Photo by Gerco Hoogeweg

- Confirmed
- Probable
- Possible
- Observed

BLACKPOLL WARBLER
Setophaga striata

Occurrence: uncommon migrant

Southerly migration period: September 11 – October 3

Northerly migration period: May 5 – June 6

The Blackpoll Warbler is our other "Black-and-white Warbler," a species it superficially resembles. In spring, it sports a broad black crown, white cheek, salt-and-pepper nape, and white underside with heavy black streaking. Its appearance changes dramatically by fall; see your field guide under "confusing fall warblers." The Blackpoll in all seasons is a small, compact bird, with short wings and tail. It forages slowly high in deciduous trees for insects, usually in the outer branches. Its song is a unique, extremely high-pitched *tsit Tsit TSIT TSIT Tsit tsit* that increases then decreases in intensity.

Migrants move through Loudoun at a leisurely pace throughout May. Most atlas sightings (over 80%) were in spring. They breed in Canada's boreal forests. Return migration is anything but leisurely, over the Atlantic in a non-stop flight of up to 3 days to South America. This still-common species is in steep decline, having lost as much as 92% of its population in the past 50 years (PIF 2017). Threats include habitat loss, climate change, and severe weather, especially during their epic fall migrations.

Written by Bruce Hill

Photo ©Dick Rowe

- Confirmed
- Probable
- Possible
- Observed

BLACK-THROATED BLUE WARBLER
Setophaga caerulescens

Occurrence: uncommon migrant

Southerly migration period: September 10 – October 16

Northerly migration period: April 23 – May 20

Photo by Gerco Hoogeweg

Approachable and inquisitive, Black-throated Blue Warblers prefer to stay low, methodically searching out insects in the forest understory and lower canopy. The sexes look dramatically different and were originally described as separate species. Males exhibit a brilliant blue crown, back, and tail; a black face, throat, and flanks; and a gleaming white underside. Females are subtler, with soft olive-brown and gray tones. A diagnostic feature of both is a small, square white spot midway down the wing (a "handkerchief"). Their slow-paced song is a buzzy *zoo-zoo-zoo-ZEEE*. Atlas sightings were spread across Loudoun relatively equally during spring and fall migration, though there was 1 rare late July sighting (2012) at the Blue Ridge Center. Their breeding range includes deciduous and mixed forests with thick understory in the higher Appalachians, New England, northeastern Canada, and the upper Great Lakes. Core winter habitat includes the northern Caribbean islands. This species has thrived over the past 50 years, with a population increase of 163% (PIF 2017). However, they remain susceptible to clear-cutting and fragmentation throughout their range.

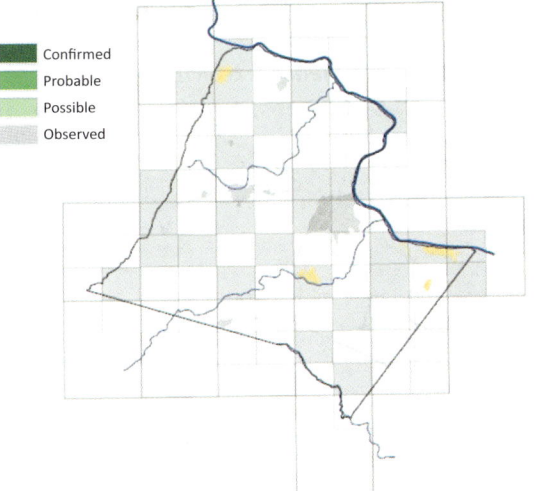

Confirmed
Probable
Possible
Observed

Written by Bruce Hill

PALM WARBLER
Setophaga palmarum

Occurrence: uncommon migrant, rare winter visitor

Earliest fall sighting: September 8

Latest spring sighting: May 15

Photo by Dave Boltz

Confirmed
Probable
Possible
Observed

Palm Warblers forage for insects or berries on the ground or in low scrub, walking actively and constantly bobbing their tail, a tell-tale clue to this bird's identity. Check out groups of ground-feeding sparrows and juncos; a Palm Warbler could be mixed in. Early to arrive and late to leave their boreal breeding grounds, this is one of a few warbler species to routinely overwinter in the southern U.S. as far north as coastal North Carolina.

The eastern form is a relatively large, round-bodied bird with a bright rusty cap, yellow eyebrow, and bright yellow underside with rusty streaking. Western form birds also sometimes show up; they are not as brightly colored, but both forms have distinctive yellow undertail coverts. Though vulnerable to habitat degradation and collisions with structures during their nighttime migrations, their numbers are relatively stable at about 13 million (PIF 2017). Most of the 80+ atlas sightings, spanning 38 blocks, were in the spring and fall, with 1 early February (2012) sighting. Palm Warblers were found on 4 of the past 20 Central Loudoun CBCs.

Written by Bruce Hill

PINE WARBLER
Setophaga pinus

Photo by Dave Boltz

Occurrence: occasional breeder and migrant, rare winter resident

Earliest/latest breeding confirmations: highest breeding evidence in Probable category, see account for details

A melodious trill from high in a grove of pines can tip you off to this species' presence. The Pine Warbler's song sounds a lot like a Chipping Sparrow's trill, but is a bit looser and less mechanical. Not always easy to spot, they work slowly through the branches of pines hunting for insects among clumps of needles. Listen and then look for them in motion as they fly from branch to branch or tree to tree. Pine Warblers are yellow to olive-green above, with an indistinct dark line through the eye, a stout pointed bill, and two bold white wingbars. Their head, throat, flanks, and breast are yellow, transitioning to a white belly and undertail coverts. They are relatively large warblers, with a long tail. Females are paler, and young birds can be mostly gray, with a white eyering.

Practically an endemic, Pine Warblers breed throughout the eastern U.S., with just a small percentage venturing into extreme southern Canada. Males establish territories early, in late winter to early spring. They sing vigorously and can be aggressive with interlopers, sometimes fighting in mid-air. Nests are usually high and well-hidden amongst clumps of cones and needles, built mostly by the female. Once the young fledge, family groups travel about together. Pine Warblers are partially migratory; more northerly breeders move into the Southeast in the winter, but no further than Florida and Texas. Below southern Virginia, many birds stay in place year-round.

They eat caterpillars and various other insects and arthropods, moving methodically to inspect the bark and needles. They also eat seeds (especially pine seeds) as well as a wide variety of berries, particularly in colder months. They may grub for seeds on the ground, and even visit backyard platform or suet feeders. Their numbers have increased slightly over the past half-century, as supported by atlas data, with a current global population around 13 million (PIF 2017). Though their pine habitats are frequently cut or otherwise altered, they are adaptable, and may in fact benefit from a warming climate as southern pine forests thrive and expand in warmer conditions. The 25 atlas blocks throughout Loudoun with Pine Warbler sightings were divided almost 50/50 into migrants and probable or possible breeders. Typically found between early spring and late fall, there was one Central Loudoun CBC record in 2010. When seeking this species out, keep in mind they are almost always in or near pines.

Written by Bruce Hill

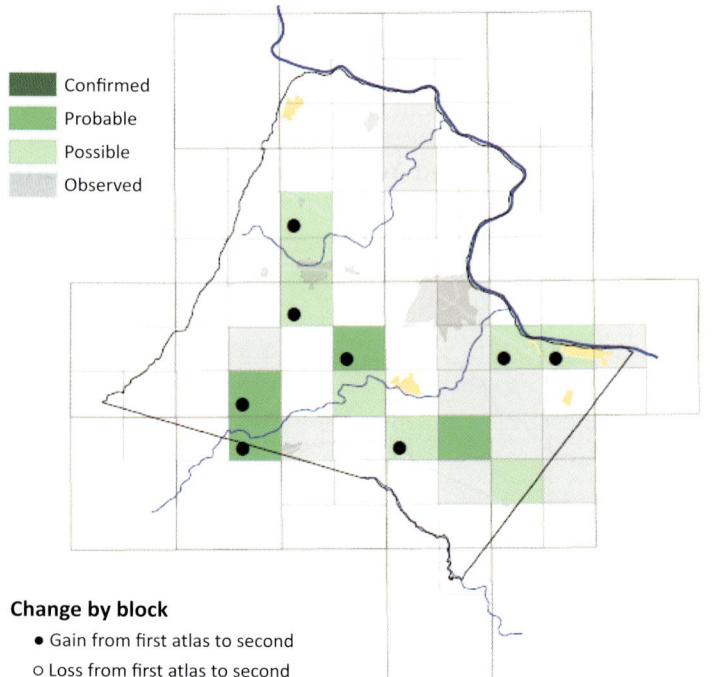

- Confirmed
- Probable
- Possible
- Observed

Change by block
- ● Gain from first atlas to second
- ○ Loss from first atlas to second

YELLOW-RUMPED WARBLER
Setophaga coronata

Occurrence: common migrant and winter resident

Earliest fall sighting: August 29

Latest spring sighting: May 25

Photo by Lisa McKew

Lovingly (or not) nicknamed "butter-butts," Yellow-rumped Warblers at times seem omnipresent, filling binoculars and distracting attention as birders try to focus on less common winter species. Though found in 85% of the atlas blocks and a fixture on Central Loudoun CBCs, familiarity should not breed contempt. This cold-tolerant, adaptable species is our only regular overwintering warbler, uniquely adapted to switch from eating mostly insects in warm weather to a more varied winter diet including fruits and hard-to-digest berries. Curious and unafraid, they respond readily to pishing as they forage in mixed-species flocks in open woodlands and thickets. Breeding across Alaska, the northwestern U.S., and Canada, there are two main subspecies: Audubon's in the West and Myrtle in the East. Our Myrtles have a busy look, with a gray crown and nape, white eyebrow, black mask, boldly streaked chest, and yellow shoulder and rump patches. The yellow rump can help quickly identify this species, as can learning its soft, warbled song and sharp *chek* call. Yellow-rumps are widespread, numerous at 130 million (PIF 2017), and seemingly stable.

Written by Bruce Hill

Photo ©Dick Rowe

YELLOW-THROATED WARBLER
Setophaga dominica

Occurrence: rare breeder and migrant

Earliest/latest breeding confirmations: highest breeding evidence in Probable category, see account for details

The aptly named Yellow-throated Warbler sports a bright yellow chin and throat that is clearly demarcated from its white breast. Its flanks are white with bold black streaking, and its back is gray. It has two white wingbars and a distinctive black and white pattern on its face. The female is only slightly paler than the male, with little sexual dimorphism. Unlike most warblers, the Yellow-throated forages for insects with slow and deliberate movement along tree limbs, much like the Brown Creeper or Black-and-white Warbler. This behavior inspired 18th-century English naturalist Mark Catesby to nickname the bird the Yellow-throated Creeper. This warbler can be found on rare occasions in Loudoun, generally from early April into September.

There was no evidence of confirmed breeding discovered during the atlas, but territorial behavior – evidence of probable breeding – was reported at Algonkian Park on July 4, 2010 and at the Blue Ridge Center on May 12, 2012. Possible breeding was documented in 2 additional blocks (2011 and 2013). There was no evidence of breeding in Loudoun during the statewide Atlas 1, although evidence of probable breeding was found in neighboring Fauquier and Fairfax Counties. The Maryland and D.C. 2002-2006 BBA reported evidence of possible, probable, and confirmed

YELLOW-THROATED WARBLER (continued)

breeding in the Harpers Ferry, Point of Rocks, and Poolesville quadrangles, respectively, so there is a good possibility of breeding just across the river in Loudoun as well.

The breeding range of the Yellow-throated Warbler extends from northern New York south and westward to Missouri, Arkansas, and eastern Texas. The bird is largely absent, however, from higher elevations of the Appalachians and Blue Ridge. Its range is expanding northward as the bird reclaims territory it inexplicably abandoned in the beginning of the 20th century. Populations increased by about 50% between 1966 and 2014 (Sauer et al. 2017). Its winter range includes parts of Central America and the Caribbean islands, as well as the coastal U.S. from South Carolina into eastern Texas.

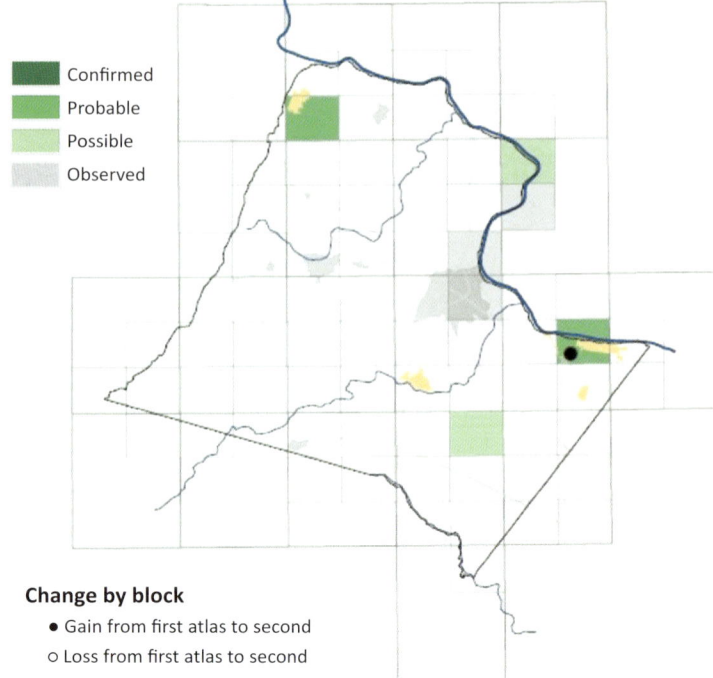

Confirmed
Probable
Possible
Observed

Change by block
● Gain from first atlas to second
○ Loss from first atlas to second

This warbler forages and nests in the canopy of mature forests, up to 100 feet high – making observation and finding breeding evidence relatively difficult. It breeds in a variety of habitats, including cypress swamps and loblolly pine stands. Riparian woodlands are the preferred breeding habitat for inland populations, with sycamores being a favored tree for nesting. The female builds the nests, incubates the eggs, and broods the young. Both males and females have been observed feeding the young.

Written by Bill Brown

Photo by Dave Boltz

PRAIRIE WARBLER
Setophaga discolor

Occurrence: uncommon breeder and migrant

Earliest breeding confirmation: June 8, parent carrying food or feeding young (CF)

Latest breeding confirmation: August 8, recently fledged young (FL)

The adult male Prairie Warbler has bright yellow underparts, bold black streaking on its flanks, and an olive back and crown. Its yellow face is marked with a black eyeline and distinctive black arc below its eye. The female appears similar, but paler, so that her facial markings can be difficult to distinguish. The male may be identified by his song, a series of quick *zh-zh-zh-zh-zh-zh-zh* notes gradually rising in pitch. They frequently bob their tail while perched.

Typical breeding habitat includes old fields, abandoned pastures, and pine woodlands with scattered trees, an open canopy, and some undergrowth. They are seldom found nesting in forest interiors. These attractive birds were reported in 42 of the 73 atlas blocks. Though some evidence of breeding was recorded in 36 of these blocks, breeding was confirmed in only 6.

Males arrive at their breeding grounds a few days before females. Older birds tend to return to previous breeding territory. The female selects the nest site and builds a neat cup nest in the fork of a tree or bush, usually less than

PRAIRIE WARBLER (continued)

10 feet above ground. She typically lays a clutch of three to five eggs. Only the female incubates the eggs, which hatch in approximately 11 days. The female broods the chicks, while both the male and female share in feeding the young. The nestlings fledge in 8-11 days. First-year birds begin southward migration before adults.

The Prairie Warbler's breeding range extends southeast of a line running roughly from southern Maine, diagonally to eastern Texas. Its winter range includes the Florida peninsula, the Caribbean islands, and the Caribbean coast of Central America. Both its spring and fall migrations begin earlier than those of most eastern warblers. The earliest atlas observation was April 9. Observations peaked in May and June then dropped sharply from July through early October, with an outlying observation on October 23.

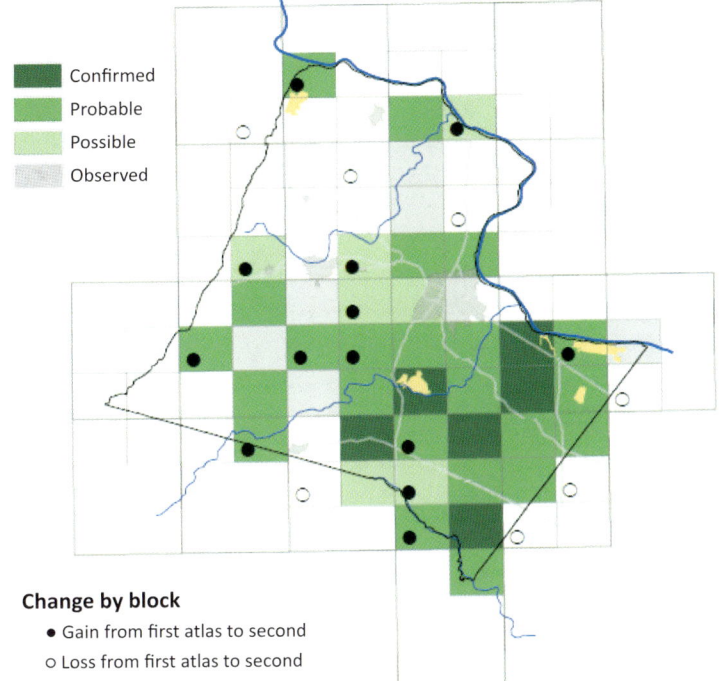

Confirmed
Probable
Possible
Observed

Change by block
- Gain from first atlas to second
- Loss from first atlas to second

The Prairie Warbler is on the 2014 State of the Birds Watch List. The apparent gain in blocks from Atlas 1 to 2 is likely influenced by the greater coverage and effort per block in Atlas 2. Reasons for their decline include loss of breeding habitat to development and natural succession of shrubby habitat to forest.

Written by Bill Brown

Photo by Dave Boltz

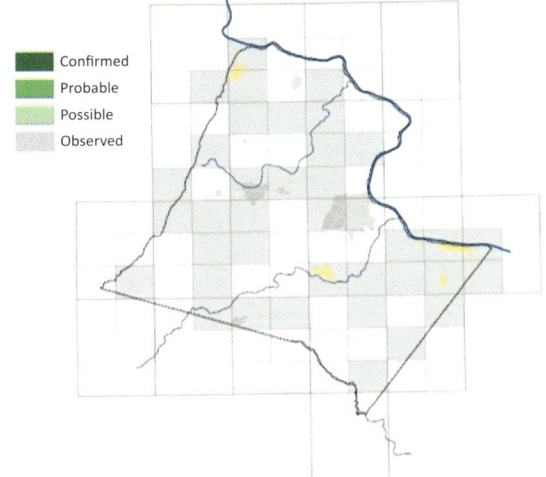

Confirmed
Probable
Possible
Observed

BLACK-THROATED GREEN WARBLER
Setophaga virens

Occurrence: uncommon migrant

Southerly migration period: August 27 – October 12

Northerly migration period: April 24 – May 19

Known for its memorable voice, migrating males tirelessly announce their presence from the treetops with one of two typical songs: a loud, buzzy *zee-zee-zee-zoo-ZEE* or an equally emphatic and more aggressive *zoo, ZEE, zoo-zoo-ZEE* (sometimes characterized as *trees, TREES, murmuring TREES*). If you can get your binoculars focused on one, you'll see a small, active warbler with a bright yellow face with a dark line through the eye, an olive-green crown and back, and black wings with two broad white wingbars. The white underside has bold black streaking on its flanks. Males have an extensive black throat, which females lack. Found in half the atlas blocks, most migrating birds move beyond Loudoun to breed in the Appalachians, northeastern U.S., and southern to central Canada. They utilize a wide variety of forested habitats, eating caterpillars and other insects. In fall, they return to tropical forests in the Caribbean and Central America, often associating in migration with other species in mixed flocks. They are common and increasing, about 8.7 million strong (PIF 2017). But as forest breeders, fragmentation remains a threat.

Written by Bruce Hill

CANADA WARBLER
Cardellina canadensis

Photo by Dave Boltz

Occurrence: occasional migrant

Southerly migration period: August 29 – September 28

Northerly migration period: May 11 – 25

Always a delightful sight, the colorful and crisply plumaged Canada Warbler forages actively in the understory, often near water, for insects and spiders. The male's solid yellow underside, necklace of thick black streaks, and steel-blue head and upper body are distinctive. Its bold eyering and yellow lores give it a bespectacled appearance. The female is a muted version of the male, with an indistinct necklace and a dull gray above. Its song is a fast jumble of notes, usually preceded by a chip note.

The Canada Warbler is primarily a boreal breeder, but some nest in the Appalachian highlands, often in hillside rhododendron thickets. Nests are built on the ground in a mossy depression or under a log or tree root. Observed in just 10 atlas blocks, they migrate through Loudoun in late spring and early fall, with only a short time on the breeding grounds. Winters are spent in northern South America. Globally uncommon and declining, Canada Warblers are a PIF Watch List species due to forested wetland declines, degraded understory, and woodland fragmentation.

Written by Bruce Hill

Confirmed
Probable
Possible
Observed

Photo by Dave Boltz

Confirmed
Probable
Possible
Observed

WILSON'S WARBLER
Cardellina pusilla

Occurrence: rare migrant

Southerly migration period: September 11 – 19

Northerly migration period: fewer than 5 atlas sightings, see account for details

Wilson's Warblers are infrequent visitors in our area, turning up just 5 times in the fall and 4 times in the spring (but at least once each year) during the atlas. All yellow below and olive above, this small, round-bodied warbler has a long tail and short, rounded wings. The male's distinguishing feature is a small black cap; the female shows a similar but less pronounced olive crown. Encountered in scrubby thickets and forest edges, they often sing during spring migration, a rapid, two-part series of chips.

This warbler nests on the ground in mountains and northern forests, mostly in Canada but also in the far northwestern U.S, upper Rocky Mountains, and Maine. They migrate largely over land to Mexico and Central America. Though relatively few are seen along the East Coast, they can be abundant out West. Foraging rapidly in low vegetation, they chase both leaf-bound and flying insects. Considered a "common bird in steep decline" (2014 State of the Birds Report), they none-the-less sustain a global population of about 60 million (PIF 2017).

Written by Bruce Hill

SUMMER TANAGER
Piranga rubra

Occurrence: rare breeder and migrant

Earliest/latest breeding confirmations: highest breeding evidence in Probable category, see account for details

Photo ©Dick Rowe

A rare treat for Loudoun birders, the Summer Tanager was documented only 5 times for the atlas, in May and September 2009-2011. A pair, both of breeding age, were banded at Banshee Reeks Nature Preserve on May 22, 2010 with a brood patch found on the female. The pair flew into the banding net together and flew off together upon release. This data provides the first evidence of probable breeding for this species in Loudoun, which is exciting but not altogether surprising since Loudoun is located along the northern edge of their mid-Atlantic and southern U.S. breeding range.

Male Summer Tanagers are dressed from head to tail in red while females and immature males are yellowish, with darker, greenish wings and upperparts; both have a large, thick, pale bill. Some females and immature males can be confused with female versions of their cousin, the Scarlet Tanager, found more commonly throughout Loudoun. Adult male Summer and Scarlet Tanagers are easier to distinguish thanks to the Scarlet's black wings and tail. Both species are members of the cardinal family.

With a year-round diet that's not for the faint of heart, the Summer Tanager specializes on bees and wasps, catching them mid-flight then beating them against a branch. The stinger is removed before eating by rubbing it on the branch. After eating the bees and wasps, they may tear open the nest to feed on the larvae. As they slowly forage through the treetops in open woodlands (especially oaks and other deciduous trees), they also eat other invertebrates and fruit. Like many forest songbirds, they are often heard before seen; listen for the male's robin-like song or the distinctive *pit-ti-tuck* call given by both sexes.

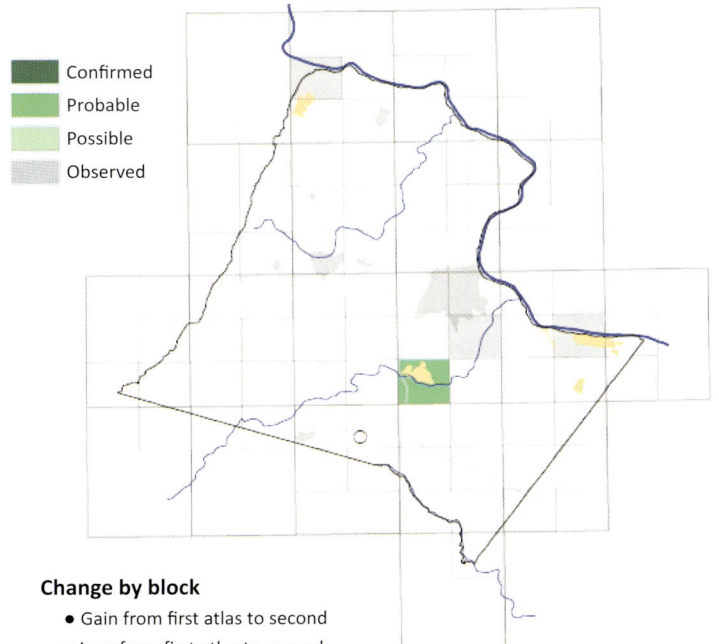

Confirmed
Probable
Possible
Observed

Change by block
- Gain from first atlas to second
○ Loss from first atlas to second

The female lays three to four eggs in a shallow cup nest that is often placed well away from the tree trunk, about 10-35 feet above the ground. Both parents feed the young and raise one to two broods per season, aggressively defending the nest from parasitic Brown-headed Cowbirds. They have an extensive winter range, including southern Mexico, Central America, and northern South America. With a tendency to be solitary outside of the breeding season, they sometimes follow mixed-species flocks of fruit-eating birds. North American populations have remained fairly stable over the past 5 decades, despite fluctuations in local populations. Local declines may be attributed to habitat conversion from open forest to agricultural and other uses.

Written by Spring Ligi

SCARLET TANAGER

Piranga olivacea

Occurrence: uncommon breeder and migrant

Earliest breeding confirmation: June 15, parent carrying food or feeding young (CF)

Latest breeding confirmation: July 19, parent carrying food or feeding young (CF)

The male Scarlet Tanager in breeding plumage makes a striking impression when discovered, but this brightly colored red bird with black wings and tail is quite elusive, noticed with difficulty in the high treetops despite its color. Its hoarse, whistled song (often described as "like a robin with a sore throat") and *chick-burr* calls alert you to its presence. Breeding was confirmed in 8 atlas blocks in more rural areas, where its favored deciduous forest habit is found.

Photo by Dave Boltz

Residing in Loudoun from late April through early October, the Scarlet Tanager was either observed or reported with some evidence of breeding in all but 8 of the 73 blocks. After breeding throughout eastern North America, this long-distance migrant departs for South American wintering grounds.

The sexes differ dramatically in their breeding plumage. The adult female is a delicate olive-green above with dull brownish-olive wings and a tail edged in green. Her underparts are olive-yellow. Yellow rings surround her eyes. The non-breeding male, after molting his bright plumage, shares some characteristics with the female, but keeps his distinctive black wings and tail. The legs and feet are pinkish olive-gray, and the bill is large and pale.

The Scarlet Tanager is monogamous and aggressively territorial. It sings out its claims from perches in the middle to upper tree canopy. Counter-singing males may also escalate into a threat pose, sometimes preceding flight and chase. Females may chase competing females from established territories. Nesting areas are most vigorously defended. The nest is built among a grouping of leaves to provide shading, well out from the trunk of the tree in a crotch or junction of smaller branches. It is often positioned to provide a clear view of the ground below, with open flyways for approaching and departing. Saucer-shaped with a shallow cup, the nest is loosely woven so that eggs may be seen from below. Both parents feed the two to five young. This tanager makes food of both flying and non-flying insects, and the larvae and spiders which it captures on leaves and bark. Flying insects are caught by hawking. In the fall the Scarlet Tanager also forages for fruit.

Fragmentation of forest habitat is of concern for this species, which requires larger-size woodland territories to breed successfully and elude Brown-headed Cowbird parasitism. While there are no conservation management efforts underway specifically for Scarlet Tanagers, habitat loss prevention and restoration of forest habitat would contribute to improving the species' viability.

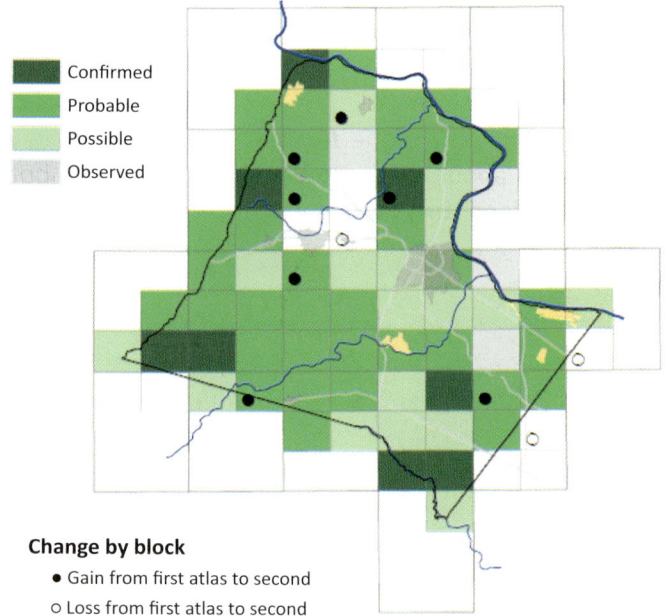

Confirmed
Probable
Possible
Observed

Change by block
- Gain from first atlas to second
○ Loss from first atlas to second

Written by Chris White

NORTHERN CARDINAL
Cardinalis cardinalis

Photo by Larry Meade

Occurrence: abundant breeder and year-round resident

Earliest breeding confirmation: March 17, adult carrying nesting material or nest building (NB)

Latest breeding confirmation: September 28, recently fledged young (FL)

Phoebe Snetsinger, known for having seen the most bird species in the world at the time of her death in 1999, said if the Northern Cardinal was a rare bird, people would go to the ends of the world to see it. Fortunately for us, the cardinal brings its cheery presence to our backyards, woodlots, and just about anywhere there are thickets for nesting. Cardinals are year-round residents; the sight of a cardinal against freshly fallen snow is a cherished image of winter in Loudoun.

Cardinals are medium-sized birds typically seen hopping on branches as well as on the ground. Food consists of fruit, seeds, and insects. They are especially fond of sunflower seeds and eagerly visit bird feeders. Males are a striking red with a red crest, red bill, and black mask. Females are subtler but equally beautiful in shades of brown with reddish tones on the bill, wings, crest, and tail.

Males defend territory by singing and actively attacking intruders. Both males and females are sometimes seen battling their reflections in windows, a behavior that may persist until breeding season ends. The cardinal female is one of the few female bird species that sings; she sings in spring before nesting and from the nest, perhaps to remind her mate to bring food. Cardinals have a wide range of vocalizations but most commonly heard are the bright *cheer cheer cheer* and *perty perty perty* songs. Cardinals can be located by their sharp, metallic chip call even when not visible.

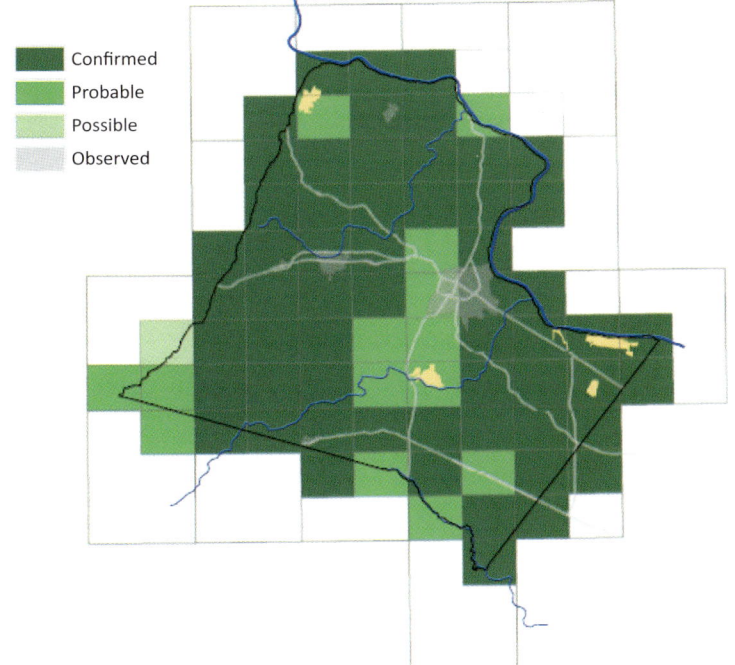

Confirmed
Probable
Possible
Observed

Nests are well-hidden in dense shrubs and thickets. The female molds a cup from twigs, bark strips, and rootlets, lined with fine grass or hair. Three to four grayish white, speckled eggs are laid, and incubation is by the female alone for 12-13 days. Young leave the nest about 10 days after hatching, and both parents feed the fledglings. A pair raises two to three broods per year. The cardinal ranked high on the top 25 list of atlas breeding species and was 1 of 14 species documented in all 73 blocks.

With its red plumage, distinctive crest, and cheery song, it is no wonder the Northern Cardinal is one of our most popular birds. Seven states, including Virginia, claim it as their state bird. Once a bird of the Southeast, it is interesting to note that cardinals have been expanding their range northward for many years and are now found as far north as southeastern Canada.

Written by Donna Quinn

ROSE-BREASTED GROSBEAK
Pheucticus ludovicianus

Occurrence: occasional breeder, uncommon migrant

Earliest/latest breeding confirmations: highest breeding evidence in Probable category, see account for details

Photo by Bill Brown

Though the Rose-breasted Grosbeak was not confirmed as a breeder in Loudoun during the atlas, there were 2 reports of probable breeding in Ashby Gap 6 (July 2009) and Bluemont 3 (June 2010), the more wooded western parts of the county, along with 4 reports of possible breeding. Post-atlas, parents were observed feeding three fledglings at a feeder in Middleburg on June 30, 2016, confirming that this species does indeed breed in Loudoun. Found in 25 of the 73 atlas blocks, most sightings were made in the months of May and September when migration to and from more northerly breeding grounds is in full swing. Early and late dates of April 25 and October 10 were reported. This long-distance migrant overwinters in Central and northern South America.

The Rose-breasted Grosbeak is a medium-sized songbird equipped with an exceptionally large, whitish seed-eating bill. The adult male in breeding plumage is resplendent with black and white upperparts and white underparts, sporting a distinct pinkish-red triangular mark on its breast. The female is streaked olive-brown and black above with a pale stripe on the crown and a whitish stripe above the eye. She has whitish wingbars, pale underparts, and dark streaking on the breast and flanks. The non-breeding male acquires some of the characteristics of the female after molt.

Often hidden among the treetops, this grosbeak may first be detected by the male's long, sing-song string of rich whistled phrases, likened to a happier version of the American Robin's song. Its squeaky *chink* call, often described as

a "sneaker squeak," is also distinctive and is given by both sexes. Males sing to establish territory and attract females. Both parents share nest building, incubation, brooding, and feeding duties. The nest is often so flimsy that eggs can be seen from below.

Preferred habitat is found in moist, open deciduous and mixed forests, thickets, river corridors, and second-growth woods; parks and gardens are also chosen. There is a tolerance for human activity, and they often visit garden feeders, especially during migration. The Rose-breasted Grosbeak is considered to be both pest and useful. It will consume buds, flowers, and small fruits, but also insects injurious to humans and crops. It forages at all levels of tree growth, on the extremities of branches as well as where leaves are thickest. According to the North American BBS, Rose-breasted Grosbeak populations have experienced a slow decline over the past 5 decades.

Written by Chris White

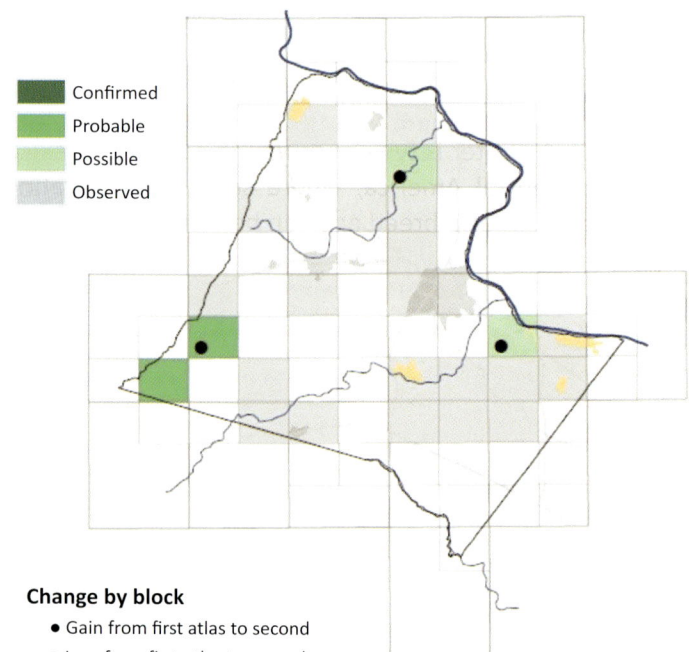

Confirmed
Probable
Possible
Observed

Change by block
- Gain from first atlas to second
○ Loss from first atlas to second

BLUE GROSBEAK
Passerina caerulea

Occurrence: uncommon breeder and migrant

Earliest breeding confirmation: June 4, recently fledged young (FL)

Latest breeding confirmation: August 27, parent carrying food or feeding young (CF)

Blue Grosbeaks are bulky sparrow-like birds with a large silvery-gray bill and double chestnut-colored wingbars, the upper one very broad. Males are a deep electric blue overall, while females are cinnamon brown above and below. They have relatively short, broad wings and a short tail. Both sexes are similar in color to Indigo Buntings, but Blue Grosbeaks are much larger and bulkier overall, and the large bill and head

Photo ©Dick Rowe

are quite obvious. They can be difficult to spot when quiet, but males often sit at the tops of trees or on overhead wires within their territory to sing. Their song is a somewhat variable musical warble that lasts several seconds, and their call is a metallic *chink*. Their oversized beak appears built to handle tough nuts, but is actually used primarily to catch and consume large insects. Grasshoppers and crickets are favorites, but many other bugs will also do. Blue Grosbeaks also eat a variety of seeds and grains, including, uncommonly, sunflower seeds when offered in backyard feeders.

These are widespread but nevertheless eagerly sought breeding birds across Loudoun, found between late April and late September in open habitats like overgrown fields and other low-growth areas with cedars, hedgerows, or nearby wooded edges for cover and nesting purposes. Transmission corridors, one of eastern Loudoun's few expanding habitat types, are also a good place to seek out this species. Blue Grosbeaks breed throughout the lower tier of the continental U.S., and farther north in the central Great Plains states up to southern North Dakota. Males arrive first in spring, and may flock together with other males in feeding groups prior to the females' arrival. Once paired off, nests are constructed in low shrubs, where the monogamous pair will typically raise two broods per year. They are a frequent victim of cowbird parasitism. Though there was 1 extraordinary Blue Grosbeak sighting on a Central Loudoun CBC (2014), winter is typically spent in southern Mexico and Central America, where some non-migrating grosbeaks also breed and can be found year-round. Their global population is stable and estimated at about 24 million (PIF 2017); populations in Loudoun are also stable and appear to have increased from Atlas 1 to 2. Human-induced habitat changes appear to be a mixed blessing for Blue Grosbeaks; they are rarely found in suburbs, but thrive in degraded areas like the aforementioned transmission corridors or abandoned agricultural fields.

Written by Bruce Hill

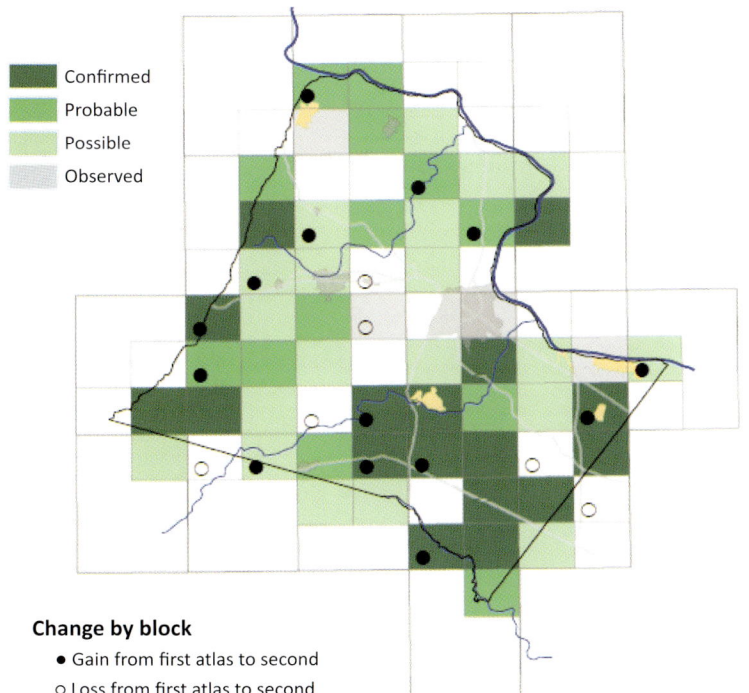

Confirmed
Probable
Possible
Observed

Change by block
- Gain from first atlas to second
- Loss from first atlas to second

INDIGO BUNTING
Passerina cyanea

Occurrence: common breeder and migrant

Earliest breeding confirmation: May 12, adult carrying nesting material or nest building (NB)

Latest breeding confirmation: September 19, parent carrying food or feeding young (CF)

The Indigo Bunting is one of Loudoun's most striking songbirds. The brilliant ultramarine blue of the male's breeding plumage results from the refraction of blue light through the feathers and is accordingly most intense in bright sunlight. This vivid blue is in sharp contrast to the drab, buffy coloration of the female. The plumage of non-breeding males resembles that of the females, although varying patches of blue in the wings, tail, and breast are distinctive.

Photo by Liam McGranaghan

Indigo Buntings begin to arrive in Loudoun in mid-April from their wintering grounds in Central America, Mexico, and the Caribbean. They prefer brushy or edge habitats in thickets, hedgerows, or old fields, though the male's cheerful song can also ring out unexpectedly in a quiet forest. The female builds the nest a few feet off the ground in a shrub or sapling. The nest is a cup consisting of layers of stalks, bark, and leaves and lined with fine grasses or hair. A pair of buntings may raise one to three broods of three to four young during the breeding season.

The Indigo Bunting's song is a rapid warble, readily identified by the tendency to pair or repeat notes (such as *sweet sweet, chew chew*), especially at the beginning and end of the song. The male sings from the tops of trees or poles and is notable for his stamina as a singer; he continues to sing through July and August and may repeat his song all day.

Following the breeding season, Indigo Buntings may form large flocks preparatory to fall migration. Although most Indigo Buntings leave Loudoun by late September, they were observed here as late as October 12. They are nocturnal migrants, using stars to guide them on their journey.

Breeding evidence for Indigo Buntings was well documented in 72 blocks, with breeding confirmed in 35 blocks. Although the population in Loudoun remained stable from Atlas 1 to Atlas 2, habitat loss through development and clearing of brush and hedgerows poses a threat to this species. According to the North American BBS, populations of Indigo Buntings have decreased by roughly 31% since the 1960s. In addition to habitat loss, vehicular collisions and parasitism by Brown-headed Cowbirds may be factors in the species' overall population decline.

Written by Christine Perdue

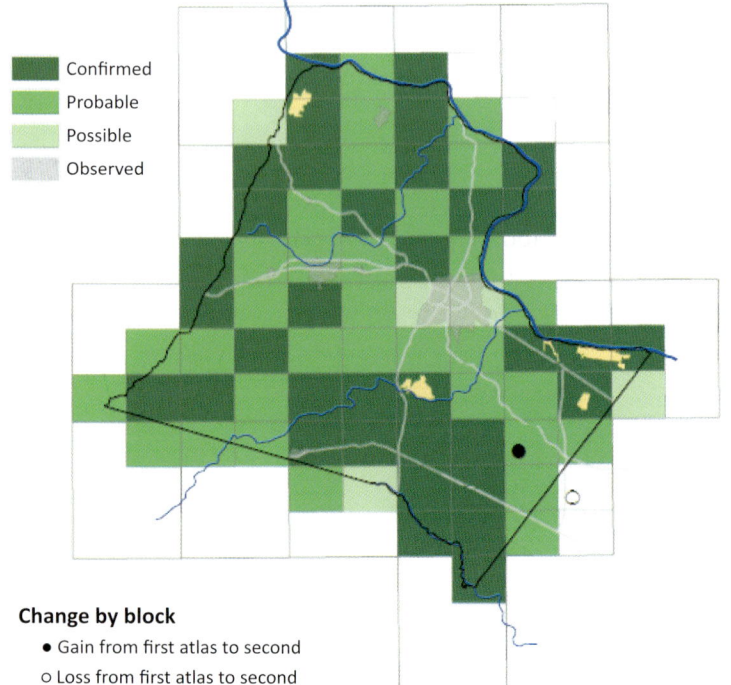

Confirmed
Probable
Possible
Observed

Change by block
- Gain from first atlas to second
- Loss from first atlas to second

DICKCISSEL

Spiza americana

Occurrence: irregular breeder

Earliest breeding confirmation: July 2, adult carrying nesting material or nest building (NB)

Latest breeding confirmation: September 2, recently fledged young (FL)

Photo by Dave Boltz

Dickcissels are sometimes confused for sparrows, but are more closely related to buntings, grosbeaks, and cardinals. With a yellow stripe over the eye and in the malars and yellow on the breast, Dickcissels are quite distinctive. Males in breeding plumage almost look like miniature meadowlarks with their bright yellow chests and black 'V' on the throat. Rusty shoulders and a conical bill complete the distinctive look. The name Dickcissel is derived from the sound of their song, *dick, dick, ciss, ciss, ciss*. Because they like to hide in scrubby, overgrown fields, they are often first detected by this unique song.

The core of their summer breeding range is the Midwest, focused around the eastern part of Kansas and stretching into parts of Oklahoma, Missouri, Nebraska, and Iowa. However, their breeding range can vary significantly from year to year. Loudoun is sometimes in this breeding range, and may be becoming more so, as reflected in the gain in blocks from Atlas 1 to 2. During the atlas, all breeding confirmations were made in 2 blocks with their preferred habitat (Poolesville 3 and Arcola 1) during only 2 years (2011 and 2013). Males are polygynous, which is uncommon among songbirds, and not likely to win a "parent of the year" award. The female builds the nest close to the ground (typically less than 4 feet up) in dense grasses, shrubs, or a small tree. She lays three to six eggs, and is solely in charge of incubating and raising the young.

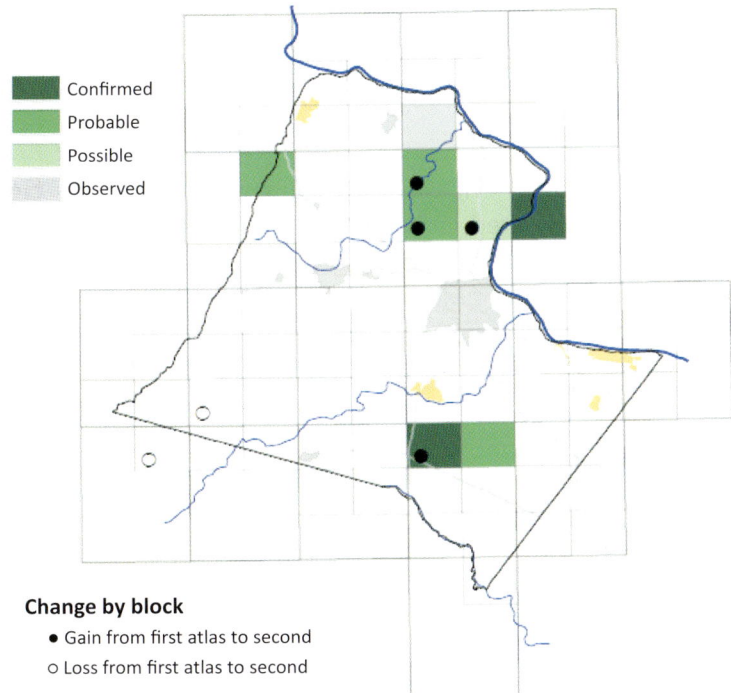

Confirmed
Probable
Possible
Observed

Change by block
- Gain from first atlas to second
- Loss from first atlas to second

In the winter, their range is much more restricted and their population more concentrated in extreme northern South America and the Pacific Coast of Central America. Much of the population winters in large flocks in the Llanos region of Venezuela, where many farmers consider it a pest. Some flocks are so large they may contain 10-30% of the global population (Temple 2002)! Their winter diet consists of many of the cultivated grains, including rice. When on their breeding grounds in the U.S., their diet is mostly composed of grasshoppers, beetles, and other insects.

The Dickcissel population has declined throughout North America in recent decades. Their preferred breeding habitat is at threat from development and changes in agricultural practices. On their wintering grounds, flocks are poisoned or shot by farmers trying to protect their crops.

Written by Bryan Henson

GREAT PLACES TO BIRD IN LOUDOUN

The following parks and nature preserves provide a sampling of great places to find a variety of birds in Loudoun. An asterisk indicates that a checklist of species documented during Atlas 2 is available on the Loudoun Wildlife Conservancy website. If you can't visit one of these great places, try birding the paths around your local patch and check out any ponds or lakes. You never know what birds are waiting to be discovered!

Algonkian Regional Park* - Part of the Virginia Birding and Wildlife Trail, this park's location along the Potomac River makes it a hot spot for birds. The park is located in Sterling and includes trails along the river and through the forest as well as a wildflower meadow and vernal pools. Atlasers documented an impressive 167 species here, including a nice variety of ducks, 29 species of warblers, Bobolink, and Rusty Blackbird.

Appalachian Trail - There are various trailheads in western Loudoun to explore, including Bears Den, Snickers Gap, and Route 9 along the Virginia and West Virginia border. The trail leads to beautiful panoramic views and is home to Wood Thrush and a variety of warblers, including Kentucky and Worm-eating Warblers.

Balls Bluff Regional Park - This Leesburg park is part of the Virginia Birding and Wildlife Trail and includes woodland trails that lead to the Potomac River. The rich diversity of spring wildflowers is worth making a trip in April. The park hosts a variety of bird species, including Bald Eagle, Barred Owl, and Red-headed Woodpecker.

Banshee Reeks Nature Preserve* - Known as the wildlife gem of Loudoun, this 725-acre preserve hosts a variety of habitats ranging from wetlands and ponds to mixed hardwood forests and meadows. The preserve is located south of Leesburg and is open to the public on Saturdays and Sundays. Barn Owl, Loggerhead and Northern Shrikes, Summer Tanager, and Rusty Blackbird highlight the 141 species documented here during Atlas 2.

Beaverdam Creek Reservoir - Located in Ashburn, this 350-acre property includes a large lake surrounded by woods with hiking trails. Bald Eagle, Ruddy Duck, seven woodpecker species, and Winter Wren are just a few of the species documented here. The reservoir is undergoing a major renovation which should be completed in the near future. As a result of a partnership with NOVA Parks, the reservoir and trails will be open to the public.

Bles Park* - This 124-acre park, located in the University Center development of Ashburn and bordering Broad Run and the Potomac River, has birding and hiking trails that run along fields, wetlands, and streams. Atlasers documented 151 species at this park, including Black-billed Cuckoo, Merlin, Bobolink, Rusty Blackbird, and 25 species of warblers.

Blue Ridge Center for Environmental Stewardship* - Located at the north-western tip of Loudoun, this 895-acre property, which will become a state park in the near future, contains vernal pools, meadows, ponds, streams, and forest. Over 150 species were documented in the preserve, including a variety of less common warblers such as Kentucky, Cerulean, and Blue-winged Warblers.

Claude Moore Park* - Part of the Virginia Birding and Wildlife Trail, this 357-acre park provides nature trails alongside wetlands, ponds, meadows, and forest. A variety of environmental education classes are offered for families and children. This park is located in Sterling and hosts 120 species, including American Bittern, courting American Woodcock, and Red-headed Woodpecker.

Dulles Greenway Wetlands* - This privately-owned 149-acre wetland, established to mitigate the loss of wetlands from the construction of the Dulles Greenway, is located south of Leesburg. Loudoun Wildlife has permission to monitor the property for wildlife and holds periodic bird walks; the wetlands are not open to the public. The wetlands hosts 158 species, including nesting Bald Eagles and numerous species that are rare to Loudoun.

Elizabeth Mills Riverfront Park - This park, located in the Lansdowne area of Leesburg, includes 122 acres of forest buffer along the Potomac River. Ducks such as Northern Pintail and Common Goldeneye may be found on the river in the winter. Barred Owl and Yellow-billed Cuckoo are among the species that may breed in the park.

Horsepen Preserve* - Located within the community of Countryside in Sterling, this privately-owned, 370-acre wetland preserve has walking and birding trails, one of which leads to the Potomac River. Three species of grebe, Prothonotary and Cerulean Warblers, and Rusty Blackbird highlight the 113 species documented here during Atlas 2.

Morven Park - This park, which includes ridge habitat that is the terminal end of the Catoctin Mountains, is now open to the public year-round. There are two main hiking and birding trails with ephemeral wildflowers, vernal pools used by frogs and salamanders, and a variety of birds including Wild Turkey, American Woodcock, Wood Thrush, and Scarlet Tanager.

Phillips Farm - This 144-acre farm is open to the public and located in Waterford, a historic, rural Quaker village. The farm's floodplain, riparian buffer, forests, hedgerows, and meadows attract a variety of species such as Belted Kingfisher, Warbling Vireo, Savannah Sparrow, and Eastern Meadowlark.

Red Rock Wilderness Overlook Park - This 67-acre park in Leesburg is part of the Virginia Birding and Wildlife Trail and offers forest trails opening up to panoramic views of the Potomac River. The park hosts a variety of species such as Great Blue Heron, Northern Rough-winged Swallow, and Scarlet Tanager.

Rust Sanctuary - Part of the Virginia Birding and Wildlife Trail, this easily accessible sanctuary is located in the heart of Leesburg and protects 68 acres of forest and meadow along with a large pond. Barred Owl, Eastern Bluebird, several species of warblers, Scarlet Tanager, and Rose-breasted Grosbeak frequent the sanctuary.

Snickers Gap Hawkwatch - Located where Route 7 crosses the Blue Ridge Mountains into Clarke County, this hawk watch site is active from September through November and typically counts about 12,000 raptors each season. Species of special interest reported at the hawk watch include Peregrine Falcon, Golden Eagle, and Rough-legged Hawk as well as Red- and White-winged Crossbills.

White's Ford Regional Park - This 300-acre property is located on the Potomac River north of Leesburg and offers hiking trails and water access. The park opened in June 2014 after data collection for Atlas 2 was complete, but atlasers obtained permission to survey this area in prior years, finding Barn Owl, Grasshopper Sparrow, and Dickcissel.

CONSERVATION: PUTTING THE DATA INTO ACTION

Data collected during Atlas 2 has been and will continue to be utilized in various ways to protect Loudoun's birds. In addition to identifying species-rich areas throughout the county, the data also provides valuable information on the status and distribution of species of special concern, such as the Loggerhead Shrike and Cerulean Warbler. Portions of the atlas dataset have contributed to other bird-related projects including grassland surveys, Christmas Bird Counts, Nightjar and Owl Surveys, Loudoun Wildlife's Audubon at Home program, and a Virginia Society of Ornithology weeklong foray. Atlas data can also serve to strengthen requests such as to the state highway department regarding the postponement of highway bridge painting projects during the breeding season for Cliff Swallow and other species.

Loudoun Wildlife is also using the Atlas 2 data to assist environmental planners in making sound decisions regarding the use and management of natural resources throughout the county. Loudoun Wildlife works closely with county representatives regarding proposed changes to county parks. Eighty-five percent of the atlas species were documented non-exclusively in seven parks and preserves throughout Loudoun (3% documented exclusively), so birds do indeed benefit from the parks, which need to be protected and managed for a variety of species. Atlas data is also available to assist property owners who are considering placing a conservation easement on their property.

Over the long term, comparing our atlas results with results from the 2016-2020 Virginia BBA will provide a valuable opportunity to document any changes in species distribution, especially in rapidly developing eastern Loudoun. As noted earlier, many of the grassland and uncommon species documented in the highest richness areas of eastern Loudoun were found during the first years of Atlas 2 in abandoned fields awaiting development. As the atlas progressed, many of these fields were developed and species were lost. Comparing the 2009 and 2016 atlas datasets may also help refine our understanding of when birds migrate through or breed in Loudoun and allow us to recognize changes in species' traditional arrival and breeding dates, perhaps tied to environmental factors such as climate change.

Outside the few public and private protected parks and preserves in eastern Loudoun, suitable habitat for many sensitive bird species is increasingly fragmented and rapidly disappearing. In 2019, Loudoun will finalize a new Comprehensive Plan to guide development throughout the county over the next decade or two. Armed with data from the atlas and other scientific sources, Loudoun Wildlife has partnered with the Piedmont Environmental Council and local conservation groups to inform county representatives of the importance of including a Green Infrastructure component in the new plan, with measurable and enforceable standards for natural areas.

Conservation isn't just a matter for policy-makers and dedicated groups — conservation starts at home! Here are a few ways each of us can benefit Loudoun's birds and wildlife:
- Plant native trees, shrubs, and flowers which provide food and shelter for wildlife.
- Buy local food and products to support Loudoun's farms and businesses.
- Reduce or eliminate pesticides and fertilizers. Look for natural alternatives instead.
- Maintain hedgerows and brush along streams, fence lines, and field borders.
- Install decals or other treatments to reduce window collisions.
- Make your yard a wildlife sanctuary by adding a nest box, feeder, or water feature and certifying it under Loudoun Wildlife's Audubon at Home program.
- Keep cats indoors.
- Attend a Loudoun Wildlife program or field trip to one of Loudoun's great places. Better yet, become a member of this enthusiastic and influential group!

ACKNOWLEDGEMENTS

We are grateful to all the atlasers who enthusiastically embraced this tremendous 5-year task. The success of the Loudoun County Bird Atlas is a direct result of their dedication and knowledge. We appreciate the hospitality of many private landowners who granted permission to atlas on their property, providing important opportunities to find some of the more elusive species. A special thanks goes to Allison Sussman and Mark Wimer from the USGS Patuxent Wildlife Research Center for graciously providing the database and distribution maps, along with invaluable advice throughout all stages of the project. We'd also like to thank Karen Coleman for the use of her Barn Owl feather painting for the atlas logo and all the photographers, especially Dave Boltz, Gerco Hoogeweg, and Dick Rowe, who graciously shared their beautiful photos.

We are particularly thankful for the authors who so eloquently portrayed the story of each species; they included Bill Brown, Joe Coleman, Mary Ann Good, Bryan Henson, Spring Ligi, Christine Perdue, Donna Quinn, Chris White, and especially Bruce Hill who wrote nearly one-third of all the accounts and, with his rich knowledge of local birds, provided an invaluable sounding board. Special mention to Mary Ann Good for tireless hours editing and reviewing accounts for readability and accuracy. Finally, the atlasers and authors would like to give a huge shout-out to Spring Ligi for her enormous devotion of time and energy in coordinating this vast effort. Her unfailing guidance, encouragement, and hard work made this unique and comprehensive end product possible. Financial support for the Loudoun County Bird Atlas came from the Loudoun Wildlife Conservancy, with a start-up grant from the Virginia Society of Ornithology.

The following list of volunteers have contributed to this project by collecting field data, assisting with data entry, or serving in an advisory capacity. The regional coordinators, truly the heart and soul of this project, are listed in bold font. An asterisk indicates that the atlaser contributed over 2,000 sightings. We apologize if we inadvertently overlooked anyone when compiling this list.

REFERENCES

American Bird Conservancy. 2016. Kentucky Warbler. <https://abcbirds.org/bird/kentucky-warbler>.

American Bird Conservancy. 2016. Osprey. <https://abcbirds.org/bird/osprey>.

American Bird Conservancy. 2017. Common Nighthawk. <https://abcbirds.org/bird/common-nighthawk>.

American Bird Conservancy. 2014. Swainson's Thrush. <https://abcbirds.org/bird/swainsons-thrush>.

American Kestrel Partnership. 2016. Declines of American Kestrel populations. <kestrel.peregrinefund.org/decline>.

Andres B.A., Smith P.A., Morrison R.I.G., Gratto-Trevor C.L., Brown S.C., and Friis C.A. 2012. Population estimates of North American Shorebirds, 2012. *Wader Study Group Bulletin* 119: 178–194.

Arcese P., Sogge M.K., Marr A.B., and Patten M.A. 2002. Song Sparrow (*Melospiza melodia*). *The Birds of North America* (A.F. Poole and and F.B. Gill, Eds.). Cornell Lab of Ornithology, Ithaca, NY. <https://birdsna.org/Species-Account/bna/species/sonspa>.

Artuso C.C., Houston S., Smith D.G., and Rohner C. 2013. Great Horned Owl (*Bubo virginianus*). *The Birds of North America* (A.F. Poole, Ed.). Cornell Lab of Ornithology, Ithaca, NY. <https://birdsna.org/Species-Account/bna/species/grhowl>.

Audubon Guide to North American Birds. 2017. <http://www.audubon.org/field-guide/bird>. Adapted from: Kaufman K. 1996. *Lives of North American Birds*. New York, NY: Houghton Mifflin Harcourt Publishing Company.

Austin J.E., Custer C.M., and Afton A.D. 2014. Lesser Scaup (*Aythya affinis*). *The Birds of North America* (P.G. Rodewald, Ed.). Cornell Lab of Ornithology, Ithaca, NY. <https://birdsna.org/Species-Account/bna/species/lessca>.

Baldassarre G. 2014. *Ducks, Geese, and Swans of North America*. A Wildlife Management Institute Book. Baltimore, MD: Johns Hopkins University Press.

Bannor B.K. and Kiviat E. 2002. Common Gallinule (*Gallinula galeata*). *The Birds of North America* (P. G. Rodewald, Ed.). Cornell Lab of Ornithology, Ithaca, NY. <https://birdsna.org/Species-Account/bna/species/comgal1>.

Baughman M. 2003. *National Geographic Reference Atlas to the Birds of North America*. Washington, DC: National Geographic.

BBC Wildlife Magazine. 2013. Discover Wildlife. 12 Barn Owl facts you need to know. London, England: Immediate Media Company Limited. <http://www.discoverwildlife.com/blog/12-barn-owl-facts-you-need-know>.

Benkman C.W. 2012. White-winged Crossbill (*Loxia leucoptera*). *The Birds of North America* (A.F. Poole, Ed.). Cornell Lab of Ornithology, Ithaca, NY. <https://birdsna.org/Species-Account/bna/species/whwcro>.

Blackwell B.F. and Dolbeer R.A. 2001. Decline of the Red-Winged Blackbird Population in Ohio Correlated to Changes in Agriculture (1965-1996). *The Journal of Wildlife Management* 65(4): 661-667. <https://www.jstor.org/stable/3803017?seq=1#page_scan_tab_contents>.

Blankenship K. 1998. Trumpeter Swans Arrive at New Winter Home on Bay. *Bay Journal*. Bay Journal Media. <http://www.bayjournal.com/article/trumpeter_swans_arrive_at_new_winter_home_on_bay>.

Breeding Bird Atlas (BBA) Explorer. 2016. U.S. Geological Survey Patuxent Wildlife Research Center. <http://www.pwrc.usgs.gov/bba>. Data compiled from: Delaware Breeding Bird Atlas 2008-2012. Delmarva Ornithological Society. Interim results used with permission.

Breeding Bird Atlas (BBA) Explorer. 2016. U.S. Geological Survey Patuxent Wildlife Research Center. <http://www.pwrc.usgs.gov/bba>. Data compiled from: Loudoun County Bird Atlas 2009-2014. Loudoun Wildlife Conservancy.

Brisbin Jr. I.L., Lehr I., and Mowbray T.B. 2002. American Coot (*Fulica americana*). *The Birds of North America* (P. G. Rodewald, Ed.). Cornell Lab of Ornithology, Ithaca, NY. <https://birdsna.org/Species-Account/bna/species/y00475>.

Brown C.R. and Brown M.B. 1999. Barn swallow (*Hirundo rustica*). *The Birds of North America* (A.F. Poole and F.B. Gill, Eds.). Cornell Lab of Ornithology, Ithaca, NY. <https://birdsna.org/Species-Account/bna/species/barswa>.

Brown C.R., Brown M.B., Pyle P., and Patten M.A. 2017. Cliff Swallow (*Petrochelidon pyrrhonota*). *The Birds of North America* (P.G. Rodewald, Ed.). Cornell Lab of Ornithology, Ithaca, NY. <https://birdsna.org/Species-Account/bna/species/cliswa>.

Buehler D.A. 2000. Bald Eagle (*Haliaeetus leucocephalus*). *The Birds of North America* (P.G. Rodewald, Ed.). Cornell Lab of Ornithology, Ithaca, NY. <https://birdsna.org/Species-Account/bna/species/baleag>.

Bull E.L. and Jackson J.A. 2011. Pileated Woodpecker (*Dryocopus pileatus*). *The Birds of North America* (A.F. Poole, Ed.). Cornell Lab of Ornithology, Ithaca, NY. <https://birdsna.org/Species-Account/bna/species/pilwoo>.

Burger J. and Gochfeld M. 2002. Bonaparte's Gull (*Larus philadelphia*). *The Birds of North America.* (A.F. Poole and F.B. Gill, Eds.). Cornell Lab of Ornithology, Ithaca, NY. <https://birdsna.org/Species-Account/bna/species/bongul>.

Carey M., Burhans D.E., and Nelson D.A. 2008. Field Sparrow (*Spizella pusilla*). *The Birds of North America* (A.F. Poole,

Ed.). Cornell Lab of Ornithology, Ithaca, NY. <https://birdsna.org/Species-Account/bna/species/fiespa>.

Cavitt J.F. and Haas C.A. 2014. Brown Thrasher (*Toxostoma rufum*). *The Birds of North America* (A.F. Poole, Ed.). Cornell Lab of Ornithology, Ithaca, NY. <https://birdsna.org/Species-Account/bna/species/brnthr>.

Ciaranca M.A., Allin C.C., and Jones G.S. 1997. Mute Swan (*Cygnus olor*). *The Birds of North America* (P.G. Rodewald, Ed.). Cornell Lab of Ornithology, Ithaca, NY. <https://birdsna.org/Species-Account/bna/species/mutswa>.

Connecticut DEEP (Department of Energy and Environmental Protection). 1999. Endangered and Threatened Species Fact Sheet Series. Barn Owl (*Tyto alba*). <http://www.ct.gov/deep/cwp/view.asp?q=325962>.

Cornell Lab of Ornithology. 2014. All About Birds. <https://www.allaboutbirds.org>.

Cornell Lab of Ornithology. 2016a. Nestwatch. All About Birdhouses. <http://nestwatch.org/learn/all-about-birdhouses/birds/great-crested-flycatcher/?region=northeast&habitat=open-woodland>.

Cornell Lab of Ornithology. 2016b. Project Feeder Watch. <http://feederwatch.org/learn/common-feeder-birds>.

Crossley R. 2011. *The Crossley ID Guide*. Princeton, NJ: Princeton University Press.

Cuthrell D.L. 2004. Special animal abstract for *Ardea Herodias:* Great Blue Heron rookery. Michigan Natural Features Inventory. Lansing, MI. <http://mnfi.anr.msu.edu/abstracts/zoology/Great_blue_heron_rookery.pdf>.

De Jong M.J. 1996. Northern Rough-winged Swallow (*Stelgidopteryx serripennis*). *The Birds of North America* (A.F. Poole and F.B. Gill, Eds.). Cornell Lab of Ornithology, Ithaca, NY. <https://birdsna.org/Species-Account/bna/species/nrwswa>.

Dellinger R., Wood P.B., Jones P.W., and Donovan T.M. (2012). Hermit Thrush (*Catharus guttatus*). *The Birds of North America* (A.F. Poole, Ed.). Cornell Lab of Ornithology, Ithaca, NY. <https://birdsna.org/Species-Account/bna/species/herthr>.

Dolbeer R.A. and Linz G.M. 2016. Blackbirds. *Wildlife Damage Management Technical Series 1*. U.S. Department of Agriculture: Animal and Plant Health Inspection Service at DigitalCommons@University of Nebraska - Lincoln. <http://digitalcommons.unl.edu/cgi/viewcontent.cgi?article=1000&context=nwrcwdmts>.

Dubowy P.J. 1996. Northern Shoveler (*Anas clypeata*). *The Birds of North America* (P. G. Rodewald, Ed.). Cornell Lab of Ornithology, Ithaca, NY. < https://birdsna.org/Species-Account/bna/species/norsho>.

Duggar B.D., Dugger K.M., and Fredrickson L.H. 2009. Hooded Merganser (*Lophodytes cucullatus*). *The Birds of North America* (P.G. Rodewald, Ed.). Cornell Lab of Ornithology, Ithaca, NY. <https://birdsna.org/Species-Account/bna/species/hoomer>.

Dunn J. and Alderfer J. 2011. *National Geographic Field Guide to the Birds of North America, 6th edition.* Washington, D.C.: National Geographic Society.

Eadie J.M., Mallory M.L., and Lumsden H.G. 1995. Common Goldeneye (*Bucephala clangula*). *The Birds of North America* (P. G. Rodewald, Ed.). Cornell Lab of Ornithology, Ithaca, NY. < https://birdsna.org/Species-Account/bna/species/comgol>.

Eastern Golden Eagle Working Group (EGEWG). 2017. What we know about Golden Eagles in eastern North America. *<www.ncwildlife.org/Portals/0/Blogs/images/WhatweKnowabouteasternGoldenEagles_v2015-1.pdf>*.

eBird. 2017. Virginia Breeding Bird Atlas 2. Cornell Lab of Ornithology. <http://ebird.org/content/atlasva>.

eBird. 2017. Species range maps and other data. Cornell Lab of Ornithology. <https://ebird.org/explore>.

Ellison W.G. 2010. *Second Atlas of the Breeding Birds of Maryland and the District of Columbia.* Baltimore, MD: The Johns Hopkins University Press.

Enders E. 2012. The Loudoun County VSO Foray of June 2012. *Raven* 83(2): 10-16.

Falls J.B. and Kopachena J.G. 2010. White-throated Sparrow (*Zonotrichia albicollis*). *The Birds of North America* (P.G. Rodewald, Ed.). Cornell Lab of Ornithology, Ithaca, NY. <https://birdsna.org/Species-Account/bna/species/whtspa>.

Frederick P.C. 2013. Tricolored Heron (*Egretta tricolor*). *The Birds of North America* (A.F. Poole, Ed.). Cornell Lab of Ornithology, Ithaca, NY. <https://birdsna.org/Species-Account/bna/species/triher>.

Gamble L.R. and Bergin T.M. 2012. Western Kingbird (*Tyrannus verticalis*). *The Birds of North America* (A.F. Poole, Ed.). Cornell Lab of Ornithology, Ithaca, NY. <https://birdsna.org/Species-Account/bna/species/weskin>.

Gardali, T. and Ballard G. 2000. Warbling Vireo (*Vireo gilvus*). *The Birds of North America* (A.F. Poole and F.B. Gill, Eds.). Cornell Lab of Ornithology, Ithaca, NY. <https://birdsna.org/Species-Account/bna/species/warvir>.

Gauthier G. 2014. Bufflehead (*Bucephala albeola*). *The Birds of North America* (P.G. Rodewald, Ed.). Cornell Lab of Ornithology, Ithaca, NY. < https://birdsna.org/Species-Account/bna/species/buffle>.

Gowaty P.A. and Plissner J.H. 2015. Eastern Bluebird (*Sialia sialis*). *The Birds of North America* (P.G. Rodewald, Ed.). Cornell Lab of Ornithology, Ithaca, NY. <https://birdsna.org/Species-Account/bna/species/amgplo>.

Greenberg R., Demarest D.W., Matsuoka S. M., Mettke-Hofmann C., Evers D., Hamel P.B., Luscier J., Powell L.L., Shaw D., Avery M.L., Hobson K.A., Blancher P.J., and Niven D.K. Understanding Declines in Rusty Blackbirds. *Studies in Avian Biology* 41: 107- 125. <https://www.aphis.usda.gov/wildlife_damage/nwrc/publications/11pubs/avery 114.pdf>.

Hawk Migration Association of North America. 2017. Snickers Gap Hawkwatch. <https://hawkcount.org/siteinfo.php?r=on&rsite=494&go=Go+To+Hawkwatch+Profile>.

Hughes J.M. 2001. Black-billed Cuckoo (*Coccyzus erythropthalmus*). *The Birds of North America* (P.G. Rodewald, Ed.). Cornell Lab of Ornithology, Ithaca, NY. <https://birdsna.org/Species-Account/bna/species/bkbcuc>.

International Union for Conservation of Nature. The IUCN Red List of Threatened Species. Version 2017-2. <http://www.iucnredlist.org>.

Jackson J.A. and Ouellet H.R. 2002. Downy Woodpecker (*Picoides pubescens*). *The Birds of North America* (P. G. Rodewald, Ed.). Cornell Lab of Ornithology, Ithaca, NY. <https://birdsna.org/Species-Account/bna/species/dowwoo>.

Jackson J.A., Ouellet H.R., and Jackson B.J. 2002. Hairy Woodpecker (*Picoides villosus*). *The Birds of North America* (A.F. Poole and F.B. Gill, Eds.). Cornell Lab of Ornithology, Ithaca, NY. <https://birdsna.org/Species-Account/bna/species/haiwoo>.

Jehl Jr. J.R., Klima J., and Harris R.E. 2001. Short-billed Dowitcher (*Limnodromus griseus*). *The Birds of North America* (P. G. Rodewald, Ed.). Cornell Lab of Ornithology, Ithaca, NY. <https://birdsna.org/Species-Account/bna/species/shbdow>.

Jin S., Yang L., Danielson P., Homer C., Fry J., and Xian G. 2013. A comprehensive change detection method for updating the National Land Cover Database to circa 2011. *Remote Sensing of Environment* 132: 159-175.

Johnson O.W. and Connors P.G. 2018. American Golden-Plover (*Pluvialis dominica*). *The Birds of North America* (P. G. Rodewald, Ed.). Cornell Lab of Ornithology, Ithaca, NY. <https://birdsna.org/Species-Account/bna/species/amgplo>.

Kamm M., Leahy C., Peters K., Servison M., and Walsh J. 2013a. *State of the Birds, Massachusetts Breeding Birds: A Closer Look*. Mass Audubon Society.

Kamm M., Walsh J., Galluzzo J., and Petersen W. 2013b. *Massachusetts Breeding Bird Atlas 2*. Scott & Nix, Inc.

Kaufman, K. 1996. *Lives of North American Birds*. New York, NY: Houghton Mifflin Harcourt Publishing Company.

Kaufman, K. 2017. *The Fascinating and Complicated Sex Lives of White-throated Sparrows*. Kenn Kaufman's Notebook. Audubon. <http://www.audubon.org/news/the-fascinating-and-complicated-sex-lives-white-throated-sparrows>.

Kessel B, Rocque D.A, and Barclay J.S. 2002. Greater Scaup (*Aythya marila*). *The Birds of North America* (P.G. Rodewald, Ed.). Cornell Lab of Ornithology, Ithaca, NY. <https://birdsna.org/Species-Account/bna/species/gresca>.

Kiere L. 2005. Orchard Oriole, *Icterus spurius*. Animal Diversity Web. <https://animaldiversity.org/accounts/Icterus_spurius>.

Kushlan J.A., Steinkamp M.J., Parsons K.C., Capp J., Cruz M.A., Coulter M., Davidson I., Dickson L., Edelson N., Elliot R., Erwin M., Hatch S., Kress S., Milko R., Miller S., Mills K., Paul R., Phillips R., Saliva J., Sydeman B., Trapp J., Wheeler J., and Wohl K. 2002. *Waterbird Conservation for the Americas: The North American Waterbird Conservation Plan*, Version 1. Waterbird Conservation for the Americas. Washington, DC. <https://iwjv.org/sites/default/files/nawcp.pdf>.

Kyle P.D. and Kyle G.Z. 2005. *Chimney Swifts: America's Mysterious Birds above the Fireplace*. Texas A&M University Press.

Laughlin S.B., Carroll J.R., and Sutcliffe S.M. 1990. Standardized breeding criteria codes: recommendations for North American breeding bird atlas projects. *Handbook for Atlasing North American Breeding Birds*. North American Ornithological Atlas Committee. <http://www.bsc-eoc.org/norac>.

Ligi S. 2011. *Loudoun County Bird Atlas Handbook*. Loudoun Wildlife Conservancy. <http://www.loudounwildlife.org Bird_Atlas.htm>.

Ligi S. and Omland K. 2007. Contrasting breeding strategies of two sympatric orioles: first documentation of double brooding by Orchard Orioles. *Journal of Field Ornithology* 78(3): 298-302.

Ligi S. and Sussman A. 2016. Results of the 2009-2014 Loudoun County Bird Atlas. *Raven* 87(1): 3-17.

Loudoun Wildlife Conservancy. 2016. Bluebird Nest Box Monitoring. Results reported to Virginia Bluebird Society. <www.loudounwildlife.org/Bluebird_Monitoring.htm>.

Lowther P. and Johnston R. 2014. Rock Pigeon (*Columba livia*). *The Birds of North America* (P. G. Rodewald, Ed.). Cornell Lab of Ornithology, Ithaca, NY. <https://birdsna.org/Species-Account/bna/species/rocpig>.

Lowther P. 1999. Alder Flycatcher (*Empidonax alnorum*). *The Birds of North America* (A.F. Poole and F.B. Gill, Eds.). Cornell Lab of Ornithology, Ithaca, NY. <https://birdsna.org/Species-Account/bna/species/aldfly>.

Lowther P.E. and Cink C.L. 2006. House Sparrow (*Passer domesticus*). *The Birds of North America* (A.F. Poole, Ed.). Cornell Lab of Ornithology, Ithaca, NY. <https://birdsna.org/Species-Account/bna/species/houspa>.

Lutmerding J.A. and Love A.S. 2015. Longevity records of North American birds. Version 2015.2. U.S. Geological

Survey. Patuxent Wildlife Research Center, Bird Banding Laboratory.

Mack D.E. and Yong W. 2000. Swainson's Thrush (*Catharus ustulatus*). *The Birds of North America* (A.F. Poole and F.B. Gill, Eds.). Cornell Lab of Ornithology, Ithaca, NY. <https://birdsna.org/Species-Account/bna/species/swathr>.

Marzluff J.A. and DeLap J. 2015. *Welcome to subirdia: sharing our neighborhoods with wrens, robins, woodpeckers, and other wildlife.* Yale University Press.

McGowan K.J. 2001. Fish Crow (*Corvus ossifragus*). *The Birds of North America* (A.F. Poole and F.B. Gill, Eds.). Cornell Lab of Ornithology, Ithaca, NY. <https://birdsna.org/Species-Account/bna/species/fiscro>.

McGraw K.J. and Middleton A.L. (2017). American Goldfinch (*Spinus tristis*). *The Birds of North America* (P. G. Rodewald, Ed.). Cornell Lab of Ornithology, Ithaca, NY. <https://birdsna.org/Species-Account/bna/species/amegfi>.

McKay B. and Hall G.A. 2012. Yellow-throated Warbler (*Setophaga dominica*). *The Birds of North America* (A.F. Poole, Ed.). Cornell Lab of Ornithology, Ithaca, NY. < https://birdsna.org/Species-Account/bna/species/yetwar>.

Michigan Bluebird Society. 2018. Nest Box Basics. <https://michiganbluebirds.org>.

Moreno M.I., Salaman P., and Pashley D. 2006. The Current Status of the Cerulean Warbler on its Winter Range. U.S. Fish and Wildlife Service Midwest Region. Species of Concern. <https://www.fws.gov/midwest/es/soc/birds/cerw/morenaetal0806.html>.

Mowbray T.B. 1999. Scarlet Tanager (*Piranga olivacea*). *The Birds of North America* (A.F. Poole and F.B. Gill, Eds). Cornell Lab of Ornithology, Ithaca, NY. <https://birdsna.org/Species-Account/bna/species/scatan>.

Mowbray T.B., Ely C.R., Sedinger J.S., and Trost R.E. 2002. Canada Goose (*Branta canadensis*). *The Birds of North America* (P. G. Rodewald, Ed.). Cornell Lab of Ornithology, Ithaca, NY. < https://birdsna.org/Species-Account/bna/species/cangoo>.

Mumme R.L. 2002. White tail spots and tail-flicking behavior enhance foraging performance in the Hooded warbler. *Auk* 131: 141-149.

National Audubon Society. 2001. Typical Owls. *The Sibley Guide to Bird Life & Behavior*. New York, NY: Alfred A. Knopf, Inc.

National Audubon Society. 2009-2013. Christmas Bird Counts (110th–114th). *American Birds*. <http://netapp.audubon.org/cbcobservation>. Loudoun County trends found at <http://loudounwildlife.org/PDF_Files/CBC/Summary_Years.pdf>.

National Eagle Center. 2015. Eagle Nesting and Young. <https://www.nationaleaglecenter.org/eagle-nesting-young>.

National Geographic. 2003. *Reference Atlas to the Birds of North America* (M. Baughman, Ed.). Washington, DC: National Geographic.

National Geographic. 2005. *National Geographic Complete Birds of North America: Companion to the National Geographic Field Guide to the Birds of North America* (J. Alderfer, Ed.) Washington, DC: National Geographic.

Naugler C.T., Pyle P., and Patten M.A. 2017. American Tree Sparrow (*Spizelloides arborea*). *The Birds of North America* (P.G. Rodewald, Ed.). Cornell Lab of Ornithology, Ithaca, NY. <https://birdsna.org/Species-Account/bna/species/amtspa>.

Nol E. and Blanken M.S. 2014. Semipalmated Plover (*Charadrius semipalmatus*). *The Birds of North America* (P. G.

Rodewald, Ed.). Cornell Lab of Ornithology, Ithaca, NY. <https://birdsna.org/Species-Account/bna/species/semplo>.

Nolan Jr. V., Ketterson E.D., and Buerkle C.A. 2014. Prairie Warbler (*Setophaga discolor*). The Birds of North America (A.F. Poole, Ed.). Cornell Lab of Ornithology, Ithaca, NY. <https://birdsna.org/Species-Account/bna/species/prawar>.

North American Bird Conservation Initiative (NABCI). 2014. *The State of the Birds 2014 Report, United States of America.* U.S. Department of the Interior. Washington, D.C. <http://www.stateofthebirds.org/2014/2014%20SotB_FINAL_low-res.pdf>.

North American Bird Conservation Initiative (NABCI). 2016. *The State of North America's Birds Report.* Species Assessment Summary and Watch List. <http://www.stateofthebirds.org/2016/resources/species-assessments>.

North American Bluebird Society (NABS). 2018. NABS Factsheet. Nest Box Recommendations. <http://www.nabluebirdsociety.org/PDF/NABS%20factsheet%20-%20Nestbox%20Recs.pdf>.

O'Brien M., Crossley R., and Karlson K. 2006. *The Shorebird Guide.* Houghton Mifflin Harcourt Publishing Company.

Oklahoma Department of Wildlife Conservation. 2011. Turkey Vulture. <https://www.wildlifedepartment.com/wildlifemgmt/species/turkeyvulture.htm>.

Parsons K.C. and Master T.L. 2000. Snowy Egret (*Egretta thula*). The Birds of North America (A.F. Poole and F.B. Gill, Eds.). Cornell Lab of Ornithology, Ithaca, NY. <https://birdsna.org/Species-Account/bna/species/snoegr>.

Partners in Flight (PIF). 2016. Partners in Flight Watch List for Continental United States and Canada. <https://www.partnersinflight.org/wp-content/uploads/2017/03/SPECIES-OF-CONT-CONCERN-from-pif-continental-plan-final-spread-2.pdf>.

Partners in Flight (PIF). 2017. Avian Conservation Assessment Database. <http://pif.birdconservancy.org/ACAD/Database.aspx>.

Paulson D. 2005. *Shorebirds of North America; the Photographic Guide.* Princeton University Press.

Peer B.D. and Bollinger E.K. 1997. Common Grackle (*Quiscalus quiscula*). The Birds of North America (A. F. Poole and F.B. Gill, Eds.). Cornell Lab of Ornithology, Ithaca, NY. <https://birdsna.org/Species-Account/bna/species/comgra>.

Pennsylvania Game Commission. 2017. Threatened and Endangered Species. Long-eared Owl. <http://www.pgc.pa.gov/Wildlife/EndangeredandThreatened/Pages/Long-EaredOwl.aspx>.

Porneluzi P., Van Horn M.A., and Donovan T.M. 2011. Ovenbird (*Seiurus aurocapilla*). The Birds of North America (A.F. Poole, Ed.). Cornell Lab of Ornithology, Ithaca, NY. <https://birdsna.org/Species-Account/bna/species/ovenbi1>.

Price C.V., Nakagaki N., Hitt K.J., and Clawges R.C. 2006. *Enhanced historical land-use and land-cover data sets of the U.S. Geological Survey.* U.S. Geological Survey Digital Data Series 240.

Project SNOWstorm. 2016. Biodiversity Research Institute. <http://www.briloon.org/raptors/snowstorm>.

Purple Martin Conservation Association. 2018. Scout-Arrival Study. <https://www.purplemartin.org/research/8/scout-arrival-study>.

Quinn T. and Milner R. 2004. Great Blue Heron (*Ardea Herodias*) in *Management Recommendations for Washington's Priority Species.* Volume IV: Birds. Last updated 1999. Washington Department of Fish and Wildlife. <https://rentonwa.gov/uploadedFiles/Business/EDNSP/planning/PHS_great_bluheron.pdf>.

Rasmussen J.L., Sealy S.G., and Cannings R.J. 2008. Northern Saw-whet Owl (*Aegolius acadicus*). *The Birds of North America* (A.F. Poole, Ed.). Cornell Lab of Ornithology, Ithaca, NY. <https://birdsna.org/Species-Account/bna/species/nswowl>.

Ritchison G.T., Grubb Jr. C., and Pravosudov V.V. (2015). Tufted Titmouse (*Baeolophus bicolor*). *The Birds of North America* (P. G. Rodewald, Ed.). Cornell Lab of Ornithology, Ithaca, NY. <https://birdsna.org/Species-Account/bna/species/tuftit>.

Robertson G.J. and Savard J.L. 2002. Long-tailed Duck (*Clangula hyemalis*). *The Birds of North America* (P. G. Rodewald, Ed.). Cornell Lab of Ornithology, Ithaca, NY. < https://birdsna.org/Species-Account/bna/species/lotduc>.

Rodgers Jr. A.A. and Smith H.T. 2012. Little blue heron (*Egretta caerulea*). *The Birds of North America* (A.F. Poole, Ed.). Cornell Lab of Ornithology, Ithaca, NY. <https://birdsna.org/Species-Account/bna/species/libher>.

Rosenberg K.V., Pashley D., Andres B., Blancher P.J., Butcher G.S., Hunter W.C., Mehlman D., Panjabi A.O., Parr M., Wallace G., and Wiedenfeld D. 2014. *The State of the Birds 2014 Watch List.* North American Bird Conservation Initiative (NABCI), U.S. Committee. Washington, D.C. <http://www.stateofthebirds.org/2014/extinctions/watchlist.pdf>.

Rosenberg K., Kennedy J., Dettmers R., Ford R., Reynolds D., Alexander J., Beardmore C., Blancher P., Bogart R., Butcher G., Camfield A., Couturier A., Demarest D., Easton W., Giocomo J., Keller R., Mini A., Panjabi A., Pashley D., Rich T., Ruth J., Stabins H., Stanton J., and Will T. 2016. *Partners in Flight Landbird Conservation Plan: 2016 Revision for Canada and Continental United States.* Partners in Flight Science Committee.

Rottenborn S.C. and Brinkley E.S. 2007. *Virginia's Birdlife: An Annotated Checklist (aka "The Gold Book").* Virginia Avifauna No. 7. Fourth Edition. Virginia Society of Ornithology.

Ruth J.M. 2015. *Status Assessment and Conservation Plan for the Grasshopper Sparrow (Ammodramus savannarum).* Version 1.0. U.S. Fish and Wildlife Service. Lakewood, CO.

Sauer J.R., Niven D.K., Hines J.E., Ziolkowski Jr. D.J., Pardieck K.L., Fallon J.E., and Link W.A. 2017. *The North American Breeding Bird Survey, Results and Analysis 1966-2015.* Version 2.07.2017. U.S. Geological Survey Patuxent Wildlife Research Center. Laurel, MD. <http://www.mbr-pwrc.usgs.gov/bbs/specl14.html>.

Savard J.L., Bordage D., and Reed A. 2015. Surf Scoter (*Melanitta perspicillata*). *The Birds of North America* (P.G. Rodewald, Ed.). Cornell Lab of Ornithology, Ithaca, NY. <https://birdsna.org/Species-Account/bna/species/sursco>.

Schablein J. 2012. Belted Kingfisher, *Megaceryle alcyon.* BioKids Animal Diversity Web. Critter Catalog. <http://www.biokids.umich.edu/accounts/Megaceryle_alcyon>.

Scharf W.C. and Kren J. 2010. Orchard Oriole (*Icterus spurius*). *The Birds of North America* (P.G. Rodewald, Ed.). Cornell Lab of Ornithology, Ithaca, NY. <https://birdsna.org/Species-Account/bna/species/orcori>.

Seng W.J. 2001. Ibises and Spoonbills. *Sibley Guide to Bird Life & Behavior* (C. Elphick, J.B. Dunning, and D.A. Sibley, Eds.). New York, NY: Alfred A. Knopf, Inc.

Sibley D.A. 2003. *The Sibley Field Guide to the Birds of Eastern North America.* New York, NY: Alfred A. Knopf, Inc.

Sibley D.A. 2009. *The Sibley Guide to Bird Life and Behavior.* National Audubon Society. New York, NY: Alfred A. Knopf, Inc.

Sibley D.A. 2014. *The Sibley Guide to Birds, Second Edition.* New York, NY: Alfred A. Knopf, Inc.

Smith R.J., Hatch M.I., Cimprich D.A., and Moore F.R. (2011). Gray Catbird (*Dumetella carolinensis*). *The Birds of North America* (A.F. Poole, Editor). Cornell Lab of Ornithology, Ithaca, NY. <https://birdsna.org/Species-Account/bna/species/grycat>.

Stokes D. 1979. Stokes Nature Guides. *A Guide to Bird Behavior*, Volume I. New York, NY: Little, Brown, and Company.

Telfair II, R.C. 2006. Cattle Egret (*Bubulcus ibis*). *The Birds of North America* (A.F. Poole, Ed.). Cornell Lab of Ornithology, Ithaca, NY. <https://birdsna.org/Species-Account/bna/species/categr>.

Temple S.A. 2002. Dickcissel (*Spiza americana*). *The Birds of North America*. (A.F. Poole and F.B. Gill, Eds.). Cornell Lab of Ornithology, Ithaca, NY. <https://birdsna.org/Species-Account/bna/species/dickci>.

Temple S.A. and Wiens J.A. 1989. Bird populations and environmental changes: can birds be bio-indicators. *American Birds* 43: 260-270.

Trollinger J.B. and Reay K.K. 2001. *Breeding Bird Atlas of Virginia 1985-1989.* Virginia Department of Game and Inland Fisheries. Richmond, VA.

Tuttle E., Bergland A., Korody M., Brewer M., Newhouse D., Minx P., Stager M., Betuel A., Cheviron Z., Warren W., Gonser R., Balakrishnan C. 2016. Divergence and Functional Degradation of a Sex Chromosome-like Supergene. *Current Biology* 26(3): 344-350.

University of Illinois at Urbana – Champaign Animal Sciences. 2015. Climate Change Creates Dramatic Decline in Red-Winged Black Bird Population. <https://ansc.illinois.edu/news/climate-change-creates-dramatic-decline-red-winged-black-bird-population-0>.

U.S. Census Bureau. 2010. QuickFacts. Loudoun County, VA. <https://www.census.gov/quickfacts/table/PST045215/51107>.

U.S. Fish & Wildlife Service. 2014. Environmental Conservation Online System. Yellow-billed Cuckoo (*Coccyzus americanus*). <https://ecos.fws.gov/ecp0/profile/speciesProfile?spcode=B06R>.

U.S. Fish & Wildlife Service. 2015. Bald Eagle. Midwest Region. <www.fws.gov/midwest/Eagle/index.html>.

U.S. Fish and Wildlife Service. 2015. *Waterfowl Population Status, 2015*. U.S. Department of the Interior. Washington, DC. <https://www.fws.gov/migratorybirds/pdf/surveys-and-data/Population-status/Waterfowl/WaterfowlPopulationStatusReport15.pdf>.

U.S. Geological Survey. 2016. *The National Map*. <http://nationalmap.gov/index.html>.

Vanderhoff N., Pyle P., Patten M.A., Sallabanks R., and James F.C. 2016. American Robin (*Turdus migratorius*). *The Birds of North America* (P. G. Rodewald, Ed.). Cornell Lab of Ornithology, Ithaca, NY. <https://birdsna.org/Species-Account/bna/species/amerob>.

Vermont Fish & Wildlife Department Agency of Natural Resources. 2002. *Guidelines for Protection & Mitigation of Impacts to Great Blue Heron Rookeries in Vermont.* <http://anr.vermont.gov/sites/anr/files/co/planning/documents/guidance/Guidelines%20for%20Protection%20and%20Mitigation%20of%20Impacts%20to%20Great%20Blue%20Heron%20Rookeries%20in%20Vermont.pdf>.

Vickery P.D. 1996. Grasshopper Sparrow (*Ammodramus savannarum*). *The Birds of North America* (P.G. Rodewald, Ed.). Cornell Lab of Ornithology, Ithaca, NY. <https://birdsna.org/Species-Account/bna/species/graspa>.

Virginia Bluebird Society. 2017. Nest Boxes, Guards, and Signs. <http://www.virginiabluebirds.org/about-bluebirds/

nest-boxes-guards-signs>.

Virginia Department of Game and Inland Fisheries. 2017. Virginia Golden Eagle Research and Conservation. <www.dgif.virginia.gov/wildlife/birds/golden-eagle>.

Weidensaul S. 2015. *Peterson Reference Guide to Owls of North America and the Caribbean.* Houghton Mifflin Harcourt Publishing Company.

Wiebe K.L. and Moore W.S. 2017. Northern Flicker (*Colaptes auratus*). *The Birds of North America* (P. G. Rodewald, Ed.). Cornell Lab of Ornithology, Ithaca, NY. <https://birdsna.org/Species-Account/bna/species/norfli>.

Wiggins D.A., Holt D.W., and Leasure S.M. 2006. Short-eared Owl (*Asio flammeus*). *The Birds of North America.* (A.F. Poole, Ed.), Cornell Lab of Ornithology, Ithaca, NY. <https://birdsna.org/Species-Account/bna/species/sheowl>.

Williams J.D. and Gilbert C.R. 1994. *National Audubon Society Field Guide to North American Birds: Eastern Region.* Knopf Doubleday Publishing Group.

Wilson Jr. W.H. 2014. Western Sandpiper (*Calidris mauri*). *The Birds of North America* (P.G. Rodewald, Ed.). Cornell Lab of Ornithology, Ithaca, NY. <https://birdsna.org/Species-Account/bna/species/wessan>.

Winkler D.W., Hallinger K.K., Ardia D.R., Robertson R.J., Stutchbury B.J., and Cohen R.R. 2011. Tree Swallow (*Tachycineta bicolor*). *The Birds of North America* (A.F. Poole, Ed.). Cornell Lab of Ornithology, Ithaca, NY. <https://birdsna.org/Species-Account/bna/species/treswa>.

Wyatt V.E. and Francis C.M. 2002. Rose-breasted Grosbeak (*Pheucticus ludovicianus*). *The Birds of North America* (A.F. Poole and F.B. Gill, Eds.). Cornell Lab of Ornithology, Ithaca, NY. <https://birdsna.org/Species-Account/bna/species/robgro>.

Zickefoose J. 2016. *Baby Birds, An Artist Looks Into The Nest*. New York, NY: Houghton Mifflin Harcourt Publishing Company.

INDEX OF SPECIES ACCOUNTS

Barn Swallows
Photo by Gerco Hoogeweg

Eastern Bluebirds
Photo by Bill Brown